D1479822

Methods for Teaching

Promoting Student Learning

Methods for Teaching

Promoting Student Learning

Fifth Edition

David A. Jacobsen
University of North Florida

Paul Eggen
University of North Florida

Don Kauchak
University of Utah

Merrill,
an imprint of Prentice Hall

Upper Saddle River, New Jersey   *Columbus, Ohio*

Library of Congress Cataloging-in-Publication Data

Jacobsen, David (David A.)
   Methods for teaching : promoting student learning / David A.
  Jacobsen, Paul Eggen, Don Kauchak. — 5th ed.
     p.   cm.
  Includes bibliographical references and index.
  ISBN 0-13-272394-8
  1. Teaching. 2. Classroom management. 3. Lesson planning.
4. Learning. I. Eggen, Paul D., (date) . II. Kauchak, Donald P.,
(date) . III. Title.
LB1025.3.J336 1999
371.102—dc21   98-2887
                                    CIP

Editor: Debra A. Stollenwerk
Production Editor: Mary Harlan
Photo Coordinator: Anthony Magnacca
Design Coordinator: Diane Lorenzo
Text Design and Production Coordination: Carlisle Publishers Services
Cover Designer: Brian Deep
Cover art: Tretiakov Gallery, Moscow, Russia: SuperStock
Production Manager: Pamela D. Bennett
Illustrations: Carlisle Graphics
Director of Marketing: Kevin Flanagan
Marketing Manager: Suzanne Stanton
Marketing Coordinator: Krista Groshong

This book was set in Galliard ITC by Carlisle Communications, Ltd. and was printed and bound by R. R. Donnelley & Sons Company. The cover was printed by Phoenix Color Corp.

© 1999 by Prentice-Hall, Inc.
Simon & Schuster/A Viacom Company
Upper Saddle River, New Jersey 07458

All rights reserved. No part of this book may be reproduced, in any form or by any means, without permission in writing from the publisher.

Earlier editions, entitled *Methods for Teaching: A Skills Approach,* © 1993 by Macmillan Publishing Company; © 1989, 1985, 1981 by Merrill Publishing Company.

Photo credits:
Scott Cunningham/Merrill/PH pp. 2, 7, 20, 35, 62, 68, 116, 228, 243, 254, and 276; Barbara Schwartz/Merrill/PH pp. 30, 88, 179, 291, and 317; Anthony Magnacca/Merrill/PH pp. 43, 84, 123, 138, 146, 164, 172, 201, 269, and 306; Anne Vega/Merrill/PH pp. 58, 102, 152, and 298; Tom Watson pp. 222 and 276; KS Studios/Merrill/PH p. 259.

Printed in the United States of America

10 9 8 7 6 5 4 3 2

ISBN: 0-13-272394-8

Prentice-Hall International (UK) Limited, *London*
Prentice-Hall of Australia Pty. Limited, *Sydney*
Prentice-Hall of Canada, Inc., *Toronto*
Prentice-Hall Hispanoamericana, S. A., *Mexico*
Prentice-Hall of India Private Limited, *New Delhi*
Prentice-Hall of Japan, Inc., *Tokyo*
Simon & Schuster Asia Pte. Ltd., *Singapore*
Editora Prentice-Hall do Brasil, Ltda., *Rio de Janeiro*

To Lorrie, Judy, and Kathy

Tell me, I forget.
Show me, I remember.
Involve me, I understand . . . Eureka!

—An Ancient Chinese Proverb

Preface

- Planning
- Implementing
- Assessing

Effective classroom teaching requires professional commitment. Although exciting experiences may occur spontaneously, such happenings serve as the exception, not the rule. If teachers are to sustain a success-oriented environment by promoting student learning throughout the academic year, they must continually and thoroughly address the teaching act, which is founded upon the planning and implementing of instructional activities and the assessing of student performance.

These planning, implementing, and assessing components represent a continual, or cyclical, process in which professional teachers strive to increase the quality of their instruction, that is, promote learning in increased numbers of students. The purpose of this textbook is to provide tools that will enable the inservice as well as the preservice teacher to plan, implement, and assess effectively. In doing so, the teacher will constantly be making decisions regarding the goals to be achieved and the resources needed, and reflecting upon whether or not the goals were met.

Needless to say, it is impossible for one textbook to cover the entire waterfront; however, we believe we are offering a foundation that will promote student learning through the fostering of effective classroom teaching and provide a solid framework for in-depth study in the areas presented.

New to This Edition

In addition to more than 100 contemporary references and updated research on teacher effectiveness throughout the text, there are a number of significant additions to the fifth edition including:

- Introductory scenarios for each chapter
- Questions for discussion and suggestions for field laboratory experiences found at the back of each chapter
- A focus throughout the text on the teacher as decision maker
- The importance of reflection in teaching
- Increased emphasis on motivating students
- Discussions of
    influences upon classroom goals and objectives
    planning and the role of goals and objectives
    the three operational levels of goals
    decision making in preparing objectives
    decision making and planning

    reasons for planning
    long-term planning: philosophical considerations
    long-term planning: specific decisions
    uses of the cognitive domain
    using open-ended questions and redirection to increase student involvement
    inclusion
    Howard Gardner's Multiple Intelligences
    alternative assessments
- Updated discussions in the areas of
    management, problem prevention and intervention
    multicultural education
    critical thinking
    cooperative learning
    mastery learning
    computers
    learning styles

Finally, as with the previous four editions, we have attempted to produce a methods book that is even more practical and applicable to classroom teaching. Revised, expanded, and additional scenarios, examples, and exercises are offered throughout the text.

Acknowledgments

We would like to express our gratitude to the hundreds of students and teachers who provided critical feedback and served as invaluable sources in the preparation of the fifth edition. We wish to thank our reviewers Leigh Chiarelott, Bowling Green State University; J. M. Dell'Olio, Hope College; Gordon E. Fuchs, University of Dayton; Stephen Lafer, University of Nevada, Reno; Donna J. Merkley, Iowa State University; Daisy F. Reed, Virginia Commonwealth University; Elizabeth Simons, Kansas State University; and Beth Stroble, University of Louisville.

We also want to thank Candy Britts, Alan Due, Emily Nolan, and Betsy Wierda, who provided suggestions and materials for the long-range planning component of Chapter 4. Finally, our thanks to Kate Scheinman for dotting all the "i's" and crossing all the "t's," and our senior editor, Debra Stollenwerk, whose input and constant support proved invaluable to the production of the work.

D. A. J.   P. D. E.   D. P. K.

Contents

UNIT TWO:
LEARNER-CENTERED INSTRUCTION   145

Chapter 6
QUESTIONING STRATEGIES   147

Chapter 7
TEACHING STRATEGIES   173

Chapter **8**

ACCOMMODATING LEARNER DIFFERENCES: INSTRUCTIONAL STRATEGIES   223

Chapter **9**

CLASSROOM MANAGEMENT: PREVENTION   255

Chapter **10**

CLASSROOM MANAGEMENT: INTERVENTION   277

UNIT THREE:
LEARNER-CENTERED ASSESSMENTS 297

Chapter 11
ASSESSING STUDENT LEARNING 299

Chapter 1

Introduction: A Model for Teaching

Mrs. Joy Warner had her kindergarten children engage in learning about dental health. She organized her room into a number of learning centers including a dentist's office where the children counted each other's teeth, cavities, and fillings and put information on a chart; a play dough center where the children made models of teeth; an art center where the children painted the different parts of a tooth; a center by the sink where students practiced correct toothbrushing strokes; and a nutrition center where she interacted with a few children at a time. Three children sat with her while an aide and a parent volunteer worked with the children in the other learning centers. To begin, she showed them a picture of some food.

"What kind of food is this?" Mrs. Warner asked.

"It looks like meatloaf," JuRelle said.

"Look a little closer."

"Cake."

"Yes, it does look like cake. And what is the stuff on top?"

"Icing," Melina said.

"And maybe nuts," Nirav added.

"Great," Mrs. Warner said. "Now what do we have here?"

"Strawberries."

"Good, Jessica. What about this one?"

"A tomato," Preston said.

"Good." Mrs. Warner then continued to hold up the pictures and have the children identify the food in each. She then turned toward the felt board upon which she had a cutout happy face.

"What we are going to do now is sort these pictures. Some of these are pictures of food that can make your teeth happy while others make your teeth not so happy. I'm going to put all the pictures in the middle and choose one and then you are going to tell us where the pictures go.

"Okay. Now let me model it first to show you. This is cake and I am going to put cake right up here under the sad tooth. Why do you think the cake would make the tooth unhappy . . . Melina?"

"Cavities," Melina replied.

"What might cause a cavity?" Mrs. Warner asked.

"Sweet things," Melina said.

"Yes. Cavities are caused by eating too many sweet things but what makes them sweet?"

"I know. It's sugar!" Melina exclaimed.

"Very good," Mrs. Warner said. "You put sugar in things to make them sweet. Now let's go back to our pictures to see if they should go under the happy face or the sad face. . . . JuRelle, you do one for us."

JuRelle reached out, picked up a picture and said, "Tomatoes."

"Can you say that in a complete sentence, please."

"Tomatoes are healthy for your teeth."

"Nice job, JuRelle. I like that word healthy. Okay . . . Preston?"

"Strawberries are good for your teeth."

"Right. A strawberry is a fruit and it does have some sugar in it but if you are go-ing to eat the natural sugar in it we know that is better than when you put sugar into foods to make them sweet like candy and cake."

Mrs. Warner continued to have the students classify the pictures and place them on the felt board. "Now," she asked, "how many things do we have that are not good for your teeth?" The children counted aloud, one through seven.

"And how many things do we have that are good for your teeth?" The children counted again, one through eight.

"So which foods do we have the most of?"

"Healthy food," the children replied.

"Good. Now I want everyone to listen. When we go over to our mural on the floor you are going to draw either one healthy food or one unhealthy food."

"I'm going to draw a strawberry," Preston said.

"And where are you going to draw it?" Under healthy things or unhealthy things?"

"Healthy."

"Good, Preston," Mrs. Warner said. "You are going to draw your strawberry under healthy and after you draw it, write the word for the food right under your drawing."

Mrs. Warner then sat on the floor next to the children and monitored their progress with a focus on an inventive spelling exercise that allowed her to diagnose the children's progress on writing and their use of phonetics. These observations gave her information for future, individualized instruction. She was also able to review with them their work in this integrated learning experience that included numbers, sets, language develop-ment, health, communication skills, writing, and art.

Introduction _____

You're probably reading this book because you're either enrolled in an undergraduate general methods course or you're a teacher interested in updating your strategies. As we write this book, we're assuming that while you've had experience with schools and classrooms—as we all have had as students, parents, aides, or tutors—you may have not done any formal teaching yourself. Based on this assumption, we're going to provide you with the background to provide the basic tools needed to make intelligent decisions about planning learning activities, implementing those activities with children, and assessing their success. We hope that when you finish your study you will have the conceptual or intellectual tools to allow you to continue to grow as a professional throughout your career.

For those of you who have had formal experience with teaching, we hope this material will help make your work more systematic and effective and will further assist you in making even better decisions about teaching.

Objectives _____

After completing your study of Chapter 1, you should be able to:

- Discuss the primary role of the teacher
- Describe a variety of strategies teachers use to promote student growth and achievement
- Identify areas that influence the act and process of teaching
- Discuss ways in which teachers serve as decision makers
- Describe the importance of reflection in classroom teaching
- Identify the components of the three-phase model of teaching

THE TEACHER'S ROLE

An often held and stereotypical view of a teacher is that of a learned person disseminating information to a group of people hungry for knowledge. The group is often viewed as passive, and the main activity in such a learning environment involves the teacher *telling* the students what they need to know. However, most educators agree that this view is extremely narrow and that *telling* is only one of many tools a teacher may employ. To begin our study of the different roles teachers play, refer to the scenario at the start of our chapter, which takes a look at a teacher implementing a primary science unit.

Promoting Growth and Achievement

There are a number of teacher roles undertaken in this teaching scenario and they are often found in the form of contrasting dualisms. For instance, by providing a number of interactive learning centers, such as the dentist's office, Mrs. Warner hoped to promote social and emotional growth in the children while the teaching strategy she employed to facilitate students' understandings of healthy and unhealthy foods promoted both the acquisition of knowledge and the processing of information. Both the social and the intellectual enhancement of children are primary aims that teachers address as a significant part of their role as professional educators. The dualism here, and in many other aspects of teaching, is not an either/or situation but one of priority. In this case, the question is, to what enhancement of the student does public education owe its first obligation? Is it his intellectual-academic or his emotional-social growth? (Noddings, 1984).

Regardless of which one might be prioritized, the central role of a teacher is to help students learn in a variety of ways. How do we learn? We learn in a number of different ways ranging from pure experiential learning to learning from others. We saw these illustrated in Mrs. Warner's scenario in the different learning activities she organized to promote learning.

Motivating Students

Another important teaching role is to increase students' desire or motivation to learn. Adults do this in a number of ways. For example, most parents reinforce and reward their children to say such things as "please" and "thank you." This can be effectively accomplished through modeling in which the parents themselves use these terms and establish for children the desirability of these socially acceptable behaviors. The initial motivation for children probably involves the concept of extrinsic worth. When using please and thank you children get what they want and also please their parents in the process. However, the parents have not actually taught the children; they have facilitated the children's ability to internalize the extrinsic worth of using these terms in their everyday speech.

Although some educators are critical of motivational factors based upon extrinsic worth, much of what we do may be founded upon or initiated by an extrinsic reward that is later internalized. Isn't it common for people, adults as well as children, to want to please their teachers? And isn't it also possible that human nature is such that we derive a great amount of pleasure by being perceived by others in a positive light? In and of itself, that may be fine, but many educators believe it is equally important to make the transition from the extrinsic to the intrinsic (Pintrich & Schunk, 1996).

For example, providing a reward for children who successfully tie their shoes can be effective in initiating the desired behavior, but our ultimate goal should be to develop intrinsic, and not extrinsic, motivation. In other words, the bottom line involves the children "feeling good" about their ability to put on their shoes, thereby enhancing their self-worth, and their positive image of themselves.

It is in this area that teachers provide a critical function. Teachers facilitate the internalization process, and they most effectively do so by promoting a positive self-concept. In doing so, the teacher may stimulate a child's interest and, more importantly, promote achievement and success.

Occasionally you may hear a teacher say, "There are kids you just can't motivate." Actually, students are never unmotivated from their own point of view. Therefore, it becomes necessary for the teacher to understand student goals and to help students perceive learning tasks differently (Hamachek, 1987). In order to be in

A wide range of motivational techniques is critical to the promotion of a student's positive self-concept.

a position to accomplish this goal, one of the most important roles of the teacher is to convince students that we are "in their corner." This requires both organizational and personal strategies.

Critical organization strategies include building meaningful and interesting curricula, providing appropriate learning experiences and materials, and allocating sufficient time to enhance student opportunities for success. These strategies promote increased student involvement, which leads to higher levels of achievement (Eschermann, 1988). In turn, achievement enhances self-esteem and a feeling of self-worth, which play an important role in student motivation (Wolery, Bailey, & Sugai, 1988). The more achievement, or success, students experience, the more likely they are to elevate their expectations and become increasingly "motivated" to stick to and attempt other tasks. A critical point to note is that research suggests that motivation is a strong variable in the learning process, perhaps an even more important variable than ability (Bardwell, 1987).

Personal strategies to enhance motivation include being sincere, positive, enthusiastic, and supportive. In addition, one of the most powerful ways of communicating our interest is simply by listening to what students are saying and letting them know that we value their thoughts and contributions to the class.

Humor can be an indispensable tool in promoting a positive relationship with your students. An ongoing teacher-student relationship, with humor as a critical component, reduces negative feelings and improves student perceptions of the teacher, thus contributing to improved attention, retention, and learning (Gorham &

Christophel, 1990). Additional research has shown that teachers who encourage laughter in their classrooms have children who learn quickly, retain more, and have fewer emotional problems in the classroom (Chenfield, 1990).

The role teachers play in motivating students is a critical factor in promoting student success, but this effort should not be limited to your classroom. Working with parents is crucial if the child's experience is to be a positive one. Suggestions you might offer parents include the following (Wlodkowski & Jaynes, 1990):

1. Be supportive with a "keep-at-it" posture.
2. Provide constructive encouragement.
3. Recognize the child's effort.
4. Communicate your confidence.
5. Help the child to pay attention to the task at hand.
6. Emphasize that mistakes are okay and that all of us learn from them.

The final point listed above is also worth focusing on in the classroom. Overemphasis on mistakes can damage a child's positive self-concept and eventually inhibit the child's desire even to attempt the task at hand. This can also happen when "winning" becomes an end goal. Although we stress the importance of cooperative learning environments, competition can promote learning if the situation is fair, if it deemphasizes winning at all costs, and if it does away with competition that dehumanizes students (Rich, 1988).

Just as there are educators who say you cannot motivate an unmotivated student, there are also educators who claim that you can't teach a child who is unwilling to learn. Once again, this would depend upon one's definition of the teacher's role. As stated earlier, teachers cannot internalize concepts or behaviors for students because internalization is a unique process that all of us must undertake for ourselves. However, there are many things we, as teachers, can do to facilitate the process.

For example, in teaching a child to ride a bicycle, we can demonstrate bicycle functions such as the use of brakes and pedaling. We can have the child sit on the bike with us, roll it slowly, and lean from side to side, thereby demonstrating balance. We can put the child on a stationary bicycle and allow him or her to experience pedaling and using the brakes. We can run alongside the child, aid in corrections, and constantly encourage and reinforce appropriate behaviors. In short, what we do is demonstrate or model riding a bicycle; provide a knowledge base regarding operation; and provide appropriate, sufficient, and supportive practical experiences. Only then does the child learn to ride a bicycle.

Mistakes are a natural part of the process. Rudolph Dreikurs provided us with a classic example of this. When many children learn to ride a bicycle, they go down a street, and if there is a rock in the middle of the road, it is much easier to miss the rock. But more often than not, they hit it because they want to experiment, to experience what it's like to hit the rock when learning to ride (Dreikurs, 1968a).

Likewise, many of our students are prone, concretely or abstractly, to hit the rock. We cannot teach them to do otherwise, but what we can do is provide educational experiences that promote positive learning environments laden with a variety of extrinsic motivational factors that, we hope, the student will transfer to the intrinsic plane. In this way, teachers enhance and, to some degree, direct the internalization process, the final product of which is determined by the child.

Throughout history, great "teachers" have facilitated that which students think or do, and an educator's value is found in paving the way for a student's transfer from what he or she does to what he or she knows or becomes.

EXERCISE 1.1

Review the discussion on motivation and list three different ways teachers facilitate student motivation. Then compare your answers to the ones given in the feedback section at the end of the chapter.

1. _____

   _____

2. _____

   _____

3. _____

   _____

TEACHING: AN ANALYSIS

What is it that effective teachers do to promote student learning? Our first step in systematically describing teaching begins with a brief look at teaching through introductory illustrations of teachers in action. To do this, let's look at three scenarios of teachers working in classrooms.

Examples

Scenario 1.   Mrs. Shafer is a pleasant woman in her middle thirties who teaches at Plainview Elementary School. Plainview is an older school in a lower-middle-class neighborhood of Laqua, Florida. While the school is not new, the administration has kept the grounds and building very attractive. Everyone cooperates in keeping the small areas of grass from being trampled on and killed, and the paved and cemented areas are kept free from debris. There are no broken windows, and the water fountains and lavatories work well and smell fresh.

Mrs. Shafer's room has a high ceiling that makes it seem big, but she has grouped large boxes to make cubbyholes and privacy corners for her children. She asked for and received permission to paint designs and graphics (sayings or pictures such as rainbows) on her walls in addition to her use of several large bulletin boards for decoration.

Mrs. Shafer is beginning a unit in geography, and students have studied various geographic regions and their physical features. The children are now familiar with regions such as the American central plains, the Russian steppes, and the Argentine pampas; and the American Rocky Mountains, the Swiss Alps, and the South American Andes. They know how the regions are similar and how they differ. She now wants her children to understand the influence of geography on people's lifestyles and culture. She decides to use pictures of people in different regions to get students to link the regions with the appearances and activities of the people. She gathers her pictures and begins the lesson. She starts by showing a picture of some children playing in front of some grass huts.

"Look at the picture, everyone," Mrs. Shafer says, smiling. "Tell me anything at all you see about the pictures."

"They're in Africa," Carol says immediately.

"Excellent, Carol, but how do you know that?"

"My dad is in the navy, and we lived in Greece, and we took a trip to Africa, and we saw houses like those."

Jimmy's eyes open wide. "You went to Africa? I've never been out of Laqua in my life."

Mike adds, "I've never been there, but I've read about it, and those children could live in India maybe 'cuz they don't wear many clothes in India either."

David is whispering and grinning at Billy as Mike is talking, and Mrs. Shafer gives him a stern look.

"What did we agree was one of our important rules, David?" Mrs. Shafer asks.

"We always respect others," David says quietly.

"And what is one way we do that?"

"We listen to what they have to say whether we agree or not, and then express our opinion when it's our turn."

"Very good, David," Mrs. Shafer says with a smile. "That's a good reminder for all of us. Now let's go on. What else do you see in the picture?"

The children continue describing what they see, and then Mrs. Shafer shows two Russian children playing with a sled in front of a mosque. Again she asks for a description of what the children see. She continues this process, showing pictures of Indian shepherds in Ecuador and Bedouin tribesmen in the Middle East. She asks the students to compare all of the pictures by showing similarities and differences. Finally she asks the children to summarize what they saw.

"Well, people live in different places and their houses are different," Joan suggests.

"Fine, Joan. Now, anything else?"

"They dress different," Kim adds.

"OK."

"They're playing different games and stuff," Susan says.

"Very good. What more can you say about what we've seen—people's houses, clothes, games they play, and so on?"

"Well," Jimmy says somewhat hesitantly, "they're things about people."

"Fine, and what things about people?"

"Oh, how they live and everything."

"Very good. So we're saying geography and climate affect people's lifestyles."

Mrs. Shafer goes into a discussion of Florida's climate, geography, and lifestyle and asks the children to compare that to how they would expect to live in northern Michigan or Minnesota.

After a number of comparisons are made, Mrs. Shafer announces, "Now, everyone, I have two short paragraphs that I want you to read. Then I want you to write four examples from the paragraph that show how geography and climate affect lifestyle."

The paragraphs she gives the children are as follows:

José and Kirsten are two children about your age who live in faraway lands. Kirsten lives in the mountains of Norway, which is quite far north. José lives on the flat plains of western Mexico where it is very hot and dry. Kirsten loves to ski and does so nearly every day in the winter. In the summer she and her brother put on light wool sweaters and go hiking in the mountains. They love to sit atop the peaks and look down over the valleys. In the evenings Kirsten's mother builds a fire, and everyone in the family reads quietly.

José loves to play, just as Kirsten does. He swims every afternoon in a pond formed by a spring near his village. He becomes impatient because he has to wait until after the nap his mother takes every day at noon. The children go outside and play in the evening, enjoying the breeze that cools the village. They usually play until it is so dark they can't see.

Mrs. Shafer collects the students' papers and ends the class by saying she will introduce the idea of culture the following day and relate culture to geography and climate. She reviews the papers during her planning period and finds the following responses:

1. Kirsten skiing in the winter
2. Kirsten's family sitting and reading by the fire in the evening
3. Kirsten and her brother hiking in the mountains
4. José's mother napping every noon
5. José playing in the evening
6. José swimming in the afternoon

Scenario 2.   Mr. Adams works in a kindergarten classroom. He has his room arranged in sections. Today is Monday, so Mr. Adams arrives at school early to set up his room for the week. He changes his activities on a weekly basis and spends his Friday afternoons and Monday mornings getting them ready. This week he wants to put particular emphasis on manipulative skills and wants to be sure all of the children can perform tasks such as buttoning coats and tying shoes. In one corner he puts some flashlight bulbs in little holders, some dry-cell batteries, and some wire. In another corner he places a large flannel board with different numbers of beans glued on it so children can match numerals such as 2 or 3 with the appropriate number of beans. He arranges similar activities in the other corners of the room.

As the children come in, Mr. Adams asks them what activities they would like to choose and sends them each to a corner to begin. He then sits down on the floor with three boys to help them learn to tie the shoelaces on a large doll they've named Fred. Each day the children button Fred's shirt, tie his shoes, brush his teeth, and wash his hands after Mr. Adams has taken him to the bathroom.

Jimmy is struggling to get Fred's shoe tied and appears slightly uninterested to Mr. Adams. He feels his forehead, which appears to be warm, and immediately takes him by the hand down to the nurse's office. Jimmy is often ill, so Mr. Adams is sensitive when he appears listless.

As he returns, he sees Scott throw a beanbag at Lisa. Mr. Adams admonishes him gently saying, "Scott, you're not supposed to throw the beanbag at Lisa; you're supposed to throw it so she can catch it."

"She threw it at me first."

"Did you, Lisa?"

Smiling shyly, Lisa nods.

"Throw it to each other and count to see if you can do it ten times each without missing."

Mr. Adams continues working with groups of children until 11:30 A.M. when it is time for dismissal. He helps the children get safely on the bus and then goes back to his room.

Taking stock of his morning, he grins to himself as he recalls that David had improved significantly in tying Fred's shoes. He takes out a sheet that has the children's names on it and puts a check by David's name. He notices as he glances at the sheet that Bobby had trouble walking the balance beam and prepares a note for his mother suggesting some exercises he could do at home. With this done, he prepares for his afternoon class.

Scenario 3.   Mrs. Tyler is a history teacher in a large high school. She is working on a unit in group processes, and while her ultimate goal is for the students to understand the effects of group processes on democratic decision making, her particular goal in this lesson is to have her students learn to understand their own views more clearly and to learn to cooperate by making decisions in groups. To accomplish this, she splits the class into two groups and presents each group with a perplexing dilemma. The situation describes a shipwreck with some sick and injured people. The party is marooned on a deserted island, short of food and water fit for drinking. Fortunately, they're rescued, but the ship can only handle part of the people in one trip. In all likelihood, many of the sick and injured won't survive the trip back to civilization, but they'll surely die if left on the island. If the healthy are left until the second trip, many will die of starvation or thirst before the ship returns. She asks the students to discuss the issue during the class period, recording notes and decisions. Each group is to report the following day.

As the groups discuss the problem, Mrs. Tyler listens and periodically raises questions if students appear to drift away from the task at hand or suggests issues that aren't considered by the group.

The next day Mrs. Tyler has the students discuss the process they went through, their feelings as they were involved in the discussion, and the bases for the decisions they made. As the year progresses, Mrs. Tyler makes short notes about each student, describing the student's progress in working in group situations.

We described three teachers involved in activities with students at three different levels and in three different content areas. Let's analyze the three scenarios and see how they illustrate the framework we want to develop for later chapters in this book.

Areas of Emphasis

First, let's look again at what the three teachers did. Mrs. Shafer wanted her students to understand the influence of geography and climate on lifestyle. Mr. Adams had his children doing a variety of things; some worked with trying to light the bulb, some counted beans, and others worked on skills like tying shoes and buttoning coats. Mrs. Tyler wanted her students to learn to cooperate in groups and did this by involving them in a decision-making activity. We can see from the earlier examples that the differences among these three areas in many classrooms are those of emphasis rather than exclusion. For example, while Mrs. Shafer wanted her students to learn about the relationship among geography, climate, and lifestyle, she also viewed respect for others as important. She demonstrated this view when she reminded David and Billy to listen when Mike was talking. Also, in order to perform psychomotor skills such as carpentry and hitting a tennis ball properly, knowledge of technique is required. All of this illustrates that the three areas—knowledge, skills, and attitudes—are closely interrelated and cannot be completely separated in any reasonable way.

Based on the three scenarios, we see that students' learning is more varied and complex than we might expect at first glance. Mrs. Shafer's students were learning *information,* or *knowledge,* and how it can be used to explain objects and events that occur in the world. By comparison, many of Mr. Adams's activities were related to *manipulative skills* such as buttoning Fred's coat and tying his shoes. Many other such skills are taught in schools—typing, carpentry, leatherwork, mechanics, and physical education skills in all the sports areas. Mrs. Tyler's activity was different from both Mrs. Shafer's and Mr. Adams's. She wanted her students to develop interpersonal communication skills and acquire certain *attitudes* and *values,* such as cooperation, willingness to listen to a contrasting view, and respect for others.

So, we see now that students can learn much more than information in schools. Student learning can roughly be described as existing in three forms: (1) information and knowledge, (2) manipulative skills, and (3) attitudes and values.

All three areas are extremely important and need to be addressed in schools. However, a complete discussion of the learning of all three—knowledge, skills, and attitudes—is beyond the scope of a single text, so we have chosen to emphasize the area of knowledge and information more than the others. The reason is simple. While attitudes and skills are important and valued by both the public and educators, relatively greater emphasis is placed on the acquisition of knowledge and the ability to think.

Learning Environments

In addition to goals, learning is also influenced by learning environments. Let's look again at the three scenarios and see how the learning environments differed. Mrs. Shafer worked with her whole class, while Mr. Adams worked with small groups and had learning centers set up. Mrs. Tyler worked with two large groups. Adding one-to-one encounters to our list, the possible grouping arrangements appear in Figure 1.1. Different group arrangements provide different opportunities for students to learn different things. We discuss these different arrangements in more detail in later chapters.

Other Influences on Learning

While group arrangements affect the way children learn, many other factors influence what children take away from school. For instance, in Mr. Adams's activity, Jimmy

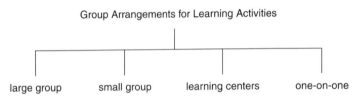

Figure 1.1   Group Arrangements for Learning Activities

appeared listless, and it turned out that he didn't feel well. Health is certainly a factor that affects learning (Berk, 1994). Nutrition is another factor, and its importance, in addition to promoting general health, is evidenced by schools implementing free breakfast and lunch programs for needy children.

Again, think about Mrs. Shafer's lesson. In discussing the picture of children playing in front of the grass huts, Carol reacted quite differently from Jimmy because she had been to Africa and had seen huts and children similar to those in Mrs. Shafer's picture, while Jimmy had no frame of reference whatsoever. Mike's reaction was somewhere in between. He had no firsthand experience but was familiar with the ideas from pictures and stories. All of this illustrates how experience can affect what children learn. In the situation just described, Carol was certainly in the best position to derive the most benefit from the lesson because of her experience, while Jimmy was in the least advantageous position. Obviously, we as teachers cannot control students' backgrounds, but we can provide the most realistic examples possible, as Mrs. Shafer did, and promote as much student involvement as possible, again as Mrs. Shafer did. This illustrates the role of the teacher in influencing student learning, which brings us to the central theme of this text.

As you reflect on your role as a teacher in the schools, you see that as an individual teacher you can do little about children's ability, health, nutrition, outside experiences, or emotional makeup. You can, however, significantly influence their learning by providing school experiences that promote thinking and by making learning as positive an experience as possible. This is what this book is all about. In succeeding chapters we will help you learn to plan, implement, and assess activities to promote as much student learning as possible. We will describe this in terms of a three-step model, or approach. This approach outlines the steps a teacher takes in developing any learning activity, and the majority of the remaining material in this text will be devoted to discussion and illustration of the three stages.

EXERCISE 1.2

Examine the following statements and determine whether they are primarily a knowledge area (k), skills area (s), or attitudes area (a). Then compare your answers to the ones given in the feedback section at the end of the chapter.

_____ 1. Students practice typing forty words per minute.
_____ 2. Students are asked to name their favorite color.

_____ 3. Students try to run a mile in under 8 minutes.
_____ 4. Students look around the room and identify examples of circles.
_____ 5. Students determine the most economical way to provide energy to a community of 2,000 people.
_____ 6. Students repair a broken television set.
_____ 7. Students exhibit their willingness to discuss AIDS as a societal problem.

THE THREE-PHASE APPROACH TO TEACHING

The model of teaching we present is simple, understandable, practical, and workable in teaching single lessons or units, and we have chosen it as a basic framework for this text.

The basic steps in the three-phase approach to teaching are:

1. Planning
2. Implementing
3. Assessing

These three phases are sequential and interrelated. In other words, a teacher, in developing any learning experience, first plans, then implements those plans, and finally assesses the success of the activity.

In each of these phases effective teachers ask themselves a series of questions that are constantly kept in mind as the process develops. We will use these questions in our development of the remainder of the text. Keep this idea in mind as we examine each of the steps more closely.

Planning

All teaching begins with planning, in which a teacher asks:

What do I want my students to know, understand, appreciate, and be able to do?

The answer to this question is the teaching goal. The first step in the planning phase is the establishment of some kind of goal. This goal may be as mundane as teaching history or math facts or as lofty as developing students' moral or spiritual values. Whatever the intent, the establishment of some type of goal or purpose is a first priority in teaching.

You may wonder or ask yourself, What determines the goals? The answer to this question can be very philosophical, and we consider this issue in Chapter 2. In addition, methods for precisely stating teaching goals are described in Chapter 3. Each of the teachers in our introductory scenarios had goals for their lessons. Mrs. Shafer wanted her students to understand the influence of geography on lifestyle and culture, Mr. Adams wanted his children to develop their manipulative or psychomotor skills, and Mrs. Tyler wanted her students to learn to work cooperatively in groups.

A second step in the planning phase is selecting a strategy and gathering supporting materials. Mrs. Shafer wanted her students to understand the relationship between climate and culture and attempted to accomplish this by showing pictures and asking questions. Her pictures were her supporting materials. Mr. Adams chose as his strategy learning centers where students developed their psychomotor skills through practice, and Mrs. Tyler's strategy was to involve her students in a group decision-making process. To accomplish her aim, Mrs. Tyler needed no materials other than pencil and paper and the problem-solving situation. Chapters 2 through 5 are all devoted to the planning process.

Research evidence supports the value of planning. Peterson, Marx, and Clark (1978) found that the actions teachers take in the classroom are influenced by the plans they make. Clark and Yinger (1979) and McCutcheon (1980) both found that planning provides teachers with both confidence and security. For those of you who have not yet taught and are approaching the experience with understandable apprehension, the research results are encouraging. The implication is to plan carefully and thoroughly so that your feelings of uncertainty can be significantly reduced.

Implementing

Having determined a goal and selected an appropriate means to reach that goal, a teacher then implements that strategy. The teacher attempts in this phase to accomplish the teaching goal through implementing the selected strategy. Mrs. Shafer implemented her strategy by showing the pictures and asking her students questions. Mr. Adams implemented his activity when he had the students participate in the learning centers, and Mrs. Tyler was in the implementation phase when her students worked on learning to make group decisions.

The success of the implementation phase depends upon clear goals. Interestingly, a surprising number of teachers do activities with little thought of the goal they're trying to reach. Mintz (1979), Peterson et al. (1978), and McCutcheon (1980) all found that teachers do not typically start the planning process with a consideration of goals but rather with a concern for activities, content, or materials. A goal for us in writing this text is for you, as preservice and inservice teachers, to make your planning, implementing, and assessing of learning experiences for your students a systematic and considered process rather than a contingency or "seat-of-the-pants" approach. Research suggests that while both planning and carrying out meaningful goal-oriented programs isn't often systematically done, such action is possible and will be rewarded with positive results.

A central question the teacher asks in implementing activities is, How will I get my students to reach the goal? The answer to the question will be the teaching procedure, or strategy, that is used. Deciding the most appropriate method to use depends on the goal, students' background and needs, the teacher's personality, strengths and style, and other factors. We formally discuss teaching strategies in Chapters 6, 7, and 8.

In addition to considering a teaching strategy to reach a predetermined goal, teachers must also organize and manage their classrooms so learning can proceed smoothly. Management ranges from something as simple as a verbal reminder to a student to pay attention to a complex set of rules and procedures that create productive learning environments.

Mrs. Shafer was involved in classroom management when she gave David a stern look for whispering while another student was talking, and Mr. Adams employed management procedures when he gently corrected Scott for throwing the beanbag at Lisa rather than to her. Additional management strategies were illustrated in the way Mr. Adams arranged his room; rather than having children organized in rows, he had them in small groups working at stations.

As the scenarios involving Mrs. Shafer and Mr. Adams illustrate, classroom management and instruction are essentially inseparable. Without attending to the learning task, students cannot learn, and organizing a learning activity invariably requires management considerations on the part of the teacher. It is for these reasons that classroom management is included in our discussion of the implementing phase of teaching. Management procedures are discussed in Chapters 9 and 10.

Assessing

The third stage in teaching is assessment. Here the teacher attempts to gather information that can be used to determine if learning has occurred. This can be done in a number of ways including administering tests or quizzes, grading homework, or noting students' reactions to questions or comments. Each of these methods can be used by the teacher in making decisions concerning whether or not the goal established in the planning stage was reached.

At this point the teacher is asking, How will I determine if the students know, understand, or appreciate the goal I identified earlier? The answer to this question specifies the way in which the students' understanding will be assessed through the use of different measurement instruments.

For instance, Mrs. Shafer gave the children an unfamiliar paragraph and asked them to identify illustrations of the relationship between geography and how it influenced the way people lived. Mr. Adams observed the children performing the manipulative tasks and checked the names of those who were successful, and Mrs. Tyler observed the students and made notes regarding their progress in group situations.

In all these instances the assessment procedures used by the teachers were chosen to be congruent with the established goals and the selected implementation strategies. We discuss assessment procedures in more depth in Chapter 11.

EXERCISE 1.3

For the following tasks, label each as being a planning phase task (p), implementing phase task (i), or assessing phase task (a). Then compare your answers to the ones given in the feedback section at the end of the chapter.

_____ 1. The teacher observes the students working on math problems at their desks.
_____ 2. A fourth-grade teacher, noting problems on the playground, decides to help her students resolve conflicts through negotiation.
_____ 3. The teacher writes a learning goal.
_____ 4. The students undertake a 10-item multiple-choice test.
_____ 5. The teacher employs a guided-discovery strategy.
_____ 6. The teacher shows a videotape depicting the settlement of the American West.

THE TEACHER AS DECISION MAKER

Teachers make a wide range of decisions that clearly impact on the effectiveness of their classroom teaching. Shavelson (1973) describes decision making as the "basic teaching skill." The argument is that, while knowledge of subject matter or teaching skills is important, being able to describe when and how to use them effectively is critical (Greenwood & Fillmer, 1997). Decision making obviously implies making choices, some of the most common examples involve deciding what to teach, how to teach it, and ways to assess student achievement. Using how to teach as an example, a number of sources influence decision making and run the gamut from *believing* a specific strategy to be the most effective way of teaching something to having case studies and hard research information establishing its effectiveness.

One way to bypass these important decisions is to implement the content, strategies, and assessments found in teacher's guides and instructional materials that often accompany textbooks. Such resources may in fact provide the most effective instruction for a given lesson, but we take the position here that anything we undertake in our classrooms should be weighed against other alternatives in a conscious and deliberate effort.

Factors Influencing Decision Making

The three major ways of evaluating these alternatives include research, experience, and context. A growing body of research provides useful information about the relationship of teacher actions to student learning (Bruning, Schraw, & Ronning, 1995; Eggen & Kauchak, 1997); we will introduce you to this research as we consider different aspects of decision making in later chapters.

A second factor influencing professional decision making is experience. Research is clear that veteran teachers draw heavily on their experiences to guide their decisions (Berliner, 1994). This has several implications for beginning teachers. First, research on the effective practices of experienced teachers needs to be considered. Second, beginning teachers need to observe and dialogue with experienced teachers as they learn to teach. Finally, beginning teachers need to reflect on their own growth as they progress and, by doing so, grow through experience and learn from their mistakes.

Context is a third factor that influences teachers' decision making. No two students and no two learning environments are alike. In addition, instructional decision making is also influenced by the kind of content being taught, the resources available, and even the time of day or point in the school year. Clearly, teaching is a very individual process in which who we are as persons influences the way we teach (Pajares, 1992). As we learn about alternative teaching methods and instructional strategies we need to continuously ask ourselves, "Will these work for me and will they effectively promote student learning in my classroom?"

The Importance of Goals

Weighing alternatives requires making choices that influence learning. This can only be done when teachers have clear goals. Teachers should always have goals in mind when they teach. Goals provide direction for teaching and guide decision making. Decision making is strategic in the sense that decisions are based upon purposeful and explicit goals. The following operations can be employed in goal-based decision making (Beyer, 1988):

- Identify the desired goal.
- Identify obstacles to reaching that goal.
- Identify options for overcoming each obstacle.
- Examine the options in terms of time, resources, costs, and constraints on their use.
- Choose the best option or combination of options.

The consideration of goals is undertaken in the planning phase, which we identified as the first of three phases in which teachers make decisions. In the planning phase, teachers not only consider goals but also design learning activities that will help students reach those goals. Decision-making questions for consideration include:

- How should I explain a given concept?
- How should I relate that concept to material we have already studied?
- How can I use concrete examples to illustrate the concept?
- What kinds of learning tasks can I design to encourage meaningful learning?

In the second phase, implementing, teachers do not engage in advanced decision making, such as the examples provided above, but are required to make a number of split-second decisions when interacting with students in classrooms. Many of these interactions are in the form of asking questions, and the effective teacher needs to know the art of asking questions and how to use different question formats—fact questions, process questions, convergent questions, divergent questions—to promote learning (Good & Brophy, 1997). Decision-making considerations include:

- What kinds of questions will encourage student thinking and also allow me the teacher to gauge student understanding?
- Should questions be addressed to the whole group or individual students?
- How long should the teacher wait for a student response?
- What should the teacher do if a student response is incorrect? Prompt (a questioning technique that will be discussed in Chapter 6 along with other questioning strategies), provide the answer, or call on another student?

The third phase, assessment, also requires teachers to make decisions. Teachers continually ask themselves whether students understand new ideas and what modifications need to be made to promote student learning. Questions that address assessment decisions include:

- What kinds of assessments can be used to determine whether or not students understand a given concept or piece of information that is being taught?
- Which aspects of the material do the students clearly understand and which require additional instruction?
- Which students need extra help and which don't?
- In what ways can the assessment results be communicated to students, parents, and other professionals in need of this information?

Teachers make curricular and instructional choices throughout the school year.

At this point, it should be increasingly obvious to you that teaching is extremely complicated and requires, among other things, continual decision making. The quality of the professional decisions you make will directly influence the kinds of learning experiences you provide and ultimately impact the degree to which you promote student learning.

THE IMPORTANCE OF REFLECTION IN TEACHING

In the above section you have seen that part of your role as a teacher involves making a series of decisions about the topics you'll teach—what you want the students to know, understand, or be able to do with respect to the topics; why they're important; and how you'll help students understand them. After you've taught the lessons, you'll want to reconsider your planning and the decisions you've made. This is the reflective role of the teacher.

Reflective teaching is complex and multifaceted. It is a review of one's practices in an attempt to determine whether you accomplished what you set out to do and to gain insight as to more effective ways of doing what you did. Both allow us to ascertain problems related to our teaching, yet we often return to our classrooms and continue to teach with little change to our practice, week after week, month after month, year after year. In short, being curious or intrigued about one's practice is not equivalent to being reflective about one's practice.

Reflective practitioners go beyond curiosity and intrigue to frame, reframe, and develop a plan for future action (Clarke, 1994). A reflective teacher is one who voluntarily and willingly takes responsibility for considering personal actions; is committed to thinking through difficult issues in depth, persistently seeking more knowledge and better ways to teach and to manage classrooms; maintains a healthy skepticism about educational theories and practices; and gathers as much information as possible about any given problem, weighs the value of the evidence against suitable criteria, and then draws a conclusion and makes a judgment (Ely, 1994).

Basically, reflection asks, "How effective were the decisions I made?" Specifically, reflection tries to answer questions such as:

- How appropriate were the topics, i.e., should they be taught again?
- Was the sequence of topics appropriate? If not, how should they be sequenced?
- Was my objective(s) appropriate for my students?
- Was my instruction aligned? Did my lesson plans facilitate my unit plan? Were the procedures and assessments I specified consistent with my objectives?
- Were the procedures I used as effective as they might have been? If not, what procedures might have been better?
- Did the materials I used adequately represent the topic?
- What representations or resources would have made the topic more understandable?
- Is there a way I could have made the overall environment more conducive to learning?

Much of what has been said to this point refers to reflection as a process of questioning in a variety of rational ways, but reflection can also be viewed as product oriented. Reflective teaching means the teacher thinks creatively about solving instructional problems confronted on a daily basis (Jarolimek & Foster, 1997). Being creative fosters the teachers' need to know or be sure they demonstrate in their teaching a sensitivity to what will be most beneficial for their students. Reflective teachers develop their potential for effective action through the process of thoughtful reflection and, in doing so, become concerned with the development of beliefs, knowledge, values, attitudes, and skills that will enable them to be aware of the implications of their actions for the current and future lives of their students (Laboskey, 1994). Current research argues that reflection should not be limited to a rational process but should also be imbued with an ethic of care and with passion (Zeichner, 1991).

A growing and recent body of research further shows that experienced teachers reflect on many different dimensions of their lessons and are able to identify erroneous assumptions and aspects of their teaching that can be improved. The opportunity for reflective thinking about teaching appears to be an activity that could assist teachers in becoming more thoughtful about why, what, and how they plan and conduct learning for the students they teach (Bean, Fulmer, Zigmond, & Grumet, 1995).

Summary

The scenarios in which the three teachers performed each of these phases can be summarized as follows:

	Planning	*Implementing*	*Assessing*
Mrs. Shafer	Wanted students to know how lifestyle and geography relate. Selected pictures and planned discovery.	Had children observe pictures and discover relationship.	Gave children a paragraph and had them identify illustrations in it.
Mr. Adams	Wanted students to develop manipulative skills. Decided on practice. Decided to use the doll.	Had students practice on the doll.	Observed students and checked their names on a checklist.
Mrs. Tyler	Wanted students to learn to work in groups. Chose a dilemma for groups to discuss.	Had students discuss the dilemma and arrive at group decision.	Observed students work in groups during the year.

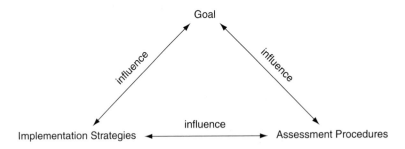

Figure 1.2   The Three Phase Approach to Teaching

Although described as three separate phases, the continuity and interrelationship of the phases should be emphasized. The goal that a teacher has for a particular group of students should determine both what is taught and how it is taught and should influence the manner in which the learning is assessed. This relationship is shown in Figure 1.2.

Some of the relationships shown in Figure 1.2 are readily apparent, while others may require some discussion. The effect of goals on implementation strategies and assessment procedures is apparent in that the goal being taught influences how the lesson is taught and how the effectiveness of the lesson is measured. However, other relationships in the diagram may not be so apparent. Assessment procedures also influence the goals chosen and the implementation procedures used. For example, if assessment procedures show that the desired learning has not taken place, the teacher may wish to reconsider both the goals and the implementation procedures. Perhaps the goals were overly ambitious or inappropriate for the students. On the other hand, the teaching strategy may have been unsuitable for attaining the chosen goal. With feedback from one phase of the teaching act, the teacher can critically examine and reflect upon the effectiveness of the other components as well as the total experience. As teachers become more reflective, they make more conscious and well-thought-out decisions about the topics they choose to teach and the procedures they'll use to teach them and, as such, is the essence of the relationship between decision making and reflection.

The role of the teacher as a decision maker is clearly established in the three-phase approach to teaching described here as a sequentially related series of steps that proceed from the establishing of goals to a verification of the attainment of these goals. Stated another way, teaching is a logical operation in which goals are determined, attempts are made to reach those goals, and the effectiveness of those attempts is assessed. Each of the steps can be identified with questions such as:

What do I want the students to know or understand?
How will I get the students to the goal?
How will I determine whether or not they know or understand what I have identified in the goal?

INTRODUCTION TO THE TEXT

Two major themes or goals serve to structure the text. The first is to develop in readers the mental tools needed to serve as a foundation for continued professional growth. The second is to describe and apply the results suggested by research on teaching.

For the first time, a substantial body of research literature is exerting a prominent influence on educational decisions. This literature falls under a somewhat general category called teacher effectiveness. Simply stated, the research identifies what "good" or effective teachers do compared to what is done by those who are less effective. The research is wide and varied and covers a multitude of controversial variables. For example, a study showed that by reducing class size, the teacher would have more time and energy for each child, would better manage the classroom, and would be able to employ a wider variety of instructional strategies (Gilman, 1988). Overcrowded classrooms are among the most talked about topics in American education today.

Another problem area is that of providing appropriate materials. Some studies found that when students were presented with information in a manner that matched their learning styles, their achievement was significantly higher than when the presentation and their learning styles were mismatched (Dunn, Beaudry, & Klavas, 1989).

Historically, education has been very vulnerable to opinion, influenced by prominent thinkers, or at the worst, even whim. This is no longer the case. Because of this second theme, we cite throughout the text appropriate studies that document teaching effectiveness.

Learning to Teach

As you've probably discovered by now, learning to teach is a complex, multifaceted process. By complex we mean that it is a complicated process that some researchers believe takes many years to master or pass from novice to expert (Berliner, 1988).

Learning to teach is multifaceted in that it requires many different kinds of knowledge. Among these are:

• Content knowledge
• Pedagogical knowledge
• Skills

Let's examine each of these.

It's long been held that, "You can't teach what you don't know." Recently research in teacher education has shown that effective teaching not only requires that teachers know something but also that they can translate this knowledge into something that students can understand and use (Shulman, 1986). Your content knowledge is based upon the hours you have spent in liberal arts courses and in courses in your major and minor. However, according to Rudolph Dreikurs, "knowledge of subject matter alone is not sufficient for being proficient in the classroom . . . or even the ability to convey that knowledge" (1968b).

Pedagogical knowledge, knowing about schools, how they work and how they promote learning is of critical concern. Evidence of pedagogical knowledge is the acquisition of a professional vocabulary that helps teachers think about educational problems and converse with other professionals about educational issues (Strahan, 1989). Some examples of concepts embedded in the domain of pedagogical knowledge include:

• Levels of learning in the cognitive domain
• Instructional goals and objectives
• Lesson planning
• Wait-time
• Inquiry
• Rules and procedures
• Criterion-referenced tests

One of our goals in writing this text is to provide you with a knowledge of these concepts that will allow you to think about and analyze your role as a teacher.

A third kind of teacher knowledge includes teaching skills, or the ability to use knowledge in strategic ways to bring about student learning. The teaching skills contained in this book are organized around the three interrelated tasks of planning, implementation, and assessment. It is our hope that this book will provide you with the necessary skills to become competent during your first years of teaching.

Organization of the Text

The material that follows has been organized into three units:

Unit 1: Learner-Centered Planning (Chapters 2–5)
Unit 2: Learner-Centered Instruction (Chapters 6–10)
Unit 3: Learner-Centered Assessment (Chapter 11)

In an attempt to streamline the readability of the text, we have implemented a standard format that is used for each chapter. The format includes the following:

1. *Introduction.* An orientation to the material and a rationale for its inclusion in the book including a scenario to focus the material to be studied.
2. *Objectives.* A listing of the general knowledge you will have upon the conclusion of the chapter.
3. *Content.* Ideas and concepts that facilitate your attainment of the objectives by providing explanations, descriptions, and examples.
4. *Exercises and Feedback.* Opportunities to practice the skills with explanations and answers provided. Feedback for all exercises is given at the end of each chapter.
5. *Summary.* Brief statement relating the work to the overall conceptualization of the book.
6. *Questions for Discussion.* A series of questions designed to stimulate in-depth discussions on key chapter topics.
7. *Suggestions for Field Experiences.* A list of activities that can be undertaken in schools and classrooms.

This text is designed to be interactive, to help you actively use the information in it to construct a comprehensive view of effective teaching. We encourage you to use the different components of each chapter as you define yourself as a teacher.

Questions for Discussion _____

1. After reading the comment from Nell Noddings found on page 6 which of the primary aims of education would you prioritize? Why?
2. Why is intrinsic motivation considered to be more powerful than extrinsic motivation?
3. Of the three forms of student learning (information and knowledge, manipulative skills, and attitudes and values) which do you believe should receive the primary focus? Why?
4. What are some of the most common decisions classroom teachers make on a daily basis?
5. What is the relationship between decision making and teacher reflection?
6. Most classroom teachers consider the three-phase approach to teaching to be cyclical or that of a closed loop. What does this mean and how does it work?

Suggestions for Field Experience _____

1. Interview a teacher and ask her to share strategies she uses in her classroom to motivate children. Also ask her to suggest ways you can increase your knowledge of a student which in turn impacts upon the success of your motivational techniques.
2. If available, look at a series or number of objectives in a lesson plan, curriculum guide, or teacher's edition and determine whether they primarily address the areas of knowledge, skill, or attitude. You might also discuss with a classroom teacher how or if she prioritizes these three areas.
3. Review some curriculum guides to see if you can identify areas in which teachers can engage in decision making. Specifically, look for opportunities for choice in the areas of content, strategies, and assessments.
4. If sharing information with other preservice teachers is possible at your school site, discuss the role of reflection as a critical part of the three-phase approach to teaching.
5. Given the opportunity, select a goal that appears in a curriculum guide, unit plan, or text and decide what available materials would provide the most effective instruction.

Exercise Feedback _____

EXERCISE 1.1

Your list could include any of the following discussed in Chapter 1:

1. provide extrinsic rewards
2. model appropriate behaviors
3. build a meaningful curriculum
4. develop an interesting curriculum
5. provide appropriate learning experiences
6. provide appropriate learning materials
7. allocate sufficient time
8. project a sincere, positive, enthusiastic, and supportive personality
9. listen to what students say
10. value what students say
11. employ humor
12. enlist the support of parents

EXERCISE 1.2

1. (s) Skill. This is a physical or manipulative behavior.
2. (a) Attitude. The student is expressing a feeling or opinion.
3. (s) Skill. Also a physical behavior.
4. (k) Knowledge. The student needs to know the characteristics of a circle to accomplish this task.
5. (k) Knowledge. The student needs to intellectually process information.

6. (s) and (k) Skill and Knowledge. This task requires both manipulative skills as well as knowledge of how a television functions.
7. (a) Attitude. Willingness to become involved is in and of itself an attitude.

EXERCISE 1.3

1. (a) Assessment. An informal observation.
2. (p) Planning. This is a rationale.
3. (p) Planning. The goal is the cornerstone of planning.
4. (a) Assessment. A formal measurement.
5. (i) Implementation. A procedure.
6. (i) Implementation. An instructional material.

Learner-Centered Planning

In the opening unit of the text, we address planning—the first of the three phases in the approach to teaching. The contents of Chapters 2 through 5, which comprise this unit, are founded upon the constructivist view that planning involves teachers making decisions regarding the most effective ways to provide varied, complex, challenging, and stimulating learning environments. Additionally, teachers strive to provide a highly interactive, student-centered focus in the classroom with an emphasis upon multifaceted views of content that students perceive to be practical and relevant.

The cornerstone of the planning phase is the goal or objective. Decisions regarding the content to be presented, the strategies to be implemented, the materials to be offered, and the assessments to be employed cannot be made until teachers have clearly determined a desired student-learning outcome.

The sources from which goals are determined are presented in Chapter 2 along with the different forms of knowledge that are focused within the objective itself. In Chapter 3, we present three formats which are used to write goals and objectives, and in Chapter 4 we establish the critical role goals and objectives play in long-term planning and the development of unit and lesson plans. Finally, in Chapter 5, we establish ways in which goals and objectives can be designed to nurture attitudinal, physical, and intellectual growth. Unit One concludes with an emphasis on the ways in which objectives can be employed to enhance the ability to process information that is critical to the promotion of student learning.

Chapter 2

The Goals of Instruction

Three middle school social studies teachers were in the teachers' lounge comparing classes over their sack lunches.

"I take a chronological approach. I want them to understand the major events that shaped our country," offered Bill Jenson, an American History teacher.

"I've tried that," replied Shawna Heider, "but my students got lost. Instead we're starting with our country today. We're looking at our society and using that as a focus for our study. I hope to get my students to start thinking about themselves as members of that society."

"I'm taking a similar approach with my class," added Tim Cairns. "I'm asking them to identify a problem that's important to them like pollution, or drugs, or minority problems. Then we're getting into groups to research each area."

Introduction

The purpose of this chapter is to help you think about your own teaching goals, or what you want students to learn in your classroom. We discuss the different types of goals found in our schools today, providing you with the conceptual tools necessary to select and analyze goals for your own teaching. These goals then will serve as the starting point for the construction of specific learning objectives (the focus of Chapter 3). In subsequent chapters we discuss the process of translating objectives into teaching strategies that can be implemented in elementary and secondary classrooms.

Before we launch into our discussion of goals, brief mention should be made of the distinction between goals and objectives. Goals are broad statements of educational intent. Typically, they are described in general, abstract terms, for example:

To understand the importance of the Civil War in U.S. history
To appreciate the importance of good study habits
To know basic principles of proper nutrition

Objectives, by contrast, are typically stated using behavioral terms, in an attempt to define educational outcomes precisely, for example:

Students will identify examples of participles, gerunds, and infinitives.
Students will match major historical events with appropriate U.S. presidents.
Students will apply the Pythagorean theorem to various word problems.

In these instances verbs like *identify, match,* and *apply* specify what is expected of students as they attain the objective. We talk more in the next chapter about the relationship of goals to objectives.

Objectives

After completing your study of Chapter 2, you should be able to:

- Understand the three major sources of goals for the school curriculum
- Describe the three domains: affective, psychomotor, or cognitive
- Understand important differences between abstractions and facts

SOURCES OF GOALS

Every teacher has some kind of goal when she teaches, but the goals selected by various teachers differ in their value to the student. For example, some teachers have as their goal keeping the kids busy and quiet until the bell rings; other teachers have as their goal getting through a textbook or covering a chapter in the following week. The value of each of these goals is questionable at best and is hard to defend from a professional standpoint. Our purpose here is to describe some possible sources for the establishment of educationally defensible goals and discuss the significance of these sources for today's schools.

The Child as a Source of Goals

Two basic questions every teacher should ask in considering the goals of instruction are, What are schools for? and, How does my class fit into the larger picture? One pair of answers to these questions is that schools are for people, and the function of both the school and its classrooms is to help young people develop to the fullest extent of their potential. In other words, one source of goals for instruction can be found in the students themselves. In tapping this source of curriculum goals, the teacher is basically asking the question: How can the knowledge and skills that I possess as a teacher help the students I'm teaching develop into healthy and functioning adults?

If you thought about this question for a while, we think you'd realize that the answer depends upon a number of factors such as the kind of student, their cultural backgrounds, the level of the students, and the subject being taught. Your educational psychology classes probably have discussed the idea of development and how teachers can adapt their instruction to meet the needs of students of different ages. In addition, special methods classes, like science or social studies methods, will help you use these content areas to meet the interests and needs of students. Tim Cairns took this approach when he asked students to investigate problems that were individually important to them. Let's see how this occurs in other areas.

Probably the area of the curriculum in which the learner has had the greatest effect on goals is early childhood. A major movement in this area is the developmental curriculum, an attempt to match the curriculum to the developmental learning needs of students (Gestwicki, 1995). Here, a large part of the school day is devoted to helping the child grow emotionally, intellectually, and physically. Special attention is paid to the developmental levels of the students, and learning tasks are designed to match these levels and help children progress to the next. In addition, special attention is paid to the emotional growth of individuals, and attempts are made to help students develop healthy attitudes about themselves and others. Some goals in the early childhood curriculum that have the student as a primary source include the following:

Kindergarten students will develop good eye-hand coordination.
Kindergarten students will understand families and how children are a part of families.
Kindergarten students will develop speaking and listening skills.

Another area of the curriculum that stresses the child as a source of goals is health science. A primary focus of the health curriculum is to help children understand their bodies and the changes that are occurring in those bodies. Some examples of student-related goals in this area of the curriculum include the following:

Health science students will understand the importance of proper nutrition in the diet.
Health science students will appreciate the importance of hygiene in preventing disease and maintaining the body's functionings.
Health science students will understand the role of exercise in maintaining physical fitness.

Each of these goals focuses on the area of health and uses the child as a starting point for that focus. Lists like these could be constructed for each subject matter area and grade level. The extent to which a particular teacher's goals approximate this list would indicate, to a large extent, the degree to which that teacher believes that schools are designed to help students develop into physically and psychologically healthy adults.

Society as a Source of Goals

Another way to approach the task of establishing teaching goals is to examine the society that students live in and will ultimately function in, and decide how schools can help students to meet the challenges of that society effectively. Proponents of this view of the curriculum claim that the role of the school is to prepare students for life, and the content of the schools should be matched to the demands of everyday living. The value of goals established by this approach is measured in terms of their usefulness to the individual in functioning in today's world. Knowledge for its own sake is rejected; instead, knowledge becomes valuable to the extent that it is practical. A present-day interpretation of this approach of selecting goals is called life management and focuses on those goals that will help an individual manage her life in a complex technological world. A major focus of this emphasis is helping students to understand how basically abstract processes like math and reading have potential use for functioning in the worlds of work and play. Shawna Heider adopted this focus when she tried to get her students " . . . to start thinking about themselves as members of society."

One of the areas of the curriculum where societal influences have had a major impact on the curriculum is home economics. Here, students are trained to attack the problem of functioning in today's modern society in a systematic and scientific way. Some examples of goals in the home economics curriculum that reflect a societal influence are:

> Home economics students will compare different loan conditions and select the one that is best for a particular situation.
> Home economics students will plan menus that are nutritionally and economically practical.
> Home economics students will understand the responsibilities and rewards of parenting.

Each of these goals has as its focus the development of skills that will be useful to each individual in living in modern-day society.

Another, more traditional, area of the curriculum where societal demands have had an influence is mathematics. With this orientation, mathematics' place in the curriculum is determined by the extent to which it can help students function in 21st-century America. Emphasis is placed on the application of math skills rather than their theoretical implications. The following are some goals from the area of math that reflect a societal influence:

> Math students will be able to balance their checkbooks.
> Math students will use ratios to adjust recipes and adapt woodworking and construction plans.
> Math students will understand distance, rate, and time problems.
> Math students will be able to use various area formulas to solve everyday problems.

In each of these examples mathematics is seen not as an end but rather as a means toward some other goal.

A third type of orientation to goal setting, the academic focus, views the various disciplines as ends in and of themselves.

The Academic Disciplines as Sources of Goals

Goals for instruction can be found by examining the various academic disciplines and determining which knowledge in these disciplines is most important or central to understanding these different content areas. Proponents of this approach to goal setting contend that the function of the schools is not so much to help students adjust to society or to give them short-range skills that will quickly become outmoded in today's rapidly changing world but rather to transmit to students the knowledge that has stood the test of time. These same people call attention to the immense number of changes that have occurred in the last 20 or 30 years and point out that anything other than an academically oriented curriculum, which transcends these changes, would soon be outmoded. In addition, they believe that a number of other institutions, like the family and the church, are much better suited to teach life-adjustment skills and that the schools should focus on basic knowledge and intellectual or cognitive skills.

If a teacher were to use an academic approach to select teaching goals, she would probably turn to the texts and notes she used as a college student and try to determine which ideas were central to her discipline. These would then become the goals of the curriculum and the major focus of her teaching. Bill Jensen used the academic disciplines as a source of goals when he approached history from a chronological perspective. Some other examples of academically oriented goals include the following:

Social studies students will know the differences between Marxism and socialism.
Economics students will understand the law of supply and demand.
Science students will know the characteristics of the major animal phyla.
Music students will be able to classify major musical works as baroque, classical, or romantic.
Math students will know how to solve for unknowns in quadratic equations.

Meeting the needs of students is one of the three sources of goals.

Sometimes goals are selected for inclusion in an academically oriented curriculum because they form the foundation or basis for other goals. For example, teaching young children the concepts of right and left, up and down, big and little, and square and circle can be justified in terms of their future value in the teaching of reading in addition to their more immediate utilitarian value. (Think for a second how you would explain the difference between a *d*, a *p*, and a *q* if kindergarten or first-grade students didn't know the difference between left and right or up and down.) These goals are called readiness skills.

Another example of the use of prerequisite goals is the common activity in preschool and kindergarten classes of having children color in figures. The major purpose of this activity is not to provide some type of artistic experience for students but rather to develop their eye–hand and small muscle coordination. Both of these are important later in learning to read and write.

These latter examples were provided to broaden the concept of an academically oriented curriculum to include the spectrum of goals that provide students with background experiences for later, more traditional, academic goals.

EXERCISE 2.1

Examine the following goals and try to determine whether their primary focus is the child (c), society (s), or the academic disciplines (a). Then compare your answers to the ones given in the feedback section at the end of the chapter.

_____ 1. Junior-high social studies students will know the 13 states of the Confederacy.
_____ 2. First-year math students will understand how to compute cost per unit when given aggregate costs.
_____ 3. Fifth-grade science students will understand the concept of an ecosystem.
_____ 4. First-grade students will understand that they have rights and responsibilities.
_____ 5. Sixth-grade health students will understand how to care for cuts and abrasions.
_____ 6. Senior-high civics students will understand the voting system in their city, state, and country.
_____ 7. Junior-high health students will know the causes, symptoms, and means of preventing venereal disease.
_____ 8. First-year biology students will know the characteristics of monocotyledons and dicotyledons.
_____ 9. Senior-high driver education students will know the driving regulations in their state.
_____ 10. Fifth-grade math students will know how to convert fractions into decimals.

THE THREE DOMAINS

When teachers think about what to teach, the nature of the learning experiences that students encounter must be taken into account. Learning can be thought of as a change in capability resulting from experience rather than growth. For example, children begin learning early and undertake many physical tasks such as tying shoes, buttoning shirts, holding pencils, and moving their eyes back and forth across a printed page. They learn intellectual tasks such as the names of objects in their home, the alphabet, and the use of mathematical principles. They also learn attitudes and values that influence their feelings and interests, such as color preference, confidence in themselves, and reactions to peers.

These are examples of learning, but they are not all the same kind of learning. Just as goals can be differentiated in terms of their sources, goals can also be described in terms of the type of learning that is intended. In this respect we can describe goals as being primarily concerned with the development of muscular skills and coordination (psychomotor), the growth of attitudes or values (affective), or the transmission of knowledge and intellectual skills (cognitive).

Understanding differences between goals in the different domains helps to clarify teachers' thinking about the goals they're trying to teach. This, then, has implications for planning, implementing, and assessing. The more clearly teachers understand what they are trying to accomplish, the greater the chance that they will achieve those goals (Cohen, 1987). Other helpful discussions of the three domains and problems encountered in establishing goals in these areas can be found in Bloom, Hastings, and Madaus (1971), and Armstrong (1989).

Unfortunately for teachers who are trying to separate and analyze behaviors, children come to the classroom as whole beings. So as we examine the three domains of learning, remember that they don't occur in isolation but rather work together to influence one whole being. Some goals are easily classifiable into one of the three domains, while others seem to overlap a great deal. This overlap appears in Figure 2.1. A good example of an integrated behavior that incorporates all three domains of learning in school is handwriting. The child must have the small muscle coordination to make the necessary intricate movements (psychomotor); he must know what movements are used to form the letters (cognitive); and he must want to perform these enough so that proficiency can be developed through practice (affective).

Many tasks taught in schools can be separated as to domain, and every teacher should know her domain of primary teaching concentration in order to plan effectively. The importance of knowing the intent of the instruction makes it imperative for the teacher to determine the focus of planned instruction as either affective, psychomotor, or cognitive. We'll consider each of these three domains further in Chapter 5 when we examine ways to classify goals and objectives at different levels. Because of the importance

Figure 2.1 The Three Domains of Learning

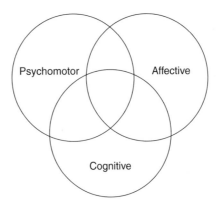

of the cognitive domain at all levels and in all disciplines, we'll continue to examine it in the next section.

CONTENT IN THE COGNITIVE DOMAIN

One way to analyze the cognitive domain is to examine the different kinds of content found in that area. The basic idea here is that not all goals within the cognitive domain are of equal worth. Some types of content are more valuable than others in helping students understand the world around them. These ideas are called abstractions.

Abstractions

Abstractions are the ideas people use to describe, understand, and simplify the world. They are in a sense the mental templates that we use to perceive and understand our environment. Abstractions form an important part of the curriculum at every grade level. In this section of the chapter we define abstractions and examine how teachers help students learn this important form of content.

> Ms. Tanya Harris was trying to teach her kindergarten students the basic shapes. She did this by cutting out squares, circles, and rectangles from felt and putting them in a paper bag. Students took turns coming up to the front of the class, pulling one piece of felt out of the bag, and putting it in the correct circle on the board.

> Mr. Kim Lawson wanted his fifth-grade students to understand basic differences among amphibians, reptiles, and mammals. They read paragraphs about different animals and looked at pictures of them and then tried to classify them into the correct area.

> Mr. Sean Harris introduced the topic of Elizabethan sonnets by placing several on a handout. He distributed this handout to his tenth-grade literature class without an introduction and asked the class to analyze them for similarities and differences.

To illustrate the notion of abstractions as ideas, imagine a small child beginning to acquire experience in her young life. She encounters an animal her mother or father identifies as a dog. The dog has a set of features such as floppy ears, wagging tail, and scruffy fur that the child reacts to without consciously being aware of it. She then encounters another dog with some similar features, then a third, perhaps a fourth, and ultimately many more. The child, again without realizing it, sees a pattern in the features. For instance, even though the dogs vary considerably, they all have four legs, say "woof-woof," are hairy, and so on. The pattern in these features common to the dogs result in the child's idea of "dog." This idea is an abstraction. The abstraction is not any particular example of dog, nor is it a sort of average of the examples encountered. It is literally an abstracted mental idea of dog (Tennyson & Cocchiarella, 1986).

Let's investigate this abstracting process a bit further. We watch or hear the weather forecast over a period of time, and we hear the meteorologist make statements such as, "The barometric pressure is dropping" and "The rain probability is 50 percent." As we watch or hear these broadcasts, we begin to notice that there is a relationship between low barometric pressure and rain probability. As with the child beginning to acquire an idea of dogs, we see a pattern emerge that could be described as "The lower the barometric pressure, the higher the probability of rain." The child has formed an abstraction and we have formed an abstraction. The difference between the two is that the child found a pattern in the features of different dogs, and we found a pattern in the relationship between pressure and rain probability. Our abstraction is broader and more encompassing than the one about dogs, but it is a pattern and an abstraction nevertheless.

The power in understanding patterns or abstractions is enormous. They greatly simplify the world for us because we need only remember the pattern, not the individual examples that fit it. For instance, the child would have to understand or know each example of dog separately if she had no pattern, but with it she has a single idea of dog, into which she fits all the examples she encounters.

As another example of the power of abstract patterns, consider the spelling rule "*i* before *e* except after *c*." (Academic rules are another form of pattern.) Knowing this academic rule allows a learner to spell individual words such as

> retrieve
> believe
> conceive
> conceit
> perceive

Admittedly, the learner must know the pattern's exceptions, but the pattern makes it unnecessary for the learner to remember all words individually.

Abstractions are formed as a result of seeing patterns in our experiences, and their value comes from their ability to summarize these experiences in an economical manner. But what is the school's role in teaching abstractions?

One way to think of education is to view it as a process in which abstract ideas of a culture are transmitted to the young people of that culture (Hirsch, 1987). For example, social studies education is concerned with teaching students to understand the following abstractions:

> democracy
> socialism
> social stratification
> The more economically diverse an economy, the more stable it is when economic changes occur.
> When supply stays constant, price is directly related to demand.

In a similar manner, teaching science involves the transmission of abstractions such as the following:

> mammal
> ion
> magnetism
> Acids neutralize bases.
> The more recent animal phyla have more complex systems.

English or language arts would incorporate abstractions such as:

adverb
metaphor
Elizabethan sonnet
When the subject is singular, add an s to the verb.
When there are several adjectives modifying a noun, the article goes first.

Similar analyses could be done for each of the subject matter areas.

We now turn our attention to the two major types of abstractions taught at the elementary and secondary levels: concepts and generalizations. *Concepts* are classes or categories that share some common characteristic. *Generalizations* are statements relating two or more concepts, typically in a causal or correlational relationship. Each of these types of cognitive goals is described more fully in the paragraphs that follow.

Concepts

Concepts are ideas that refer to a class or category in which all the members share some common characteristics. For example, *adverb* is a concept that has the characteristic of modifying a verb, an adjective, or another adverb. We use these defining characteristics to decide whether a particular word belongs in the category or not. In addition to the essential or defining characteristics, examples of concepts also contain irrelevant or nonessential characteristics. In the case of the concept *adverb,* the irrelevant characteristics include the length of the word, its sound, and the number of consonants or vowels in it. These irrelevant characteristics tell us nothing about whether a word is an adverb or not. In trying to learn a concept, these nonessential characteristics represent noise that the learner must filter out to focus on the essential characteristics. These essential characteristics are important to remember because they make up the rule for class membership; they help to determine whether something is a positive or negative example of a concept. Many of the abstractions that have previously been mentioned are concepts. For example, *dog, adverb, democracy,* and *ion* are all concepts. Typically we think of concepts as being single words that represent ideas. Another way of representing concepts is by a definition; for example, a democracy is a form of government in which the power to make decisions resides in the governed. Some additional examples of concepts from various disciplines are found in Table 2.1.

Let's look again at the idea of forming patterns. Suppose a learner sees sentences such as:

The boy ran <u>quickly</u> to his locker.
Their conversation was <u>abruptly</u> interrupted.
The material was <u>appropriately</u> analyzed.

Learners recognize on their own, or with the help of the teacher, that in each case the underlined word tells something about the verb. This represents a pattern that is the characteristic of "modifying a verb." The pattern will be expanded to include modification of adjectives and other adverbs, and the result is the concept *adverb.*

Table 2.1   Concepts from Various Disciplines

Language Arts	Science	Mathematics
homonym	nucleus	set
antonym	mitosis	rational number
syllable	evaluation	lowest common denominator
alliteration	mesoderm	quadratic equation
quatrain	metamorphosis	exponent
inference	acid	base
tragedy	base	tangent
gerund	algae	angle
plot	fruit	axiom
prefix	energy	
	plant	

Social Studies	Music	Art
federalism	melody	line
climate	rhythm	texture
tax	syncopation	batik
inflation	harmony	realism
boycott	a cappella	cubism

Notice as we've discussed abstractions in general and concepts in particular that we've consistently referred to examples. Research supports the value of examples in concept learning (Tennyson & Cocchiarella, 1986). The use of nonexamples is also important in learning concepts. By analyzing the positive examples and noting what they have in common, and by contrasting these with negative examples, the learner is often able to figure out the essential characteristics for himself. In addition to providing the student with data from which to extract the important characteristics, examples also provide concrete referents in the world. In a sense, they make abstract ideas less abstract.

Another way of teaching someone about a concept is by relating it to other concepts. For example, if you were to ask someone what a bird is, a typical reply would be that it's a kind of animal. In a similar way, a social studies teacher might define a democracy as a form of government. In both instances the concept being explained was related to a larger, more inclusive—or *superordinate*—concept. Superordinate relationships can be illustrated either through the use of conceptual hierarchies or through the use of Venn diagrams, as shown in Figure 2.2.

Knowing that a concept is a member of a larger set or concept is useful because it allows us to apply characteristics of the larger to the smaller. For example, if a person knows a lemur is a mammal, a superordinate concept, then she could infer that lemurs have mammalian characteristics such as having fur, being warm-blooded, giving live

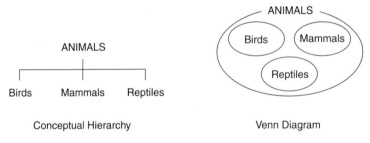

Figure 2.2   Illustrations of Superordinate Relationships

birth, and nursing their young. In a similar manner, if someone tells you that cilantro is an herb, then you know that it's a plant that is used for seasoning. Superordinate concepts help to make concepts more meaningful by contributing their characteristics to the definition. This is why most dictionaries define concepts in terms of a superordinate one. For example, if you were to look up the term *wok*, you would find it described as a pan for cooking Asian food dishes. The superordinate concept *pan* allows you to infer that this object is probably made of metal and is meant to be heated.

In addition to allowing us to infer characteristics, superordinate concepts also help to show relationships between concepts. For example, in the case of the concept *birds*, linking this concept to *animals* establishes the fact that *birds* are related to other concepts like *mammals* or *reptiles*. Linking concepts in our teaching is important so that students learn to see the larger relationships between ideas. One of these relationships is between coordinate concepts.

Coordinate concepts are abstractions that are subsumed by the superordinate concept and that are different from the concept under consideration. In the previous examples with birds, *mammals* and *reptiles* would be coordinate concepts to *birds* because they are types of animals that are different from birds. To integrate ideas, knowing the coordinate concepts of a given concept is important because it is coordinate concepts that are most easily confused with the concept under study. For example, in a lesson involving the concept *reptiles*, students are most likely to get examples of this concept confused with examples of coordinate concepts such as *amphibians* or *mammals* rather than unrelated concepts like *cars, balls*, or *books*.

A third type of relationship that exists between concepts is a subordinate relationship. A *subordinate concept* is a subset or subcategory of a concept. If you understand superordinate concepts, subordinate concepts are easy to understand because they are reciprocal relationships. For example, in the case of animals and birds, *animals* is superordinate to *birds*, and *birds* is subordinate to *animals*. In a similar manner, the concept *noun* is superordinate to the subordinate concept *proper noun*.

Superordinate, coordinate, and subordinate concepts are discussed again in Chapter 7 when we describe strategies for teaching concepts. Those wanting to read more about concept teaching in the classroom are referred to Slavin (1997) and Bruning, Schraw, and Ronning (1995).

Providing the students with the ability to undertake a concept analysis allows them to relate one concept to other concepts.

EXERCISE 2.2_____

Answer the following questions by circling your choice. Note that more than one response may be correct. Then compare your answers to the ones given in the feedback section at the end of the chapter.

1. Consider the concept *horse*. Which of the following could be superordinate to the concept?
   a. cow
   b. domestic animal
   c. Shetland
   d. beast of burden
   e. none of the above
2. Consider the concept *radio*. If *electrical instructional tools* is superordinate to *radio,* which of the following is coordinate to *radio?*
   a. encyclopedia
   b. overhead projector
   c. textbook
   d. teacher
   e. none of the above
3. Consider the concept *bread.* Which of the following could be subordinate to the concept?
   a. rye
   b. wheat
   c. meat
   d. white

   e. vegetable
   f. food
4. Which of the following could be superordinate to *bread?*
   a. banana
   b. rye
   c. food
   d. fruit
   e. vegetable
5. If *fried bacon* and *hot oatmeal* were coordinate to *bread,* which of the following could be superordinate?
   a. banana
   b. food
   c. cooked food
   d. raw food
   e. prunes
   f. none of the above

Generalizations

Generalization is the second major type of abstraction taught in our schools. Again, generalizations are statements about patterns in the world that are either correlational or suggest a causal relationship. Other terms used to refer to these patterns are *rule, principle,* or *law.* For our purposes, we will consider these terms synonymous in that all of them describe patterns in the ways that objects and events in our environment operate.

Here are some examples of generalizations describing causal relationships:

Smoking causes cancer.
Lack of sunlight makes plants grow tall and spindly.
Heat makes molecules move faster.

These generalizations describe a relationship between concepts in which something causes something else to occur. The other type of generalization describes a relationship between concepts in which a given condition is usually accompanied by another condition. For example, the following generalizations describe situations in which one type of condition is typically followed by or correlated with another:

The time spent studying a subject is related to achievement in that area.
Lower socioeconomic families have more children than upper socioeconomic families.
More management problems occur during individual student work than in large-group activities.

Note that these generalizations don't imply causality; for example, time itself does not cause learning to occur. Instead, greater time spent on a subject allows other processes like attention, rehearsal, and meaningful processing to occur.

As can be seen from the examples presented, generalizations vary in terms of their validity or accuracy, with some being very probabilistic and others, invariant. For example, heat always makes molecules move faster. This would be an invariant relationship in that it always happens. Contrasted with generalizations like this are probabilistic generalizations like time is related to learning. Obviously there are a number of instances in which more time is not related to increased learning (for example, the student may be unmotivated or may not be concentrating on the topic at hand). But on the whole this generalization is valid.

This brings us to a discussion of how generalizations are formed. People make generalizations by observing the world around them and by trying to see patterns in the things that they observe. As an illustration of this process, look at Table 2.2 and see if you can make any general statements about trends or patterns in the data.

Here are several generalizations that could be made:

The sun rises later each day in the autumn.
The sun sets earlier each day in the autumn.
Days get progressively shorter each day of autumn.

Generalizations like these are formed by people who are observant enough to see patterns in the world around them. In a sense, these patterns can be said to be discovered, in that they have always existed, and one person or group of persons finally noticed the pattern. One of the major goals of science is to formulate generalizations about the world (Lawson, 1995). What differentiates scientists from other people who form generalizations is that scientists approach this task in a much more systematic fashion than the person on the street. However, all of us form generalizations about the world.

Often generalizations are learned in the same way that they are formed, by observing a number of examples and noticing trends or patterns in them. Generalizations are quite similar to concepts in this regard. The generalizations that you formed from observing the sunrise and sunset data were learned this way. An alternate way of learning generalizations is to have someone tell them to you. This is often quicker, and perhaps it is for this reason that this is the most common way of teaching generalizations in schools today. However, the teaching of generalizations through strictly verbal means has drawbacks. One is related to developmental considerations. The work of Piaget and others who have studied the way children learn shows us the importance of providing children with concrete, tangible experiences in the learning of abstractions (Berk, 1994). In the absence of such experiences, children learn words and not ideas. A classic example of this was noted by William James.

> A friend of mine, visiting a school, was asked to examine a young class in geography. She said, "Suppose you should dig a hole in the ground hundreds of feet deep, how should you find it at the bottom—warmer or colder than on the top?" None of the class replying, the teacher said, "I'm sure they know, but I think you don't ask the question quite rightly. Let me try." So taking the book she asked, "In what condition is the interior of the globe?"

Table 2.2   Times for Sunrise and Sunset

Date	Sunrise	Sunset
10/14	7:14	6:42
10/15	7:15	6:41
10/16	7:16	6:40

and received the immediate answer from half the class at once, "The interior of the globe is in a condition of igneous fusion" (1914, p. 150).

Obviously, the students in that class had learned a string of words rather than a meaningful abstraction. Situations like this occur all too frequently in our schools when teachers forget that concepts and generalizations are meaningful only to the extent that students can relate them to the real world. Forgetting this, teachers teach abstractions as a string of words and are satisfied when students can recall these words without their meanings during class discussion or on a test. The teaching strategies discussed in Chapter 7 describe a number of techniques to ensure that this doesn't happen.

In trying to decide which generalizations should be included in the curriculum, the teacher has several things to consider. Fraenkel (1980) suggested the following criteria be used in deciding whether a particular generalization should be included in the curriculum:

- To how many varied areas, events, people, ideas, objects, etc., does the generalization apply? (Applicability)
- How likely is it that the relationship that the generalization suggests does indeed exist? (Accuracy)
- To what degree does the generalization, as stated, lead to other insights? (Depth)
- To what extent does (do) the relationship(s) that the generalization suggests describe important aspects of human behavior and explain important segments of today's world? (Significance)
- How much information does it encompass? (Breadth)
- How many powerful (complex) concepts does it include? (Conceptual strength)

The use of these criteria can be illustrated by comparing the following two generalizations:

Tree-ring size is related to the amount of rainfall in that year.
How quickly any change comes about depends not only on the nature of the change itself but also on the pressures for and against that change.

Obviously, the second generalization is preferable to the first on the basis of a number of the criteria listed. It is more widely applicable and provides students with greater opportunities to understand their worlds.

This concludes our discussion of abstractions. In the following section we describe facts, discuss how facts are different from abstractions, and explore the implications of these differences for teaching. Before that, however, let's focus on two exercises involving abstractions.

EXERCISE 2.3

Read the following teaching episodes and answer the questions that follow. Then compare your answers to the ones given in the feedback section at the end of the chapter.

1. Mr. Waters, a fifth-grade teacher, was preparing for his first-period language arts class. His goal for that period was to teach his students transitive verbs. He began his lesson by saying, "I'm going to show

you two sentences, and I want you to look at them and tell me how the sentences are different." He wrote the following sentences on the board:

The infielder, bobbling the ball momentarily, threw it in the nick of time.
They were late again for the start of first-period English.

"The first one is longer," said Jim.
"The second one has a plural subject," offered Mary.
"Isn't the verb in the first sentence in the past tense?" asked Kathy.
"But so is the verb in the second sentence. And we're supposed to be looking for differences," corrected Dick.

After writing these ideas on the board, Mr. Waters commented, "Those are all good ideas. Let me give you another example of the first kind of sentence and see if you can narrow your ideas down." To his list he added:

The children ate the oatmeal cookies.

"Look at the sentences again," directed Mr. Waters, "and tell me how the first and the third are similar."
The lesson continued until the students saw that the first and the third both had direct objects. Then Mr. Waters discussed the idea of transitive verbs, relating this idea to the examples the students had used.

a. What abstraction was Mr. Waters trying to teach?

_____

_____

b. What kind of data did the teacher use for examples?

_____

_____

2. Mrs. Jones, another English teacher, was also trying to teach her sixth-grade students about verbs. She started the lesson by saying, "All of you remember what verbs are. We've been working with them all year. Now we're going to learn about a special kind of verb called the intransitive verb. Intransitive verbs are verbs that can't take a direct object. Who remembers what a direct object is? Johnny?"
"I think they are words that receive the action of the verb," Johnny responded. "Like, 'He hit me.' *Me* is the direct object."
"Fine, Johnny," said Mrs. Jones. "Now remember, intransitive verbs are verbs that can't take a direct object. Some examples of intransitive verbs are different forms of the verb be, such as *am, were, was,* and *has been.* I'm going to put a sentence on the board. See if you can tell me whether the verb is intransitive or not."

He was late.

"Yes," offered Sally, "because it's a form of *be* and can't have a direct object."
"Good," said Mrs. Jones, "and how about this one?"

The woodsman chopped the tree down.

"That can't be intransitive," Rachel said.
"Why not?" Mrs. Jones asked.

Because it has a direct object. *Tree* is the direct object."
"Good, Rachel."

The lesson continued until Mrs. Jones felt assured that the students understood intransitive verbs.

a. What abstraction was Mrs. Jones trying to teach?

_____

b. What kind of data did the teacher use for examples?

_____

_____

c. How were Mr. Waters's and Mrs. Jones's teaching approaches different? How were they the same?

_____

_____

3. Mr. Black wanted his fourth-grade students to know biodegradable objects so that they would know what kinds of things could be thrown away and not cause litter. He began the lesson by saying, "Today I'm going to teach you about biodegradable objects. Everybody say, 'biodegradable objects.' " He then wrote biodegradable on the board. "Orange peels and cigar butts are biodegradable. However, bottles and cigarette filters are not. Neither is aluminum foil or bottle caps. Can you tell me what biodegradable means?"

Jerry said, "It must be something to do with plant products."
Chris added, "Or it could be things that are soft."
"Well, let me give you some more information to help you decide."
With that, he took out a container that was filled with moist dirt and other objects. In the container were a number of biodegradable objects like wood chips and paper that had already started to disintegrate, along with other objects like plastic cups and pop tops. As he took each of these objects out of the pail, he labeled them as either biodegradable or not. On the basis of this information the class was able to come up with a definition.

a. What abstraction was Mr. Black trying to teach?

_____

b. What kind of data did the teacher use for examples?

_____

_____

Facts

Facts are statements about the world that are directly observable and typically singular in occurrence, either in the past or in the present. Some examples of facts are:

Johnson was one of Lincoln's vice presidents.
Emil von Behring discovered how to control diphtheria.
Japan bombed Pearl Harbor on December 7, 1941.

Each of these statements is or was directly observable and is singular in occurrence in the past. As such, they are factual reports of what happened at a particular place and time. This differentiates them from abstractions in that abstractions are statements about general patterns. Concepts describe categories and classes which are, in a sense, timeless in that what was an adverb yesterday will be an adverb tomorrow. Generalizations describe patterns that were not only valid in the past but are also valid now and should also be valid in the future. Facts, by contrast, occur only once. This characteristic of facts places severe limitations on their use to students, as we'll see shortly.

Let's look now at a series of facts and their relationship to patterns or abstractions. Consider the following:

President Roosevelt was from New York.
President Johnson was from Texas.
President Nixon was from California.

Each of these statements is a fact. Consider also the fact that each state mentioned has a large population. We might then suggest the pattern, "Presidents tend to come from populous states." While there are obvious exceptions to this pattern, it tends to be generally valid. Our point in this example is to illustrate the relationship between facts and abstractions. Abstractions are formed by having learners process facts into recognizable patterns. This is one reason for including facts in the curriculum.

The other major reason for learning facts is that some facts are considered valuable to know, in and of themselves, apart from any relationship of abstractions. Examples of these facts are

The Declaration of Independence was signed in Philadelphia on July 4, 1776.
Alexander Graham Bell invented the telephone.
Herman Melville wrote Moby Dick.

The reason that facts such as these are considered inherently valuable is that they make up part of the general store of knowledge that is shared by most Americans and considered one of the marks of an educated person. In the book *Cultural Literacy*, Hirsch (1987) equates cultural literacy with knowledge of a certain number of key facts and concepts. However, relative to their use and importance in the curriculum, facts probably receive an undue amount of emphasis in most classrooms (Goodlad, 1984).

Facts and Abstractions: Their Value in the Curriculum

If our biases haven't already crept through in our writing, let us make them explicit. We feel that the major amount of time and effort spent in the classroom on cognitive goals should involve the teaching of abstractions rather than facts. The reason for this is that abstractions can be used to summarize large amounts of information, can be used to predict the future, and can be used to explain phenomena. Each of these reasons and its relevance to the classroom is discussed in the paragraphs that follow.

Abstractions serve a summarizing function in that they describe large amounts of information in a statement that is easier to remember than all the individual facts. An example from mathematics helps to illustrate this point. One of the authors was helping his son with his 9s addition facts. The son was having trouble remembering each of the separate facts, so the father taught him the generalization, "When you add 9 to any number, your last number is always one less than the original." (For example, in adding 6 and 9, you get 15, the 5 of which is 1 less than the original 6.) By understanding this generalization, the boy was able to bypass the need for memorizing each of the combinations that 9 could make. Instead, he remembered a general pattern that could apply to all instances. The earlier illustration with the spelling rule "*i* before *e* except after *c*" is another example of the benefits of learning patterns as opposed to isolated facts.

So the first argument against learning many isolated facts is that their sheer number makes them hard to remember, as attested to by anyone who has taken a course that consisted primarily of the rote memorization of facts. Typically in courses like this, students memorize the facts for a test and forget the facts shortly after, since these facts aren't integrated with other ideas and often aren't ever used again.

A second reason why abstractions have particular value in the curriculum is that we can use them to make predictions about the future. To illustrate this process, analyze the following facts in Table 2.3 and make a prediction about the tides on June 7.

Three generalizations can be formed from the facts in Table 2.3:

High tides and low tides are 6 hours apart.
There are 12 hours between occurrences of high tides and 12 hours between occurrences of low tides.
High and low tides occur 45 minutes later each subsequent day.

On the basis of these generalizations, we can predict that high tides would occur on June 7 at 4:15 A.M. and P.M. and low tides at 10:15 A.M. and P.M. This type of information is valuable to fishermen, sailors, or people just wanting to walk on the beach and not get wet. Note that on the basis of the facts alone, you could not make this prediction. These facts first needed to be processed into abstractions, and then predictions could be made.

The process of making predictions from abstractions is a common and often unconscious everyday occurrence. For example, what time do you expect it to get dark tonight, and where will the sun be when it sets? Also, how do you expect the temperature this evening to compare to the temperature during the day? Your answers to all of

Table 2.3   High and Low Tides

Date	High Tides	Low Tides
6/4	2 00 A.M.	8:00 A.M.
	2:00 P.M.	8:00 P.M.
6/5	2:45 A.M.	8:45 A.M.
	2:45 P.M.	8:45 P.M.
6/6	3:30 A.M.	9:30 A.M.
	3:30 P.M.	9:30 P.M.

these questions were predictions based on generalizations that you have formed either consciously or unconsciously about the environment. The same type of predictions can be made with concepts, the other major type of abstraction. For example, if you purchase a mystery novel, what do you expect to find in it? Or if you order crepes in a restaurant, how do you expect them to taste? Or if you rent a car, where do you expect the steering wheel, the gas pedal, and the brakes to be? These and other questions like them are fairly easy to answer if we are familiar with the concepts involved. Knowing the characteristics of a concept allows us to apply these characteristics to examples of that concept. Therefore, a mystery novel that we pick up should have some kind of mystery to solve, clues to help solve the mystery, and a resolution by the end of the story. Again, it should be emphasized that facts alone do not allow us to make such predictions.

A third use of abstractions that makes them a valuable component in the curriculum is their ability to explain phenomena. For example, lower insurance rates for married people and nondrinkers can be explained by the generalizations linking these categories of drivers and accident rates. An additional example from teaching further illustrates this explanatory function.

Two elementary teachers taught geometric shapes to their classes. Teacher A pointed out different kinds of circles, squares, rectangles, and triangles around the room, while Teacher B prepared shapes from cardboard and used these as examples. The students in Teacher B's class seemed to learn the concept faster, but on a posttest the students in Teacher A's class did better at identifying shapes that were embedded in complex designs. Both of these results can be explained by referring to generalizations that psychologists have found in the research on concept learning (Eggen & Kauchak, 1997; Slavin, 1997). The fact that Teacher B's class learned the concept more quickly could be explained by the generalization that simplifying examples when initially teaching a concept speeds up the learning process. Because of the simple shapes provided by Teacher B, her class had less difficulty in seeing the characteristics of the concepts in the examples. The fact that Teacher A's class performed better on the embedded figures task can be explained by the generalization that the closer the criterion task is to the learning situation, the better the score on the task. Because Teacher A's class had already had practice in finding shapes embedded in other shapes, they did better on this aspect of the posttest.

Several final comments should be made about the teaching of facts. As already mentioned, one rationale for the inclusion of facts in a curriculum is that some facts constitute a body of knowledge that is generally considered to be a necessity for life in modern-day America (for example, knowledge about our country's history or governmental operations). A second justification for their inclusion in the curriculum is that they are a means of teaching abstractions by serving as the raw material that students process into abstractions. Unless one of these criteria can be applied to a particular fact, we question its inclusion in the curriculum. All too often a proliferation of facts in the curriculum indicates that teachers don't know the difference between facts and abstractions and, consequently, treat all content the same. When this is done, students are inundated with minutiae, and their ability to discern and learn the major ideas in a discipline is severely hampered.

Fantini and Weinstein had the following comments to make about the proliferation of facts in the curriculum:

> Considering that so many of the largest problems facing the world and the United States today are predominantly a matter of inadequate human relations and lack of cooperation among different peoples, one wonders why we spend so much time trying to get our young children to memorize such facts as the order of American Presidents, the precise dates on which this or that event occurred, the area in square miles of this or that state (or nation or continent), and the locations of natural resources in the world. We do not deny the importance of knowledge in these areas but we become concerned when schools emphasize these areas to the exclusion of others.
>
> How many of us can remember these facts now? Name even two products of Chile. Can you, right off the top of your head, so to speak, list all the Presidents from Washington through Johnson in perfect order? Can you remember the year in which Texas was admitted to the Union? (1968, pp. 139–140)

More is said on this topic when teaching strategies are discussed in Chapter 7.

EXERCISE 2.4

Now let's see if you understand the difference between facts and abstractions well enough to differentiate between examples of each. (By the way, the ideas of a fact and an abstraction are both abstractions themselves.) We tried to teach essential characteristics of these ideas and provided you with a number of examples. We now are attempting to determine if you've learned these two abstractions by asking you to classify additional positive and negative examples of them.

Classify the following statements as either fact (f) or abstraction (a). Then compare your answers to the ones given in the feedback section at the end of the chapter.

_____ 1. A geometric figure with four equal sides is called a rhombus.
_____ 2. Extinction is the cessation of responding caused by lack of reinforcement.
_____ 3. The gravitational pull between two bodies is directly related to their mass and inversely related to the square of the distance between two objects.
_____ 4. When asking a question in the English language, the verb comes before the subject.
_____ 5. Pavlov discovered the phenomenon of classical conditioning.
_____ 6. The older a musical piece or composition, the fewer instruments in it.
_____ 7. Questions placed before a text increase learning directly related to the questions but decrease incidental learning (content not directly related to the question).
_____ 8. There are five national parks in Utah.
_____ 9. A novel is a form of literature that narrates a story.
_____ 10. Community helpers are people who perform important jobs in their neighborhoods.
_____ 11. Water boils at a lower temperature at higher elevations.
_____ 12. Sentences that state a fact or give information are called declarative.
_____ 13. Antibodies are body globulins that combine specifically with antigens to neutralize toxins and other harmful substances in the body.
_____ 14. Adagio refers to a way of playing music in an easy, graceful manner.
_____ 15. Ford Motor Company stopped making Edsels after a short time of production.

Summary

This chapter began with a discussion of goals, and you should remember that describing the three orientations to goal setting as mutually exclusive is an oversimplification, in that a particular goal could be defended from several perspectives. For example, knowing how to compute the areas of different geometric shapes could have a strictly academic focus or could be presented as a practical law with a number of applications in the real world—knowing how to compute the area of a rectangle could be used to tell how much fertilizer to buy for a garden plot, and knowing how to compute the area of a circle could be used to adjust a pizza dough recipe for a 9-inch diameter pan to an 18-inch pan. (Hint: you don't just double the recipe.) In addition, teaching students about the biological changes that occur during puberty could be defended from all three perspectives. From a student-oriented perspective, this knowledge helps developing adolescents understand and deal with the changes that are occurring in their bodies. From a societal perspective, this information is essential for young people who will soon attempt to assume adult roles in society. And from an academic viewpoint, these changes are interesting in and of themselves as they illustrate the functioning of a number of complex systems within our bodies.

Proponents of all three orientations could claim this content area as their own, and a particular goal could serve several orientations and could be philosophically defended from a number of perspectives. What is important is that you understand the major sources of teaching goals and that you are able to defend intelligently your choice of goals in terms of a well-thought-out rationale.

The second area of study in this chapter involved a discussion of the three domains. The purpose here was to introduce you to and familiarize you with the psychomotor, affective, and cognitive domains. We discuss the three domains further in Chapter 5.

Finally, we summarize our discussion of facts and abstractions by referring to Table 2.4. In our discussion we treat concepts and generalizations as singular entities, abstractions. In doing so we emphasize similarities between these two content forms that include their formation, the importance of examples in teaching, the measurement of what is learned, and their use. Take a second now to glance over this table.

Probably one of the biggest differences between these two types of cognitive content is in terms of how they are taught. Facts can be thought of as stimulus-response connections in which the stimulus is a question and the response is the answer. The major goal of instruction is the strengthening of the S–R bond. A major way of strengthening this bond is through repetition, which can be accomplished by repeating a fact (Now remember, students, there were 13 states in the Confederacy), by asking a question (How many states were there in the Confederacy?), or by inducing students to study their notes or reread the text. In contrast to facts, abstractions are learned by presenting a number of different examples that either the teacher or the students analyze for commonalities.

A second major way that facts and abstractions differ is in terms of how they are measured. Facts are typically measured as they were learned, with one part of the fact

Table 2.4   Comparison of Facts and Abstractions

Examples	How Taught	How Measured	Uses
FACTS The closest planet to the sun is Mercury.	Question/Answer S—R	Question/Answer S—R	Can be formed into abstractions.
There were 13 states in the Confederacy.	(The stimulus is the question, and the response is the answer.)	(Either the S or R is presented, and the student has to provide the missing term.)	(Cannot be used to summarize, explain, or predict.)
ABSTRACTIONS People who exercise regularly have lower pulse rates.	Examples/ Abstractions	S⟍ S—R S⟋	Can be used to summarize, explain, and predict.
The stopping distance of a car is inversely related to its speed.	S⟍ S—R S⟋	(New examples are provided, and students generate correct classification.)	
A herbivore is an animal that eats only plants.		(Abstraction is given and student provides new examples.)	

acting as the stem (for example, Who was the first president of the United States?) and the second part serving as the answer. Abstractions, by contrast, are measured by asking students either to recognize examples of the abstraction (for example, in the case of the concept *verb,* What do the underlined words have in common?) or to provide new examples (for example, List three verbs not discussed in class). In both instances it is important that new examples are used to ensure that the abstraction learned generalizes to new situations. (Note how we did this in the exercises in this chapter.)

Questions for Discussion

1. How does the relative importance of the three sources of goals—the child, society, and academic disciplines—change in terms of grade level?
2. Which content areas stress the following sources of goals the most: the child, society, or academic disciplines? The least? Why?
3. What are the most important concepts and generalizations at your grade level or content area? Why are they important?

4. What would be the optimal mix of concepts, generalizations, and facts at your grade level or in your content area? Why?
5. What are some possible reasons why facts are overemphasized in schools?
6. How should the optimal mix of facts, concepts, and generalizations (e.g., 50% facts, 25% concepts, 25% generalizations) change over the K–12 continuum? Defend your position with specific content areas or disciplines.

Suggestions for Field Experience

1. Interview a teacher at the grade level and/or in the content area in which you plan to teach and ask them about the importance of different sources of goals in their classrooms.
   a. Which is most important? Why?
   b. Which is least important? Why?
   c. Does this order change with different types of students (e.g., minority or at-risk)?
   d. Does this order change with different topics (e.g., Revolutionary War versus voting in elections in Social Studies)?
2. Examine a chapter from a textbook at your grade level or in your content area. List the following:
   a. facts
   b. concepts
   c. generalizations.
   What proportion of the chapter is devoted to each? Is this an optimal mix?
3. Examine a chapter from a textbook at your grade level or in your content area. Identify two concepts and describe how well they identify the concepts:
   a. characteristics
   b. examples
   c. superordinate concept
   d. subordinate concept.
   Using this information evaluate how well the book does in teaching concepts.
4. Identify a concept from a unit that has just been completed. Interview a student to see how well he or she understands the concept. Specifically ask the student to describe:
   a. characteristics
   b. examples
   c. superordinate concept
   d. subordinate concept.
   What does the student's response tell you about the depth of learning?
5. Examine a text that a teacher has administered. What proportion of the exam focused on:
   a. facts
   b. concepts
   c. generalizations?
   Comment on this mix.

Exercise Feedback

EXERCISE 2.1

Like previous examples, most of these goals could be defended from several perspectives. However, we believe the primary focus of these goals to be the following:

1. (a) Academic.
2. (c) Child. This would be a skill that would help students shop more economically and use their money more wisely.
3. (a) Academic.
4. (s) Societal. This goal is designed to help students interact in a constructive and positive fashion with other people.
5. (c) Child. A basic knowledge of first-aid techniques provides students with the knowledge and skills to care for their bodies when accidents occur.
6. (s) Societal. This information should prove valuable as students become citizens.
7. (c) Child. We consider the primary focus of this goal to be student oriented but consider a societal interpretation to be valid.
8. (a) Academic.
9. (s) Societal. Again, the focus here is on surviving and functioning in a world of other people.
10. (a) Academic.

EXERCISE 2.2

1. b and d. A horse is a kind of domestic animal and beast of burden.
2. b. An overhead projector is the only one of these that is an electrical instructional tool.
3. a, b, and d. Rye, wheat, and white are all kinds of bread.
4. c. Bread is a type of food but isn't a subset of any of the others.
5. b and c. Fried bacon, hot oatmeal, and bread are all types of food and cooked food.

EXERCISE 2.3

1. a. The abstraction being taught was *transitive verb.*
   b. The data Mr. Waters used to illustrate his abstraction were the sentences with transitive and intransitive verbs.
2. a. The abstraction being taught here was *intransitive verbs.*
   b. The data Mrs. Jones used to illustrate her abstraction were also the sentences.
   c. Mr. Waters and Mrs. Jones both used examples to teach the concepts. Mr. Waters showed the examples first and helped the students discover the concept, while Mrs. Jones first defined the concept and then had students identify and analyze the examples. We discuss each of these sequences in Chapter 7.
3. a. The abstraction being taught here was the meaning of *biodegradable.*
   b. The data Mr. Black used were the words and the biodegradable and nonbiodegradable objects in the container.

EXERCISE 2.4

1. (a) Abstraction. This abstraction defines the concept rhombus.
2. (a) Abstraction. Again, this is a concept definition.

3. (a) Abstraction. This abstraction is a generalization.
4. (a) Abstraction. This is a generalization about a pattern in our language.
5. (f) Fact. Note how this occurred in the past and was a singular occurrence.
6. (a) Abstraction. Note how you could use this generalization to date the age of a given musical piece.
7. (a) Abstraction.
8. (f) Fact.
9. (a) Abstraction. This is a definition of a concept in which the target concept is defined in terms of the superordinate concept form of literature.
10. (a) Abstraction.
11. (a) Abstraction. This is a generalization that can be used to predict why it takes longer to cook vegetables in the mountains, for example.
12. (a) Abstraction.
13. (a) Abstraction. This is a concept.
14. (a) Abstraction.
15. (f) Fact.

Chapter 3

Formulating Goals and Objectives

Mrs. Dolores Salazar began her lesson by asking her students to take out their notes in order to review yesterday's work. The 20 plus students enrolled in this high school Chemistry in the Community class were seated in a U-shaped arrangement with the laboratory stations lining the walls of the classroom. Her method of soliciting involvement in a Q&A (question and answer) was to toss a koosh to students when they raised their hands. Toni made the first catch of the day!

"We have been working on water purification and we said that back in the 1800s people obtained their water in three different ways. What was one of those ways . . . Toni?"

"Wells," Toni said.

"I couldn't quite hear you."

"WELLS!!"

"Wells. Good. Rob, a second way?"

"Ponds."

"Good. Along with ponds, what else?"

"Rivers, oceans, stuff like that," Bianca added.

"Great!" Mrs. Salazar said. "And a third source?"

"Rain," Paul said.

"Right, so those were basically the sources of water. Now, water has to be discarded so what were three ways they got rid of waste water?"

"Cesspools," Nancy said.

"Okay, what are cesspools?"

"Pits."

"Good, and what were they lined with?"

"Stones or rocks," Nancy added.

"Okay. Now a second way in which water was discarded . . . Alina?"

"How about just using the ground," Alina said.

"Right. A lot of times people just dumped it outside so it went into the ground. And, finally, a third way?" Mrs. Salazar asked as he tossed the ball to Gabe.

"A dry well."

"And what is a dry well, Gabe?"

"A well that doesn't have any water in it."

"Exactly, Gabe. Simply a well that has dried up. Now, what happened if somehow discarded or waste water got into the wells or rivers meaning the drinking water . . . Josie?"

"It got contaminated," Josie said.

"Which means?"

"If you drank it you got sick."

"Right. Now, today, what are two things we can do with water to prevent sickness or other negative effects?"

"We can filter it," David replied.

"Okay," Mrs. Salazar said, "but what does filtering do? When we filter something out, what are we actually doing?"

"Taking stuff out," David said.

"How?"

"By holding back the stuff that is too big to pass through the filter," David added.

"Great . . . so filtering is one method. What is a second . . . Melissa?"

"Chlorinating," Melissa answered.

"Chlorinating. Why do you think we need to chlorinate water?"

Vince caught the ball. "In order to kill bacteria," he said.

"Okay, good," Mrs. Salazar said. "We also talked about the way nature purifies water if left alone and given enough time. However, we don't have that kind of time because we are using water quicker than the time it takes to naturally replenish itself. In addition we talked about hard and soft water and that hard water has an excess of calcium, magnesium, or ions. Therefore, water purification can also involve the removal of these excess minerals.

"In today's lab, I am going to give you a sample of hard water which has an excess amount of calcium ions. Your job is to soften, or purify this water using filtering techniques."

Mrs. Salazar then provided the students with a filtration procedure handout and demonstrated the placement of filters in test tubes. She went on to briefly discuss how the test would show whether or not they had gotten rid of the calcium. For the remainder of the class, Mrs. Salazar assisted the students at their laboratory stations.

Introduction

In Chapter 1 we introduced the content of this text by presenting a model of teaching described in three interrelated phases—*planning, implementing,* and *assessing.* The planning phase begins when a goal is identified, and we introduced you to sources of goals and domains of instruction in Chapter 2. We now want to look at goals in more detail and put them into operational form for instruction. In other words, we are preparing to state goals to use them as guides for teaching. They mark the beginning of the planning process which will be fully developed in Chapter 4.

The use of goals and objectives is certainly not new. Ralph Tyler (1949), in his classic text *Basic Principles of Curriculum and Instruction,* proposed an instructional model that included objectives as an integral component. Because of his influence, objectives, their form, and the ability to express them have been major components of teacher-preparation courses, and much time and energy are devoted to developing preservice teachers' skills in preparing objectives. Tyler suggested that the most useful form for stating objectives "is to express them in terms which identify both the kind of behavior to be developed in the student and the content or area of life in which this behavior is to operate" (p. 46). Thus, behavioral objectives were born.

Another powerful teacher-training influence followed Tyler's when Robert Mager first published *Preparing Instructional Objectives* in 1962. His highly readable book has been popular for years and thousands of teachers have been taught his principles for stating behavioral objectives. His objectives have been criticized as being incomplete, however, and an alternative is called *the goals approach* to preparing objectives.

A popular approach to preparing objectives in this way has been suggested by Norman Gronlund (1991). He believes objectives should first be stated in terms of general goals such as "understand," "appreciate," "know," "evaluate," or "apply," which are then followed by observable behaviors specifying evidence that the learner has met the objective. We examine both these approaches in this chapter.

Objectives

After completing your study of Chapter 3, you should be able to:

- Recognize the influence of national, state, and local goals on what is taught in classrooms
- Discuss the function of goals regarding annual, unit, and lesson planning
- Prepare original behavioral objectives
- Prepare original goals objectives
- Describe the current emphasis on the use of objectives in classrooms

INFLUENCES ON CLASSROOM GOALS AND OBJECTIVES

As you have seen in Chapter 2, the three sources of goals are the child, society, and the academic disciplines. Within each source, goals are generated at the national, state, and local level, the former being the most global or general and the latter being the most specific. An example of a national goal, as presented at the national education summit in 1989, is that American students will be first in the world in math and science. At the state level, such a goal becomes more concrete and at the local or classroom level, the goal is presented in terms of specific outcomes. We can see how these three levels provide direction as we look back at our chapter-opening scenario in which we see a classroom presentation in terms of the goals and objectives of the lesson.

Levels and Perspectives

Mrs. Salazar undertook a number of goals in this lesson ranging from the general to the specific. On a national or more global scale, she was concerned with the need for students to become aware of the critical problem of and need for replenishing the world's water supply. Obviously, this issue is one of international concern and it is important for American students to not only be aware of such an issue but to develop a potential expertise to pragmatically address this issue as a participant in tomorrow's scientific community.

On possibly a state or regional scale, she wanted to introduce the students to methods that are commonly employed in the effort to replenish existing sources of water. Issues such as water shortages, agricultural and industrial utilization, and the debate between a number of states over river rights (i.e., Wyoming and Nebraska over the use of the Platte River) are common agenda items in many state legislative houses, all of which lend support to her teaching of this lesson.

In the classroom, specifically, Mrs. Salazar designed a lesson that required the students to actually employ a given procedure and successfully filter a sample of water. Notice how concrete and measurable her classroom objective is as opposed to the general and ambiguous nature of the national goal.

Additionally, regarding the source of her overall goal, Mrs. Salazar was primarily focused on the need of society which is dependent upon an abundant and healthy water supply. As you can see, the format of the goals and objectives is *founded* on the sources of goals and the levels at which they are formulated and is *determined* by their function and their amount of, or lack of, specificity.

National goals are global and provide direction for long-range student learning.

PLANNING AND THE ROLE OF GOALS AND OBJECTIVES

The Three Operational Levels of Goals

The role or purpose of a goal is determined by the level at which it is written. In that goals are directly concerned with student achievement and growth, teachers need to identify desired learner outcomes at the beginning of the school year. The purpose of the first of the three operational levels, *annual* or *long-range goals*, is both philosophical and conceptual in that the goal must provide direction regarding what knowledge students should acquire. With this in mind, decisions regarding the development of long-range goals require the teacher to determine terminal behaviors in a very general way. For example, primary school teachers realize reading is critical and that it is their responsibility to focus on ways in which they can increase their students' ability to read. At the high school level, an American History teacher realizes the need for students to understand the role wars played in the growth and expansion of the nation.

These two examples of long-range goals become less global and more focused at the second, or *unit,* level. The purpose of these goals is to provide a focal point for a unit of instruction without being too specific or directly measurable. Returning to our reading example, at the unit level a teacher will be concerned with word recognition strategies that will facilitate the annual goal of increasing reading ability. Likewise, the American History teacher might have the students become more familiar with the Spanish-American War in terms of expansionism. The third level is found in *lesson planning.* It is at this level that the purpose is very specific and observable. Again, regarding our reading example, the lesson plan might call for the student circling all the words with two syllables in a given list. In doing so, word recognition strategies are enhanced (unit level) and the ability to read is increased (long-range level). Turning to our history example, the teacher might have the students write an essay discussing three causes of the Spanish-American War (lesson-plan level) which increases familiarity with the war (unit level) and promotes understanding of the role of war played in the expansion of the United States (long-range level.) Note the behaviors in the examples of the objectives at the lesson-plan level; circling words and writing an essay, are specific, concrete, and observable.

Decision Making in Preparing Objectives

From these examples we can see how decision making is involved in preparing objectives. In this process they answer two important questions: (1) In both a general and specific sense, what does the teacher want the students to know, understand, or be able to do after completing the units and lessons? and (2) How will the teacher determine that the students know, understand, or can do this? Answering the first question assists in identifying the end product and helps the teacher remain focused on the lesson. Brophy (1987) found that teachers play a key role in determining the curriculum students actually receive, even when clear curriculum guidelines and materials are in place. Regarding the second question, objectives help both the teacher and the students assess learning because the objectives at the lesson-plan level specify performances in specific terms. Let's now take a look at how these objectives are prepared.

SELECTING FORMATS

Mager's Behavioral Objectives

As we said in the chapter introduction, Robert Mager was enormously influential in his approach to the preparation of objectives. In his attempt to focus teachers' attention on observable outcomes, he suggested that an objective ought to clearly state "what it is that students are expected to be able to do, and that each intended performance be directly visible and/or audible; you can see or hear someone doing it" (Mager, 1997).

Mager suggests that a good objective has three parts: (1) an observable behavior, (2) the conditions under which the behavior will occur, and (3) criteria for acceptable performance. The following are examples of objectives written according to Mager's format.

1. Given six sentences, fifth graders will identify each that contains a simile.
2. Given 10 addition problems requiring regrouping, second graders will successfully solve 8.
3. Given 15 compounds written with the correct chemical formula, chemistry students will identify the valence of the ions in each.

Mager's system, with its emphasis on final behavior, requires a great deal of specificity. Mager contends that the effort required to achieve this specificity is worthwhile, and he has even gone so far as to suggest that students often can teach themselves if they are given well-stated objectives.

Mager's objectives, sometimes called an *outcomes approach,* can be criticized as being incomplete, however, in that they are only evaluation statements; that is, they specify the *student outcome* or how students will be evaluated but do not identify the educational intent of the teacher. An alternative that addresses this criticism is called the *Goals Approach to Preparing Objectives,* or more simply, *goals objectives.* We turn to a discussion of them now.

Goals Objectives

A goals objective can be described as a statement that answers two questions for the teacher:

1. What do I want the learner to know, understand, or appreciate (or some other educational goal)? and
2. How will I know if the student knows, understands, or appreciates?

Mager's outcomes approach to preparing objectives answers the second question. Answers to both are important, however, particularly if you're a beginning education student developing your understanding of the teaching process. For this reason we have adopted the goals approach in this text. This approach combines Mager's objective, which is an evaluation statement, with a goal. This is how a goals objective subsumes Mager's objectives. Keep in mind that from this point on when we refer to an evaluation statement, we mean a Mager objective. Let's look now at goal statements within a goals objective.

Goal Statements.   A major purpose for writing this text is to help you begin to think like teachers. With this notion in mind, imagine that you are responsible for a class in a certain grade level or subject matter area. You are planning a specific lesson for the next day. Your first step in planning is to ask yourself, What do I want the students to know, understand, or be able to do? All your planning, and ultimately your actual work with the students, derives from the answer to this question. This question is particularly important for people who are now beginning to study and understand education. At this point, your understanding is best served by formally and explicitly stating goals in writing. As your thinking and understanding develop, your goals will become less formal and more implicit.

Planning begins with teachers' consideration of what they want their students to accomplish during one or more lessons. This desired result is called a *goal statement,* which is a statement of educational intent that is usually given in general terms. The goal statement answers the question, What do I want my students to know or understand? The following are examples of goal statements:

1. For kindergartners to know the basic colors.
2. For eighth-grade science students to understand Newton's first law.
3. Senior trigonometry students will solve written problems involving right triangles.

As we examine the goal statements, we see that they have three common characteristics. First, each identified the particular student population for which it was designed—kindergartners, eighth-grade science students, and senior trigonometry students, respectively. Second, the learning outcome or task was identified. The kindergartners' task is to know colors, the eighth graders' is to understand Newton's first law, and the trigonometry students' is to be able to solve problems with right triangles. Finally the goal's attainment in each case must be inferred rather than observed. We never observe "understanding"; we can only infer it, and it can mean different things to different people. The same is true for "know," "appreciate," and other desired educational goals. When we discuss the evaluation component of goals objectives, we will see how we gather the information needed to infer knowledge, understanding, appreciation, and so forth.

Goal statements should be written as simply and efficiently as possible. They may be simply an introductory phrase, as in the first two examples just cited, or they may be a complete sentence, such as our third example. Let's examine some additional examples.

1. For senior literature students to understand the impact of personal experience on an author's work.
   Learner: senior literature students
   Learning Task: understand the impact of experience on authors' works
2. Sixth-grade science students will understand the concept of density.
   Learner: sixth-grade science students
   Learning Task: understand the concept of density
3. For second graders to understand the rule for adding -*ing* to words.
   Learner: second graders
   Learning Task: understand the rule for adding -*ing* to words
4. Eighth-grade algebra students will be able to solve simultaneous equations.
   Learner: eighth-grade algebra students
   Learning Task: solve simultaneous equations

5. Seventh-grade geography students will know the locations of the countries of Europe.
Learner: seventh-grade geography students
Learning Task: know the locations of the countries of Europe

You will note that each of the objectives we've written for this text refers to *you* as a reader and student, and it has been stated in each case. We've done this so our objectives can serve as appropriate models for you as you study. Specifically stating the intended learner group is useful when designing curriculum at the school or district level. If a teacher has the same audience for an extended period of time, however, it wouldn't be necessary to repeat the learner component in each objective once the learner is clearly established. Notice also that although the goals are written in nonobservable terms such as *know* and *understand,* they are specific. Goals such as the following are too general to be useful.

For students to understand American literature.
Algebra students will be able to solve problems.
Geography students will know about Europe.

Because of their lack of specificity, these disintegrate into a series of words. Compare the examples you've just read with the first, fourth, and fifth of the preceding examples to see the difference.

EXERCISE 3.1

Identify the learner and the learning task in each of the following goal statements. Then compare your answers to the ones given in the feedback section at the end of the chapter.

1. For fifth graders to know the parts of the digestive system.

   Learner: _____

   Learning Task: _____

2. American history students will understand Andrew Jackson's philosophy regarding states' rights.

   Learner: _____

   Learning Task: _____

3. Seventh-grade life science students will know the different types of bacteria.

   Learner: _____

   Learning Task: _____

4. First graders will like reading.

   Learner: _____

   Learning Task: _____

5. For kindergartners to be able to walk a balance beam.

Learner: _____

Learning Task: _____

Although each of the goals in Exercise 3.1 appears in a conventional format, remember that the key elements of a properly stated goal are identification of the learner and specification of the learning task. The precise wording of the goal is not critical.

Evaluation Statements

When we introduced goals objectives, we said they provide the answer to two questions:

1. What do I want the learner to know, understand, or appreciate?
2. How will I know if the student knows, understands, or appreciates?

The goal statement answers the first question, and we are now prepared to consider the second. The answers can and often do vary, and teachers must make decisions about how they will determine whether or not their students know or understand. Again, we are encouraging you to begin to think like a teacher. For instance, consider the following goal:

For third graders to understand the concept *noun*

This is a simple and straightforward goal. However, when we begin to ask ourselves how we will know if they understand nouns, even this simple goal becomes more complex. The following are some possibilities we might use to determine whether they understand the concept.

1. Have them define *noun* in writing from memory.
2. Have them write a list of nouns that were not used as examples in class.
3. Have them identify examples of nouns from a list of words.
4. Have them identify nouns in a series of sentences.

Even with a concept as simple as *noun*, we see that the evaluation question requires thought. For instance, if students can define *noun*, does this mean they understand the concept? Probably not. However, as the teacher, you are the one who ultimately must answer the question.

Imagine instead that you had the following goals for your students:

For senior English students to analyze a writing sample critically
or
For junior high math students to learn to problem solve.

Both are worthwhile goals, but deciding how to evaluate them is a complex process. These are questions teachers must answer every day, and this is what it means to "think like a teacher."

Let's consider evaluation statements. This statement reflects the teacher's answer to the question, How will I determine if the student knows, understands, or appreciates? For instance, by stating

For third graders to understand the concept *noun,* so that when given a list of sentences they will underline all the nouns in each,

the teacher has decided that she can infer that the students understand nouns if they can underline all the nouns in a series of sentences she provides.

Let's look carefully now at the entire objective. It contains a specific goal that identifies the learner and the learning task, and it includes an evaluation statement that designates (1) the expected performance, (2) the conditions under which the student is to perform, and (3) the standard for the performance. Each of these helps the teacher clarify his thinking while also communicating clearly with students and other professionals. Let's examine the performance component further.

Specifying Observable Performances.   In one of our examples we see that the students will demonstrate their understanding of nouns by *underlining* the nouns in a series of sentences. The key feature of the performance is that it is *observable* by the teacher. As with all inferences, if we are to conclude that students understand, we must have something observable on which to base this conclusion. This observable behavior is the *performance.* When we considered different ways of assessing students' understanding of nouns, the performances were *define, write,* and *identify,* respectively.

When developed for classroom lessons, objectives are very specific in terms of what students will learn.

In addition, verbs such as the following are also observable and can be used as performance statements:

state	select	list	label
classify	solve	construct	compare
describe	recite	derive	name
identify	draw	underline	organize

Many more could be added to the list, but this gives you a sample of observable performances. Although the approach to writing objectives varies among educators, most adhere to the need for including an observable behavior in the objective's description. In addition, each objective should contain a single performance; if more than one is desired, a second evaluation statement should be written.

EXERCISE 3.2

This exercise reviews your understanding of goal statements and checks your ability to recognize observable performances. Enclose the goal statement for each of the following goals objectives in parentheses and underline the performance in each. Place an X in front of each objective that *does not* include an observable performance. Then compare your answers to the ones given in the feedback section at the end of the chapter.

____ 1. For life science students to know the parts of a cell, so that when given a picture of a cell, they will label each part.

____ 2. Physics students will understand the law of conservation of momentum, so that when given a series of problems involving momentum, they will identify all the cases where momentum is conserved.

____ 3. Second graders will understand how to make plurals for words ending in *y*, so that when given a list of ten words, they will know the plural for each.

____ 4. Earth science students will comprehend the importance of topsoil in agriculture, so that when given a series of photographs illustrating erosion, they will appreciate the importance of conservation.

____ 5. Geometry students will understand the construction of circles, so that when given a compass and three points, they will construct a circle through the points.

____ 6. For kindergarten students to know the letters of the alphabet, so that when shown written letters, they will verbally state the name of each.

Specifying Conditions. Let's look again at our example with the concept *noun*. The four possibilities we listed for evaluating the goal were

1. Have them define *noun* in writing from memory.
2. Have them write a list of *nouns* that were not used as examples in class.
3. Have them identify examples of *nouns* from a list of words.
4. Have them identify *nouns* in a series of sentences.

Notice that in both examples 3 and 4 the students were asked to identify nouns. In one case they were asked to identify them from a list of words, however, and in the other case in a series of sentences. The *conditions* under which the students were to perform the behavior were quite different. Specifying the evaluation condition helps us clarify our own thinking about what we're trying to accomplish, which makes it easier to communicate more clearly to students exactly what we want them to learn. Some examples of common conditions are

> From memory
> Without aids
> Given a list
> Given a compass, volleyball, jump rope, pictures (or other materials needed to demonstrate the performance)

By contrasting conditions such as

> After instruction,
> After exposure to, or
> Given experience with

are *not* acceptable conditions. Rather than specify the conditions under which the performance will be demonstrated, they describe a learning condition. Also, conditions such as

> Given a test,
> Given multiple-choice items, or
> When asked

are so vague that they're not useful. Although they're technically correct, they don't give us any specific information about the evaluation condition. The learner is always asked, told, or required to respond. The solution is to specify the form of the test item. For instance, "identify nouns in a list of sentences" accomplishes exactly that. A portion of a test would include a series of sentences, and the student would be asked to identify nouns by circling, underlining, or providing some other indicator. As another example, consider the following objective:

> For American government students to understand different forms of government so that when given a case study describing a political ideology, they will identify the form of government it represents.

The measurement of this objective could be in the form of a multiple-choice item where the stem would illustrate the ideology and choices, such as (a) democracy, (b) monarchy, (c) communism, (d) fascism. The objective specifies the form of the item and doesn't merely say, "given a multiple-choice item."

EXERCISE 3.3

For the following objectives enclose the goal statement in parentheses and put a GS over it, enclose the condition in parentheses and put a C over it, and underline the performance. Then compare your answers to the ones given in the feedback section at the end of the chapter.

1. Second graders will be able to subtract with regrouping, so that when given 10 problems requiring regrouping, they will correctly solve 7.
2. Prekindergartners will know their colors, so that when given individually colored shapes, they will correctly identify the color of each.

3. World history students will know what kind of impact the Crusades had on Europe, so that without aids they will list four cultural outcomes resulting from the Crusades.
4. Tenth-grade chemistry students will understand ionization potential, so that when given lists of elements and the periodic table, they will identify the element from each list with the highest ionization potential.
5. Earth science students will know different types of minerals, so that when given mineral specimens and written labels, they will match the labels with the specimens.

Specifying Criteria.   As a theme for this chapter, we have been describing the thinking process a teacher must go through when making professional decisions. When the teacher asks how he'll find out if the student understands what he identified in the goal, the teacher should observe the student's performance. The performance is critical because different performances tell you very different things about the learner. We've also seen how the condition under which the performance is demonstrated can have an impact on the goal and the evaluation process.

Let's take the process one step further. Look again at the first three items in Exercise 3.3.

1. Second graders will be able to subtract with regrouping, so that when given 10 problems requiring regrouping, they will correctly solve 7.
2. Prekindergartners will know their colors, so that when given individually colored shapes, they will correctly identify the color of each.
3. World history students will know what kind of impact the Crusades had on Europe, so that without aids they will list four cultural outcomes resulting from the Crusades.

We see that in the first example the teacher concluded that solving *7 of 10* correctly was sufficient for students to demonstrate their ability to solve problems with regrouping. However, in the second example the teacher decided that the children should identify the color of *each;* and in the third, students could demonstrate their knowledge by listing *four* outcomes. The teachers specified not only the condition and performance but also how well the students were to perform. This level of performance represents the criteria, and it is the final dimension to be considered as you develop your thinking about goals objectives.

As with conditions and performances, criteria vary and depend on the judgment of the teacher. Additional examples of criteria are:

With 100 percent accuracy
With no more than three errors
Within 20 seconds
Four times in 10 seconds

The value of criteria as a tool depends on the topic and activity. For example, consider the objective

For physical education students to demonstrate muscular strength, so that on a horizontal bar they will do 10 pull-ups in 20 seconds.

Here the performance is to do pull-ups, but the objective has little meaning until we specify the criterion. Without it we would immediately ask, How many? and In how much time? On the other hand, look at the objective

> For language arts students to understand the concept hyperbole, so that when given examples of figurative language, they will identify 80% of the examples of hyperbole.

This objective reflects two important teacher decisions: (1) that understanding hyperbole is an important goal, and (2) that we will infer that the students understand if they can identify the examples of hyperbole from among a number of cases of figurative language. In addition, the teacher has set the criteria at 80%, reflecting a professional judgment that this level would be sufficient to demonstrate mastery of this concept.

In typical classroom practice, teachers rarely set explicit criteria in advance. Instead, they establish grading systems, such as those we've all experienced as students, and the criteria are implicitly incorporated within the system. However, most school districts continue to move toward school accountability through competency testing, and setting criteria is important in these cases. Therefore, an understanding of criteria is important as you develop your thinking about teaching.

EXERCISE 3.4

Identify the four components of goals objectives by enclosing each in parentheses and labeling them GS, C, P, and CT for the goal statement, condition, performance, and criteria, respectively. Then compare your answers to the ones given in the feedback section at the end of the chapter.

1. Vocational technical students will demonstrate carpentry skills, so that when given a saw, square, and 2 × 4s, they will make a 90-degree joint in the boards to within 1 degree.
2. Middle school music students will know the fingerings for the recorder, so that when given an excerpt of music, they will demonstrate the correct fingerings for each note.
3. Elementary physical education students will demonstrate hand–eye coordination, so that when given a basketball, they will dribble it 25 consecutive times in place without losing control.
4. Eleventh-grade oceanography students will know the zones of the ocean floor, so that when given an ocean topographic map, they will label each zone correctly.
5. Physics students will understand components of forces, so that when given the magnitudes and angles of forces on objects, they will calculate the horizontal components of the forces in each case.

EXERCISE 3.5

You are now ready to analyze the quality of goals objectives. Consider each of the following and mark them as follows:

> A —— Objective is accurate and acceptable as written
> GS —— Missing or inappropriate goal statement
> C —— Missing or inappropriate condition

P —— Missing or inappropriate performance
CT —— Missing or inappropriate criteria

After identifying the problems in the objectives, rewrite each in appropriate form. Then compare your answers to the ones given in the feedback section at the end of the chapter.

_____ 1. Fifth graders will understand the calculation of volume of solids, so that after seeing sample problems, they will solve 9 of 10 similar problems correctly.

_____

_____

_____ 2. For vocational technical students to understand common problems in small gas engines, so that given a stalled lawn mower, they will fix the causes of stalling with 80% accuracy.

_____

_____

_____ 3. To demonstrate understanding of figurative language, so that when given a series of statements, students will identify the figure of speech in each case.

_____

_____

_____ 4. Prealgebra students will understand order of operations, so that when given problems involving the four operations, they will correctly simplify each.

_____

_____

_____ 5. Seventh-grade geography students will know the geographical location of countries in Europe, so that when given a map and multiple-choice items, they will answer each correctly.

_____

_____

_____ 6. For ninth graders to appreciate the use of verbals, so that when given a series of descriptions, students will know appropriate examples of gerunds, participles, and infinitives for each.

_____

_____

_____ 7. American government students will understand the concept of governmental checks and balances, so that on an essay test they will present a written example of a check and balance.

_____

_____

_____ 8. Biology students will understand genetics, so that when given case studies with dominant and recessive traits, they will identify the characteristics of each offspring.

_____

_____

_____

Gronlund's Instructional Objectives

In the last two sections we described Mager's behavioral objectives and the goals approach to preparing objectives. They are very similar in that the goals approach is essentially a Mager objective attached to a goal statement.

We turn to another alternative, popularized by Norman Gronlund (1991). Let's examine some examples of objectives written according to Gronlund's principles and see how they compare to those we've already illustrated.

Consider the following example taken from elementary school language arts.

General Objective: Knows spelling rules for adding suffixes
Specific Behaviors:

1. States rule in his or her own words
2. Distinguishes rule from closely related rule
3. Applies rule to unique example

Now consider a second example taken from algebra.

General Objective: Solves word problems
Specific Behaviors:

1. Describes problem
2. Identifies relevant information
3. Specifies variables
4. Writes solution equation
5. Calculates solution

Let's look now at the characteristics of the objectives.

1. Gronlund (1991) suggests that objectives should be first stated in general terms, such as *know, understand, apply, evaluate,* or *appreciate,* which are then followed by specific behaviors providing evidence that the learner has met the objective. In this regard Gronlund's objectives are similar to the goals approach; he suggests that a general objective that identifies the instructional intent should be stated first. The general objective is similar to the goal statement in the goals approach. "Knows spelling rules for adding suffixes" and "solves word problems" were the statements of intent in our examples. The specific behaviors listed below each general objective then provide the evidence that the students have met the intent. This approach differs from Mager's in that his objectives specify the evidence but do not include the intent.

2. The objectives are stated in terms of student outcomes rather than teacher performance. For instance, "teach spelling rules for adding suffixes" is a teacher performance and not a student outcome. Virtually all objectives, regardless of the approach, share this characteristic, and both county curriculum guides and state-level curriculum frameworks state objectives in terms of student outcomes.

3. Objectives are not stated in terms of the learning process, such as "students learn spelling rules for adding suffixes." "Learns" is a student process rather than a student outcome, and Gronlund discourages this description. Both Mager's and the goals approach share this characteristic.

4. Objectives are limited to a single performance. Again, this is consistent among the three approaches. We suggested in the last section that a teacher should write two different evaluation statements if more than one performance was involved, and Gronlund would make a similar argument.

5. Gronlund believes that conditions and performance criteria are too specific and limit teacher flexibility. For example, consider the objective: Given a drawing of a flower, the student will label in writing at least four of the five parts shown. By specifying the condition "given a drawing," the teacher has excluded the use of a slide or a real flower in the testing condition. In a similar way, by specifying four out of five, the teacher limits instructional flexibility that might suggest lower standards for slower students and higher ones for brighter students.

Gronlund's approach or a modification of it is probably the most popular one among curriculum writers. Its primary advantage is one of economy; his objectives are more inclusive than those written according to the other approaches. Content requiring literally thousands of objectives written according to Mager's approach could be expressed in less than a hundred using Gronlund's.

The compromise Gronlund makes is in terms of specificity. He doesn't identify either the conditions for acceptable performance or the criteria, and he discourages the use of specific subject matter topics. This latter feature is often modified by curriculum writers. They typically include specific topics in their objectives, as we discuss in the next section.

EXERCISE 3.6

Consider each of the following objectives and identify those that are inappropriately stated according to Gronlund's criteria. Rewrite each of the inappropriately stated objectives in acceptable form. We are purposely sidestepping the issue of content specificity, so do not evaluate them on that basis. Then compare your answers to the ones given in the feedback section at the end of the chapter.

1. Learns concepts in chemistry
   1.1 Defines concept in own words
   1.2 Identifies examples of concepts

2. Teach students parts of speech
   2.1 Define parts of speech for students
   2.2 Provide students with examples
   2.3 Have students identify parts of speech in context

   _____

   _____

3. Understands subtraction with regrouping
   3.1 States rule for borrowing
   3.2 Solves problems requiring regrouping

   _____

   _____

4. Understands geographical terms
   4.1 States definition in own words and writes definition
   4.2 Identifies examples in paragraphs
   4.3 Identifies examples on maps

   _____

   _____

5. Understands Newton's second law
   5.1 States the law
   5.2 Writes the law mathematically
   5.3 Solves problems using the law

   _____

   _____

IMPLEMENTING GOALS AND OBJECTIVES IN CLASSROOMS

Current Emphasis

Let's look at what you will likely encounter when you leave the college or university and enter a public school classroom. What role do objectives play there, and how do they appear? For instance, consider the following objectives taken from the *Student Performance Standards of Excellence for Florida Schools* (1984, p. 85).

STANDARDS	SKILLS—*The student will*
G. The Student Will Acquire Skills To Participate Effectively In A Democratic Society And Apply Problem-Solving Skills To The Democratic Political Process.	1126. Explain the function of the Cabinet 1127. Relate political elections to processes used to choose leaders in the school and community 1128. Contrast what it means to be a good citizen in the United States with what it means in an authoritarian society

Table 3.1 Grade Level: Six Theme: Matter and Energy

Primary Idea: The interaction of matter involves energy and causes change.

Secondary Ideas	Objectives
All matter can be classified into three general categories: elements (atoms of the same kind), compounds (elements that undergo chemical reactions), and mixtures (solids, liquids, and gases).	Given proper materials and directions, the students will 1. State that all matter is made of tiny parts called atoms. 2. Identify the principal parts of an atom and describe their relationship to one another. 3. Contrast the different states of matter in terms of molecular motion. 4. Describe the conditions under which a mixture may be produced. 5. Compare elements and compounds. 6. State the purpose of chemical symbols and formulas. 7. Compare chemical and physical changes. 8. State the function of group tests. 9. Give examples of how chemistry can affect one's own life.

This excerpt was taken from a state-level document that serves as a guide for instruction. The document was written by teams considering educational goals for Florida. They have what amounts to a goal statement, which they describe as a *standard*. The evaluation statement is labeled a *skill*.

Table 3.1 is based on a county curriculum guide (*Science Curriculum Guide*, 1982). We see here that primary and secondary ideas rather than goals are presented. Understanding these ideas, however, amounts to the goal. The statement they identify as an *objective* is an *evaluation* statement, as we've discussed it in this chapter. Notice in these objectives that a general statement of conditions is written and that an observable performance is specified.

As the teaching profession continues to move toward holding teachers accountable for student learning, some districts place descriptions of objectives in teachers' hands and require that they specify the date when the objective is taught. For example, consider the following taken from skill sheets for St. Johns County, Florida.

15. Compare fractions using $<$, $>$, and $=$.
16. Add 2 fractions with unlike denominators 2, 3, 4, 6, 8, and 12.
17. Subtract fractions with unlike denominators 2, 3, 4, 6, 8, 12.
18. Read and write decimals in tenths and hundredths.
(Minimum Skills—Fifth Grade)

We have suggested that performance objectives are a way of life in education today, and the examples we've presented support this contention. There are obvious compromises, such as the use of labels and explicit goal statements as opposed to topics lists, but performance objectives are certainly used in the real world of the public schools. They serve as guides and are designed to aid teachers in their instruction.

Objectives and Reflection

We are discussing objectives at this point in our text because we want them to serve as guides to aid your thinking. Having you state goals serves this purpose. We believe you will benefit from the process of explicitly considering and writing both goal and evaluation statements at this point in your studies. When you get into the classroom, a topic, as opposed to a goal, may be more appropriate.

There is one exception to what we've said so far. If you look again at the excerpts, you see that none of the examples we've presented have criteria as described in this chapter. As we've said repeatedly, objectives serve as guides for thinking by requiring you to ask yourself what you want the learner to know or understand, and further, how you will determine this knowledge or understanding. This is common practice. However, the explicit statement of criteria can be difficult to determine and is often quite artificial. The measurement of the objective is most often done with a paper-and-pencil test, and judgments about achievement are based on the test results. If the test items are consistent with the objectives—and they will be if the teacher used objectives as a guide for instruction—we find the practice very acceptable. In other words, we support the practice of not explicitly stating criteria. Our position is that objectives should guide a teacher's thinking but should not restrict it. However, we believe it is worthwhile for you to understand how to specify criteria if it should ever be necessary, and we also recognize that there will be instructors using this text whose position will differ from ours. We are presenting both sides of the issue for this reason.

In either event, the last function of objectives in terms of providing a guide for instruction is found in reflecting upon the objective in terms of whether it is achieved or mastered by the students and the degree to which it is perceived as being relevant and practical. When considering goals and objectives within the planning process, reflection, once again, establishes the cyclical nature of effective teaching and is a powerful tool for promoting student learning.

Summary

The purpose of Chapter 3 has been to help you understand the reasons for preparing objectives; to introduce you to the ways in which objectives are influenced at the national, state, and local level; to establish the long-range, unit, and lesson levels of objectives; and to help you develop your skill in writing them. We presented three different approaches to their preparation. Of those three we emphasized the goals approach because of the advantages it provides in developing your thinking about instruction.

A goals objective has two primary parts. First is the goal statement, which is a description of the teacher's intent stated in general, nonobservable terms. It identifies the learner and the learning task. The evaluation statement, which is identical to an objective written according to Mager's approach to preparing objectives, includes the condition, the performance, and the criteria. The goal statement answers the question, What do I want the learner to know, understand, or be able to do? and the evaluation statement answers the question, How will I determine whether the learner knows or understands?

Gronlund's instructional objectives are similar to goals objectives in that a general statement of intent is first identified, which is followed by specific behaviors providing evidence that the general objective has been met. Gronlund's objectives, however, are much more general than goals objectives.

Examples taken from state and district curriculum materials indicate that although specific procedures for preparing objectives vary, and some of the principles are compromised, objectives play a central role in the "real world" as a guide for instruction.

Objectives are critical to the planning and implementation of instruction. They increase effective communication, aid teachers in developing learning strategies, and encourage thinking about assessment and reflecting upon whether or not the objectives were achieved. The importance of objectives is further illustrated when we study the development of lesson plans in Chapter 4.

Questions for Discussion

1. Of the three determining influences upon objectives (national, state, and local), which do you believe will have the most impact on you as a classroom teacher?
2. What are the key structural differences between annual or extensive objectives, unit objectives, and lesson objectives?
3. What are some of the reasons for the extensive practice of providing teachers with prepared objectives in materials such as curriculum guides and textbooks?
4. What are some of the significant differences between Mager's behavioral objective and Gronlund's instructional objective?
5. Does a goals objective address the major concerns of both Mager and Gronlund? If so, how?
6. Why are objectives considered to be the cornerstone of planning?

Suggestions for Field Experience

1. Interview teachers at the grade level and/or subject matter area in which you plan to teach and ask them about the ways in which national, state, and local goals and objectives are incorporated into their curriculum.
   a. Which impacts upon them the most? Why?
   b. Which impacts upon them the least? Why?
2. Examine a curriculum guide and a textbook at your grade level or in your academic discipline focusing on whether or not objectives are presented in these materials. In the event they are present, determine if they are
   a. Mager objectives
   b. Gronlund objectives
   c. Goals objectives
   d. Other formats
3. Locate a textbook at your grade level or in your subject field that does not have prepared objectives. Select a chapter and for the content in that chapter, prepare a
   a. Mager behavioral objective
   b. Gronlund instructional objective
   c. Goals objective
4. Interview teachers at your grade level and/or in the academic subject area which you plan to teach and ask them what styles they employ when writing objectives for their original units and lesson.

Exercise Feedback

EXERCISE 3.1

1. *Learner:* fifth graders
   Learning Task: know the parts of the digestive system
2. *Learner:* American history students
   Learning Task: understand Jackson's philosophy regarding states' rights
3. *Learner:* seventh-grade life science students
   Learning Task: know different types of bacteria
4. *Learner:* first graders
   Learning Task: like reading
5. *Learner:* kindergartners
   Learning Task: walk a balance beam

EXERCISE 3.2

_____ 1. (For life science students to know the parts of a cell), so that when given a picture of a cell, they will <u>label</u> each part.

_____ 2. (Physics students will understand the law of conservation of momentum), so that when given a series of problems involving momentum they will <u>identify</u> all the cases where momentum is conserved.

  X   3. (Second graders will understand how to make plurals for words ending in *y*), so that when given a list of ten words, they will know the plural for each. The goal in this case is for students to understand the rule for forming plurals. "Knowing" the plural for each is not an observable performance. It puts us right back where we started, and again we must ask, How will I determine if they "know" the plural for each?

  X   4. (Earth science students will comprehend the importance of topsoil in agriculture), so that when given a series of photographs illustrating erosion, they will appreciate the importance of conservation. Again, "appreciating" the importance of conservation is not observable, and we must have some observable indicator to help us determine whether the students understand the importance of erosion to agriculture.

      5. (Geometry students will understand the construction of circles), so that when given a compass and three points, they will <u>construct</u> a circle through the points.

      6. (For kindergarten students to know the letters of the alphabet), so that when shown written letters, they will verbally <u>state</u> the name of each.

EXERCISE 3.3

1. (Second graders will be able to subtract with regrouping)^{GS}, so that (when given 10 problems requiring regrouping) they will correctly <u>solve</u>^{GS} 7.^{C}

2. (Prekindergartners will know their colors)^{GS}, so that (when given individually colored shapes) they will correctly <u>identify</u> the color of each.^{C}

3. (World history students will know what kind of impact the Crusades had on Europe)^{GS}, so that (without aids)^{C} they will <u>list</u> four cultural outcomes resulting from the Crusades.

4. (Tenth-grade chemistry students will understand ionization potential)^{GS}, so that (when given lists of elements and the periodic table)^{C} they will <u>identify</u> the element from each list with the highest ionization potential.

5. (Earth science students will know different types of minerals)^{GS}, so that (when given mineral specimens and written labels)^{C} they will <u>match</u> the labels with the specimens.

EXERCISE 3.4

1. (Vocational technical students will demonstrate carpentry skills)^{GS}, so that (when given a saw, square, and 2 × 4s)^{C}, they will (make)^{P} a 90-degree joint (in the boards to within 1 degree)^{CT}.

2. (Middle school music students will know the fingerings for the recorder)^{GS}, so that (when given an excerpt of music)^{C}, they will (demonstrate)^{P} the (correct fingerings for each)^{CT} note.

3. (Elementary physical education students will demonstrate hand–eye coordination)^{GS}, so that when (given a basketball)^{C}, they will (dribble)^{P} it (25 consecutive times in place without losing control)^{CT}.

4. (Eleventh-grade oceanography students will know the zones of the ocean floor)^{GS}, so that (when given an ocean topographic map)^{C}, they will (label)^{P} (each zone correctly)^{CT}.

5. (Physics students will understand components of forces)^{GS}, so that (when given the magnitudes and angles of forces on objects)^{C}, they will (calculate)^{P} the horizontal components of the forces in (each)^{CT} case.

EXERCISE 3.5

In each case of an inaccurately written objective, we've presented an appropriate alternative. As you rewrite the objectives, they may look a bit different from ours and still be acceptable. If you're uncertain, discuss your objectives with your instructor.

__C__ 1. "After seeing sample problems" is a learning condition rather than an evaluation condition. A better objective would be

Fifth graders will understand the calculation of volume of solids, so that when given 10 pictures of solids with their dimensions, they will correctly determine the volume of 9.

__CT__ 2. To fix the causes of stalling "with 80% accuracy" doesn't make sense. The engine still won't start. The objective would be appropriately written as

For vocational technical students to understand common problems in small gas engines, so that when given a stalled lawn mower, they will eliminate all the causes of stalling.

__GS__ 3. The learner is not identified in the goal statement. An improved description would be

For sixth-grade English students to understand figurative language, so that when given a series of statements, they will identify the figure of speech in each case.

__A__ 4. This objective is accurate and appropriate as written.

__C__ 5. "Given . . . multiple-choice items" is an inappropriate condition. A more precise description would be

Seventh-grade geography students will know the geographical location of countries in Europe, so that when given a map with numbered locations and lists of countries, they will identify the appropriate country for each number.
    This objective is a bit lengthy, but we've presented it to illustrate one way that multiple-choice items can be specified in an objective. The students would be given a map with each country numbered. The "lists of countries" would be the four or five choices that would go with each number. There are other appropriate ways to write the objective, of course.

__P__ 6. "Will know" is not an observable performance. A better objective would be

For ninth graders to understand the use of verbals, so that when given a series of descriptions, students will identify all those that are gerunds, participles, or infinitives.

__C__ 7. "On an essay test" is an inappropriate condition. An objective with an appropriate alternative would be

American government students will understand the concept of governmental checks and balances, so that without aids they will present a written example of a check and balance.

__GS__ 8. "Will understand genetics" is a goal statement that is so broad that it is no longer meaningful. An improved objective would be

Biology students will understand dominant and recessive patterns, so that when given case studies with dominant and recessive traits, they will identify the characteristics of each offspring.

EXERCISE 3.6

1. "Learns . . ." is a learning process rather than a student outcome. The subobjectives are properly stated according to Gronlund. An acceptable general objective would be

   Understands concepts in chemistry

2. Both the general objective and the subobjectives are stated in terms of teacher performance rather than student performance. An improved objective could be stated as

   Understands parts of speech
   2.1 Defines parts of speech in own words
   2.2 Generates examples
   2.3 Identifies parts of speech in context

3. This objective is properly stated. Gronlund would be critical of specifying content, but as we noted, we have set this issue aside.
4. Subobjective 4.1 identifies two performances. Otherwise, the objective is properly stated. The subobjective could be written as two objectives and could appear as

   States definition in own words
   Writes definition

5. The objective is properly stated.

Chapter *4*

Planning for Learning

Mr. Harry Armendariz, a middle school science teacher, sat at his desk at the beginning of the school year and thumbed through the science books spread out in front of him. The study of the causes and prevention of erosion appeared on both the state and district science curriculum guides and he was trying to decide what the best way to introduce the concept erosion *would be.*

"Sheesh," he thought to himself, "They're gonna croak when I try this out on them. They aren't too crazy about science to start with, and 'erosion' for crying out loud. That'll seem about as relevant to a bunch of sixth graders as . . . ," as his thoughts trailed off.

"This stuff is important. . . . It can help them understand how important it is to try and protect the environment," he muttered almost audibly with an air of determination, continuing to flip through the pages and take notes.

"Exactly what do I want them to know about it?" he thought as he wrote the word erosion *down on his notes.*

"How does it [erosion] fit my unit on land forms?" he continued, jotting down "erosion—land forms" in his notes.

"What can I show them, so they'll understand it? How hard will it be to get the materials?" he continued talking to himself.

"Now, how can I make them see that it's actually relevant?" he thought shaking his head.

He sat for several more minutes, and then wrote "sand-table demonstration" in his notes as he thought, "I'll start with that demonstration. It's concrete and actually fairly interesting—it'll give them a good reference point. It's a microexample of erosion at work, and they'll even see little canyons and deltas. It's also big enough, so the whole class will be able to see it without being too crowded. . . . Yeah, that's where I'll start."

Mr. Armendariz then decided to supplement his demonstration with a video that further illustrated the process of erosion in different locations around the world.

Having planned for his initial illustrations, "I'll try to get them to see how erosion relates to volcanoes and earthquakes—other factors that change the landscape," he thought to himself. Finally, he identified relevant pages in the text and made a note to himself to assign them for reading.

"Later on," Mr. Armendariz further mused, "I'll take them down to Black Creek, a local stream in the area, to see how erosion is working right here in town."

Introduction

Can you imagine a surgeon beginning an operation without specific knowledge of the patient's problem and what he or she will try to do to correct it? Can you imagine an engineer building a bridge without detailed blueprints, knowing what it will cost, and understanding how it will impact the environment? Does a pilot go into the air without consulting weather reports, charts, and maps? In each case, the results would be disastrous. While it doesn't seem as dramatic, teaching is similar. To facilitate intellectual, emotional, social, and physical growth in students, teachers must carefully plan and prepare, just as the surgeon, engineer, or pilot. Simply stated, you must plan, and you must plan thoroughly! Planning is the way teachers turn their thinking and decision making into tangible teaching strategies.

Research indicates that a teacher's preparation and systematic approach to instruction are variables that strongly affect student motivation, academic performance, and perceived teacher effectiveness (Pittman, 1987). Helping you learn to make decisions that will result in as much student learning as possible is the focus of this chapter.

Objectives

After completing your study of Chapter 4, you should be able to:

- Identify the most important factors to be considered in long range planning
- Illustrate ways that unit planning can be used to frame and connect a series of specific lesson plans
- Construct effective daily lesson plans
- Identify the advantages and disadvantages of different lesson plan formats
- Describe modifications in planning for inclusive classrooms

DECISION MAKING AND PLANNING

To begin our discussion of this chapter, refer back to the chapter opening scenario. Let's think about some of the decisions that Mr. Armendariz made as he planned. At least three decisions are significant:

- He made decisions about ways to illustrate or demonstrate the concept *erosion* for his students (his sand-table demonstration, the video, the text, and a field trip).

- He made a decision about sequence, that is, he decided to start the lesson with the sand-table demonstration.
- He made a decision about relating the lesson on erosion to his unit on land forms.

By definition, a decision involves a resolution or a conclusion that requires the professional judgment of the person making it—Mr. Armendariz in this case. He could have made a different set of decisions; for example, instead of using the sand table and video, he could have used different representations; he could have chosen to sequence the lesson differently; and he could have related the concept to the unit on land forms in a different way. In making his decisions, he took three important factors into account. First, he considered both short- and long-term goals. In asking himself, "Exactly what do I want them to know about it?" he was establishing a clear short-term goal for himself and the students; in wondering, "How does it [erosion] fit my unit on land forms?" he was considering his long-term goals.

Second, he considered the way students learn—the learning process itself. He asked himself, "What can I show them, so they'll understand it?" and "How hard will it be to get the materials?" He also decided to start with his sand-table demonstration because ". . . It's concrete, and . . . it'll give them a good reference point." These decisions indicated that Harry was consciously and systematically taking into account the way students learn as he planned.

Finally, he considered student motivation as he made his decisions. His first reaction was, "Sheesh, . . . They're gonna croak when I try this out on them. They aren't too crazy about science to start with . . . ," and his subsequent decisions involved trying to make his presentation interesting and helping the students see the relevance of the topic. This kind of thinking is typical for veteran teachers (Zahorik, 1996).

From this description, we begin to see that planning is a complex process that involves making a number of important decisions, and these decisions must take a number of factors into account. With these ideas in mind, let's reconsider the reasons teachers plan.

Reasons for Planning

Professionals plan for a variety of reasons, which can be classified into four categories:

- Conceptual
- Organizational
- Emotional
- Reflective

Conceptual Reasons for Planning.   We introduced the chapter by asking about surgeons, architects, pilots, and teachers, suggesting that each must carefully plan in order to do their work effectively. When architects, for example, make decisions about the best materials to use in designing a building, they're involved in the conceptual aspect of planning. Mr. Armendariz, as another example, made decisions about goals—exactly what he wanted his students to know, what he would use to represent the topic, and how he would sequence the lesson. This conceptual planning allows teachers to present ideas in a coherent and connected way.

Thorough planning allows teachers to know what students will learn, how they will learn, and the degree to which they have learned.

Organization and Planning. When a surgeon or pilot makes decisions about schedules in surgery or flights, they're involved in the organizational dimension of planning. Teachers, in addition to making conceptual decisions about goals and learning activities, also consider classroom rules and procedures, how they will use their time, and the optimal use of the physical environment. These are also part of the organizational concerns of planning.

Emotional Reasons for Planning.   A third important reason for planning is emotional. McCutcheon (1980) found that careful planning provides a source of security and confidence for teachers, and Neale, Pace, and Case (1983) found that beginning teachers tend to be quite extensive with their written plans. Even veteran teachers take extra care in planning when they face content that is new to them or difficult for students. These findings have important implications for us all—we should plan with extra care when content is new or when we are uncertain or insecure.

Reflection and Planning.   Planning is also important for reflection. It helps teachers make clear decisions about their goals, why the goals are important, and how they'll go about trying to help students reach the goals. This establishes reference points that allow them to reflect on the appropriateness of the goals and how effective they were in helping students reach them. Without careful planning, the process of reflecting becomes murky and uncertain at best.

Having examined decision making in planning and considered different reasons for planning, we turn now to planning at three different levels. We begin with long-term planning, then consider unit planning, and finally we examine daily lesson planning.

LONG-TERM PLANNING

Philosophical Considerations

Decision making during planning involves philosophical considerations about the value of different goals and objectives. At a very broad level, philosophers concern themselves with that which is "ultimately knowable." Teachers then focus on the subset of "knowable" information that is considered to be necessary and desirable. By definition, education is the acquisition of desirable knowledge and dispositions (Frankena, 1965).

As you saw in Chapter 2, the knowledge students are expected to learn is intended to satisfy the needs of the individual, the needs of society, and the need to understand essential bodies of information. We saw these views reflected in Mr. Armendariz's planning. He was considering the needs of individual students when he took the nature of learning and student motivation into account; he considered the needs of society when he decided that an understanding of erosion was important to protecting the environment; and the important aspects of the body of knowledge were reflected in the curriculum materials.

Specific Decisions

Teachers begin to operationalize or make these philosophical goals happen through long-term planning that includes both the philosophical considerations we just discussed together with each of the four reasons for planning that were outlined in the previous section. However, its primary focus is more on the conceptual and organizational dimensions than on the emotional and reflective ones. In the conceptual dimension, for example, it broadly outlines a year or semester of content and serves as a framework for more detailed planning that will come later. During the summer or pre-planning—the time in the fall when teachers prepare for the year, but students are not yet attending school—teachers commonly examine their text and other books, curriculum guides, and district- or state-level curriculum frameworks. Based on these materials, they often write lists of broad topics in an approximate sequence. For example, a ninth-grade geography teacher wrote the following:

First Term

1. Basic map skills—latitude, longitude, time zones, map projections
2. What is geography—the five fundamental concepts of geography
3. The earth's resources: geography and the environment
4. World climates

Second Term

5. Biomes, soil, and vegetation
6. Landforms
7. Seasons
8. Culture

Third Term

9. Cultural regions
   a. Western Europe
   b. Eastern Europe
   c. Russia and the former Soviet Union
   d. North Africa and the Middle East
   e. Africa south of the Sahara

Fourth Term

   f. South and East Asia
   g. The Pacific World
   h. Anglo-America
   i. Latin America

In addition to these topics, the teacher also considered available videos, worksheets, possible field trip locations, potential guest speakers, and projects.

We can see three important decisions involved in this simple set of notes. First, the teacher made decisions about what topics would be taught; second, she made decisions about sequence; and third, she considered—in a broad sense—resources and learning activities. Her planning and decision making were similar to Harry Armendariz's, only on a broader scale. During long-term planning, the conceptual dimension of planning remains broad; more specific decisions come later. Even though they're broad, however, these decisions help the teacher by reducing the number that must be made later, which helps simplify the overall planning process. For instance, the teacher can look at her outline and conclude, "Oh, yeah, I'm moving into world climates next, so I need to schedule those videos right away." Her decision about the topic to be covered next had already been made.

In the organizational aspect of long-term planning teachers also consider at least three additional factors:

- Characteristics of the students—their ability levels, needs and interests, and previous experiences. To gather this information, they talk to other teachers and look at cumulative folders.
- The physical environment. They try to create an environment that will induce positive emotions, and they also consider arrangements that will allow all students to see the board, screen, and television, as well as traffic lanes and access to facilities, such as storage cabinets and the pencil sharpener.
- Classroom management. They establish the rules and procedures that will set the patterns for the year.

Management deserves further mention. The structure provided by routines "played such a major role in the teacher's planning behavior that planning could be characterized as decision making about the selection, organization, and sequencing of routines" (Yinger, 1977, p. 165). Some of these routines are outlined in Table 4.1.

As with the conceptual dimension of planning, making decisions about organization and management during long-term planning reduces the number of decisions that will have to be made later.

Table 4.1   Areas for Establishing Routines in Long-Term Planning

Area	Example
General routines	• Checking attendance • Monitoring tardiness
Room use	• Teacher's desk and storage areas • Student desks and storage of personal items • Storage for class materials used by all students • Sink, pencil sharpener, waste basket • Learning centers and/or lab stations • Distributing and collecting materials • Expected behavior during interruptions • Class helpers in elementary schools • Computer use
Transitions in and out of room	• Beginning the school day or period • Procedures for leaving the room and returning (e.g., drinking fountain, bathroom breaks, lunch, school grounds, library, main office) • Ending the school day or period • Fire and disaster drills
Groupwork procedures	• Moving to and from groups • Expected behavior in groups
Seatwork and teacher-led instruction	• Student attention • Student participation • Procedures for leaving seats • Asking for help • Activities after seatwork is completed

UNIT PLANNING

Unit planning is the intermediate step between long-term planning and the process of constructing specific lesson plans. A unit can last anywhere from a week or two to a month or more depending on the topic and the age of the students.

While unit planning is an individual matter and the components of teachers' units vary, units commonly include the components outlined in Table 4.2.

Let's examine these components now.

Unit Title

A unit is a series of interrelated lessons that focus on a general topic. Some examples of unit topics in different content areas are shown in Table 4.3

If long-term planning has been effective, the decisions about unit topics have, for the most part, already been made, because these decisions have been based on an examination of national curriculum guides, state and district guidelines, the text, and

Table 4.2   Unit Components and Descriptions

Component	Description
Unit title	Identifies the unit topic
Unit goal	Generally describes what learners should accomplish
Rationale	Specifies why the unit is important
Content outline	Identifies and sequences the topics that are included in the unit
Specific lesson plans	Provide specific guidelines for each lesson within the unit

Table 4.3   Unit Topics in Different Content Areas

Language Arts	Social Studies
Nouns	The Civil War
Punctuation	The Colonial Era
Short Stories	Capitalism and Socialism
Paragraph Writing	Industrial Movement in America

Health	Science
Respiratory System	Reptiles
Drugs	Plants
Nutrition	Electricity
Exercise	Nuclear Energy

other resources. For instance, from our list of geography topics that appeared in the section on long-term planning, *basic map skills, world climates, landforms,* and *Russia and the former Soviet Union,* all could be converted into units.

Chapter divisions in textbooks commonly correspond to approximate unit lengths. This doesn't mean that teachers should mechanically follow the text as the primary organizer for unit topics, however. In some of their most effective units, teachers take only portions of text chapters, add material that doesn't appear in the text, or change the sequence of the text topics.

Unit Goal

Having identified the unit topic, the teacher is now ready to consider the overall goal or purpose for the unit. Some examples of unit goals are outlined in Table 4.4.

The goals form the core of the unit. In specifying the goal, the teacher makes decisions about what they want students to understand or be able to do with respect to the topic. In the unit on plants, for instance, knowing that understanding "why plants are critical to life" is a component of the goal, helps the teacher make deci-

Table 4.4   Unit Topics and Goals

Unit	Goal
Word endings (fourth grade)	The purpose of this unit is to help students understand the rules for adding suffixes to words.
Plants (seventh grade)	The purpose in this unit is for students to understand the parts of plants and their functions, the necessary conditions for healthy plants, and why plants are critical in ecosystems.
Civil War (eighth grade)	This unit is designed to help eighth-grade American history students understand the causes, events, outcomes, and aftermaths of the Civil War.
Solving equations (Algebra)	At the end of this unit algebra students should be able to solve two or more simultaneous equations.

sions about specific objectives and learning activities as specific lesson plans are prepared.

Rationale for the Unit

At no point in the planning process is professional decision making better illustrated or more critical than in considering the rationale for the unit. This decision making is critical for at least two reasons. First, we hear a great deal about the "knowledge explosion," which is reflected in the ever-increasing amount of information included in textbooks. It has become literally impossible to cover—even superficially—all the topics that appear in books, so teachers must make judicious decisions about what topics are most important to teach and in what sequence they should be taught. Teachers must think carefully about the reasons for selecting the topics they teach, promoting more important goals and topics over others.

Second, consciously considering rationales for selecting topics in the planning process provides a framework for reflection that will occur after the unit is taught, making the process of reflection more meaningful.

Content Outline

Having wrestled with the unit goal and its rationale, the teacher is now ready to outline the major ideas in the unit. This process breaks the general topic down into more specific and teachable subtopics. In introducing the unit, the teacher can provide the outline as a type of advance organizer to help students understand where the unit is going and the connections among the ideas. In addition, as daily lessons are introduced, the teacher can refer to the outline to help students understand the relationship of that lesson to previous and future ones.

Different ways of outlining the content of two different units are illustrated in Figures 4.1 and 4.2. The format you choose will depend on your own preferences and the content being considered.

Using either outline as a planning guide, the teacher is now ready to consider specific objectives for the unit. The task at this phase of the planning process is to translate content topics into measurable goals objectives. In addition, once constructed, these objectives need to be sequenced in terms of Bloom's taxonomy. This provides a suggested order for teaching as well as a way to clarify the kinds of behaviors expected of students. An example of this process applied to one segment of the plant unit is shown below.

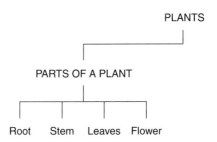

Interdisciplinary and Thematic Units

The discipline-centered single-topic approach to planning that we've described so far has at least two advantages, especially for beginning teachers. The first is simplicity; because individual lessons focus on a single topic or skill, it is easier for a beginning teacher to plan learning activities around that topic. A second advantage is that it presents a simpler and clearer picture of the discipline to students. When students leave a math lesson on equivalent fractions, for example, hopefully they will have a clear understanding of the topic and how to use it.

However this approach to planning also has problems and limitations, probably the most serious of which is fragmentation of the curriculum. For example, students study land forms and climate in earth science or geography, and they study historical events such as the American Civil War in history. Strong links exist, however, between the geography and climate, economies of the North and South, and the causes and outcomes of the war. Studying these topics separately doesn't help students see connections between different content areas.

Integrated planning attempts to organize learning activities so that lines separating subject matter areas are blurred or erased entirely, and distinct and discrete subject matter areas disappear (Wolfinger & Stockard, 1997). Integrated planning helps students see links between ideas from different content areas by consciously planning learning activities that encourage students to see connections.

There are at least three approaches to integrated planning (Wolfinger & Stockard, 1997):

- Combining disciplines
- Identifying themes
- Exploring issues

Figure 4.1   An outline of a plant unit content

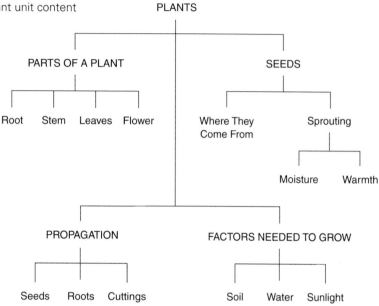

Figure 4.2   Outline of Dairy Product Unit Content

MILK AND DAIRY PRODUCTS
I. History
II. Nutritional Composition of Milk
    A. Fats, Proteins, Carbohydrates
    B. Vitamins
    C. Minerals
III. Processing of Milk
    A. Pasteurization
    B. Homogenization
IV. Variety of Milk Products
    A. Milk
        1. Whole
        2. Skim
        3. Cream
        4. Half and half
        5. Buttermilk
    B. Butter
    C. Yogurt
    D. Cheese
    E. Sour Cream
    F. Ice Cream
V.   Storage and Care of Milk and Milk Products
VI. Uses of Milk in Menu Planning

Let's look at them.

Combining Disciplines.   One of the simplest ways to integrate content areas is to start with a topic and explore possible connections in another discipline. For example, a teacher who is planning a social studies unit on different Native American cultures might look to art and music for ways that students could use to describe those cultures. In a similar way, a teacher planning a unit on graphing might look to science or social studies for topics that could be counted, measured, and graphed. A simple way to remind yourself of these opportunities is to pause after you've planned a lesson or unit and ask yourself, "How might I connect this content with other topics and skills my students are learning?"

Identifying Themes.   A second way to integrate your planning is around themes. Children's common interests at a particular grade level provide one source of themes. For example, children at the lower elementary levels have widely varying interests, such as holidays, their communities, or dinosaurs. Students at the middle school and high school level are often fascinated by topics such as their changing bodies, interpersonal relationships, and health issues such as drugs, smoking, and alcohol. Thematic units, organized around topics such as these, can be used to pull lessons together from a number of different content perspectives.

Exploring Issues.   A third way to integrate planning is through the use of issues or problems. As students study issues such as pollution, terrorism, the arms race, or hunger and poverty, teachers can encourage them to use different disciplines to understand the issues and propose solutions to the problems posed by these issues.

Interdisciplinary planning is admittedly demanding. It requires thorough understanding of content, learners, and goals. However, starting with relatively simple processes, such as the example with graphing information from social studies (Civil War) and science (land forms, climate), is a good beginning point. From there, as you gather experience, you'll see more and more opportunities for making connections among the disciplines. Having specified and sequenced the unit topics, the teacher is now ready to prepare specific lesson plans.

EXERCISE 4.1_____

Look at the following series of goals, each of which provides a topic for a daily lesson plan. For each, identify a unit into which the topic would fit. Then compare your answers to the ones given in the feedback section at the end of the chapter.

1. You want your language arts students to understand homonyms.

    _____

2. You want your American History students to know the causes of the American Revolutionary War.

    _____

3. You want your kindergartners to understand the difference between squares and rectangles.

    _____

4. You want your life science students to understand the characteristics of paramecia.

_____

5. You want your technology students to understand factors affecting wood strength.

_____

EXERCISE 4.2 _____

A fifth-grade teacher is beginning to plan a unit on Native American cultures. Write a unit goal and outline for this general topic. Then compare your answers to the ones given in the feedback section at the end of the chapter.

UNIT GOAL: _____

_____

_____

OUTLINE: _____

_____

_____

LESSON PLANNING

Having specified the unit topic, goal, rationale, and topic outline, the teacher is ready to plan individual lessons. In this phase of the planning process, the teacher is thinking about a single class period. This might be as little as 15 or 20 minutes or as long as 90 or 100 (since some middle and secondary schools have gone to "block" scheduling).

Although there is no one "right" lesson plan, the format that we recommend has seven components:

- Unit topic
- Objectives
- Rationale
- Content
- Procedures
- Materials
- Assessment

Each of these components is intended to contribute to teaching effectiveness and student learning. After describing the seven components we examine different ways of thinking about the planning process.

Unit Title

Individual lessons aren't planned in isolation; they should exist in the context of the unit and other lessons that come before and after it. The unit title simply reminds the teacher of the relationship between the individual lesson and the unit as a whole. For example, a lesson on the parts of a flower would exist in the context of the overall unit on plants. A lesson on rules for adding *-ing* endings to words would fit into the overall unit on adding suffixes, and identifying reasons that the South lost the Civil War would be one or more lessons from a unit on the Civil War.

Objectives

Objectives form the core of the lesson plan. They serve three functions:

- They expand the unit goal by describing it in greater detail.
- They specify what the students should know or be able to do at the end of the lesson.
- They translate the content outline of the unit into measurable outcomes.

For instance, the unit goal for the unit on plants was,

> The purpose in this unit is for students to understand the parts of plants and their functions, the necessary conditions for healthy plants, and why plants are critical in ecosystems.

Objectives for single lessons within the unit might appear as follows:

1. Life science students will know the parts of a plant, so when given an unlabeled picture of a unique plant (one they haven't previously encountered), they will identify and label each part.
2. Life science students will understand the functions of each of the parts of a plant, so when given a list of plant parts, they will describe the functions of each.

As another example, the goal for the unit on suffixes was,

> The purpose of this unit is to help students understand the rules for adding suffixes to words.

Objectives for lessons in this unit might appear as follows:

1. Fourth graders will understand the rule for adding *-ing* endings to words, so when given a topic of their choice they will write a paragraph in which each part of the rule is illustrated.
2. Fourth graders will understand the rule for adding *-ed* endings to words, so that given a topic of their choice, they will write a paragraph in which each part of the rule is illustrated.

- Objectives help teachers plan learning activities with precision.
- Objectives help learners become self-regulated, because they understand what is expected of them.

A rule of thumb in making decisions about the number of objectives is, *When in doubt, err on the side of too many.* You have nothing to lose. If you've planned more content than you can cover, you have less planning to do for the following lesson. On the other hand, a lesson completed when half the period remains can lead to uncertainty, classroom management problems, and embarrassment. This is one of the more challenging tasks for interns and beginning teachers.

Rationale

Imagine a visitor to your classroom asking, "*Why* are you teaching this to your students at this time?" Your answer would be the *rationale* for your lesson. Typically, it involves a philosophical reason for teaching the lesson. For instance, a teacher might feel that understanding the rules for forming suffixes will make students better writers, which in turn will help them in the world of work—knowledge that satisfies the needs of the individual. Understanding the causes of the Civil War are important in helping students become responsible citizens—knowledge that satisfies the needs of society.

As we said in the introduction to this chapter, planning helps teachers *think* about their teaching, and in our discussion of unit planning we said that the rationale was critical. The same is true at the lesson level; the *rationale* is perhaps the most important part of a lesson plan. If you don't have a clear reason for teaching a topic, maybe it should be eliminated from the unit.

A rationale for knowing the parts of a flower, and identifying the reasons the South lost the Civil War might be stated as follows:

- Understanding the parts of a plant is important for understanding how plants and animals interrelate in ecosystems.
- Understanding the reasons the South lost the Civil War helps students see the interrelationships among geography, politics, agriculture in particular, and industrial strength among nations in general.

Rationales also help us get at the idea of *relevance*—one of the most popular and often-used terms in education today. When establishing a rationale, you are considering the applicability of the topic you're having the students study. The more applicable the work, the more relevant it is for them.

The rationale can also be viewed as a defense for teaching the content in the lesson. As noted earlier, if you can't confidently defend the lesson, to yourself, to students, to their parents, and to administrators, you should rethink the objectives for that particular plan. We will return to this idea in the section on "Planning and Reflecting."

Content

The lesson's content component describes the major ideas you plan to teach. If someone were to walk into the room and ask you, "*What* are you teaching?" you would respond by describing the content of the lesson plan. Having already decided at the beginning of the year what your broad goals are, the content component of the lesson requires you to be more specific. In some cases, the process is simple. If the lesson focuses on a concept, the content is a definition of the concept, its characteristics, examples and nonexamples of the concept, and the relationship of the concept to other concepts. When the lesson involves a generalization or academic rule, it's a statement of the generalization or rule and illustrations and applications of it. For example, in the lesson on adding *-ing* to words, the content is simply the rule with some examples:

> When adding *-ing* to a word, you double the final letter if it's a consonant preceded by a short vowel sound, but you do not if it's preceded by another consonant or involves a long vowel sound.

flop	flopping	sing	singing
trip	tripping	jump	jumping
fly	flying	play	playing
read	reading		

On the other hand, if the lesson involves a more complex concept, such as the parts of a flower, the content may exist in outline form:

Pistil (female)
   Stigma
   Style
   Ovary (ripened ovary becomes fruit)
   Ovules (later become seeds)

Stamen (male)
   Anther
   Filament

Petals (add color and attract birds and insects)

Sepals (protect reproductive organs)

The content outline serves as a guide for teachers and helps remind them of what is to be covered. They may refer to it as the lesson progresses to be certain that they haven't forgotten anything, and they may even check off the items as they are covered. The outline also allows teachers to emphasize the parts of the lesson that are most important or those parts that may present problems for students.

How much detail should you put in the content section of the lesson plan? This is another illustration of one of the text's themes. It involves a decision made by professionals. Inexperienced teachers or those who aren't familiar with the topic may decide to prepare a point-by-point outline, whereas a few key words or phrases might be enough for a tenured educator.

Procedures

In the content section, you list *what* you intend to teach. In this section, you consider *how* you intend to teach it. The procedures component of the lesson plan can be viewed as a set of directions or instructions on how to present the lesson. If you were absent from school on a particular day, the substitute should have enough information from the procedures section to teach the lesson as you planned it.

As with the content section, how detailed the procedures section will be involves decisions made by the teacher. The procedures section for novices will probably be very detailed; for veterans it may be quite sketchy.

One effective planning strategy is to write the procedures as a series of steps or directions for a possible substitute. For example, a procedures component for the lesson on adding *-ing* endings to words might appear as follows:

1. Display the following passage on the overhead for the students.

   > *"Would you like to read* the paper?" Latanya's mother asked, handing her the paper.
   >   "No," Latanya replied, *jumping* up from her chair, "I've been *reading* all day." I'm going to *jump* into the shower."
   >   "Don't *trip* on the rug in there. I've been *tripping* over it every time I go in there," her mother warned.
   >   "You're *flying* around the house all the time," Latanya retorted. "I only *fly* around when I'm getting ready for school."
   >   "Well be sure you *lay* it down when you leave. I don't want it *laying* in a heap."

2. Ask the students to get together with their partners.
3. Direct the groups to try and identify any patterns that they find in the underlined words. Give them 5 minutes.
4. Reassemble the class, and ask the groups to report on what they've found.
5. Prompt the class if necessary to notice that half the words end in *-ing*.
6. Guide the class to conclude that the final consonant in each root word is doubled if it is preceded by a short vowel sound, but it isn't doubled if it's preceded by another consonant or a long vowel sound.
7. Call on a student to articulate the rule.
8. Write the rule on the board as the student states it.

As another example, the procedures section for the lesson on parts of a flower might appear as follows:

1. Display a transparency showing the parts of a flower.
2. Write the name of each part on the display and link it to the diagram.
3. Describe the function of each part.
4. Show the students an actual flower.
5. Ask individuals to identify verbally the different parts of the flower.
6. After each part is identified, have the students describe the function of the identified part.
7. Give the students a colored drawing of a flower. Have them independently (or in small groups) identify in writing the parts of the drawing and their functions.

Notice how the content and procedures portions of the lesson plan relate. We see that the content is the *what* of the lesson and the procedures are the *how*. In our example with the flower, when the procedure calls for identifying each part, the content outline provides a reference for the specific parts.

As with other parts of planning, the procedures reflect a great deal of decision making. For example, in the procedures for teaching the rule for adding *-ing* to words, the teacher made three significant decisions. First, she chose a guided discovery approach. (We will examine guided discovery in detail in Chapter 7.) She could have decided instead to first state the rule, provide some examples, and explain them, which would have been a more teacher-centered expository approach.

Second, the teacher decided to embed the examples of the rule in the context of a short passage, instead of illustrating it in isolated sentences or words, which would have involved a different decision. And third, she decided to first have the students work collaboratively and then as a whole group, instead of deciding to conduct the entire lesson with the whole class. As with other parts of planning, the decision-making process is very much a part of selecting procedures.

Materials

The purpose in listing materials in the lesson plan is simple; it reminds the teacher of any *special* equipment, resource books, illustrations, demonstrations, transparencies, videotapes, computer software, etc., that must be gathered or prepared before the lesson. For instance, the passage illustrating the rule for adding *-ing* to words, the transparency showing the parts of the flower, and the actual flower would be listed in the materials sections of the lesson plans.

By "special" we mean materials other than textbooks, pencils, notebook paper, and similar items. Although they're technically materials, listing them in a lesson plan isn't necessary because they're always available, and students are supposed to have them. (Students failing to bring necessary materials is another issue, which we discuss in Chapter 9.)

Teachers should carefully consider the procedures and materials that will most effectively facilitate student learning.

Assessment

The assessment component of the lesson plan encourages the teacher to consider—before the lesson—how to evaluate student learning. This is relatively simple if the objective is complete and includes an assessment statement.

When planning your lesson, try to be as specific as possible in describing what you want students to learn and how you'll assess whether or not this happened. Don't just say, "I'll evaluate on the basis of student responses." Of course you will, but what student responses will you be looking for? Thinking this through will help you be clear about what is targeted and what students will be able to do when you are through.

As examples of the link between objectives and assessment, consider the following:

Objective:
Fourth graders will understand the rule for adding *-ing* to words, so that when given a topic of their choice they will write a paragraph in which each part of the rule is illustrated.

Assessment:
Have the students select a topic and write a paragraph—that makes sense—in which each part of the rule is illustrated.

Objective:
Seventh-grade life science students will know the parts of a flower, so that when given a drawing showing the structure of a flower, they will correctly label each part.

Assessment:
Give the students a handout with a drawing showing the structure of a flower. Have them label each part identified with an arrow.

The point here is that the assessment must be consistent with the objective. If the objective calls for a listening behavior, it would be inappropriate to call for a discussion in the assessment. A detailed discussion of the preparation of items to measure students' attainment of goals is presented in Chapter 11.

Don't confuse this component of the lesson plan with reflection or critique, which is your evaluation of your own teaching performance. Although the critique is not actually one of the components of a lesson plan, it is an important step and a critical part of the planning and reflecting process that aims at you evaluating *your* performance.

EXERCISE 4.3

Provide a rationale for each of the goals in Exercise 4.1 Then compare your answers to the ones given in the feedback section at the end of the chapter.

1. _____

_____

2. _____

_____

3. _____

_____

4. _____

_____

5. _____

_____

EXERCISE 4.4 _____

For each of the goals found in Exercise 4.1, provide an assessment component of the lesson plan. Then compare your answers to the ones given in the feedback section at the end of the chapter.

1. _____

_____

2. _____

_____

3. _____

_____

4. _____

_____

5. _____

_____

The Total Lesson Plan

A simple way of organizing all the components of a lesson plan is presented in Figure 4.3. Turn ahead to Exercise 4.5, and you will see that we have listed the procedures below the content, whereas in Figure 4.3, they are listed side by side. This arrangement is a matter of personal preference, and one is no more correct than the other.

Personal preference is not only found in arrangements but can also be found in the components of a lesson plan. For example, Madeline Hunter (1982) developed a lesson plan model consistent with the one we've presented in this chapter but provided additional elements as you can see in Table 4.5.

Her objective and purpose parallel our objective and rationale, her input compares to our content component, and modeling is similar to procedures. In addition, Hunter's model includes specific plans for attracting student's attention (anticipatory set), checking for understanding, and two kinds of practice. In our lesson on plants,

UNIT: Social Classes in America

OBJECTIVE: For the high school history student to understand social stratification in America, so that when given a list of characteristics of a certain family, the students will choose one of the three classes that best represents the family, giving at least three examples of proof.

RATIONALE: It is necessary for a history student to understand that America's social stratification is a fluid division of people. It is part of this country's social makeup to have little classification of people, although there are noticeable differences in this country's people.

Content	Procedures
I. Upper Class	
A. Income	1. Identify characteristics of upper class.
B. Education	2. Discuss relationship of characteristics with each other. Ask "How are education and income related? How about education and occupation?"
C. Occupation	
D. Political affiliation	
E. Residence	3. Ask "What characteristics separate them most from other classes?"
II. Middle Class	4. Repeat steps 1, 2, and 3 for middle and lower classes.
A. Income	
B. Education	5. Present case study 1 on overhead. Have class try to identify class in terms of characteristics discussed above.
C. Occupation	
D. Political affiliation	
E. Residence	6. Present case study 2 on overhead. Discuss characteristics.
III. Lower Class	
A. Income	7. If time permits, present case study 3 as a quiz. If there is not enough time, have students prepare for a quiz tomorrow.
B. Education	
C. Occupation	
D. Political affiliation	
E. Residence	

MATERIALS: Dittos of characteristics for each student.

ASSESSMENT: Students should be able, in short essay form, to describe why a certain family could fit into one of the social classes studied, giving reasons why and characteristics of that class.

Figure 4.3   Sample Lesson Plan

Table 4.5   Madeline Hunter's Elements of Lesson Design

Component	Function
1. Anticipatory Set	How will student's attention be focused?
2. Objective and Purpose	What will students learn and why?
3. Input	What new information will be discussed?
4. Modeling	How can the teacher illustrate the new skill or content?
5. Checking for Understanding	How can the teacher ascertain whether students are learning new material?
6. Guided Practice	What opportunities are students given to practice new materials in class?
7. Independent Practice	How can assignments and homework be used for long-term retention?

for example, a teacher might display an apple and an orange and ask the students to try and explain where they come from. This would be a form of anticipatory set. Hunter also suggests that we consciously plan for a way to check students' understanding of the content as we deliver it. One way of accomplishing this is through questioning, which we discuss in detail in Chapter 6.

Practice, both guided and independent, can be accomplished by preparing additional examples and having students work with the examples. For instance, look again at the sample procedure we presented for the lesson on plants (p.101). In steps 5 and 6, the procedure called for having the students verbally identify different parts of a flower and the function of each part. This process is a form of *guided practice*. This was followed by *independent practice* in step 7, where the procedure provided for the teacher to give the students a colored drawing of a flower and have them identify the parts in writing on the drawing.

EXERCISE 4.5

Using the lesson plan format presented in the chapter, develop a lesson plan for the concept "mammal." Then compare your answers to the ones given in the feedback section at the end of the chapter.

UNIT: _____

OBJECTIVE: _____

_____

RATIONALE: _____

_____

CONTENT: _____

_____

PROCEDURES: _____

_____

MATERIALS: _____

_____

ASSESSMENT: _____

_____

PLANNING FOR STUDENTS WITH EXCEPTIONALITIES IN INCLUSIVE CLASSROOMS

Increased numbers of students with exceptionalities are being included in regular classrooms in today's schools. This is due in part to a growing body of research suggesting that these students benefit from as much time as possible in regular environments instead of in restricted settings (Hardman, Drew, & Egan, 1996). As a result, instruction on inclusion is being included in many preservice education programs. One of the most critical of these components involves adapting unit and lesson planning for the needs of students with exceptionalities.

One adaptation utilizes *task analysis,* or the process of breaking complex skills down into simpler ones. A sample task analysis is presented in Figure 4.4.

As we see in Figure 4.4, the first task involves assessing the student, which requires identifying the student's level of academic, social, emotional, and physical functioning. Pretests, recommendations, reviews of reports on successive visits, observation, and consultations with external resources such as counselors or physicians can be used for this purpose.

This information makes it possible to state a terminal objective for the student. Once you've accomplished this task, you are ready to write "enroute" objectives, which are more specific objectives designed to help the student reach the terminal objective.

Next, you will focus on organizing the special education lesson plan designed to facilitate the Task Analysis. A sample is presented in Figure 4.5

We see that the lesson plan in Figure 4.5 includes only enroute objective #6. In reality, a lesson plan will be prepared for each of the enroute objectives listed in the task analysis. Also, you need to employ a wide and varied selection of classroom methods and learning materials in order to facilitate the diverse needs of the students. In addition, the focus should not be totally academic but should also employ elements that are applicable, real, and relevant. Evaluations need to be flexible enough to measure both these elements and acceptable individual performance.

As often occurs in Individualized Education Plans (IEPs) (which we discuss in Chapter 8), our examples focused on a single student, Eric. When developing IEPs, you will frequently be addressing the needs of three, four, or more students with exceptionalities in your classroom whose instructional needs may or may not overlap. Here is where help from a consulting special education teacher is essential.

SPECIAL EDUCATION
Task Analysis (Unit Plan)

Entering Behavior for Each Student: Enrolled in the second grade, Eric is an EMH (educably mentally handicapped) child who is functioning at a 4–5 year preschool level in reading and writing. Spelling is slowly being introduced and he is functioning at a kindergarten level in math. Eric has been diagnosed as having A.D.D. (Attention Deficit Disorder) and is borderline hyperactive. He is currently receiving Ritalin three times a day. He receives his second dose at lunchtime (11:00 A.M.). Approximately 45 minutes before lunch, his frustration level is low, and he has a difficult time maintaining attention to a particular task.

Enroute Objectives:

1. Given five pictures of different types of trains, the student will identify the engine, car, and caboose in all five trains (circle the engine, cross out the car, and underline the caboose).
2. Given a worksheet containing 10 words with the *sh, ch, th,* and *wh* diphthongs, the student will identify the diphthongs in all 10 words (circle).
3. Given a worksheet containing 10 compound words, the student will distinguish between the 2 component words with 80% accuracy (drawing a vertical line).
4. Given a handout of a short train story, the student will identify five of the seven contractions contained within (circle).
5. Given a worksheet with five words and their definitions, the student will identify the word with the appropriate definition with 100% accuracy (match).
6. Given a worksheet comprised of six sentences that describe particular events in the text, the student will state the correct sequence of events with 100% accuracy (by numbering).
7. Given a worksheet containing three short statements, the student will identify the correct statement depicting the main idea (circle).

Terminal Objective:

Cognitive: For the second-grade EMH student to internalize the use of word-attack skills, so when given a copy of a page from *The Little Engine That Could,* the student will identify all the diphthongs, contractions, and compound words (circle).

Affective: For the second-grade EMH student to know there are differences in what individuals can accomplish, so when given crayons and drawing paper, the student will describe (drawing) at least one task that is difficult and one task that is easy to accomplish.

Figure 4.4   Sample Special Education Task Analysis (Unit Plan)

ADAPTING LESSON PLANNING FOR EVERYDAY USE

Both the basic format we've presented here, the Hunter planning model, and the Special Education Model are more detailed than formats you're likely to encounter in the schools. Experienced teachers typically use an abridged format that looks something like Figure 4.6 (at the top of p. 110).

SPECIAL EDUCATION
Lesson Plan

Date   February 23

A.   ENROUTE OBJECTIVE #6: Given a worksheet comprised of six sentences that describe particular events in *The Little Engine That Could,* the student will state (by numbering) the correct sequence of events with 100% accuracy.

B.   METHODS AND MATERIALS:

MATERIALS: *THE LITTLE ENGINE THAT COULD*
Teacher-made trains depicting Nos. 1–10
Pictures of sequence of events
Pictures of: the happy little train, the toys, the shiny new engine, the big strong engine, the old and tired engine, the little blue engine
string
pencils
crayons
handouts depicting sequence of events

METHODS:

1. Read *The Little Engine That Could* to the class.
   *Early in the morning because of Eric's attention span.
2. Review the numbers 1–10 using teacher-made trains and have them put in proper order.
   *Emphasize tactile with Eric using beads to help him to count.
3. Discuss terminology such as first, then, after, and finally.
4. Hang pictures and have them put in correct order.
   *To avoid confusion, let Eric do the first and the last items.
5. List unfamiliar words and review meanings.
6. Pass out handouts.
   *Eric receives handout with visual cues.

Application of Lesson to Pupil Interests and/or Real Life:

It is important for students to understand the concept that events occur in a particular order in stories as well as in real life. The attainment of this concept will assist them in their communication skills (retelling an event or story) as well as their comprehension skills (recalling a story or event). This concept assists the EMH students in organizing events in their minds, thus enabling a deeper understanding.

C. EVALUATION

Pupil: Teacher-made handout
         *revised version of handout

Eric: Eric completed the revised handout with 100% accuracy but exhibited a high level of frustration and was restless while doing his work. He also needed teacher assistance.

Figure 4.5   Special Education Lesson Plan Example

	Monday	Tuesday	Wednesday	Thursday	Friday
Period 1					
Period 2					
Period 3					
Period 4					
Period 5					
Period 6					
Period 7					

Figure 4.6   An abridged planning format.

Figure 4.7   A completed cell from an abridged planning format.

Period 1

Hand back quiz Introduce adjective clauses p. 125 Assign exercises p. 127 Begin individual conferences

Planning books blocked out in days and periods are useful tools for keeping track of the week's activities. A quick glance at the page tells the teacher the major activities for that period of that day. This can be helpful after a long weekend or as a means of keeping track on a particularly hectic day. For an example of what a cell commonly looks like, see Figure 4.7.

This brief format and the sketchy information it includes is likely to be misleading. Because we see only a brief outline and don't see objectives, rationales, and procedures, we might conclude that veteran teachers don't think about these things. Nothing could be further from the truth. Master teachers have very precise goals in mind, they have clear reasons for teaching the topics they teach, and they know in detail what procedures they will use. Because of their experience, much of this information isn't written down. Further, as teachers acquire expertise, some of the procedures are virtually automatic, meaning they require little conscious thought.

Our goal in writing this chapter is simple. The long-term, unit, and lesson planning that we've described in detail is intended to give you concrete illustrations of the *thinking* and *decision making* that all effective teachers engage in. We want you to think and make decisions about content, goals, rationales, procedures, materials, and assessments. As you acquire experience, you too will write less information down. The information in this chapter is intended as a starting point, designed to help you make your thinking clear and systematic. Now, you should be planning in detail and writing down a considerable amount of information. This forces you to be specific and concrete. At this point, if information isn't committed to paper, many of the planning decisions tend to be vague and ill-formed. As you acquire experience, your thinking will become clearer, more of what you do will be automatic, and you won't have to write as much down.

PLANNING AND REFLECTING

You've made a series of decisions about the topics you'll teach; what you want the students to know, understand, or be able to do with respect to the topics; why they're important; and how you'll help students understand them. After you've taught the topics, you want to consider the kind of thinking and the decisions you've made. This is the reflective aspect of planning. In a basic sense, reflection asks, "How good were the decisions I made?" Specifically, reflection might try to answer questions such as:

- How appropriate were the topics, i.e., should they be taught again?
- Was the sequence of topics appropriate? If not, how should they be sequenced?
- Were my objective(s) appropriate for my students?
- Was my instruction aligned? Did my lesson plans facilitate my unit plan, and were the procedures and assessments I specified consistent with my objectives?
- Were the procedures I used as effective as they might have been? If not, what procedures might have been better?
- Did the materials I used adequately represent the topic? What representations would have made the topic more understandable?
- Is there a way that I could have made the overall environment more conducive to learning?

No one can answer these questions better than you can. In addition, the actual answers are less important than developing the inclination to ask the questions. Teaching a topic because it's in the book, or because it's been taught before, is not an adequate reason for teaching it now. As teachers become reflective, they make more conscious and well-thought-out decisions about the topics they choose to teach and the procedures they'll use to teach them. This is the essence of the relationship between decision making and reflection.

Summary

Planning exists at three levels: long-range, unit, and lesson planning. Each requires a series of decisions that must be made before instruction actually begins. Long-range planning is an overall blueprint within which unit and specific lesson planning occur. Unit planning then converts broad goals into sequences of topics with rationales for teaching those topics. Specific lesson plans then convert the topics into teachable and learnable parts.

Written lesson plans follow a variety of formats. One includes a seven-part sequence including the unit, objectives, rationale, content, procedures, materials, and assessment. The Hunter Model is consistent with this format but also includes additional elements, such as anticipatory set, checking for student understanding, guided practice, and independent practice. Planning for working with students with exceptionalities requires more detailed plans, such as task analysis and individual education plans.

As teachers acquire experience, they are likely to write less information down on paper. This can be misleading, however, because master teachers think carefully about topics, goals and objectives, rationales, procedures, and assessments.

Reflecting about planning involves asking questions about the inclusion of topics and the way they've been sequenced, the appropriateness of objectives, the alignment of objectives, learning activities and assessments, the effectiveness of procedures, and the extent to which the materials adequately represented the topics. Trying to answer these questions provides the link between decision making and reflecting in the planning process.

Questions for Discussion

1. What are some examples of decisions that you might make during long-term, unit, and lesson planning. What might be some alternative decisions? Provide rationales for the different decisions.
2. How might administrators and colleagues influence the planning decisions that you make? Offer an example in each case.
3. Offer an example that describes how federal, state, and local agencies will influence your planning decisions.
4. Describe the different kinds of knowledge that teachers must possess in order to make the most effective decisions possible about planning. Offer examples for each of the kinds of knowledge.
5. Would veteran teachers be more effective if they wrote more detailed plans? Provide a rationale for your position.
6. Since veteran teachers typically don't prepare plans in the detail presented in this chapter, is requiring that you go through this process a waste of time? Why do you think so, or why do you think not?
7. An alternative to the planning process we've presented in this chapter might be for you to work as an "apprentice" with a veteran teacher, and imitate the process that he or she goes through. How effective would that likely be in helping you learn how to plan? Provide a basis for your thinking with respect to this question.

Suggestions for Field Experiences

1. Interview a teacher. Ask her to describe her thinking when she is involved in long-term, unit, and lesson planning. Ask her to show you some written samples of her plans and describe how she uses them. Ask her what questions she asks herself after she has planned and conducted lessons.
2. Review some curriculum guides and see if you can identify elements of long-term, unit, and lesson planning in them.
3. Assuming you have been placed at a school site with other preservice teachers, compare the content of this chapter with the planning you've seen at your school.
4. Given the opportunity, select a goal that appears in a unit plan in your field experience and develop a complete lesson plan for that goal.

5. Given the opportunity, develop and teach a lesson plan to a class or small group of students in your field placement. Then, using the list of seven suggestions found on page 111, reflect on what you did and how you might revise or improve the presentation.

Exercise Feedback

EXERCISE 4.1

Listed below are possible units for the topics in the exercise. Remember there are a number of ways to organize topics, so more than one unit is possible. Identifying the unit is designed to help you think about the way you're organizing your content. The thought processes are more important than the particular form of organization that results.

1. One possibility is "Word Pairs." Another would be "Basic Vocabulary." A third might be "Using context to improve understanding."
2. The unit could simply be "The Revolutionary War." A second might be "Causes of Wars."
3. "Basic Shapes" might be the unit here. Other possibilities would be "Visual Discrimination" or "Reading Readiness Skills."
4. A unit here would likely be "Protozoans." Another possibility might be "Simple animals and plants."
5. "Building Materials" could be a unit in this example.

EXERCISE 4.2

Your unit goal and outline for the unit on Native American cultures might appear as follows:

UNIT GOAL: The purpose of this unit is to help fifth graders understand the cultures and lifestyles of various Native American cultures prior to the time that Europeans came to the New World. At the completion of the unit, the students should understand influences that caused some of the differences in the cultures.

CONTENT OUTLINE: The content outline depends on decisions made by individual teachers. The following represents one possibility.

1. Native Americans of the Northeast
    a. Culture
    b. Climate and geography
    c. Economy
    d. Lifestyle
2. Native Americans of the Plains
    a. Culture
    b. Climate and geography
    c. Economy
    d. Lifestyle
3. Native Americans of the Northwest
    a. Culture
    b. Climate and geography

      c. Economy
      d. Lifestyle
  4. Native Americans of the Southwestern Deserts
      a. Culture
      b. Climate and geography
      c. Economy
      d. Lifestyle

A different content outline might appear as follows:

1. Components of cultures
2. Geography, climate, and culture
3. Geography, climate, and economy
4. Native American groups
    a. The Northeast
    b. The Plains
    c. The Northwest
    d. The Southwest Deserts

We can see that the content represented by the two outlines is essentially the same, but the organization is different. This illustrates how significant the decision-making process is in planning.

EXERCISE 4.3

As with the unit, the rationale may vary. The important thing is that the rationale exists, showing that the teacher has thought about the lesson. Possible rationales are as follows:

1. Homonyms are important as basic building blocks in vocabulary. It is important that students understand that words that sound alike and are spelled alike don't have the same meaning.
2. The causes of the Revolutionary War are important to a total perspective on the war. Also, an understanding of the Revolutionary War's causes can lead to an understanding of the causes of other wars.
3. Visual discrimination is a critical reading readiness skill. The ability to discriminate between shapes is an indication of visual discrimination ability.
4. Paramecia are common and widely known protozoans, and understanding a protozoan is the foundation for understanding the animal kingdom.
5. Understanding wood strength allows a carpenter to select the proper materials for a job at the most reasonable cost.

EXERCISE 4.4

As with the other components, assessments may vary and we are providing only possible ones.

1. Present the students with word pairs in the context of a written passage and have them identify the homonyms.
2. Give the students a description of the conditions in the colonies before the Revolutionary War. From this description, have them identify the factors that contributed to the war.

3. Give the children a sheet with shapes drawn on it. Have them color the squares red and the rectangles blue.
4. Have the students draw a paramecium and label all its parts.
5. Show the students a series of three wood samples. Have them order the three from strongest to weakest.

EXERCISE 4.5

Although your responses will differ somewhat from those that follow, here is how the lesson plan might appear:

UNIT: Warm-Blooded Animals.

OBJECTIVE: First graders will understand mammals, so when given a series of pictures of animals, they will identify all the mammals.

RATIONALE: Mammals are the most advanced members of the animal kingdom, and humans are mammals. Understanding mammals will contribute to children's understanding of different ways that animals adapt to ensure their survival.

CONTENT: Mammals are warm-blooded animals that have hair, suckle their young, and give live birth. Some examples are cows, horses, people, wolves, seals, whales, kangaroos, and tigers. (Notice here that the teacher is making decisions about the content she is including based on the developmental level of the children. Not all mammals give live birth, for example. Some, such as the duckbilled platypus are egg-layers. Understanding the more precise characteristics of mammals will come at a later age.)

PROCEDURES:

1. Show the students a guinea pig, and have them touch and feel it.
2. Have them describe what they saw and felt.
3. Show them a picture of a cow with a calf.
4. Ask them to describe the picture.
5. Show them a picture of an eagle sitting on a nest of eggs.
6. Ask students to identify the similarities and differences in the pictures and the guinea pig.
7. Show the students a picture of a tiger.
8. Ask the students to compare all of the pictures and the guinea pig.
9. Continue showing pictures of mammals and other animals.
10. Prompt the students to identify the characteristics of the mammals.
11. Call for a definition of mammals based on the characteristics they've described.

MATERIALS:

A student's pet guinea pig
Pictures of mammals and nonmammals

ASSESSMENT: Show the students a series of pictures of animals. Have them circle those that are mammals.

Chapter 5

The Affective, Psychomotor, and Cognitive Domains

Three kindergarten teachers were sharing their short lunch break and talking about their different views of teaching.

"Have I got a group this year," offered Jan Hansen. "They are really immature. I'm working with them on real basic eye–hand coordination activities in my learning centers. They're cutting and pasting and coloring and it seems to help."

"I know what you mean," replied Rita Sanchez. "I tried teaching my kids the letters in each of their names as a starting point for learning the alphabet, but they had problems with left and right and up and down. So I figured back to the drawing boards. There's no point in trying to teach letters when they don't know concepts such as big and little and straight and curved. So that's what we do in our learning centers."

"I think you're both pushing the kids too much. Haven't you heard of the developmentally appropriate curriculum?" Alice Trang asked jokingly. "You're trying to turn these kids into junior academians. Kindergarten is the time for kids to learn about themselves and learn to like school. I have lots of exploration activities that require small group cooperation. That way students can explore their own individual interests while learning to get along with each other."

"Right, Alice. So they just drift through life liking themselves but never learning anything. Great idea," Jan replied mockingly.

"Oh, you know what I mean," Alice responded with a smile, "You're exaggerating."

"Cool it, both of you," interjected Rita. "We all know how hard it is to deliver a balanced curriculum."

Introduction

In this chapter we examine learning in the affective, psychomotor, and cognitive domains and analyze the different types of learning involved in each. As we emphasize throughout the book, it is crucial for teachers to match the academic challenge, methods, and materials employed in the classroom to our intended teaching goals. In doing so, teachers can more efficiently meet the individual needs of their students and facilitate the concept of a balanced curriculum referred to in the above scenario. Understanding learning in the three domains contributes to this effort not only in the area of formulating objectives, as discussed in Chapter 2, but also in the development of questions. For example, an instructional goal might call for students to increase their knowledge of trees. In implementing this goal, the teacher might ask any of the following questions:

> What are the names of three trees found in this geographical area?
> Can you think of an example of a deciduous tree?
> What is a major difference between a pine tree and an oak tree?
> Look at these pictures of trees. What do they all have in common?
> What is one way in which we economically utilize trees in this area?
> Which tree does not belong on this list?
> Can you devise a plan that will make better use of the trees from this area that are cut for lumber?
> How do you feel about the lumber industry in this area?

As you will see in this chapter, the preceding questions ask students to think about and learn very different forms of content, and they employ and promote a wide and differing range of student learning activities.

Another reason for understanding the three domains relates to the emphasis educators are placing on the promotion of critical thinking (Jones, 1995). A major concern here is that an overabundance of the memorization of information delimits the quantity and quality of opportunities that students have to think about content in a deep and analytical manner. Additionally, students who memorize material may not retain it as effectively as those who learn material in other ways (Bruning et al., 1995). Finally, there can be little doubt that questions (as well as objectives) that require more than simple recall are essential for exercising or stimulating thinking (Marzano, 1992).

The domain that has the most impact on the critical-thinking issue is the cognitive domain, but it is important to note that critical thinking also has ramifications for both the affective domain and the psychomotor domain. As we mentioned earlier, we can divide goals into domains, but when we teach children, their attitudes, beliefs, and goals as well as their developmental levels all influence learning (Berk, 1994). The cognitive domain will be examined in depth because the central goal of most schools is to make students more knowledgeable and intelligent. However, we urge some caution here. The cognitive domain should not be the be-all and end-all in the curriculum. All three domains must be considered if we are to meet the commonly held goal of maximizing student potential.

Objectives

After completing your study of Chapter 5, you should be able to:

- Understand the affective domain and how its different levels influence learning
- Describe the major goals of the psychomotor domain
- Understand how the different levels of the cognitive domain influence both learning and teaching activities
- Explain the relationship between the different levels of the cognitive domain and critical thinking

THE AFFECTIVE DOMAIN

The affective domain is probably the most pervasive in terms of implicit inclusion in the curriculum. This domain deals with feelings, likes, and dislikes. It is implicit in that virtually all teachers want their students to go away from their classes with a more positive attitude toward the subject, themselves, and others, but it is seldom made explicit and then consciously translated into teaching procedures. We will say more about this later.

The primary focus of the affective domain is the development of two major attributes: attitudes and values. Attitudes are feelings of like or dislike toward objects, people, or ideas in our environment (Eagly & Chaiken, 1993). We can have attitudes about educationally unimportant things like spinach and baseball or more educationally important things like minority groups and the environment. Like most aspects of human behavior, attitudes are learned and result from experiences. For example, students typically develop some type of attitude toward school. If their experiences with school have been pleasurable, with opportunities for growth and reward, then their attitudes will be positive. On the other hand, if they constantly encounter boredom and frustration in school, then their attitudes about school will tend to be negative (Pintrich & Schunk, 1996; Stipek, 1993). A significant finding from classroom research is that positive attitudes toward school are related to achievement and success; when students learn more, they feel better about themselves and school (Berliner, 1987; Wang, Haertel, & Walberg, 1993).

The fact that attitudes are formed through experiences is fortunate in the sense that it allows teachers to positively influence them, but it also places a burden of responsibility on teachers not to contribute to the development of negative attitudes toward various aspects of schooling.

A word should be mentioned about how attitudes are measured. Attitudes are what psychologists call theoretical constructs. This means that we don't really believe that there is a place in a person's body where a particular attitude, knowledge, or skill actually exists. Instead, we infer the existence of an attitude or skill by the person's behavior or performance on some task. For example, we would infer that a person has the skill of converting ounces to pounds if she is able to do this on a test. In a similar way we would infer the existence of a negative attitude toward school by behaviors such as truancy, tardiness, and eagerness to leave school as quickly as possible. So one of the major ways that we infer the existence of positive and negative attitudes toward something is by observing behaviors. To use a mundane example, it makes sense that if a student has a positive attitude toward ice cream, this positive attitude will be reflected in the way he or she acts around ice cream.

An alternate and more systematic way of measuring peoples' attitudes is through the use of some type of formal instrument. Probably the most common type of instrument used in this regard is a Likert scale. The key elements in a Likert item are (1) some type of statement to which students are asked to react and (2) a response scale that typically varies from "strongly agree" to "strongly disagree." For example, an item measuring students' attitudes toward a course's textbook might look like this:

The text was appropriate for the content and objectives of the course.

1	2	3	4	5
Strongly disagree	Disagree	Agree and disagree	Agree	Strongly agree

While fairly easy to prepare, the intent of items like this is fairly apparent, and students who are either eager to please or displease an instructor can influence their responses in spite of their true attitudes. In this respect, other less obtrusive measures such as student comments and willingness to read the book might give a teacher a more valid indicator of the students' true feelings. Readers wanting to pursue this topic further are referred to Eagly and Chaikin (1993).

A second major goal in the affective domain is the development of values. Values differ from attitudes in that they are more global, referring not to specific objects such as school, ice cream, or a textbook, but instead to aims of existence or ways of leading a life. Some typical values taught in our schools are honesty, cleanliness, wisdom, self-respect, and broad-mindedness. Each of these is an abstract idea about how people ought to act or lead their lives rather than a feeling about specific things or objects.

In addition to being broader in terms of focus, values also differ from attitudes in terms of how they are measured. We don't typically think of values as being accepted or rejected but rather in terms of their relative importance to an individual. For example, it would be hard to find students in our schools who would outwardly reject values such as self-respect or broad-mindedness. To some, however, these qualities would be of less significance than to others. Try the following exercise yourself.

Rank the following values in terms of their relative importance to you by placing a 1 in front of the most important value, a 2 in front of the second most important value, and so on down the list:

_____ Pleasure
_____ Honesty
_____ Self-respect
_____ Social recognition
_____ An exciting life
_____ A sense of accomplishment

If you're like other people who have completed similar exercises, you probably had to think a while before ranking the items. This is because many, if not all, of these values are important to most people. The difficulty resides in having to prioritize them in terms of your own life. One of the benefits of this exercise, in addition to the information it can provide to the teacher, is the help it can provide to students in clarifying their own value structures.

One way that a teacher can use this information is by noting the relative importance students place on different values. For example, teachers who note that students rank pleasure, social recognition, and an exciting life above values such as honesty, self-respect, and a sense of accomplishment gain insight into the minds of their students and are in a better position to do something about this if they choose to do so.

Creative Thought and the Affective Domain

Educators are placing increased emphasis on creativity because of growing recognition of its importance in problem solving as well as artistic endeavors. Creativity involves the ability to produce work that is both novel and functional (Sternberg & Lubart, 1995). It is critical for you to understand that all students are creative thinkers. Learning environments that encourage creativity must be provided in which children feel safe to express their ideas and voice their opinions. The importance of being accepted and feeling valued is essential for children at all levels (Berk, 1994). Teachers can promote creativity in their classrooms by using the affective domain to encourage and support student fluency, originality, flexibility, and elaboration.

Strategies that can assist you in this endeavor include (Hagaman, 1990)

- Listening carefully to comments by each member of the class and being willing to reconsider their judgments and opinions, realizing that consensus is often not possible or even important.
- Helping students learn that knowledge, judgment, and opinions are greatly influenced by the context of the situation.
- Encouraging children to examine and explain why they think as they do in order to teach them to appraise and evaluate ideas.

The Levels of the Affective Domain

The basic organizing principles behind the affective domain is internalization. As we proceed through the taxonomy we see that each higher level requires a deeper or more thorough degree of internalization or personal integration. For example, if the focus is appreciating and valuing other cultures, the lower levels of the affective domain focus on openness or willingness to learn about other cultures, while higher levels involve valuing these cultures. Let's see how this works in terms of the specific levels.

Receiving.   The lowest level of the affective domain is receiving. The key element at this level is that students exhibit a degree of open-mindedness, for without this trait they may not be receptive to the new information under study. We know from cognitive psychology that perceiving a message is an essential first step in understanding and encoding any information (Bruning et al., 1995). It is important to note that although the students may be aware of the material being presented and are willing to listen to a presentation, they may not change their behavior because of the material or absorb it in a positive way. The critical factor at this level is that the students are open to ideas. Some examples of behaviors at this level include being willing to listen to others' points of view and being receptive to new information about a controversial topic.

Responding.   The significant difference between responding and receiving is that the former assumes a somewhat positive attitude whereas the latter implies neutrality. At the responding level students are exhibiting some interest, involvement, or even commitment. Again, there is the matter of degree, for students may be willing to undertake an activity but may not actually have bought into it. However, it is hoped that the students will perceive the experience positively and to some degree enjoy what they are doing even though they did not initiate the activity or topic. Some examples of behaviors at this level include being willing to dialogue about a controversial topic or being willing to participate in a new activity introduced in physical education class.

Valuing.   This level of the affective domain implies that students perceive an attitude, value, or belief as having worth and that their behavior has been internalized and reflected on a continual basis. Unlike the two levels of the affective domain previously discussed, at the valuing level the teacher does not initiate the behavior. It is initiated by the student who is committed to a particular position and is willing to discuss and support that position openly. Some examples of behaviors at this level include voluntarily going to an art museum after a presentation on artists displayed at this museum or arguing for a particular position on a controversial topic.

Organization.   The organization level builds upon the valuing level in that the latter is singular and the former implies an organized and integrated system. In other words, valuing implies a commitment to a specific belief or position, but in most cases, a value does not exist as a separate entity. Organization requires the student to justify, accept, or reject other values that may conflict with a value orientation and thereby adopt a more complex point of view. Examples here would include integrating something learned at school, such as racial tolerance, into a more comprehensive view of people and how we should all treat each other.

Characterization by a Value or Value Complex.   The previous levels of the affective domain have made it possible for the student to group complex objectives and operate at the characterization level, which allows the students to develop personal yet global views about such things as the nature of the universe or a philosophy of life. At this level, students have arrived at and exhibited a coherent group of attitudes and, more importantly, have incorporated them on a consistent basis and reflected them as an integral part of their character. For example, in a health class students operating at this level would integrate attitudes and views about healthy lifestyles into a coherent and comprehensive plan for living.

Character Education

This brings us to a final comment about the place of the affective domain in teaching. As mentioned previously, probably every teacher at every grade level and in every subject matter deals with affective goals either implicitly or explicitly. Every teacher wants students to exit from her class with at least as positive an attitude toward that subject as when they entered. All the teachers that we've met would like to develop values in their students including honesty, open-mindedness, and ambition; but few teachers make affective goals an explicit part of their curriculum, preferring instead to keep them implicit.

Part of the reason for this is that many educators aren't quite sure about the appropriateness of affective goals in the curriculum. Some critics of these goals contend that they have no place in schools and that teachers ought to be spending their time teaching students to think rather than feel. Other critics point to the subjectiveness of these goals and raise the question of whether teachers should impose their own attitudes and values on students. These same critics contend that this is a role best left to other institutions such as the family or the church. Responses to these critics typically focus on the fact that schools can't help but teach attitudes and values and that, unless these attitudes and values are critically examined and made explicit, we may be teaching students undesirable things or teaching desirable things improperly. Like other issues covered in this book, this is a topic all teachers should think about, and, we hope, adopt a position consistent with their personal values. Students interested in reading more about the place of the affective domain in the curriculum are referred to Tom (1984), the Association for Supervision and Curriculum Development (1962), and Raths, Harmin, and Simon (1966).

Teachers employ the taxonomy in order to vary student experiences in the classroom.

THE PSYCHOMOTOR DOMAIN

Developing muscular strength and coordination is the primary focus of goals within the psychomotor domain. This domain probably receives the least emphasis of the three in our schools, but the accuracy of this generalization will vary with the subject and age level of students taught.

Probably the most obvious exception to this generalization is in the area of physical education, where the primary focus is on the psychomotor domain. It should be mentioned, though, that cognitive and affective goals do form an important part of the physical education curriculum. For example, students must know how to perform a certain skill before they can properly execute it and must understand the rules of a game before they can play it; both of these are cognitive goals. Also a major affective goal of the physical education curriculum is to develop positive attitudes and values about the importance of keeping our bodies healthy and physically fit. Examples of psychomotor goals within the physical education curriculum include the following:

> Physical education students will serve a volleyball with speed and accuracy.
> Health students will develop cardiovascular strength and endurance.
> Physical education students will know how to swim using the breast stroke.
> Physical education students will do a forward roll in gymnastics.

As can be seen from these examples, the psychomotor domain involves not only the development of strength and endurance but also the teaching of skills and the development of coordination.

Another area of the curriculum where psychomotor goals are emphasized is in the area of vocational-technical education. Here goals like learning to type, operate a wood lathe, and splice two wires all involve the development of manipulative skills and abilities. A third area of the curriculum emphasizing psychomotor goals is the area of music. Here students are training different parts of their bodies to perform in the proper way at the proper time. In the music curriculum these goals vary from being able to keep time with the music to learning how to place the fingers on the keyboard in different piano pieces to forming the lips and breathing properly while playing wind and brass instruments.

The three groups of examples from different subject matter areas illustrate how the content being taught influences the relative emphasis placed on the psychomotor domain. Grade level also influences this emphasis, with relatively greater emphasis being given to psychomotor goals at lower levels. For example, most early childhood curricula have as goals the development of sensorimotor skills and eye–hand coordination (Papalia & Wendkos-Olds, 1996). Activities aimed at accomplishing these goals include skipping, walking on a balance beam, and playing catch with beanbags. Later on, students are taught additional psychomotor skills like printing, writing, and coloring. At an even later time in the curriculum, psychomotor skills don't receive as much explicit attention because teachers assume that skills such as handwriting have already been mastered. Harrow (1972), Jewett and Mullan (1977), and Moore (1992) have developed systems to sequence learning within this domain. Readers interested in this topic may wish to consult these sources.

The Levels of the Psychomotor Domain

Level 1—Reflex Movements.   Reflex movements or actions are elicited in response to some stimulus without conscious volition on the part of the learner. They are not voluntary movements but may be considered an essential base for movement behavior.

Level 2—Basic-Fundamental Movements.   Basic-fundamental movement patterns occur in the learner during the first year of life. The common basic movement behaviors, such as visually tracking an object, reaching, grasping, and manipulating an object with the hands, and progressing through the developmental stages of crawling, creeping, and walking, emerge in learners in a highly patterned and predictable way. All of these fundamental movement patterns are built upon the foundation of reflex movements listed in the first classification level of this model. Many of these fundamental movement patterns, which develop early in the learner's life, literally unfold from within and are not taught.

Level 3—Perceptual Abilities.   Though level 3 appears to suggest cognitive as well as psychomotor behaviors, it is included in the psychomotor domain because many investigators claim that perceptual and motor functions are inseparable, and enriched movement experiences usually enhance children's abilities to structure and perceive more efficiently the many events to which they are exposed.

Efficiently functioning perceptual abilities are essential to development of the learner in the affective, the cognitive, and the psychomotor domains. These abilities assist the learner in interpreting stimuli, thus enabling her to make necessary adjustments to her environment. Present-day society places high premiums on cognitive excellence and superior performance in psychomotor activities; both depend upon the development of perceptual abilities. Developmental research suggests that the learner should have maximum opportunities to engage early in sensory stimulating activities and to explore a variety of movement tasks to facilitate the development of these essential perceptual abilities (Papalia & Wendkos-Olds, 1996).

Level 4—Physical Abilities.   Physical abilities are essential to the efficient functioning of the learner in the psychomotor domain. Proper functioning of the various systems of the body enable the learner to meet the demands placed upon him by his environment. These physical abilities are in fact an essential part of the foundation for the development of skilled movements. Physical abilities include the following components: endurance, strength, flexibility, and agility.

Level 5—Skilled Movements.   Skilled movement can be thought of in several ways. It can mean proficiency in performing a task; skill can also connote the economy of effort a learner displays while perfecting a complex movement. Skill can also mean that an integration of learner behavior regarding a specific task has occurred. In other words, proficiency at this level includes a degree of efficiency in performance of a specific, reasonably complex movement behavior.

Level 6—Nondiscursive Communication.   Nonverbal communication plays a central role in everyday life and is an important aspect of the learner's psychomotor development. At this level each learner develops a style of moving that communicates her feelings about her affective self to the perceptive observer. Accurately interpreting communicative movement behaviors of a learner heightens an educator's perceptions of the learner's feelings, needs, and interest, thereby enabling the educator to make more meaningful selections of learning strategies for that particular learner.

This completes our discussion of the affective and psychomotor domains. Now take a few moments to complete the exercise that follows. It is designed to see if you can differentiate between goals in these two domains.

EXERCISE 5.1

Examine the following goals and determine if their focus is primarily affective (a) or psychomotor (p). Then compare your answers to the ones given in the feedback section at the end of the chapter.

_____   1. Third-grade students will learn respect for the American flag.
_____   2. First-grade students will print the letters of the alphabet in upper- and lowercase.
_____   3. High school literature students will develop an appreciation for poetry.
_____   4. Physical education students will improve their putting ability.
_____   5. Fourth-grade health students will become convinced of the importance of proper eating and sleeping habits.
_____   6. Kindergarten students will develop their scissor-cutting skills.
_____   7. Advanced shorthand students will be able to take dictation at the rate of 120 words per minute.
_____   8. Driver education students will develop an appreciation for safe driving habits.
_____   9. Preschool children will be willing to share toys in a free-play situation.
_____   10. Elementary music students will be able to clap with their hands to simple rhythms found in songs.

THE COGNITIVE DOMAIN

Probably the most common types of instructional goals found in our schools are cognitive. This is because the cognitive domain focuses on the transmission of knowledge and strategies, which constitute the most prevalent view of the role of the school both today and in the past. We estimate that anywhere from 80 to 90% of the average elementary and secondary student's school time is devoted to the achievement of cognitive goals. This emphasis can be seen in the goals teachers have, in their teaching strategies, and in the kinds of tests that teachers give. Virtually all of the items of both teacher-made and standardized tests are devoted to the measurement of cognitive goals. This will, of course, vary with the grade level and with individual courses, but we believe that, on the whole, our estimates are accurate.

However, because schools focus on the cognitive domain doesn't suggest that we believe the affective domain is not important. In fact, when parents send their children to school initially, they most often ask the child upon returning, "How was your teacher? Is she nice?" Rarely do parents ask, "Well, what did you learn on the first day of school?" While this is only one small example, it suggests that parents are concerned about their children's learning, but they are also concerned with how their children are treated and their growth as individuals. Furthermore, at the high school level, a study sponsored by the National Association of Secondary School Principals involving 1,500 public and private school students showed a teacher's caring attitude toward students to be more important than a vast knowledge of the subject (Cromer, 1984).

The cognitive domain is sometimes confused with the affective domain. One way of differentiating between the two is to think of the cognitive domain as involving rational and analytical thinking processes, whereas the affective domain deals with feelings and likes or dislikes. Metaphorically, we can think of the focus of the cognitive domain as being in the mind, whereas the focus of the affective domain is in the heart. Another way of differentiating between the two domains is by asking these questions: (1) Does the person know how to do it? and (2) Will the person do it freely, without any type of coercion? The first question implies a cognitive answer, whereas the second implies an affective answer. For example, when students fail to follow a school rule or policy, these two questions could be asked to determine the cause of the problem. If students are unaware of the rules, then the solution to the problem is cognitive, involving teaching or informing students of the rules. However, if students know what the rules are but choose to ignore them, then the problem is affective and involves their willingness to follow these rules. This is a clear example of how understanding the difference between the cognitive and affective goals can help to make teaching more effective.

As another example, lecturing, which implies a cognitive goal, is a fairly inefficient way of changing people's attitudes, which is an affective goal. Consequently, lecturing students who have chosen to disregard a particular rule is a fairly ineffective way to change their behavior. A teacher who understands these distinctions can more readily analyze a problem situation and select a teaching strategy that is appropriate for the task at hand.

Uses of the Cognitive Taxonomy

Like the other taxonomies, the cognitive domain is hierarchical, which means that successful performance at the higher level is dependent upon success at the lower levels. The broad scope of the cognitive domain and the fact that the steps are cumulative make the cognitive taxonomy useful in three ways:

- *Expand our view of learning.* All too often classrooms focus on memorization at the expense of higher level goals such as problem solving and critical and analytical thinking. Through emphasis on processes such as application, analysis, and evaluation, the taxonomy provides not only a reminder of the existence of these processes but also tangible ways to make them happen in the classroom.
- *Sequence learning activities.* Because the taxonomy is hierarchical the sequence of the levels provides teachers with a means to structure learning activities. For example, research on both problem solving and critical thinking suggest that a solid background knowledge base is essential for successful performance in these activities (Eggen & Kauchak, 1997). The cognitive taxonomy suggests that before teachers involve students in these higher level activities, they should plan for opportunities for students to acquire the necessary background knowledge.

- *Assist teachers in analyzing their practice.* Teaching is a complex process, and one way that teachers become more efficient and effective is through the process of reflection. The cognitive taxonomy provides an analytical tool for teachers to think about the goals they choose, the learning activities they design, and the evaluation methods they use to assess learning.

EXERCISE 5.2 _____

Examine the following goals and determine whether they are primarily cognitive (c), affective (a), or psychomotor (p) in their orientation. Then compare your answers to the ones given in the feedback section at the end of the chapter.

_____ 1. In an unsupervised setting, third-grade students will follow traffic rules on foot, on bicycle, or on another conveyance.
_____ 2. Junior-high social studies students will recite the Gettysburg Address.
_____ 3. The middle school student will, during a classroom discussion, listen to another's ideas, evidencing this by using the other's ideas in his comments.
_____ 4. The first-year history student will be able to paraphrase the definition of constitutional monarchy.
_____ 5. Senior-high driver education students will be able to parallel park.
_____ 6. Senior-high driver education students will know the major traffic signs.
_____ 7. The reader will understand the differences among the cognitive, affective, and psychomotor domains.
_____ 8. Seventh-grade students will behave properly in the cafeteria.
_____ 9. Beginning secretarial skills students will type at a minimum of 45 words per minute.
_____ 10. Auto mechanics students will know how to read a schematic diagram of a diesel engine.
_____ 11. Advanced algebra students will construct a proof to prove the commutative property of real numbers.
_____ 12. Middle school students will listen to students who disagree with their points of view.
_____ 13. Advanced American literature students will spend at least 1 hour a week reading unrequired American literature classics.
_____ 14. Second-grade students will follow classroom rules as prescribed by the teacher.

The Levels of the Cognitive Domain

The cognitive domain includes a large number of diverse goals, but its primary focus is on intellectual development. Within the domain, goals can be divided into two major areas: (1) knowledge and (2) the processing and manipulation of information. Knowledge goals in the cognitive domain involve learning and remembering of basic facts, concepts, generalizations, and theories, whereas processing goals involve using or applying this knowledge in some type of problem-solving situation. The examples in Table 5.1 are designed to illustrate the relationships of these two areas.

Knowledge.   Knowledge is one of two major areas of the cognitive domain and the first or foundational level for the levels that follow (Bloom, Englehart, Furst, Hill, & Krathwohl, 1956). This area is sometimes referred to as a low level because it does not

Table 5.1   Knowledge-Level Goals and Their Related Processing Activities

Knowledge	Related Processing Activity
Knowing the formula for the area of a rectangle	Being able to apply the formula in a problem-solving situation
Knowing the definition of a noun	Being able to identify nouns in a sentence
Knowing the definition of a controlled variable	Being able to design an experiment with a controlled variable in it
Knowing the terms *rhythm, meter, personification,* and *alliteration*	Using these terms to analyze a poem

call for the processing or manipulation of information. Simply stated, knowledge involves recall or recognition of previously learned material. The range of goals at this level can be quite broad and commonly includes such things as

Knowledge of terminology.
Knowledge of specific facts.
Knowledge of trends and sequences.
Knowledge of classification systems and categories.
Knowledge of principles and generalizations.
Knowledge of theories.

The most common vehicles that provide the material to be learned at this level are reading of printed materials and listening to teachers disseminating information. Then, at a later time, the learner recalls or recognizes material when provided with a cue.

For example, most of us were told that George Washington was the first president of the United States, and we have stored this information. When confronted with a verbal cue (for example, Who was the first president of the United States?), we retrieve the information and respond accordingly. Psychologists speculate that most of what we have learned is stored in our brains, but sometimes it can be very difficult to retrieve the information (Ashcraft, 1989). For instance, who was the second president of the United States? Most of us have learned this isolated fact—John Adams—at one time or another, and most of us simply cannot recall it. This is particularly so when information is learned in an isolated or disconnected fashion on a singular basis. In other words, the less use we make of information learned and the less we connect it to other information, the less likely we are to recall that information (Bruning et al., 1995).

Knowledge differs from other levels of the cognitive domain because the act of retrieving types of information—facts, for example—does not require us to do anything with the data. The other levels of the cognitive domain require us to alter or employ information in one form or another.

Although knowledge may imply very little in the form of intellectual activity, the memorization of such things as trends, classifications, principles, and theories can be very difficult and can require a great amount of practice (Schunk, 1991; Ormrod, 1995). Furthermore, if the student does not have a sound foundation of available and retrievable information, utilizing the higher levels of the domain may become a difficult if not impossible task (Eggen & Kauchak, 1997). Examples of knowledge-level objectives include

> The student will identify the author of the *Iliad*.
> The student will be able to provide the formula for finding the area of a rectangle.
> The student will describe Newton's third law.
> The student will be able to match important events in U.S. history to their dates.

EXERCISE 5.3

Read the following behavioral objectives and place a (k) in front of all those written at the knowledge level. Then compare your answers to the ones given in the feedback section at the end of the chapter.

_____ 1. Social studies students will match a list of historical events with their dates.
_____ 2. Elementary students will be able to draw a rabbit that has two long ears and four short legs.
_____ 3. Middle school social studies students will remember the last three presidents of the United States.
_____ 4. High school English students will remember major plays written by Shakespeare.

EXERCISE 5.4

Write a knowledge-level objective for each of the following concepts. Then compare your answers to the ones given in the feedback section at the end of the chapter.

Mammals: _____

_____

Presidents: _____

_____

Comprehension.   Comprehension is the next level in the taxonomy and requires students to alter or manipulate information to demonstrate that they understand something. It represents a step beyond the knowledge category because it asks students to transform information into a form that is understandable to them. Students can do this in several ways.

Restating information in one's own words is perhaps the most basic form of comprehension. For example, Mr. Johns defined the concept war for his students by saying, "War is an armed hostile conflict between opposed forces which is accompanied by death and destruction and which usually involves an economic factor." Mr. Johns then asked his class to consider their own definitions in light of his observation. Georgianne replied, "War occurs when one country wants something another country has and is willing to kill and destroy to get it." Georgianne has redefined the concept of war in her own terms and, in doing so, has manipulated or processed infor-

Figure 5.1   A Bar Graph Handout

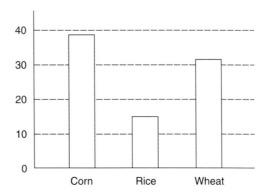

mation. This might not be a very difficult task, but it is surely one that goes beyond memorization.

Students can demonstrate that they understand something by interpreting it from presented material. For example,

Given a bar graph representing the major crops grown in the United States (see Figure 5.1), the students will orally name the most widely produced crops.

In meeting this goal students would need to interpret the information from the graph and verbalize it.

Translation is another form of comprehension. This cognitive activity requires a change in format so that the information can be presented in a different way. Students regularly accomplish this task when taking arithmetic problems in the form of words and changing them into numerical symbols. What we find here is a conceptualization not found at the low level of the cognitive domain.

The following list contains some examples of comprehension questions:

Look at this pie chart. Which piece of the federal budget consumes the most tax-payer dollars?
Glance around the room. Can you find an example of a circle?
In your own words, can you tell me what hybridization means?

Keep in mind that when working at the comprehension level, students will not have prior knowledge of the desired outcome and will in some way have to alter the material with which they are confronted.

EXERCISE 5.5

Read the following goals and place a (c) in front of all those written at the comprehension level. Then compare your answers to the ones given in the feedback section at the end of the chapter.

_____ 1. The student will be able to describe, in order, the 10 original amendments to the Constitution.
_____ 2. Kindergarten students will understand the characteristics of squares and rectangles.
_____ 3. Algebra students will be able to differentiate between quadratic and nonquadratic equations.
_____ 4. Kindergarten students will be able to tell the names of different farm animals.

EXERCISE 5.6

Write a comprehension-level objective for each of the following concepts. Then compare your answers to the ones given in the feedback section at the end of the chapter.

Mammals: _____

_____

Presidents: _____

_____

Application.   Application, the next level in the cognitive domain, requires problem solving. There are two critical characteristics involved in terms of the application level. The first is that the situation confronting the students should be one that has not been encountered before or practiced during the unit of instruction. Otherwise, the students would simply be recalling the desired answer or solution.

The second characteristic is that the students must select the appropriate tool, solution, equation, or algorithm that in turn is correctly applied to the problem at hand. The following example shows how these two features work hand-in-hand.

Given a drawing of a house and yard (see Figure 5.2), the students will correctly determine the area of the backyard.

The first thing students have to do is determine the nature of the problem, i.e., one involving the area of a rectangle. Then they have to recall the appropriate formula

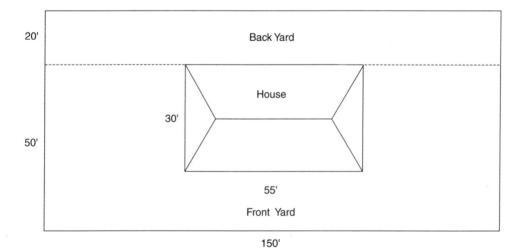

Figure 5.2   A House/Yard Handout

and apply it to the data in order to solve the problem. Again, it is assumed that the students have not been confronted with this specific problem at a prior time.

The following are some examples of application-level objectives:

Given a swimming pool with a diameter of 16 feet and a depth of 30 inches and the instructions from a bottle of chlorine, the student will determine the appropriate amount of chlorine to be poured into the pool.

Given the appropriate tools and a specific set of instructions, the wood-shop student will build a coffee table that clearly reflects the specifications.

Given the necessary culinary equipment, all or some of which may be used, the student will make three crepes that will fold without breaking and hold a cottage cheese mixture.

In each case, students must produce an answer or a finished product. It is important to note at this point that although the students are solving problems, they are not doing anything that is new or unique. To do so would place the students at a more complex level, as discussed shortly.

EXERCISE 5.7

Read the following objectives and place an (ap) in front of all those written at the application level. Then compare your answers to the ones given in the feedback section at the end of the chapter.

_____ 1. Given an amount of energy consumed and the rate per consumed unit, the student will correctly determine the total amount due on an electric bill.

_____ 2. Given five written passages, the student will determine all those that represent propaganda.

_____ 3. Without aid, the student will define *generalization* as described in class.

_____ 4. Given 20 subtraction problems, the student will solve 80% of them correctly.

EXERCISE 5.8

Write an application-level objective for each of the following concepts. Then compare your answers to the ones given in the feedback section at the end of the chapter.

Mammals: _____

_____

Presidents: _____

_____

Analysis.   In its basic form, analysis involves the process of taking an entire or whole entity or phenomena and breaking it down into its separate parts, or determining its particular characteristics. A common laboratory exercise involving analysis occurs when a student is provided with a substance and is asked to determine its constituent elements.

This might involve weighing, dissolving, splitting, flaming, and testing with various chemicals and compounds. In most academic situations, however, it is more common to analyze printed materials in the form of essays, speeches, editorials, poems, and books.

In working at the analysis level, there are a number of key words that students might consider, such as

assumptions
implications
fallacies
central themes
persuasion
consistency.

For example, let's say that the students are assigned the task of reading selected editorials from the local newspaper. In most editorials, the columnist is using persuasive techniques, such as the selective presenting of factual information or data. An analysis-level task would ask students to identify the writer's position and explain how the editorial selectively used data to support that position.

Pinpointing a central theme is another very common analysis-level operation and often can present quite a challenge. For instance, the student might be asked to read Plato's *Republic* and ascertain the role of the individual in a perfect state.

Visuals can also be used to promote analysis-level thinking. For example, Ms. Fry was teaching a third-grade science class. She showed them pictures of three groups of animals and asked the students to figure out which group did not belong. Drawings of animals in the pictures included

1. horse	2. pig	3. chicken
cow	goat	wolf
sheep	dog	colt

The students then began the process of comparing the animals and through the process of analysis concluded that of all the animals,

Only a colt is a baby animal.
Only the chicken has feathers.
Only the chicken is not a mammal.
Only the wolf is a meat eater.

Additional examples of analysis-level tasks, written in the form of questions, include

How do the facts in this passage support the author's message?
What is the main ingredient in this mixture? Why is it essential?
On what assumption has the author based his position? How can you tell?
What is the major difference between Gina's point of view and Mike's point of view?
Look at these two paintings. Compare at least two characteristics of the artists' styles.

EXERCISE 5.9

Read the following objectives and place an (an) in front of all those written at the analysis level. Then compare your answers to the ones given in the feedback section at the end of the chapter.

_____ 1. Given a list of 10 automobiles, the students will circle their favorite one.
_____ 2. When given a concept and superordinate concept in diagram fashion, the student will write one coordinate concept.
_____ 3. Without aid, the student will determine one assumption upon which Darwin's theories are based.
_____ 4. Given 10 pictures, the student will identify all those that are farm animals.

EXERCISE 5.10

Write an analysis-level objective for each of the following concepts. Then compare your answers to the ones given in the feedback section at the end of the chapter.

Mammals: _____

_____

Presidents: _____

_____

_____

Synthesis.   Synthesis involves the creative integration of elements into a unique entity. Synthesis is more or less the opposite of analysis. Whereas analysis requires us to take something apart, synthesis involves the process of putting things together to produce a new and unique whole. There are two critical considerations when assigning students synthesis-level activities. The first is that the finished product must be new and unique to the student, not the world.

The second point is that a criterion must be present in order to allow us to apply a standard of success. For example,

> Given the use of any materials of their choice, the wood-shop students will design and build an original boat that will be at least 14 feet in length, will accommodate up to four adults, and will be capable of handling a small electric engine.

The fact that the finished product may resemble other boats is immaterial; the students designed it, and it is theirs. In that it is a creative exercise, there is room for subjective evaluation regarding excellence, but a clear-cut criterion is used to determine whether or not the task has been accomplished successfully. The same holds true for the following goal:

> Without aids the student will write an original haiku poem that contains the correct number of syllables and deals with nature.

EXERCISE 5.11

Read the following objectives and place an (s) in front of all those written at the synthesis level. Then compare your answers to the ones given in the feedback section at the end of the chapter.

_____ 1. Given any materials of her choice, the homemaking student will create a dress that is sleeveless and below knee length and that contains at least two different kinds of material.

_____ 2. Given appropriate materials, the student will construct a model of an airplane that clearly reflects a set of preexisting specifications.

_____ 3. Given a variety of art materials, the student will develop an original design that incorporates a single geometrical shape.

_____ 4. Without aid, the student will list two characteristics of a republic.

EXERCISE 5.12

Write a synthesis-level objective for each of the following concepts. Then compare your answers to the ones given in the feedback section at the end of the chapter.

Mammals: _____

_____

Presidents: _____

_____

Evaluation.   This highest and most complex level of the cognitive domain requires the student to make a value judgment about some product or project. However, the judgment in and of itself is insufficient; it must be supplemented with a reasoned explanation for the evaluation. For example, let us say a teacher asked his children, "What is the best type of dog for a pet?" The children responded excitedly with examples such as labrador, boxer, cocker spaniel, and poodle. At this point, the children were merely expressing a feeling or opinion and therefore were operating in the affective domain.

Although making a judgment is important, when considering the evaluation level we need something else—a criterion. A critical process necessary at the evaluative level is the intellectual support or defense of judgment. Let us continue our example and see how this is accomplished.

After the children had provided examples, the teacher then asked them to be very specific when thinking about the characteristics a "best" pet dog might need. After the teacher facilitated the discussion, the list was as follows:

1. The best dog should be under 50 pounds, or it will cost too much to feed.
2. The best dog should have a gentle disposition.
3. The best dog should be short-haired if in a warm climate.
4. The best dog should be short-eared because a moist climate would promote ear infections.

Having established some criteria, the teacher then helped the children to apply the criteria to the list of four dogs. The children then were operating at the evaluation level. This example illustrates that a criterion must be employed if the students are working at the evaluative level. Now let us examine a few additional examples of evaluative-level objectives.

> Given a list of famous 20th-century figures, the student will select the one he or she believes had the greatest impact on the 1900s and document the choice by citing two of that person's major achievements that had an impact on the world's population.
>
> Given five paintings completed by grand masters, the students will select the one they consider to be the most outstanding and support the selection by discussing (1) the style of the artist's work and (2) the contemporary value of the artist's work.
>
> Given geographical and geological information regarding a mountain river, the student will determine the most logical place to erect a dam and will cite data on soil composition, terrain, and water pressure in support of the selection.

EXERCISE 5.13

Read the following objectives and place an (e) in front of all those written at the evaluation level. Then compare your answers to the ones given in the feedback section at the end of the chapter.

_____ 1. Given a list of computer models, the students will select the one they consider to be the best.

_____ 2. Given specifications and road tests of five major automobiles, the students will select the one they consider to be most efficient and will support their choice by discussing cost, maintenance, gas consumption, and road handling.

_____ 3. Without aid, the student will name three Native American reservations found in the southwestern United States.

_____ 4. Given any art materials of their choice, the students will create an oil painting using no more than three colors.

_____ 5. Given a list of 10 books, the students will select the one they would most like to read.

EXERCISE 5.14

Write an evaluation-level objective for each of the following concepts. Then compare your answers to the ones given in the feedback section at the end of the chapter.

Mammals: _____

_____

Presidents: _____

_____

The use of the cognitive domain promotes student ability to engage in critical thinking.

CRITICAL THINKING AND THE COGNITIVE DOMAIN

One essential characteristic of an effective teacher is the ability to integrate both higher and lower level cognitive objectives into meaningful lessons (Porter & Brophy, 1988). These higher order, or process, levels of the cognitive domain promote higher order thinking that is complex, yields multiple solutions, involves the application of multiple criteria, involves uncertainty, requires self-regulation of the thinking process, and requires effort (Schrag, 1989).

Teachers can promote critical thinking in their classrooms by involving students in cognitive activities such as identifying main ideas, fostering and monitoring comprehension, constructing and representing meanings, analyzing text structures and constructing spatial networks.

Current views of intelligence stress the importance of higher level processes in thinking and problem solving (Sternberg, 1994). One specific theory, Sternberg's Triarchic Theory of Human Intelligence, classifies intelligent behavior into three major thinking processes:

1. legislative—creating, formulating, planning
2. executive—implementing and doing
3. judicial—judging, evaluating, comparing

When encountering a problem students use the legislative process to attack the problem, monitor the actions with the executive functions, and evaluate success through judicial processes. Connections with processes in the different levels of the cognitive taxonomy are clear.

Problem-solving strategies, founded upon the application level, can be effective when employing practical life experiences for instruction. One such strategy (Buser & Reimer, 1988) includes the following steps:

1. discovery activity
2. discussion
3. conclusion
4. follow-up activities
5. integration into existing body of student knowledge

In implementing this view of problem solving, the cognitive taxonomy provides activities and questions for the teacher to follow in guiding the process.

In addition to more complex and integrated strategies, you can also use specific procedures to promote critical thinking. Some examples include analyzing media coverage, comparing newspaper editorial accounts, classifying games, using puzzles, employing verbal analogies, and improving overall classroom discussions (Carr, 1988).

Critical thinking should be an integral goal in student acquisition of knowledge. However, the focal point is not so much in terms of "what" the student learns. "How" the student learns and the goal of improving the student's critical-thinking abilities provide the rationale for this crucial educational objective.

Finally, recent research in the area of high-risk adolescents supports the belief that problem-solving training enhances student learning by increasing the students' abilities to self-regulate behavior during classroom activities. A positive relationship may exist between problem-solving training and social and academic success (Larson, 1989). If additional research continues to corroborate these findings, the application of the process levels of the cognitive domain to the promotion of critical-thinking skills may have a significant impact on developing more than the student's intellectual abilities.

Summary

In Chapter 5 we have familiarized you with the three domains, with a heavy emphasis upon the cognitive domain. This was not because we believe that domain to be the most important but because it is the focus in so many educational programs. Although objectives involving the affective domain are fewer in number, we are convinced that they should play a critical role in the development of youngsters. This is particularly true at the primary level, where socialization is such an important factor.

Regarding the psychomotor domain, pediatricians throughout the country have become increasingly disturbed with the cardiovascular development in children who are not engaged in a constant, sequential physical education program. In addition, the drive toward academics in the upper grade levels has clearly limited the amount of time spent in physical activities.

As stated early in the chapter, we believe all three domains have to come into play to promote the healthy growth of children, and even though we have presented only a brief overview of the affective and psychomotor domains, we urge you to incorporate them in your curriculum whenever possible.

Whether or not the cognitive domain is the most critical source of objectives and questions is immaterial, for this domain is surely the most commonly employed in schools; and that provides the rationale for our treatment in this chapter. We have clearly delineated low- and high-level behavior because we take the position that the low-level area, knowledge, often dominates the curriculum and that we need to shift our emphasis to the higher, or process, levels of the cognitive domain, which are crucial to the promotion of critical thinking. Whether or not we can teach critical thinking is a controversial point, but we believe there is general agreement that if we fail to provide a learning environment that requires the meaningful processing of information, we will be doing our students a major disservice.

Questions for Discussion

1. How should the relative importance of the affective, psychomotor, and cognitive domains change over the course of the K–12 curriculum?
2. Which of the three areas—affective, psychomotor, or cognitive—should receive more emphasis in today's schools? Less?
3. How do current changes in today's society (e.g., poverty, increase in reliance on technology) influence the relative importance that should be devoted to the three areas?
4. What are the most important values that schools should be teaching? Why? How can or do schools teach these values?
5. Take and defend a position on the following statement, "Because of society's increased reliance on technology, there is less need for emphasis on the psychomotor domain."
6. In terms of your future teaching goals (i.e., first grade or high school biology teacher) which level of the cognitive taxonomy should receive the most attention? Least?

Suggestions for Field Experience

1. Interview a teacher and ask him or her about the relative importance of the three domains in the classroom. Ask what factors influence this ranking.
2. Examine a teacher's edition of a textbook or a state or district curriculum guide. Identify an example of a goal or objective in each of the three domains. What domain receives the most emphasis? Why?
3. Use the cognitive taxonomy to analyze the goals or objectives of a chapter in a text or a unit in a curriculum guide.
   a. Identify an example at each level if possible.
   b. At what level are most of the goals or objectives?
   c. Is this an optimal mix? Why or why not?

4. Use the cognitive taxonomy to analyze a test or quiz. (This could be a teacher's or one from a teacher's edition.)
   a. How do the test items correspond to the levels of the taxonomy?
   b. Is this an optimal mix? Why or why not?
5. Use the affective taxonomy to design a lesson. (Use the lesson plan format found in Chapter 4.) What did you learn about teaching and learning in this domain?
6. Use the cognitive taxonomy to design a lesson targeting one of the higher areas of the taxonomy. What kinds of prerequisite experiences did you need to provide to help students read the higher one. What did you learn about teaching and learning at higher levels?

Exercise Feedback

EXERCISE 5.1

1. (a) Affective
2. (p) Psychomotor. In interpreting this goal in this way, we are placing primary emphasis on students' ability to form letters, which assumes that they already know how to form the letters. This latter component is a cognitive skill that is discussed in the next section.
3. (a) Affective
4. (p) Psychomotor
5. (a) Affective. Here the teacher is trying to develop positive attitudes toward good health habits.
6. (p) Psychomotor
7. (p) Psychomotor
8. (a) Affective
9. (a) Affective
10. (p) Psychomotor

EXERCISE 5.2

1. (a) Affective. The key word here is *unsupervised.* Note how this goal assumes that students already know these rules, the cognitive component.
2. (c) Cognitive
3. (a) Affective
4. (c) Cognitive
5. (p) Psychomotor. Note, too, how this goal assumes that students know the proper procedure for parking, again, the cognitive component.
6. (c) Cognitive
7. (c) Cognitive
8. (a) Affective. Again, note how an affective goal assumes the necessary prerequisite cognitive knowledge.
9. (p) Psychomotor
10. (c) Cognitive. This goal would probably be a prerequisite to the goal of actually applying this knowledge to work on an engine, which has psychomotor components.
11. (c) Cognitive
12. (a) Affective. This goal is probably related to the value of open-mindedness.

13. (a) Affective. This goal is aimed at developing positive student attitudes toward American literature.
14. (a) Affective

EXERCISE 5.3

1. __(K)__ This material requires remembering connections between dates and events.
2. _____ Although the student may recall characteristics, the drawing will require higher level skills.
3. __(K)__ The key phrase here is *from memory,* which identifies this behavior as recall.
4. __(K)__ This material was probably memorized.

EXERCISE 5.4

Mammals: Given a list of animals, the student will circle all those that are mammals.
Presidents: Without aid, the student will name, in order, the first three presidents of the United States.

EXERCISE 5.5

1. _____ The fact that the student will recite implies memorization.
2. _____ Remembering characteristics is a knowledge-level task.
3. __(c)__ Pointing out *examples* is a comprehension task.
4. _____ This would be a knowledge objective *if* the students had prior access to the pictures.

EXERCISE 5.6

Mammals: Given a bar graph of mammals living in Africa, the student will determine the mammal group having the largest population.
Presidents: Given a variety of materials, the student will summarize the current president's first two years in office by including areas of domestic policy, defense, and foreign affairs.

EXERCISE 5.7

1. __(ap)__ This is assumed to be a new problem. The student will have to take into account the data and then solve the problem.
2. _____ This behavior goes beyond problem solving.
3. _____ Recall
4. __(ap)__ If the students have not seen these problems before and must select an appropriate strategy, they are working at the application level.

EXERCISE 5.8

Mammals: Given the characteristics of a specific mammal and the characteristics of a specific environment, the student will determine three physiological changes that would have to occur for the mammal to survive.
Presidents: Given economic data on trade, foreign markets, and world currency applicable for the current presidential administration, the student will determine the amount of trade deficit for the coming year.

EXERCISE 5.9

1. _____ Affective objective
2. _(an)_ The student would have to determine the characteristics of the superordinate concept and the concept in order to generate a coordinate concept.
3. _(an)_ Determining assumptions is an analysis-level task.
4. _____ This is a knowledge objective if the student had prior contact with the specific pictures.

EXERCISE 5.10

Mammals: Given materials on Darwin's theories, the student will project two implications for human beings living in the 21st century.
Presidents: Given a wide range of printed and mediated materials, the student will pose two probable motives behind John F. Kennedy's response to the Cuban missile crisis.

EXERCISE 5.11

1. _(s)_ The student is not creating a predetermined dress.
2. _____ This is a predetermined product and therefore involves application at best.
3. _(s)_ Once again, this involves an original creation with a criterion.
4. _____ Recall

EXERCISE 5.12

Mammals: Given the properties of an alien environment, the student will design a life-support system for humans that will deal specifically with the problems of air, food, and shelter.
Presidents: Given a wide range of material regarding the current administration, the student will develop a Mideast peace plan that will address the issues of borders, settlements, and peoples.

EXERCISE 5.13

1. _____ There is no criterion, and therefore the students may be working at the affective level.
2. _(e)_ A judgment is accompanied by a criterion.
3. _____ This involves memorization and therefore is a knowledge-level behavior.
4. _____ A synthesis-level objective
5. _____ Again, a criterion is not present and therefore this is not evaluation, by definition.

EXERCISE 5.14

Mammals: When supplied information on a given physical environment and a list of 10 mammals, the student will determine which mammal would be most likely to survive based upon diet, reproductive capability, and physical features.
Presidents: Given a choice of materials and a list of the five most recent presidents of the United States, the student will select the one that has been most successful based upon achievements in the areas of domestic and foreign policy and technology.

Learner-Centered Instruction

In the second unit of the text we analyze instruction from a learner-centered perspective. The contents of the chapters in this section—6 through 10—have been influenced by several sources. One of these is the Learner-Centered Principles, published by the American Psychological Association (Presidential Task Force on Psychology in Education, 1993). A summary of these principles highlights the following generalizations about learning and teaching (Alexander and Murphy, 1994):

- *Students' prior knowledge influences learning.*
- *Students need to think about their own learning strategies.*
- *Motivation has a powerful effect on learning.*
- *Development and individual differences influence learning.*
- *The classroom's social context influences learning.*

A second influence on the chapters in this section is constructivism, a view of learning that emphasizes four key components:

1. *Learners construct their own understanding rather than having it delivered or transmitted to them.*
2. *New learning depends on prior understanding.*
3. *Learning is enhanced by social interaction.*
4. *Authentic learning tasks promote meaningful learning.*

(Eggen & Kauchak, 1997)

Like the Learner-Centered Principles, constructivism refocuses our attention on the learner and reminds us that all true learning must ultimately reside within and be influenced by the learner.

As we write about questioning strategies in Chapter 6, teaching strategies in Chapters 7 and 8, and management in Chapters 9 and 10, we try to emphasize the centrality of learners in our instruction. Ultimately our success as teachers is measured in the growth of our students.

Questioning Strategies

A high school physical science teacher begins a lesson on chemical compounds by saying, "In front of each of you are two containers, each with a different substance. Look at the substances carefully and try to make some comparisons between them. How are they similar and different? Jim?"

"Well, they're both whitish colored."

"OK, good. Nancy?"

"They look sort of grainy. They both look sort of grainy."

"Could you explain what you mean by grainy?"

"Well . . ."

"Would you say they're chunky or powdery, Nancy?"

"Chunky."

"What do you call these chunks? Anyone?"

Manny answers, "Crystals."

"Good. They're both made of crystals. What else can we say about the two as a comparison? Tom." . . .

"Tom, what could we do with the substances besides look at them?"

"Well, we could rub them in our hands."

"OK, let's try that. Here," the teacher says, passing Tom the containers. "How do they feel?"

"This one is finer grained," Tom responds as he holds one up.

"Fine. How could you relate that to what we said about crystals?"

"The crystals of this one are smaller."

"OK, good, Tom. Now, Jacinta, what else could we do with the substances to make comparisons?"

"I'm not sure."

"Well, we've looked at them, and we've rubbed them in our hands to utilize the senses of touch and sight. What other senses could we use to extend our observations?"

"We could smell them."

"OK, try that." The teacher says passing the crystals to Jacinta. "What do you smell?"

"I don't smell anything."

"What do you suppose we should try next? Anyone?"

"We could taste them," Murray replies.

"Your idea is good, but remember I've said that for safety you should never put anything into your mouth until you're sure what they are. However, I know what these are, and these are harmless substances, so, Juan, you taste this one, and Peter, you taste the other. How do they taste?"

Juan replies first. "This one tastes bitter."

Peter follows quickly with, "This one tastes just the opposite."

"Whoa! Could you clarify that statement, Juan?"

"OK. It tastes like salt."

"How about yours, Peter?"

"It must be sugar."

"OK. So what is the formula for salt, Juan?" . . .

"Let's try this, Juan. What is salt composed of?"

"Sodium and chloride, I think."

"That's right. What might the formula be then?"

"NaCl?"

"Right, good! Now, anyone, what is sugar composed of?"

Murray says, "There's carbon in it."

"Yes. What else? Nancy?"

Nancy looks confused.

"What is there a lot of in the atmosphere?"

Nancy offers tentatively, "Oxygen?"

"Right! Do you suppose there might be some oxygen in sugar, Nancy?"

"Yeah. . . . There might be."

"You're right; there is. What else might there be? It's the lightest element. Tran?"

"Hydrogen?"

"Right. Now, using all this information could anyone guess at the formula for sugar?"

"CHO?" Helene offers.

"Good thinking, Helene. It's consistent with what we said about salt. Suppose, though, that there are twice as many atoms of hydrogen as there are carbon or oxygen in sugar. What might the formula be then. . . ."

Introduction

Teaching is basically a combination of art and science. While research tells us in a systematic way differences between effective compared to less effective teaching strategies (the science of teaching), teachers must practice and apply what is known according to their own personality and to a certain extent their own intuition (the art of teaching). There is no one best way to teach, no super strategy. This chapter and the ones that follow are based on this premise.

We are now beginning the second phase, *implementation,* of our three-step model. You may want to review Chapter 1 briefly to refresh your understanding of implementation. Simply stated, having identified goals, you are now prepared to attempt to help learners reach these goals. The specific experiences and learning tasks you design for students to reach or master your goals fall under the umbrella of implementation. Implementation is simply *how you teach.*

A cornerstone of all effective teaching is classroom questioning. It is an essential teaching strategy that can be used with virtually any subject matter area, grade level, or teacher personality. When done effectively it can promote involvement, enhance learning, motivate students, and provide both teachers and students with valuable feedback about learning progress (Eggen & Kauchak, 1997). Questioning also helps a teacher become and remain flexible and responsive to students, a critical characteristic of effective teaching (O'Keefe & Johnston, 1986). It helps promote a student-centered learning environment while maintaining a goal-focused activity. Because of these factors, we discuss questioning specifically first in this chapter and then describe how questioning can be incorporated into complete teaching strategies in subsequent chapters. After completing this chapter and Chapter 7, we hope you will have the background to begin forming a personally effective way of interacting with your students.

We begin our discussion with a description of question level and its influence on learning followed by explanations and illustrations of specific questioning strategies designed to meet specific goals. We conclude the chapter with a discussion of links between questioning, critical thinking, and motivation.

Objectives _____

After completing your study of Chapter 6, you should be able to:

- Explain the role of low- and high-level questions in learning
- Understand differences between convergent and divergent questions
- Explain how different questioning strategies (redirection, prompting, probing) contribute to learning
- Increase your awareness of ways to promote critical thinking through questioning

QUESTION LEVELS

The key to effective questioning is to ask questions that allow you to reach your instructional goal most effectively. The difference between good and effective teachers is that in addition to doing all the things good teachers have always done, effective teachers direct their instruction at a clear and specific goal (Berliner, 1985).

Different types of questions are effective at different times, depending on the goals of the lesson, characteristics of the learner, and the topic being taught (Duffy, Roehler, Meloth, & Vavrus, 1985). At certain times, questions that establish a knowledge of informational foundation recall are required, whereas at other times we want students to link information and apply it to thinking about our world. For instance, consider these questions:

What is 9 × 6?
What present-day significance does studying the play *Julius Caesar* have for us?

The demands on the learner are obviously much different, but for an elementary teacher whose goal is for students to know their multiplication facts, the first question is valid and important, as is the second one for a secondary literature teacher who wants students to analyze moral dilemmas.

Low-Level Questions

In our discussion of the cognitive domain in Chapter 5, we said that the knowledge level requires students to recall information that has been learned and stored in long-term memory. Low-level questions tap this knowledge. For example,

What are the three most common tools in a metal shop?
How much is 5 + 5?
What is the Pythagorean theorem?
Who was the pacifist leader of India after World War II?
How do you spell *anonymous*?
What is one animal that survived the prehistoric age?

Teachers use low-level questions to accomplish several goals:

• To assess students' background knowledge.
• To remind students of important information.
• To establish an informational base that will be used in higher level operations, which we discuss in the next section.

High-Level Questions

For certain goals low-level questions are important and valuable, but at other times we want students to connect ideas and expand their thinking. This leads us to the topic of *high-level questions*. As already discussed in Chapter 5, the characteristic that separates a low- from a high-level question is that the latter requires intellectual processing or the connecting or transforming of ideas by students, whereas the former is limited to memorization with the information being recalled upon demand. In terms of the cognitive taxonomy, low-level questions target the knowledge level. The remaining five levels (comprehension, application, analysis, synthesis, and evaluation) are all considered to be high level.

A high-level question is any question that requires the student to do more than recall previously learned information. Obviously, high-level questions vary in difficulty and demands placed on the student, but the key characteristic they possess is that they require more than mere recall.

Research on the relative merits of high- and low-level questions underscores the complexity of teaching and the importance of clear goals (Good & Brophy, 1997). While it might seem that higher level questions are intrinsically better than lower ones because they are more challenging, the research on this topic is mixed (Redfield & Rousseau, 1981; Dillon, 1981). What this research says to teachers is to first consider your goal or reason for asking a particular question. If the purpose is to identify or reinforce a particular bit of information, such as math facts, lower level questions are appropriate. If instead your goal is to encourage students to *think* about the content they're learning, higher level questions are more effective at accomplishing that goal.

Let's see how this works in the classroom.

> A teacher begins, "In looking at balance of power arrangements through history, we have seen most such arrangements rarely last more than a few decades. Why do you suppose these arrangements collapse?" . . . "Carlos?"
>
> "I think the foreign policies of many countries are changing rapidly, and, as their goals change, the nations have to seek new alliances."
>
> "How about the United States? How does the United States seek out these alliances? . . . Lavonda?"
>
> "We try to find out who agrees with our position. This would include not only countries who would support us but also those in need of our support."

By asking students questions beginning with phrases such as "why do you suppose" and "how does the United States seek," the teacher extends student thinking beyond rote memory. Both students had to integrate prior information and were therefore working at a high level.

An alternate way to encourage student thinking is to ask students to provide and explain examples of abstract ideas. Consider the statement "Give me an example, that we haven't previously discussed, of a simile." A student responding to this question must generate, on the basis of previous information, a new example of the concept *simile*. Because it requires students to think about content in a deep, rather than superficial manner, it is another excellent way to stimulate higher level thinking.

Another effective high-level question asks students to state an idea or definition in the student's own words. For example, "Tell me in your own words what we mean by the statement, 'Literature reflects the time and society of the authors.' " The answer to this question could be followed by the teacher asking for an example of an author, his or her work, and the characteristics of the society—another high-level question.

Another valuable high-level discussion question is the consideration of author motive, perspective, or reference frame, as in this example: "We've read the column by the noted journalist William F. Buckley. Where do you suppose Buckley is coming from in the column?" The discussion would involve consideration of his conservative orientation, probable motives, and basic philosophical stance.

High-level questions can also require students to provide the solution to a problem, such as "An item originally selling for $20.00 is marked 20% off. What is the sale price?" The solution to the problem requires a high-level response. There is one caution we should mention, however. It is a quite common practice in math texts to include a series of problems identical to each other in form. The students solve each as they solved the first, and the level of the task after the first problem is no longer high but, in fact, is merely recall of process. While this occurs more often in assigned work than in an interactive questioning situation, it can occur in both, and teachers think they are getting a high-level response when the opposite is actually occurring. The solution is simple. Mix up the types of problems, and students will be required to give high-level responses.

Probing, or asking students for additional information, is a very useful questioning technique.

EXERCISE 6.1

Read the following scenario and identify each teacher statement as being either a low-level (l) or a high-level (h) question. Then compare your answers to the ones given in the feedback section at the end of the chapter.

_____ 1. "On the board are three lists of words I'd like for you to analyze for a minute. What is special about the first two lists? Amy?"
"All the words are alike."

_____ 2. "Could you explain what you mean by are alike?"
"Well, they're all words that I would use to mean something good about somebody."

_____ 3. "That's right. Does anyone notice anything else about these words? Bob?"
"You could use one of them to mean the other."

_____ 4. "Can you give me an example of this?"
"I could say, 'You are a very competent teacher,' or I could say, 'You are a very skillful teacher,' and, either way, I'd mean the same thing."

_____ 5. "Good, Bob. So the terms in column 1 are more or less interchangeable with those in column 2, right?"
There is general agreement as evidenced by student nods.

_____ 6. "What term do you use to designate this type of relationship?" (No response.)

_____ 7. "OK. Think back to your study of prefixes, suffixes, and root words. Can anybody remember the prefix that means same? Sally?"
"Syn-."

_____ 8. "Good. Now, can anyone remember the one for name?"
"*-Onym.*"

_____ 9. "So, Sally, when you put them together you get . . ."
"*Synonym.*"

_____ 10. "Very good. Can you find some relationship between the words in column 1 and those in column 2? Bob?"
"*Those in column 2 are synonyms of those in column 1.*"
Amy adds, "*And those in column 1 are synonyms of those in column 2.*"

_____ 11. "Yes. Now look at column 3." (Pause.) "How do these words relate to those in the first two columns?" (No response.)

_____ 12. "OK. Does odious mean the same thing as pleasant? Samantha?"
"*No.*"

_____ 13. "Does it mean the same thing as agreeable? Jared?"
"*No, it's the opposite of agreeable.*"

_____ 14. "Good, Jared. Now, Bob, can you see another set of words in the column that has a similar relationship?"
"*Yes, ugly means just the opposite of pretty and attractive, and mean is just the opposite of kind.*"

_____ 15. "So can someone tell us the relationship between the first two columns and the third? LaDawn?"
"*Those in column 3 are opposites of those in columns 1 and 2.*"

_____ 16. "Good. Do you recall the word that expresses this relationship, Kareem?"
"*Antonym.*"

_____ 17. "Can someone make up a sentence using words that are antonyms? Bob?"
"*Hot is the opposite of cold.*"

_____ 18. "Class, is Bob's example correct? If so, why?"

QUESTION FOCUS

Convergent Questions

Another way to think about the effects that questions have on student thinking is in terms of convergent and divergent questions. Convergent questions are those that require one correct answer. Convergent questions are useful for establishing facts or ascertaining answers to problems that have one correct answer. In general, they are questions of fact or recall and are often of a low level, as described in the previous section. For example, the following are convergent questions:

1. What is 6×9?
2. What part of speech modifies a noun or pronoun?
3. A turtle is in what animal class?
4. What is the chemical formula for table salt?
5. What is the most populous country in the world?

Note in each of these that there is only one correct answer for each question, and the answer requires recall of previously learned information.

An exception to this rule involves solutions for problems requiring application, or analysis. For example, if you ask, "I have 400 feet of fence, and I want to enclose the maximum area in a four-sided figure. What should the dimensions be?" this is a high-level question but is still convergent in that only one answer to the problem is correct.

Divergent Questions

While convergent questions require one correct answer, divergent questions are just the opposite, in that many different answers are appropriate. This allows the teacher to assess student understanding while involving a large numbers of students. For instance, consider the following questions:

1. How are Julius Caesar and Hamlet alike?
2. Give me an example of a first-class lever.
3. Give me one of the most significant dates in world history.

Notice that each of the questions can be answered in several ways. For example, in the first case, responses might include

1. "They're both written by Shakespeare."
2. "They're both tragedies."
3. "Both have male central characters."

In the second example:

1. "Screwdriver prying open a paint can lid"
2. "Crowbar prying up a rock"
3. "Scissors"

And the third:

1. "1588—the defeat of the Spanish Armada"
2. "1215—the signing of the Magna Carta"
3. "1066—the Battle of Hastings"
4. "1776—the American Declaration of Independence"

Obviously, many more answers could be given in each case, but the illustrations show how divergent questions can be used to promote student involvement by allowing a number of students to respond to the same question.

EXERCISE 6.2

Return to the scenario offered in Exercise 6.1. Decide whether each of the 18 teacher questions is convergent (c) or divergent (d). Then compare your answers to the ones given in the feedback section at the end of the chapter.

_____ 1.	_____ 6.	_____ 11.	_____ 16.
_____ 2.	_____ 7.	_____ 12.	_____ 17.
_____ 3.	_____ 8.	_____ 13.	_____ 18.
_____ 4.	_____ 9.	_____ 14.	
_____ 5.	_____ 10.	_____ 15.	

EXERCISE 6.3

As a review for both the level and the direction of questions, label the following statements as low level/divergent (l/d), low level/convergent (l/c), high level/divergent (h/d), or high level/convergent (h/c). Then compare your answers to the ones given in the feedback section at the end of the chapter.

_____ 1. How is architecture influenced by culture?
_____ 2. What were some of the possible economic motives of the United States that added to its conflict with Japan prior to World War II?
_____ 3. What assumptions can you make about a novel that is referred to as a classic?
_____ 4. Name the major organs of the digestive system.
_____ 5. What may have caused Achilles to choose youth and fame over long life?
_____ 6. What are the two elements found in salt?
_____ 7. Put into your own words what effect the philosophies of Aristotle and Plato had upon the generations that followed them.
_____ 8. What would be the implications of an average world rate of 5.1 births per woman?
_____ 9. Giving equal weight to all points discussed in the readings, what was the main argument favoring separatism?
_____ 10. You want to get from Jacksonville to Miami, which is 360 miles. The speed limit is 55 mph. If you stay within the speed limit and drive at a steady speed, what is the minimum amount of time the trip will take?
_____ 11. Can anyone give us an example of *iambic pentameter?*
_____ 12. What fallacies appeared in the theory that the earth was the center of the universe?
_____ 13. List the steps involved in operating a lathe.
_____ 14. Based upon three historical events of your choice, to what degree do you believe JFK's "New Frontier" was a success?
_____ 15. In Orwell's *Animal Farm* what techniques are used to persuade the animals to devote their all to the farm?

QUESTIONING STRATEGIES

Using Open-Ended Questions and Redirection to Increase Student Involvement

A major goal in developing effective questioning strategies is to increase the amount of student participation. Typically, interaction patterns involve a teacher asking a question and a student volunteering a response to the question. As the activity proceeds, more knowledgeable or verbally aggressive students continue to be involved, while others not participating drift away from the activity (Eggen & Kauchak, 1997; Good & Brophy, 1997). These patterns can become well-established, with those volunteering being the primary participants and the others rarely responding and often not even attending to the activity. As a result, a teacher often only has a portion of the class paying attention, which, in turn, means only that portion is learning.

In general, teachers do not direct questions to particular students. Further, when questions are asked of individuals, perceived high achievers are called on much more often than perceived low achievers (Good & Brophy, 1997). An interesting and somewhat ironic aspect of both these phenomena is that teachers are quite unaware of the patterns and will often deny their existence, even to an observer who has pointed them out to the teachers immediately after a lesson.

To create a learning environment that invites the participation of all students it is very important that teachers break these patterns. When different interaction patterns are established, powerful results can occur. In one project, teachers were trained to call on *all* students in a class approximately equally (Kerman, 1979). The results were very impressive. Not only did student achievement increase but also both discipline referrals and absenteeism decreased.

There are two other forms of open-ended questions that are easy to ask, quite easy to answer, and excellent for promoting student involvement. These are *descriptive* and *comparative* questions. The first type asks learners to observe and describe an object or event such as an illustration, demonstration, map, graph, table, or statement. Dialogue is initiated by the teacher making a directive such as the following:

1. "What do you notice here?"
2. "Tell me about this."
3. "What do you see?"
4. "Describe the object in front of you."

Descriptive questions provide an effective way to promote involvement, success, and thinking.

The second type, comparative questions, requires the learner to look at two or more objects, statements, illustrations, or demonstrations and identify similarities or differences between them. As students identify similarities, they are moving toward the establishment of a pattern that ultimately results in a concept or generalization. For example, suppose students are shown the following three sentences:

1. He is quiet as a mouse.
2. He was as large as a mountain.
3. They ran as fast as the wind.

The question, "What is similar about the sentences?" requires the learners to identify patterns that ultimately specify the characteristics of the concept *simile*. The word *as* appears in each, as well as a nonliteral comparison between two objects or ideas.

Redirection can be a useful questioning strategy to help establish positive patterns and high levels of interaction in a classroom. This strategy involves the framing of a single question for which there are many possible responses and acknowledging and accepting different responses from several students. The following is an example of how this can occur in the classroom:

> "Having completed our overview of the presidents, who do you think was the greatest American chief executive? Tran?"
>> "Abraham Lincoln."
>> "Sharif?"
>> "Woodrow Wilson."
>> "José, another one?"

"George Washington."

"Those are all excellent choices. Let's talk about them now."

Notice that the teacher does not respond to or discuss the students' replies. Instead the teacher redirects the original question. In doing so, she eliminates possible domination of the discussion and increases the frequency of questions and student participation, both of which are related to increased student achievement and motivation (Brophy & Evertson, 1976; Denham & Lieberman, 1980; Soar, 1973).

Open-ended questions can also be used to elicit high-level thinking. In the next sequence, pay close attention to the ways in which the teacher redirects the question.

"We mentioned different presidents you believe to have been great. Why do you think they were great men? Yes, Betty."

"I think Lincoln was great because he was able to hold the country together, and Washington was great because he got the country started."

"Do you have something to add, Daniella?"

"I think Wilson was great because he was a man of peace and could see the problems beyond his time."

"Maria, can you add anything else?"

"They were all great men because they were strong and had the courage to fight for what they believed in."

It is important to note that, although the three students may not have been dealing with the same individual, they were all responding to a single question posed by the teacher.

Notice in the preceding example that all the redirected questions were divergent. While most redirected questions will be divergent, it is possible to redirect a convergent question as well:

"We have been working on our 5 times tables, children, so my first question is how much is 5 times 2? Myron?"

"5 times 2 is 10."

"What do you think, Suzanna?"

"I think that is right."

Teachers can use convergent redirects to (1) check other students' understanding, (2) involve other students in the lesson, and (3) communicate that the lesson content belongs to students as well as the teacher.

Other questions that are easy to redirect are those that require description and comparison. For example, using the illustration of the concept *simile* provided earlier, the teacher could present the sentence, "He is quiet as a mouse," and direct a number of individuals to describe the sentence, requesting that each say something different about it. The interaction patterns might appear as follows:

Teacher: What do you notice about the sentence? . . . Tim?

Tim: It has six words in it.

Teacher: What else, Sue?

Sue: He is the subject.

Teacher: And what else, Steve?

Steve: It's about a boy.

This process can go on as long as the teacher desires or until it looks as if the class is ready to move on.

A sensible following step would be for the teacher to present a second example and ask for comparisons. For instance, students now have displayed before them the sentences: "He is quiet as a mouse" and "She was a rock of strength." The teacher could then ask, "What is the same or different about the two sentences?" Responses would vary, and the question could be redirected to several students.

In summary, we have defined redirection as any question that is asked of several different individuals. It is a powerful strategy to increase student involvement and motivation and also promote achievement.

EXERCISE 6.4

Read the following scenario and identify the teacher's questions that are examples of redirection by marking them with an X. Then compare your answers to the ones given in the feedback section at the end of the chapter.

_____ 1. "We've been discussing immigration this week, and I want to see if we can tie things together at this point. Just for review, thousands of people came to America during the late 1800s. Name some of the countries they came from." . . . "Bob?"
"Ireland."

_____ 2. "Pablo, another one?"
"Germany."

_____ 3. "Do you have one, Pam?"
"Italy?"

_____ 4. "Fine. All good answers. Now let's use these countries as representative examples. What can we say about the people from these countries? Jim?"
Jim doesn't respond.

_____ 5. "Well, let's take a close look, Jim. Do you think they have the same religious structure?"
"No."

_____ 6. "Anything else, Jim?"
"Their languages are different."

_____ 7. "Right. That's a good one. Anybody want to add another one? Shanda?"
"Oh . . . I can think of a lot of things like clothes, food, economic factors, political structure, and attitudes."

_____ 8. "Fine, fine. What is the obvious point we can draw from this, Bonita?"
"That American immigrants were different."

_____ 9. "Different from what, Bonita?"
"From each other."

_____ 10. "Good, now let's break off for just a second. How did the book define immigration? . . . "Miguel?"
"People who leave their country immigrate from their homes."

_____ 11. "OK, let's look at the word closely. Does immigration make you think of in or out? Miguel?"
"In."

_____ 12. "So a person who is an immigrant . . . ?"
       "Comes into a country," Miguel finishes.
_____ 13. "And to emigrate . . . ?"
       "Is to leave a country."
_____ 14. "Very good!"

Prompting

What happens when we ask a student a question, and she either fails to reply or she responds incorrectly? Generally, teachers move on to another student in order to maintain interest and momentum (Eggen & Kauchak, 1997). Unfortunately, doing so has problems. The student who was unable to respond often becomes confused, discouraged, and psychologically removed from the discussion. We have stressed desirability of total involvement, but how can we deal with students who cannot answer questions or whose responses are wrong? The following sequence between a teacher and one student illustrates one way to deal with this problem:

> "Regarding our discussion on international power patterns, which pattern does this equal arms scale demonstrate? . . . Pat?"
>
> Pat does not respond.
>
> "Any idea?"
>
> "I don't know."
>
> "OK, let's take another look at the scale. If this object is 2 ounces and the one on the other tray is 2 ounces, they are said to be . . . ?"
>
> "Equal."
>
> "Right. Equal in what?"
>
> "Weight."
>
> The teacher nods. "Now, if we have these equal weights, one on each tray, what happens?"
>
> "They balance each other."
>
> "Fine. Let's suppose each weight represents three countries and that the groups are basically opposed to each other. If they are equal in strength or power they would be . . . ?"
>
> "Balanced."
>
> "Great! Then this demonstration represents what pattern of power?"
>
> "The balance of power pattern."
>
> "Now you've got it!!"

The preceding example demonstrates the strategy referred to as *prompting* which involves the use of hints, or clues, that are used to aid the student in responding successfully. This method can also be employed when a response is incorrect. For example,

> "To be specific, the pattern of power called balance is one in which two or more nation-states form a coalition in order to protect themselves from a specific enemy. Coalitions of equal power oppose each other; they are in balance and peace is preserved. However, once the balance is broken and one coalition tips the power scale in its favor, the likelihood of war is increased. As with our scale, if too much weight is added to one side, the

other side will be overpowered. Now, let's examine this idea. Does the United Nations represent a balance of power arrangement? . . . Marisha?"

"I think it does."

"Let's analyze it and find out. Marisha, does the UN aid and support any group member attacked by an enemy?"

"It's supposed to."

"OK. Is the UN a coalition of two or more nations?"

"Yes."

"Is the UN pledged against a specific enemy?"

"I'm not sure."

"Is there another organization of equal size and power with which the UN is locked in mortal combat?"

"No."

"Then what do you conclude?"

"The United Nations is not an example of balance of power."

"Good thinking."

After giving an incorrect response, students benefit most by the teacher asking a series of simple questions that give clues to help them arrive at the correct answer. This is often preferable to merely giving the student the correct answer and moving to another student or asking another student to help immediately after the incorrect response because it makes public the logic behind the correct answer.

Consider one more example. In the previous section we used the sentence, "He is quiet as a mouse," and "She was a rock of strength." The teacher wants the students to identify the first as a simile and the second as a metaphor. She probably has asked a series of divergent questions—descriptions and comparisons—that have been redirected to several individuals. However, let's assume that students don't recognize the sentences as examples of the respective concepts. One way to correct this problem is to prompt students to arrive at the correct answer:

"What do you notice about 'she' and 'rock' in the second sentence? Shin?"

"It says she is a rock."

"Does the sentence mean she really is a rock?"

"No, not really."

"So we say this is what kind of a comparison?"

(Pause.)

"Literal or nonliteral?"

"Nonliteral."

"Okay. Good. We have a nonliteral comparison of two ideas. The same is true about the first sentence, but there is a special word in it. What word?"

"As."

"Yes. The word *as* is added. Otherwise, the two sentences are similar. What are they called?"

"The first is a simile, and the second is a metaphor."

"Excellent. We have identified the key differences between the two sentences."

As the research literature indicates, prompting is an important technique employed by effective teachers. However, our experience in working with teachers suggests that it can be difficult to implement and isn't employed as often as would be desirable. The reason for the difficulty probably is that prompting requires thinking on your feet. While many other teaching procedures and skills can be planned and practiced in advance, prompting can only be practiced in the context of an actual lesson.

There will be times you simply assume the student's response will be correct, and you will draw a blank when the student is incorrect. How would you prompt a student who did not know the largest known planet? Would you refer to Roman mythology, or perhaps suggest it begins with a "J"? Would you enlist another student's support or possibly throw in the towel and answer your own question? Regardless of your choice, let us suggest that, assuming the student did not succeed, you keep that student in mind so that you might be able to facilitate a successful response during the remainder of the session.

Prompting can be enormously rewarding and enjoyable to help learners construct responses they previously could not provide. For these reasons we encourage you to persevere. With practice you will become skilled and will reap the intrinsic rewards of feeling that you have had a positive, direct, and tangible influence on student learning.

Careful preparation can be an aid that will help your prompting efforts. For instance, if a teacher knows in advance that she wants the students to identify "nonliteral comparison without *as* or *like*" as the key characteristic of metaphor and "nonliteral comparison using *as* or *like*" for simile, that awareness will help her to think on her feet because she knows what she wants from the students. She can then ask whatever questions it takes to get them to the idea.

EXERCISE 6.5

Turn back to Exercise 6.4 and identify all of the teacher's statements that are prompts by marking their numbers here with an X. Then compare your answers to the ones given in the feedback section at the end of the chapter.

_____ 1.   _____ 4.   _____ 7.   _____ 10.   _____ 13.
_____ 2.   _____ 5.   _____ 8.   _____ 11.   _____ 14.
_____ 3.   _____ 6.   _____ 9.   _____ 12.

EXERCISE 6.6

Read the following anecdote and identify all of the teacher's statements that are either redirections (r) or prompts (p). Then compare your answers to the ones given in the feedback section at the end of the chapter.

_____ 1. "Today we're considering the properties of numbers. Here is a list of some numbers." The teacher points to a list on the board. "From the list identify a prime number. Mariko?"
"Three."

_____ 2. "Another, Shalynne?"
"Two."

_____ 3. "Another one, Angela?"
"Five."

_____ 4. "Now, give me a number that is not prime. Pedro?"
"Six."

_____ 5. "Another one, Rudy?"
        "Eight."
_____ 6. "OK. Let's try something we haven't done yet. Six can be reduced to the product of two
            prime numbers. What are they, Bob?"
            Bob doesn't respond.
_____ 7. "Let me help you, Bob. Now remember your times tables. What times what equals six?"
            "Oh, three times two."
_____ 8. "OK, good. Now, from this list, select a number that is a perfect square."
            Bob adds, "Nine."
_____ 9. "Good, Bob. Another one, Sarina?"
            "Sixteen."
_____ 10. "OK. Another one? Ralph?"
            "Twenty-four."
_____ 11. Let's check this one. First let's back up a step. A perfect square is some number that can be
            broken down into the product of another number times itself. What number did we say times
            itself equals nine?"
            "Three."
_____ 12. "Good, Ralph. Let me continue to help you with this. What number times itself equals six-
            teen?"
            "Four."
_____ 13. "Now, does any number times itself equal twenty-four?"
            "Hmmm. No, twenty-four isn't a perfect square."
_____ 14. "OK. Then can you name a perfect square from this list."
            "Twenty-five?"
_____ 15. "That's the way!!"

Probing

At this point, we have discussed ways to increase student involvement through open-ended questions, redirecting, and prompting strategies. The first two involve increased numbers of students, and the latter allows the teacher to deal with incorrect responses in an informative and humane manner. Sometimes however the student's reply is correct but insufficient because it lacks depth. In such a case, it is important for the teacher to have the student supply additional information in order to have better, more complete answers. This strategy is called probing. Let's take a closer look at probing in action:

The teacher begins, "Do you think trees are important to the land?" . . . "Carmelina?"
"Yes."
"Why, Carmelina?"
"Because they help hold things together."
"What do you mean by that?"
"Well, the roots and all go down into the ground and help the ground stay in one place."
"That's very good, Carmelina, and as we learned yesterday, when the earth begins to move away to a different place, it's called . . ."
"Erosion."

Through the process of probing the teacher attempts to get students to justify or further explain their responses, thereby increasing the depth of the discussion. It also helps to move students away from surface responses. All too often, we don't take our students beyond the simple yes, no, or correct answer response. We need to provide our students with increased opportunities to process information, to deal with the *why*, the *how*, and the *based upon what* of their answers.

The function of a probe is to provide an opportunity to support or defend a simply stated position or point of view intellectually. By doing so, the student not only gains experience in dealing with high-level tasks but also experiences a greater feeling of success.

Wait-Time

When we ask students thought-provoking questions we want them to think. One way to do this is through the process of wait-time. Based on the work of Mary Budd Rowe (1974, 1986), *wait-time* is the amount of time teachers wait after asking a question until they intervene by prompting or redirecting the question to another student. It also can include the time after a student response for students to think about and wrap up their answer.

Researchers found that teachers typically wait 1 second or less for students to answer. Think about that for a moment. Suppose you as a student studying this book were asked in a class discussion, "Under what conditions would it be inappropriate to use prompting as a strategy?" and your instructor gave you less than 1 second to answer before asking another question or turning the question to someone else? This is the situation students face continually. By contrast, if given more time to think, the quality of student answers improve. These are the results Rowe found in examining the effects of increased "think time." She found that when teachers waited approximately 3 seconds or longer that the quality of student responses improved, and this simple process of giving them more time to answer also positively influenced learning. Slow down your questioning; make sure the questions are direct, clear, and require deeper thought; and wait, wait, wait for a response (Fairbain, 1987).

The implications of this research are obvious. As we question students, we should make an effort to wait a few seconds for them to answer. At first a period of silence may seem awkward, but both you and the students will quickly get used to it.

However, as with the others, this strategy should be implemented with judgment and sensitivity. Earlier in the chapter, we said that teachers need to be responsive to their students (O'Keefe & Johnston, 1986). Imagine, for example, that you call on a student and she appears to draw a blank. As you wait, she panics. In this case you wouldn't wait as long as you would in another where the student appears to be "really thinking" about the answer. Also, in asking low-level, convergent questions, such as, "What is 4×7?" or "What city is at the tip of Lake Michigan?" you wouldn't wait as long as you would in asking a more thought-provoking question such as, "Why do you suppose Chicago developed into such a major city?"

Our primary goal in this discussion is to make you aware of the value of wait-time, so you will make an effort to practice it when you teach. None of us employs the technique perfectly, and we aren't suggesting that you silently count after every question you ask. However, with effort you can increase the amount of time you give your students to think and this will increase your questioning effectiveness.

Effectively employing "wait time" in classrooms provides opportunities for students to process questions being asked by the teacher.

QUESTIONING SKILLS: THE COGNITIVE DOMAIN AND CRITICAL THINKING

When we use questioning strategies in the classroom we not only want students to learn content but also want to teach them to think more critically and analytically. The high-level questions referred to above can promote deeper thought and critical thinking through the application of the five process levels of the cognitive domain. Asking questions that require students to apply, analyze, and evaluate information is a major goal in promoting higher order thinking skills.

Asking such questions, however, is not enough. It is equally important that you establish a classroom climate in which thinking and analyzing are valued (Rodriguez, 1988). A positive classroom questioning environment requires

- Being sincerely interested in what students say.
- Being curious about students' ideas.
- Building on and paraphrasing students' ideas.
- Using divergent follow-up questions that encourage students to expand and "dig" into the problem or subject at hand.

As we've seen earlier in this chapter, the use of divergent questions prevents the overuse of factual, yes/no responses that often delimit opportunities for critical thinking. Although recalling facts is sometimes important, both achievement and motivation can be enhanced when teachers ask questions that require students to apply, analyze, synthesize, and evaluate information.

In addition, questioning is a critical component, along with summarizing, clarifying, and predicting, to involve students in reciprocal teaching. This teaching strategy focuses on learning that involves students in a dialogue or discussion about what they're reading. This allows the teacher to "hear" students' thinking and to diagnose sources of comprehension problems and, in doing so, to boost students' comprehension of the material they're reading (Palincsar, 1987).

Studies of critical thinking have also established relationships between the way students think about information and their academic success. One study showed that more successful students tend to search for similarities and differences, compare and contrast ideas, and critically analyze relationships (Miller, Alway, & McKinley, 1987). Teachers can do a lot to promote these inclinations in students by asking thought-provoking questions in their classrooms.

Clearly, the utilization of the higher, or process, levels of the cognitive domain, detailed in Chapter 4, will provide you with the foundation to frame and ask questions that will promote many of the critical-thinking behaviors cited in the above research. Often you will find that just a few such questions strategically interspersed in your lesson plans will provide sufficient challenge and stimulation for an entire lesson. We suggest that when you develop a question or discussion lesson plan, you include these key questions under the section of the plan labeled "content." These questions will provide a focal point for the intent of your lesson and will ensure that your students are engaged in activities that go beyond the recall of data, thereby enabling them to experience first hand the process of critical thinking.

MOTIVATING STUDENTS

We have to this point presented specific and separate discussions of the different question levels; convergent and divergent questions; and prompting, probing, and redirection, and have illustrated how they can be applied in various teaching situations. However, when they are synthesized and systematically applied to classroom activities, they can also become powerful techniques in motivating students. We turn now to this topic.

Skill in motivating students to learn is central and basic to teacher effectiveness (Good & Brophy, 1997). Interestingly, however, it has only been within the last few years that motivation has received systematic attention from educators. Prior to that time many teachers felt that it was their job to teach and that they couldn't also be expected to motivate reluctant learners. In other cases, motivation was a haphazard bag of tricks. Now, all that has changed. Concern about alienated youth, unsuccessful students, and high dropout rates has contributed to this renewed focus.

Although there is certainly more to motivation than questioning, a skilled teacher can do much to enhance student attention and interest through classroom interaction. We have observed teachers achieve striking results with systematic application of the strategies described in this chapter. Questions can motivate students, elicit deeper processing of information, and tell students how well they are mastering the content (Strother, 1989). How can this be accomplished?

Conceptually, the process is actually quite simple, although putting it into practice requires diligence and effort. Essentially, when we use questioning strategies to motivate students we want to establish two expectations.

First, we want to put them in a position where they know with certainty that they each will be called on during the course of a learning activity. Earlier in the chapter we noted that Kerman (1979) found impressive results when teachers were trained to call on all students equally. This communicates to all students that they are part of the learning community and that you as a teacher expect all to participate and learn. To accomplish this, call on all students equally, calling on volunteers only 10 to 15% of the time in a learning activity. This means that much of the time you will be calling on students who don't have their hands raised. This can be accomplished by extensively using open-ended questions and redirection. These can be particularly effective when redirection is combined with divergent questions calling for description or comparison. The type of question, however, is not as important as putting students in a position where they know they will be called on. When they know for certain that they will be called on at some point in the process, their attention improves markedly.

"I can't do that," some people might argue. "I put the kids on the spot, and they're worse off than they were before." This brings us to the second expectation: when students are called on, they know that you will arrange the question so they can give an acceptable answer. Notice that we said acceptable answer. We didn't say that they will give you *the* answer you want to the original question, but they will give you an answer that you can acknowledge as acceptable. For example, consider the following dialogue taken from a lesson on adverbs.

> Mrs. Wu is involved in a lesson where her students are learning to identify adverbs in sentences. She went through a series of examples, calling on the students to analyze the sentences. She continued by writing the following on the board:
> Steve quickly jumped over the hedge to get out of sight.
> She then continued, "What is the adverb in this sentence, Tim?"
> "Umm . . . I don't know."
> "What did Steve do?"
> "He jumped over the hedge."
> "Yes, indeed! He certainly did! Good, Tim."

At this point, Tim has given an acceptable answer. He admittedly didn't identify the adverb in the sentence, but his answer nevertheless moved the lesson forward and also gave the teacher a chance to praise him. Mrs. Wu could then continue prompting and probing by asking Tim, "How did he jump?" or she could let him off the hook and continue the process with another student. Either way, Tim has had a successful and positive experience.

For students who are rarely called on and who even more rarely give a correct answer, this experience can be very positive. As a result, they will be less uncomfortable the next time they are called on and will also be more inclined to try and answer. Motivational experts believe that an emotionally safe learning environment is critical to student motivation, and Mrs. Wu helped create a safe environment for Tim (Pintrich & Schunk, 1996; Wlodkowski, 1984).

Obviously, you won't turn a hostile or seriously unmotivated student around immediately with these techniques. However, if the pattern in the classroom becomes one in which all students are called on—and when they are, they are able to answer—in time you can markedly improve their attention and their inclination to participate in class. Good questioning is essential to good teaching and effective motivation. Skillful questioning can arouse student curiosity, stimulate the imagination, and motivate students to problem solve. In addition, good questioning can clarify concepts and challenge students to think (Ornstein, 1987).

Consider also the kind of classroom climate you're establishing with this process. You're communicating to students that they all are capable of learning, you expect them to be able to answer, and you're there to help them. This climate, together with using the strategies of redirection and prompting to help you involve your students and promote success, can do much to enhance their motivation.

Summary

We began this chapter by stating that questioning strategies are the cornerstone of effective teaching. The different levels, direction, and strategies contribute to teachers' overall repertoire of instructional strategies. At times high-level questions are most desirable, and at others low levels are preferable. You will ask some questions that are convergent and some that are divergent. The levels and direction of your questions will be determined by your goals for the lesson.

Open-ended questions combined with redirection, prompting, probing, and wait-time are all strategies that can be used to promote student involvement, enhance success, and promote a positive and emotionally safe learning environment. As with the levels and direction of your questions, the strategies should be employed to help you reach the goals of your lesson. However, you also have additional goals for every lesson—to involve and motivate your students and promote critical thinking skills. When systematically integrated, the specific strategies can help you reach these goals.

Questions for Discussion

1. Should low-level questions always precede high-level ones? Why or why not? In your answer provide specific examples.
2. Should the mix or ratio of high- and low-level questions vary with grade level? How does content area influence this optimal mix?
3. Based on your experience in classrooms, should teachers ask more or fewer divergent questions? Why?
4. Some teachers assert that prompting students only further embarrasses students who have failed to respond correctly in the first place. How would you respond to these teachers?
5. How should wait-time vary in terms of the following variables:
   a. type of question
   b. age of student
   c. place in unit (i.e., early or late)
   d. teacher's goals?
6. Think about the most effective teacher you've encountered in terms of questioning. How would you describe the teacher in terms of the concepts in this chapter? What else did he or she do in terms of questioning that wasn't discussed in this chapter?

Suggestions for Field Experience _____

1. Interview a teacher in terms of questioning.
   a. How do they plan for questioning ahead of time?
   b. How do they know who to call on during a lesson?
   c. What do they do to encourage participation from all students?
   d. What do they do when a student can't answer?
   e. What is the hardest part of questioning?
2. Observe an interactive lesson and list the questions the teacher asks. (You may want to record the lesson on an audiotape to make the task easier.)
   a. How many questions were high and low level?
   b. Was there any pattern to the use of high and low level questions?
   c. How successful were students in answering these questions?
   d. What suggestions do you have to improve this aspect of questioning?
3. Take the questions you listed in Activity #2 and analyze them in terms of convergent and divergent.
   a. How many of each were used?
   b. Was there any pattern to their use?
   c. How did students respond to these different questions?
4. Observe a lesson and, using a watch with a second hand, compute the wait-time for different teacher questions.
   a. What was the average wait-time?
   b. Did wait-time vary with the type of question (e.g., high versus low level)?
   c. Did wait-time vary with the type of student?
   d. What suggestions do you have to make wait-time more effective?
5. Design a lesson plan for an interactive questioning lesson. In the lesson plan write out specific questions you will ask to reach your goal. Analyze these in terms of the concepts in this chapter (e.g., high versus low level, convergent versus divergent).
6. Teach the lesson you designed in Activity #5.
   a. How well did the questions work in stimulating thinking?
   b. How often did you have to rephrase or explain a question?
   c. How often did you have to change or adapt your questioning plans?
   d. What did you learn about the use of questioning to promote learning?

Exercise Feedback _____

EXERCISE 6.1

1. (h) High. The teacher has asked an analysis-level question.
2. (h) High. This asks for clarification.
3. (h) High. This again involves clarification.
4. (h) High. This is a comprehension question.
5. (l) Low. The teacher has probably led the students.

6. (l) Low. This is a memorization recall task.
7. (l) Low. This is, once again, recall.
8. (l) Low. This, too, is recall.
9. (l) Low. This is a prompt leading to a right answer.
10. (h) High. Finding relationships is definitely not a recall task.
11. (h) High. Again, making comparisons is not a recall task.
12. (l) Low. This is a comparison of memorized definitions.
13. (l) Low. This, too, is a memorized comparison.
14. (h) High. Searching for similarities is not recall.
15. (h) High. Again, this is finding a relationship.
16. (l) Low. This is a recall task.
17. (h) High. This is a comprehension or application level question.
18. (h) High. An explanation is required.

EXERCISE 6.2

1. (d) Divergent. There may be other things than likeness.
2. (d) Divergent. Self-expression would be varied.
3. (d) Divergent. There is still a range of possibilities.
4. (d) Divergent. Examples would vary.
5. (c) Convergent. The teacher leads the students to only one conclusion.
6. (c) Convergent. The answer is a specific term.
7. (c) Convergent. This is a question with only one answer.
8. (c) Convergent. This is recall also.
9. (c) Convergent. The teacher is leading to a single answer.
10. (d) Divergent. There might be more than one relationship.
11. (d) Divergent. Again, there might be several relationships.
12. (c) Convergent. This is recall of definitions.
13. (c) Convergent. There is only one answer.
14. (d) Divergent. This is assuming there is more than one set. The question is convergent
        if there is only one.
15. (d) Divergent. There may be more than one possible relationship.
16. (c) Convergent. A single response is correct.
17. (d) Divergent. Hundreds of original sentences could be stated.
18. (c) Convergent. This is a yes/no situation.

EXERCISE 6.3

1. (h/d) High level/Divergent
2. (h/d) High level/Divergent
3. (h/d) High level/Divergent
4. (l/c) Low level/Convergent. There is only one correct list of major organs.
5. (h/d) High level/Divergent
6. (l/c) Low level/Convergent
7. (h/d) High level/Divergent
8. (h/d) High level/Divergent
9. (h/c) High level/Convergent
10. (h/c) High level/Convergent

11. (h/d) High level/Divergent
12. (h/d) High level/Divergent
13. (l/c) Low level/Convergent
14. (h/d) High level/Divergent
15. (h/c) High level/Convergent

EXERCISE 6.4

1. _____ No
2. __x__ After Bob had answered, "Ireland," the teacher posed the same question to Pablo.
3. __x__ After Pablo's response, the teacher once again posed the original question, this time to Pam.
4. _____ No
5. _____ No
6. _____ No
7. __x__ After Jim's response the teacher asked if anybody wanted to generate additional examples for the question posed.
8. _____ No
9. _____ No
10. _____ No
11. _____ No
12. _____ No
13. _____ No
14. _____ No

Note that in each case of redirection the teacher is getting more than one student to respond to a question. Once the teacher poses a new question, redirection is no longer being used unless that new question is then redirected.

EXERCISE 6.5

1. _____ No
2. _____ No, redirection.
3. _____ No, redirection.
4. _____ No
5. __x__ After Jim could not respond, the teacher gave him a leading question for consideration.
6. __x__ In this same sequence, the teacher is urging Jim to think of other examples.
7. _____ No, redirection.
8. _____ No
9. _____ No
10. _____ No
11. __x__ Although Miguel has already defined *immigration,* the teacher is beginning a sequence where he is given hints so he can use the two terms appropriately.
12. __x__ An unfinished question is a form of prompting.
13. __x__ Miguel is prompted to define a term he may not already have known.
14. _____ No

EXERCISE 6.6

1. _____ Neither
2. __(r)__ Redirection
3. __(r)__ Redirection
4. _____ Neither
5. __(r)__ Redirection
6. _____ Neither
7. __(p)__ Prompt. The teacher is getting Bob to recall his times tables so that he can generate an appropriate answer.
8. _____ Neither
9. __(r)__ Redirection
10. __(r)__ Redirection
11. __(p)__ Prompt. Statements 11 through 14 represent a prompt sequence. The teacher begins by providing additional information and helping the student to respond with appropriate examples.
12. __(p)__ Prompt
13. __(p)__ Prompt
14. __(p)__ Prompt
15. _____ Neither

Chapter 7

Teaching Strategies

Cassie Jones walked through the halls of the inner city middle school where she is the principal and listened to the sounds coming from the different classrooms. As she walked by Ben Carlson's social studies class she heard him say, "Yesterday we talked about the strengths and weaknesses of the North and South at the outbreak of the Civil War. Who remembers one of these?"

As Cassie proceeded down the hall, she stopped in front of Sarah McCarthy's science class. Sarah was at the front of the room swinging a set of keys from a piece of string. "Hmm," Cassie thought, "no wonder her class is so quiet—she's got them hypnotized." As she listened further she heard Sarah ask, "Class, this is a simple pendulum, just like the one we find in grandfather clocks. Who can tell me what factors influence the rate at which a pendulum swings?"

"Good question," thought Cassie. "Maybe that's why her kids are so quiet."

When Cassie turned the corner she was greeted by a steady stream of student voices arguing about something.

"I don't care what you say, stealing is wrong."

"But his family didn't have enough to eat. They were hungry—he couldn't let them starve!"

"What's Hector up to today?" Cassie thought as she listened more closely to Hector Sanchez's English class.

"Class," Hector broke in with a booming voice, "it's not enough just to disagree with your partners. You have to explain why. Remember, one of the reasons we read books like Sounder is to help us understand our own lives. So, you have three more minutes in your discussion groups to explain why the father was right or wrong to steal food for his family."

Cassie chuckled as she heard Hector's class rejoin the battle. "He's sure got them stirred up today. I guess I'm lucky to have such a talented teaching staff that has so many different strengths."

Introduction

We are now at the implementation phase of the general teaching model. Here teachers use different strategies to help students reach the objectives identified earlier in the planning phase of instruction. In this chapter we incorporate the questioning strategies described in Chapter 6 and show how these microstrategies can be incorporated into more comprehensive macrostrategies. The specific strategies discussed are *expository, guided discovery, discussion,* and *inquiry,* which we illustrate with examples from different disciplines. Similarities exist among the strategies, of course, and they aren't exclusive of one another.

As a teacher, you will design and teach lessons that incorporate features from more than one teaching strategy. This is desirable as you develop a personal style. However, we discuss them separately for the sake of clarity and the development of your understanding. As your thinking develops and your teaching evolves, you will make adjustments in the strategies to fit your personality and style and your students' needs.

Because expository and discovery are closely related in terms of goals, content, and procedures, we present an overview of both in the first section. They are separately described in greater detail later.

Objectives

After completing your study of Chapter 7, you should be able to:

- Understand major differences between expository and discovery teaching strategies
- Understand how to plan and implement expository lessons in different content areas
- Explain the role of examples in furthering student understanding in expository and discovery lessons
- Describe how to plan and implement discovery lessons
- Explain how to plan and implement inquiry lessons
- Understand how to plan and implement discussions

EXPOSITORY AND DISCOVERY TEACHING

An Overview

As an introduction to these two teaching strategies, let's look at a math teacher working with her fifth-grade class.

> Ms. Jane Morton had been working with her class for the past few weeks on different geometric shapes. Today her lesson focused on circles. To begin the lesson, she gave the students rulers, string, and a handout containing a number of circles like the one shown in Figure 7.1.

Figure 7.1 A Circle Handout

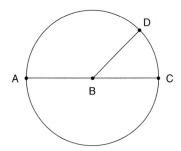

Table 7.1 Chart Handout

Circle	Radius	Diameter	Circumference
A			
B			
C			
D			
E			
F			

In addition to the handout containing the circles, she passed out a sheet that looked like Table 7.1. She began her lesson by saying, "Look at the circles you have on the handout I've given you. What do you notice about them? Shareen?"

"There's a line with an *A* and a *B* and a *C* on it."

"Yes indeed," Ms. Morton smiled. "And what do we call that line? Kevin?"

". . . The radius?" Kevin responded hesitantly.

"Does this line go all the way across the circle or only halfway across, Kevin?"

"All the way across."

"Yes, good. And what do we call that?"

"Oh, yes! I've got it. It's the diameter. I remember you told us that *diameter* sort of sounds like dime, and it goes all the way across the dime."

"Yes, good memory, Kevin. What else do you notice about the circles? Juan?"

"Well, we have a line *BD,* which is called the radius."

"Excellent, Juan. Now look at the columns in your handout. We've talked about the radius and diameter of the circles. What else do you see in the handout? Kim?"

"The word *circumference?*"

"And what does that mean?"

(Pause.)

"Look again at your circle, Kim. You've identified the diameter and the radius. What is the only thing left?"

". . . The distance around it. The circumference is the distance around!"

"Good thinking, Kim!"

"And how could we measure that? Could we use a ruler? Tanya?"

"We could, but it wouldn't be very easy because of all the curves. Instead, we could put string around the outside and measure the string afterward with a ruler."

Table 7.2   Completed Chart

Circle	Radius	Diameter	Circumference
A	1	2	6.3
B	1.9	4	12.5
C	2.95	6	18.9
D	4.1	8.1	24.9
E	5	10.1	32.5
F	6	11.8	38.0

"Excellent, you remembered how we did that with other geometric shapes. Well, today we're going to see if we can find out some things about circles. To do this, I want you to measure the circles on the handout that I've given you and put these measurements in the chart. When you're finished, we'll talk about what you've done."

With that, the class went to work measuring the circles that Ms. Morton had handed out. When she noticed that most of the class had completed the assignment, she drew the chart from the handout on the board (see Table 7.1) and asked the students to tell her what measurements they had gotten. As the class did this, they realized that different people got different answers, which provided an opportunity to talk about the idea of measurement error. In discussing this concept, the class decided that one way of handling the problem would be to average measurements, which they did.

Once the chart on the board was completed (see Table 7.2), Ms. Morton continued the lesson by saying, "Now let's look at our chart on the board. What patterns do you see there? Davon?"

". . . The values are all different."

"Yes they are," Ms. Morton smiled. "What else? Jacinto?"

"The diameters are all about twice as big as the radiuses," noted Jacinto.

"Good, Jacinto. And why do you think that is? Maria?"

Maria hesitated.

"How are the diameters and radiuses related?"

"The diameter is twice as long as the radius."

"Yes, exactly! Good, Maria. That's why the measurements are twice as long. Now let's look at the diameter and circumference columns. What do you notice here? Jamal?"

". . . When the diameter gets bigger, so does the circumference."

"That's right, Jamal," Ms. Morton smiled. "Okay—anything else? . . . Anyone?"

Not hearing a response, she continued, "Well, let's see if we can figure out how the two change. Let's have this half of the class divide the circumference of circles A, C, and E diameters while the other half of the class does the same for B, D, and F."

When the class finished, Ms. Morton added a new column with their results so the chart looked like Table 7.3.

"What do you notice about the numbers in the column labeled C/D? Juanita?"

"They're all just over three."

"Good, we see that the measurements aren't all exact. Why do you suppose that happened? Juanita?"

"Well, we talked about measurement error, so maybe that's it."

"Good thinking, Juanita. So what should we do? Leroy?"

". . . Average the numbers?" Leroy responded hesitantly.

Table 7.3   Chart with *C/D* Added

Circle	Radius	Diameter	Circumference	C/D
A	1	2	6.3	3.15
B	1.9	4	12.5	3.120
C	2.95	6	18.9	3.15
D	4.1	8.1	24.9	3.07
E	5	10.1	32.5	3.14
F	6	11.8	38.0	3.22

"Good work, Leroy! Okay everyone, let's do that. Use your calculators and quickly get an average."

After allowing a few moments, Ms. Morton said, "All right, what did you get? John?"

"Three point one four three."

"Fine, John. Is that what everyone got?"

She waited a few seconds while two of the students rechecked their answers, and having confirmed that 3.143 was the average, she continued.

"That is a very good average, everyone. We were very close. The actual number is three point one four. This number is called *pi,* and the symbol is this."

She then wrote the word and drew the symbol on the board.

"Now, think about a formula that we could use to find the circumference if we know the diameter. Anyone?"

"I think I know," Lacey said tentatively. "Multiply the diameter times pi."

"Good idea, Lacey," Ms. Morton smiled at her. "Let's everyone try that to see if it works."

With that, she drew a circle on the board using chalk and string. She measured the diameter for the class and gave them the value. While they were multiplying, she had two members of the class come up to measure the circumference for comparison. After the class discussed the results of this problem, she passed out another worksheet that contained additional circles, and the class measured these to see if they too follow the $C = \pi d$ equation.

Let's pause now to consider this lesson. It involved a teacher using a guided discovery approach to help students learn abstractions. In this lesson they learned both the concept pi and the formula $C = \pi d$. We call these lessons *guided discovery* because students are provided with information, and through the guidance of their teachers they "discover" the abstraction the teachers identified in their objectives.

Expository lessons are more teacher-centered than discovery lessons in that the teacher is the major provider of information, relating the examples to the abstraction being taught. The abstraction is stated by the teacher before examples are given, and then the examples are provided to help illustrate the abstraction. To show what we mean by expository teaching, read the following scenario, which describes a teacher using this strategy to teach a similar lesson.

Mr. Carl Hite wanted to teach his class the formula $C = \pi d$. He began by saying, "Today we're going to learn the formula for computing the circumference of a circle. When you're finished you'll be able to find the circumference when you're given the diameter."

He then wrote $C = \pi d$ on the board and said, "Go ahead and read this, Antonio."

"C equals pi times d," Antonio responded.

"OK, fine, Antonio," he smiled. "Now what is the C? Jan?"

"It's the circumference."

"And what is the circumference? Derek?"

"It's . . . I'm not sure," Derek stammered.

Carl then drew on the board a circle like the one in Figure 7.1.

"Now, look at the circle. What is the circumference?" he asked as he pointed to the board and made an imaginary circle in the air.

"It's the distance around the circle," Derek said, grinning at Mr. Hite's arm movement.

"That's right, Derek," Mr. Hite grinned back.

"Now what is the d in the formula? Sasha?"

"It's the diameter."

"And where is it on our circle?" he said, pointing to the board. "Cal?"

"It's the line AC," Cal responded after studying the circle.

"All right, good, Cal. Now we have one part left in the formula. What is it, Shanda?"

"It's that little squiggly thing that is three point one four," she said.

"Good, Shanda. What did Antonio say we called that when I wrote the formula on the board? Anyone?"

"Pi," three students said together.

"Okay, terrific. Now we're all set."

With that he gave each of the students a ruler, string, and a handout with three circles drawn on it.

"Look at the circles on the handout, everyone. I want you to measure the diameter and calculate the circumference. Then check your calculation by measuring the circumference with the string."

The students went quickly to work, computed the circumference of each circle, and checked their answers by measuring each.

These scenarios illustrate two of the teaching strategies discussed in this chapter. The first involved a teacher using guided discovery to teach the concept of pi and the formula for computing the circumference of a circle. The second used an expository method to teach the same formula. Our discussion turns now to a comparison of the two strategies.

A Comparison

In examining Jane Morton's and Carl Hite's lessons, we see that they are similar in several ways:

1. The goal was nearly the same for each. The scope of Jane's lesson was slightly greater in that she taught her students both the concept of pi and the formula $C = \pi d$, whereas Carl only taught the formula. Otherwise, the goals were the same.
2. The prerequisite planning for each was the same. Both teachers provided the students with the same materials, and the goal of having them understand the formula for circumference was identical.
3. Both teachers effectively used questioning to interact with their classes, which is critical for increasing student involvement and learning (Good & Brophy, 1997;

Positive examples enhance conceptualization and are important when employing an expository strategy.

Eggen & Kauchak, 1997). Jane prompted Kevin, Kim, and Maria when they were unable to answer, and Carl did the same when Derek had difficulty. In each case the teacher gave students ample time to answer. In doing this both teachers created a climate of support and promoted success through their questioning skills. As a result, the psychological safety and atmosphere conducive to motivation that we discussed in Chapter 6 were present in both lessons.

4. Both lessons were strongly teacher-directed, and both teachers were active in involving students in the learning activity (Good, 1983). Teachers sometimes misinterpret the discovery strategy as being one in which students are put essentially on their own to "discover" relationships among different items of information. This was not at all the case in Jane's lesson. She had a very clear goal in mind, and her lesson was strongly directed toward the goal. Carl was equally clear in his lesson's goal and direction. Both teachers used examples and questioning to guide students during the lesson.

Despite these similarities, the following differences existed in the lessons:

1. Although the objectives and planning for the lessons were essentially the same, the sequence each teacher followed in implementing the activity was reversed. Jane

Morton began by providing the students with examples and information and guided them into deriving the formula (in addition to forming the concept of pi). By contrast, Carl Hite started with the formula and then proceeded to calculations of the examples.

2. To increase involvement Jane used redirection more extensively than did Carl. She also asked a number of divergent questions, whereas Carl's questions were all convergent.

3. Although we can't determine length from written case studies, Jane's use of redirection and divergent questions likely resulted in a longer lesson.

4. Carl's lesson was more narrowly focused on the specific content goals of the lesson. For example, the students in Jane's class also dealt with the concept of radius in their discussion, whereas those in Carl's class did not. Depending on factors such as time and the teacher's own teaching style, these digressions can be either positive or negative.

Based on these comparisons, we see that each of the strategies has its own advantages and disadvantages.

Expository teaching has two primary advantages—time and control. Because the questioning is convergent, expository lessons tend to be more time-efficient, allowing the teacher to cover more content in the amount of time allocated for the topic. Also, for inexperienced teachers who are not yet sure of their skills in leading classroom interaction, the strong content focus is often a source of security. They don't have to cope with channeling students' divergent responses toward the content goal. This control and efficiency can come at a price, however. Teachers using expository methods commonly slide into lecture monologues that are deadly for maintaining student attention and motivation. This need not be the case, as Carl Hite's lesson illustrates, but expository strategies encourage this problem to occur more readily than do guided discovery strategies. Guided discovery strongly promotes student involvement and success and, as a result, helps create the safe emotional environment needed for motivation (Pintrich & Schunk, 1996).

Guided discovery also affords more opportunity for acquiring incidental information than do expository techniques. We saw an example of this in our comparison of Jane Morton's and Carl Hite's strategies. Jane's students dealt with the concept of radius, whereas Carl's did not. Guided discovery activities, with their emphasis on observation, comparison, and explanation, are also more conducive to the development of thinking skills than are expository strategies. We discuss the topic of developing student thinking in more detail in the last section of this chapter.

On the other hand, enhanced motivation, thinking skills, and incidental learning have their price as well. As noted earlier, guided discovery lessons typically require more time because of the divergent student responses, and teachers who use them often complain that they don't have enough time to "get in" all the content required by their curriculum guides or published lists of objectives.

The biggest problem with guided discovery strategies, however, may be the demands they place on teachers. Teachers using guided discovery must constantly be involved in decision making and thinking on their feet. They must decide when to begin channeling the divergent responses toward the goal, pose the right question at the right time to begin to narrow the responses, prompt when necessary—and do all this while monitoring the students' responses in order to formulate appropriate follow-up questions. Most teachers can learn to become adequate lecturers, but it takes diligence and practice to develop expertise with guided discovery.

Perseverance pays big dividends, however. Our goal in this discussion is to help you develop your expertise with both methods, so that you will have a larger repertoire of strategies, which, in turn, results in increased student interest and achievement (Good, 1983; Rosenshine & Stevens, 1986). Researchers found in analyzing the behavior of superior teachers that one important characteristic they had in common was the ability to vary their teaching methods. This allows teachers to reach students with different learning styles more effectively, and variety alone is stimulating and motivating. We turn now to a detailed description of the planning and implementing phases of each, but before continuing, please complete Exercise 7.1.

EXERCISE 7.1

Read the following teaching anecdotes and determine whether they involve expository (e) or discovery (d) teaching. Then compare your answers to the ones given in the feedback section at the end of the chapter.

_____ 1. Mr. Hames was teaching a lesson on geometry. He began the lesson by passing out protractors and a sheet with a number of triangles on it. Then he said, "Today we're going to study some properties of triangles. Now, I'd like you to measure the angles of the triangles I've given you." After doing this, the class concluded that the sum of the interior angles of a triangle was equal to 180 degrees.

_____ 2. Mr. Jones, a language arts teacher, was trying to get his class to understand how rules govern the pronunciation of our language. He began by writing the words *cold, can't,* and *cut* on the board. He had the students describe, compare, and pronounce the words. He continued by writing *cell, center, city,* and *civil* on the board and repeated the process he had used with the first list. He prompted the students to identify the letter following the *c* in each case and helped them conclude that when a *c* at the beginning of a word is followed by an *e* or *i,* the *c* is pronounced like an *s,* but when it is followed by an *a, o,* or *u,* it is pronounced like a *k.*

_____ 3. Mrs. Smith was teaching a lesson on the concept of *set.* She began the lesson by gathering her kindergartners around on the rug and placing three clothespins in a yarn circle on the floor. Then she said, "This is a set. It's a group of objects that belong together." Then she put other objects in the yarn circle and described how they were also examples of set. At the end of the lesson, the students in the class were asked to make up their own set.

_____ 4. Miss Kirk was trying to teach her reading class to recognize inferences in written materials. She did this by going through a story and identifying a number of statements in it. Then she asked what all these had in common. After the class decided that inferences were ideas in the story that weren't actually stated, Miss Kirk gave them another story and asked them to find inferences.

EXPOSITORY TEACHING

Planning

There are three essential steps involved in planning for expository lessons. The first step is to identify a topic, which is often suggested by textbooks or curriculum guides. The general topic in both Jane Morton's and Carl Hite's lessons was *circles*.

Once the topic is identified, the second step in the planning process is to determine exactly what you want your students to know, understand, or be able to do in reference to the topic. In other words, you specify an objective. For instance, Carl Hite's objective could be stated as follows:

> Given a ruler and four circles with the diameter drawn in, fifth-grade students will calculate the circumference of each without error.

The third step in the planning phase involves the selection or preparation of examples. The selection process is quite simple conceptually, but in practice it can be difficult to accomplish. The simple part is recognizing the traits of a good example. A good example includes the important characteristics if you are teaching a concept; it will illustrate the relationship or connection between concepts if you are teaching a generalization. The hard part involves finding examples that accomplish this task. For some simple concepts, the task is simple. For instance, the concept *quadrilateral* has the characteristics four-sided, plane, and straight lines. See Figure 7.2.

Each of the figures is composed of straight line segments, is a plane figure, and is four-sided. These examples are simple to prepare. On the other hand, finding examples for a concept such as *communism* can be quite difficult. In fact, this concept is rarely illustrated with examples. Instead, it is often only defined, and how well students learn the concept depends upon the quality of the definition. As research has shown, the problem with using only a definition is that a student may memorize the definition without understanding the concept (Tennyson & Cocchiarella, 1986). Regardless of how hard it is to find or prepare examples, they are the key to learning both concepts and generalizations.

In cases where the concept can easily be confused with a closely related concept, both positive and negative examples are necessary (Tennyson & Cocchiarella, 1986). Positive examples tell the learner what the concept is, while negative ones illustrate what the concept is not. For example, if a teacher wants his students to understand the concept *metaphor*, he would include *similes* as negative, or nonexamples.

In selecting positive examples to teach concepts, the essential characteristics can be used as a checklist to compare the adequacy of the examples in conveying a complete and accurate concept. For example, suppose you are teaching the concept *ad-*

Figure 7.2   Examples of the Concept *Quadrilateral*

verb and have determined that the key characteristics of the concept are that it is a word that modifies a verb, an adjective, or another adverb. Examine the following list of positive examples to determine their adequacy:

1. The boy ran quickly across the lawn.
2. The boulder thundered loudly down the mountain.
3. She didn't know the answer to the vaguely phrased question.
4. The shark tugged relentlessly at the thin line.

In the list, there is no example showing an adverb modifying another adverb. Consequently, the concept that students will form from this lesson will be incomplete and inaccurate. By checking examples such as these against a list of essential characteristics, a teacher can avoid these potential pitfalls.

An additional aid in selecting examples is to analyze the concept in terms of coordinate and subordinate concepts. The subordinate concepts can be used to generate positive examples, while the coordinate ones can provide negative examples that can be confused with the positive ones. Presenting these as negative examples helps students understand the difference between these closely connected ideas. Negative examples generated in this manner are much more helpful to the student than other types of negative examples. For example, if a teacher were trying to teach his class the concept of *reptile,* the negative examples of amphibians, mammals, and birds would be much more helpful to the learner than negative examples like car, tree, ball, or boat. These latter examples are so far removed from the concept that they contain few characteristics in common with the concept and consequently provide little valuable information about what the concept is not.

In planning for teaching a generalization, the teacher should also ensure that the examples used accurately illustrate the generalization. This is a slightly more complex process because the examples must illustrate the interaction between concepts in the generalization. For example, if you were a psychology teacher trying to teach the generalization that the amount of time between a behavior and its reinforcement is inversely related to the speed with which that behavior is learned, you would need to provide examples in which behavior was being reinforced with different time lapses and different related results. This could be done with either written anecdotes or live or videotaped examples or data in a chart or table.

In summary, the planning process when teaching abstractions, amounts to identifying a topic, forming an objective, and carefully selecting examples. It is a very logical and analytical task that requires thought and insight.

In Carl Hite's lesson, examples were used as students calculated the circumference and compared their results with a string and yardstick. The use of string and rulers was important in this case because it helped make concrete a relationship that would be quite abstract based on the calculation alone.

In addition to teaching concepts and generalizations, expository lessons can also target facts. When we teach facts it is important that the ideas are linked in a logical, interconnected fashion. For example, if we want students to remember facts connecting the Revolutionary War, the Declaration of Independence, and July 4th, our questioning strategies should help students forge connections between these ideas. In the next section we discuss how to do this in the implementation phase, but before turning to that section complete the exercises that follow.

EXERCISE 7.2

Answer the following questions involving the selection of examples. Then compare your answers to the ones given in the feedback section at the end of the chapter.

1. A health instructor was trying to get his students to understand the generalization that the more strenuous the exercise, the more calories used. To illustrate the generalization, he selected a number of pictures of people playing sports requiring differing degrees of strenuousness. Analyze the quality of his examples.

_____

_____

2. An English teacher was trying to teach that a *verb* is a word that denotes action or a state of being. To illustrate the concept, he selected the following sentences:

A dog came along and chased the cat up the tree.
The man hit the car when it wouldn't start.
The ship caught the breeze and wheeled to port.
She hadn't had a decent meal in ages.

Analyze the quality of the examples.

_____

_____

3. A teacher was trying to teach his class the concept *fruit.* What do the following two sequences suggest about the goals of the lesson or the ability level of the students?

Sequence A	Sequence B
apple	tomato
cherry	avocado
orange	mango
mango	orange
avocado	cherry
tomato	apple

_____

_____

Implementing

In implementing expository lessons the first step is for the teacher to write the abstraction on the chalkboard or display it on an overhead. For example, if a teacher's topic were the law of supply and demand, he might display the statement, "If the supply of a material remains constant, the price will go up as the demand goes up," or if the topic were the concept of acids, he would write, "Acids are compounds that taste sour and release a hydrogen ion into solution." Writing the abstraction on the board or displaying it on an overhead is important because the written or displayed information gives the student something to focus their attention on visually, and it also serves as a point of reference during the development of the lesson.

The next step in implementing an expository lesson depends upon the objectives. If they involve learning factual relationships, then the primary role for the teacher is to make these facts meaningful and connected (Gage & Berliner, 1992). This should be done in an interactive manner, as illustrated in the following dialogue involving a social studies lesson.

> "OK, today we are going to talk about the Declaration of Independence. Who knows what the word declaration means? Kathy?"
>
> "Oh, it means kind of like to tell something, like a declarative sentence."
>
> "Okay, and what were we telling people? Jerry?"
>
> "We were telling people that we wanted to be independent or free."
>
> "And to whom were we primarily interested in telling this? Sue?"
>
> "England."
>
> "Good. What date did we do this? Mary?"
>
> "July 4th. That's why it's called Independence Day."
>
> "And why did we want to be independent? How does this relate to what we talked about yesterday in terms of the taxes?"

A lesson like this, in which students are helped to see not only the meaning of a fact but also its significance in terms of a larger context, is quite different from one in which facts are mentioned in a lecture, to be memorized and repeated on a test.

When teaching concepts in an expository manner, the teacher follows a number of sequential steps based upon the characteristics of the concepts (Eggen & Kauchak, 1996). After defining the concept, the second step is to clarify the terms in the definition and relate the concept to a meaningful superordinate concept. This can be done by asking students to define the terms in their own words or by asking students to cite examples of the terms. The third and perhaps most critical step is to present positive examples that are linked to the definition. Negative examples should also be provided to help students understand what the concept is not. In presenting these examples, the teacher should try to get students to relate these to the essential characteristics listed in the definition. This ensures that the characteristics are meaningful to students and that they are linked to the examples in the students' minds.

After teachers feel that students understand the concepts they're teaching, they can provide additional examples for students to classify. In doing this, they should encourage students to explain their classifications based on the concepts' characteristics. Having students classify examples and defend their answers serves several functions:

- It reinforces the concept.
- It encourages active student participation.
- It helps the teacher assess the students' understanding. If the students can successfully classify examples, the teacher can ask them for their own examples; if not, he can provide some additional ones.

These steps are reflected in the lesson plan in Figure 7.3.

Unit: Types of sentences

Goals Objective: Fifth graders will understand imperative sentences, so when given a list of sentences they will identify all those that are imperative.

Rationale: Students need to understand imperative sentences in order to make their writing accurate and expressive.

Content: Imperative sentences are sentences that give a command or order.

Procedures:
    Present the following outline on the board:

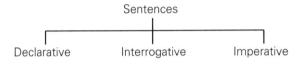

Present a definition of imperative sentences
Present the examples:

        Don't do that!
        Please pick up your clothes.

Identify the characteristics of imperative sentences.
Relate examples to the definition.
Show the examples:

        He didn't want to go.
        Go or else I'll call the police!
        Don't tell me any more lies!

Have the students identify those that are imperative and explain their reasoning.
Ask students for additional examples.

Materials: Outline the types of sentences
        Examples of types of sentences

Evaluation: Have students identify imperative sentences from a list of sentences.

Figure 7.3   Expository Lesson Plan for Imperative Sentences

Now let's see how the plan is implemented in a learning activity.

Kathy Hutchins begins her lesson on imperative sentences by saying:
    "The last few days we've been talking about different kinds of sentences. Yesterday we talked about interrogative sentences, and the day before, we talked about declarative sentences. Today we're going to talk about imperative sentences. When we're all through, you should be able to pick out the imperative sentences from a list of mixed sentences."

Figure 7.4 Diagram of Concept and Subordinate Concepts

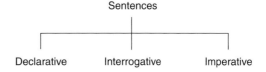

Sentences

Declarative   Interrogative   Imperative

Then she drew the diagram shown in Figure 7.4 on the board:

She continued, "Imperative sentences are a special kind of sentence that gives a command or an order, like these." She wrote the following on the board.

> Don't do that!
> Please pick up your clothes.

"Often the subject of the sentence, you, is understood. In the first example, the word 'you' isn't in the sentence, but we understand that it means, 'Don't you do that.' You can see in both of these examples that someone is telling somebody else to do something. Also, almost always the verb in imperative sentences is in the present tense. Sometimes imperative sentences have exclamation marks in them to show that someone really wants something done. An example of this would be, 'Stop, or I'll shoot!' You would put an exclamation point at the end. Also, the verb is in the present tense, and you is understood."

Then she wrote the following on the board:

> He didn't want to go.
> Go or else I'll call the police!

"Now look at these two sentences and tell me if they are imperative sentences, Jenny."

"I think the second one is, but the first one isn't because the second one gives a command, and the first doesn't."

"Also," added Tom, "the second one is in the present tense, and the first isn't."

"Anything else? Fran?"

"Yes, you can see the subject in the first sentence. It's *he*. But in the second, the subject is understood because we can't see it."

"Excellent."

She wrote one more sentence on the board.

> Don't tell me any more lies!

"How about this sentence? Is it an example of an imperative sentence? Cal?"

"Yes, because it gives a command. Also, the subject is understood, and there's an exclamation point at the end."

"Good. Now who can give me some additional examples of imperative sentences?"

From this example, we see that Kathy closely followed her plan. Note, too, that she made her objective clear at the beginning of the lesson and told students what they should be able to do when the lesson ended. In addition, she made the content organization clear by illustrating the relationship between this new concept and the old ones with a diagram. All of these help to make the logic of the lesson more apparent to students, which should result in better initial learning and better retention. The steps she followed are summarized in Table 7.4.

Because generalizations are so similar to concepts in that they are both abstractions, the steps to follow in teaching them are quite similar to those involved in teaching concepts. The only added dimension involves making sure that the concepts contained in the generalization are understood by students. This should be done at the beginning of the lesson when the generalization is being introduced. The formula $C = \pi d$ is a form of generalization, and Carl Hite clarified the terms within it when he asked Jan what the C meant, then asked Derek what the circumference was, and then continued the process as he had the students identify and describe the diameter and pi.

The steps involved in teaching an abstraction in the form of a generalization are shown in Table 7.5 and illustrated in the following elementary science lesson.

> Mrs. Swenson's class had been studying about sounds and how they are made. In this lesson, she wanted her class to understand factors that influence the pitch of a sound. She prepared for the lessons by gathering together a number of sound-making objects like a bamboo flute, a guitar, and some rubberband instruments.
>
> She began her lesson by saying, "We've been talking about how sound comes from vibrations. Now we're going to learn how to make different kinds of sounds that are high and low. Today we're going to learn that the longer the vibrating column, the lower the pitch; the shorter the vibrating column, the higher the pitch." She wrote this on the board and continued.

Table 7.4   Steps in the Expository Teaching of Concepts

Teacher:	1. Define concept and clarify terms.
	2. Link to superordinate concepts.
	3. Present positive and negative examples.
Students:	1. Classify or explain additional teacher examples as either positive or negative.
	2. Provide additional examples.

Table 7.5   Steps in the Expository Teaching of Generalizations

Teacher:	1. State generalization.
	2. Clarify concepts within generalization.
	3. Present positive and negative examples.
Students:	4. Classify and explain additional teacher examples as either positive or negative.
	5. Provide additional examples.

"When we're through, you should be able to tell me how pitch is affected by the length of the vibrating column and show me how this works with an instrument. Who knows what *pitch* is? (pause) No one? It's how high or low something sounds."

She then illustrated the concept of *pitch* with a pitch pipe, having her students listen to different sounds and identifying these as being high or low in pitch. Once she felt that the students understood this concept, she continued.

"Look at this pitch pipe closely." She showed how it had different holes in it. "These are the openings for the different vibrating columns. The noise is made here and vibrates through these columns. That's what makes different kinds of pitch."

She next took the bamboo flute and showed the class how the different holes affected the length of the vibrating column. As her next illustration of the generalization, she went to the piano and played the same key hard and softly, as well as fast and slowly, and asked the class if the pitch had changed. When they said no, she proceeded to lift up the top of the piano for the class to see. She explained how the hammer hitting the strings caused the sound and explained how strings could also form a vibrating column. Then she asked them to predict which of the strings would make high and low sounds.

As a test to determine whether the class understood the generalization, she brought out a guitar and plucked the strings several times. Then she asked the class what would happen if she held down the strings part of the way down the neck. Some of the class members could answer the question, but others couldn't, so she thought another example might be helpful. She brought out empty soda bottles and had two students in the class blow into them to make sounds. After determining that the class understood what the vibrating column was, she asked them what would happen to the pitch if they put water in the bottles.

Let's pause a second and analyze this lesson in terms of the steps suggested in Table 7.5. The teacher began the lesson by stating the generalization and determining that the students understood the concepts of *pitch* and *vibrating column*. She then illustrated the generalization with a number of positive examples and a negative one. The negative example in this case was hitting the same piano key in different ways so that students could see that this was unrelated to pitch. (In teaching abstractions, positive examples are more useful than negative examples in helping students learn the abstraction, but negative examples still help clarify what the abstraction doesn't include [Tennyson & Cocchiarella, 1986].) The teacher followed the presentation of positive and negative examples with examples in which the students had to make predictions, which essentially involved classifying examples. The lesson ended, however, before the students had an opportunity to suggest additional examples of their own.

This concludes our discussion of expository teaching strategies. Complete the following exercise on expository teaching. We then turn to a discussion of guided discovery.

EXERCISE 7.3

Read the following description of a lesson focusing on the concept of hyperbole and then answer the accompanying questions. Then compare your answers to the ones given in the feedback section at the end of the chapter.

Mr. Kida wanted to teach his English class about figures of speech so that they would be able to understand and appreciate literature better. He began his lesson by saying, "For the last week we've been studying about different figures of speech. Who remembers what figures of speech are? Kristin?"

"They're devices in literature to make the writing more interesting."

"OK, and who remembers some of these that we've discussed? Lorenzo?"

"Simile and metaphor?"

"That's correct, and, Lorenzo, do you remember the difference between the two?"

"Similes compare two things using *like* or *as,* and metaphors compare things but don't use these terms."

"Fine. Well today we're going to learn about a third figure of speech called hyperbole. A hyperbole is a figure of speech that uses vivid, nonliteral exaggeration." With that he wrote the definition on the board and drew the diagram shown in Figure 7.5.

"When we're through with this lesson, you should be able to tell the difference between hyperboles and other figures of speech. Now you all know what figures of speech are, but you may not know what nonliteral means. Let me give you an example to help you."

He then placed the following sentence on an overhead:

I had a ton of homework to do last night.

"This would be an example of a hyperbole because the boy didn't really have a ton of homework to do. That's what we mean by nonliteral. It isn't actually or literally true. Let me give you another example." He added this sentence to the overhead:

When we broke up, I cried for weeks.

"This is another example of a hyperbole because it's an exaggeration that isn't literally true. The person didn't really cry for weeks, but the hyperbole is a colorful way of communicating how broken-hearted the person was. Let's try another one." He wrote on the overhead,

I could talk with her forever.

"This is another hyperbole. Can someone tell me why? Sandy?"

"Because it's a nonliteral exaggeration. The person couldn't really talk with her forever; he just said that for effect."

"Fine, now here's a sentence that isn't a hyperbole." He wrote,

Bill and Jim are going to see Mary.

"Can someone tell me why? Jake?"

"Oh that's easy—because the words mean exactly what they say."

"Good. Now it's your turn. Can anyone give me an example of a hyperbole? Shanda?"

"Hmmm. How about, 'I was so embarrassed I felt like dying'?"

"What do the rest of you think? Is that a hyperbole, Jan?"

"I think so because the person didn't really want to die but just said that to make an effect. And I think I've got one too. Is this a hyperbole? 'If I've told you once, I've told you a million times not to exaggerate!' "

"I think so, Jan, because the person didn't really tell the other person a million times."

Figure 7.5

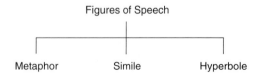

Figures of Speech

Metaphor   Simile   Hyperbole

1. What kind of abstraction was Mr. Kida trying to teach?

   _____

2. How did he organize his content?

   _____

   _____

3. Mr. Kida made one mistake in his lesson. What was it?

   _____

   _____

GUIDED DISCOVERY TEACHING

Planning

Many teachers have the misconception that discovery lessons don't require planning and that teachers only need to turn their students loose to "discover" things about the world. While it is true that children are capable of discovering abstractions about the world on their own, this process is often inefficient and frustrating for students (Weinert & Helmke, 1995). A far more effective way of ensuring that students will learn an abstraction is to explicitly plan for such learning and to provide enough guidance to be sure it takes place. For this reason we have chosen the term guided discovery (DiVesta, 1987).

A comparison of expository and discovery teaching reveals that the planning phases for each are nearly identical. As with expository teaching, planning for discovery strategies also begins with the preparation of an objective. Jane Morton's objective could have been identical to Carl Hite's. A consideration of background is also critical. Considering adjectives again, you can see that a student could not view the sentence "He was a tall boy" and observe any relationship between tall and boy unless he had some idea of the terms *modification* or *description*. Having this background would allow the student, when prompted, to say, "Tall describes boy," or "Tall modifies boy." The selection of examples is all the more important in guided discovery lessons because students must rely solely on the data to form the abstraction being taught. In expository lessons, the teacher can make allowances for the lack of adequate examples by explaining the abstraction more thoroughly (though the dangers of excessive teacher talk have already been discussed). This option is not as viable in guided discovery lessons because the students depend more heavily on the examples than they do in an expository lesson. If the examples are inadequate, learning the abstraction becomes more difficult.

The first question the teacher asks in planning for a guided discovery lesson is, "What illustrations can I provide to help the students understand the concept or generalization?" In either case, this amounts to selecting good examples—ones that have observable characteristics in them for concepts or ones that illustrate an observable relationship in them for generalizations.

For instance, a picture of a cow is much better than the word *cow* for teaching the concept *mammal,* because the characteristics of the concept are more observable in the picture. The same criteria for selecting examples for expository lessons apply to selecting examples for guided discovery lessons. The next step in the planning process is to order the examples you will use in the lesson. Placing obvious examples of an abstraction first will lead to quicker attainment of the abstraction, whereas placing less obvious examples first provides students with more practice in analyzing data and forming hypotheses. The sequence of examples can also be varied to match the difficult level of the task with the ability of the students. A more difficult sequence might be used to challenge brighter students, while an easier one might be used to help less academically talented students.

One final consideration in planning for guided discovery lessons should be mentioned. Because students don't have a definition or generalization written down to focus on, their initial responses will tend to be more divergent than those in expository lessons. Therefore, the lesson may take longer than an expository lesson covering the same material. The extra time is well spent in terms of motivation and the possibilities for incidental learning, but time, nevertheless, is a factor the teacher should consider in planning guided discovery activities.

As a postscript to the planning phase, a comment needs to be made about facts. As we noted earlier, facts are either observed, heard, or read. Thus, there is no discovery method for acquiring them (unless you call observing facts "discovering" them), so we will focus our discussion of the guided discovery method on abstractions.

Implementing

While the planning phase for expository and discovery lessons is virtually the same, the implementation phase is markedly different. In an expository lesson, the abstraction is defined or described for the student, whereas in guided discovery teaching it is not. This doesn't mean, of course, that the teacher is less concerned with the students' acquiring the abstraction. It merely means that students are to construct it themselves using the teacher's guidance.

Let's see how this process is reflected in the lesson plan illustrated in Figure 7.6 and the following case study.

Helen Cane wanted to teach her students a generalization about pronouncing words. To do this, she put the following words on the board:

beat　　boat
meet　　main
beak

She then said, "Class, look at the words on the board and tell me what you see. Henry?"
"They all have four letters."
"Good, anything else? Pam?"
"Some are verbs, and some are nouns, and some are adjectives, like *main.*"

Unit: Rules for pronouncing words

Goals Objective: Third graders will learn the rule "When two vowels are together, the first is long and the second is silent," so when given a list of words, they will pronounce each correctly.

Rationale: Students need to understand rules in order to pronounce words correctly.

Content: When vowels are placed together in words, the first is long (says its name) and the second is silent.

Procedures:

Display the following words on the board:

beat	boat
meet	main
beak	

Have the students describe the words.
Have a student pronounce one of the words.
Ask the student what he or she hears.
Ask if it is a long or short sound.
Prompt the students to notice that the other vowel is silent.
Have the class compare the other words to the first one.
Identify the generalization (rule).
Show the students the following words:

pain
late
meat
man

Ask them which ones follow the rule and why.
Ask them how *boat* would be pronounced if it were spelled b-a-o-t.

MATERIALS: List of words

EVALUATION: Have students pronounce a series of words based on the rule.

Figure 7.6   Guided Discovery Lesson for Word Pronunciation

"They could be all nouns," interjected Geraldo, "because *main* could be a noun like *water main*, and *meet* could be a noun like *track meet*."

"Good observation, Geraldo. Anything else? How about you, Jimmy?"

Jimmy paused.

"Say the word *beat*, Jimmy."

"Beat."

"And what do you notice about the sound?"

Jimmy didn't respond.

"Say it to yourself again and tell me which letters you hear."

"The *b,* the *e,* and *t.*"

"Excellent, Jimmy. And was the sound of *e* long or short, Pam?"

"Long."

"And what other letter is in the word, Will?"

"*a.*"

"What do you notice about the *a,* Stephanie?"

"You don't hear it at all."

"Good, so we say it's . . ."

(Tentatively) "Silent."

"Yes! Super, everyone. Now look at the other words and compare them to *beat.* Mike?"

"They all have two vowels."

"And what about the sound of the vowels, Judy?"

"The first one is long in each case."

"Can anyone describe the pattern we see in all these words? Missy, you have your hand up."

"If you have two vowels together, the first one is long."

"What about the second vowel?"

"Oh, yeah, you don't say it."

"That's correct. It is silent. How about the rest of you? Does what Missy says agree with the words that we have on the board? Do all of you agree? Listen again, and I'll say it, 'When two vowels go together, the first is long and the second is silent.' Is that an accurate generalization, Anne?" Anne nods. "Tell me why, using a word on the board."

"Well, boat. It has a long *o* and a silent *a.*"

"Can you do the same with the last word on the list, Jason?"

"Yes, in that word, the *a* is long and the *i* is silent."

"Excellent, now I'm going to give you some more words to see if they follow the rule." She wrote the following on the board:

pain
late
meat
man

"Some do, like pain, because the *a* is long and the *i* is silent," Janet said.

"Also, late, because the *a* is long and the *e* is silent," Jess added.

"What about man? Antonio?"

"It doesn't fit the rule," Antonio said hesitantly. "It only has one vowel in it."

"Good, Antonio. The rule doesn't apply in this case. Now, give me an example that fits our pattern. Anyone . . . Go ahead, Kathy."

"How about meat?"

"OK. Does Kathy's example fit, Kim?"

"Yes."

"Why do you say so?"

"We hear the sound of a long *e,* and we don't hear the *a* at all." "Excellent, Kim. Now let's look at one more. Suppose that boat were spelled *b-a-o-t.* If we were following this rule, how would we pronounce the word? Ken?"

"I think it would be . . . bate," Ken said, considering his answer.

"Excellent, Ken! Very well thought out."

Helen then reminded the class again of the way *boat* is actually spelled, reviewed the rule, and closed the lesson.

Now let's analyze Helen's lesson in terms of the basic steps in the guided discovery procedure as outlined in Table 7.6. First, we see that she displayed four examples of the generalization she was trying to teach. By doing so she actually departed slightly from the procedure as described, but sometimes alternate procedures are equally effective. All the strategies discussed in this chapter are designed to be flexible and allow for the teacher's judgment and preference.

Questioning skills are an integral part of guided discovery lessons, as we saw with Helen. She began by asking her students to describe the examples—a form of open-ended question. She redirected the question to several students to promote involvement and asked for comparisons of the examples. She also did a very good job of prompting when the students didn't identify the pattern in the examples immediately.

Consider also how Helen's questioning strategies were designed to motivate learners by encouraging them to participate in the lesson. Typically, teachers ask questions that have one right answer, and the same bright students are the quickest to answer these questions. This leaves a significant part of the class without the opportunity to participate, and consequently, their interest often wanes. This is a natural reaction. It's not much fun to sit back all the time and watch others get reinforced for giving the right answers. Guided discovery lessons provide opportunities for students to make observations with little fear of being wrong and induce typical nonparticipants to join in the discussion. By asking students to make observations, all of which are correct at that time in the lesson, the teacher allows everyone in the class to participate with minimum danger of failing.

A final comment should be made about Helen's teaching. Note how, at the end of the lesson, she placed the abstraction on the board for the class to see. This is important for several reasons. Most importantly, it provides a concrete record for the class to view. This is crucial because most classes are composed of students of different interests and abilities, and even the best-prepared lesson can leave some students behind. Placing the abstraction on the board or on an overhead allows all students to see it and provides them with the opportunity to relate it to the examples. Writing the abstraction somewhere for all the students to see also provides an alternate channel for learning.

Table 7.6   Steps in Guided Discovery Teaching

Teacher:	1. Present example
Students:	2. Describe example
Teacher:	3. Present additional examples
Students:	4. Describe second example and compare to first example
Teacher:	5. Present additional examples and nonexamples
Students:	6. Compare and contrast examples
Teacher:	7. Prompt students to identify characteristics or relationship
Students:	8. State definition or relationship
Teacher:	9. Ask for additional examples

EXERCISE 7.4 _____

Read the following, which describes a teacher using guided discovery to teach an abstraction, and then answer the questions that follow. Then compare your answers to the ones given in the feedback section at the end of the chapter.

Mrs. Steere, a kindergarten teacher, was trying to teach her students the concept *set equality*. She prepared to do this by gathering together objects from around the room and asking a number of students to come work with her in a small group on the floor. The lesson began with her saying, "Today I've got some things for us to look at and talk about. I'm going to show you some of them, and I want you to tell me what you see."

With that, she brought out two books and two blocks and put them in two separate piles beside each other. Then she said, "Who can tell me what you see?"

"There are two blocks over here."

"One of them is blue."

"The other is red."

"There's the book we read the other day, Mrs. Steere."

"Right, and what else do you see?"

"The other book is about animals."

"And it has a picture of an elephant on the cover."

"And how many books are there altogether? Jamie?"

"Two."

"Good. Now I want you to look at some more things."

She then moved the two groups of objects to the side, placing each group inside a circle of yarn, and brought out three trucks and three spoons, which she placed in two distinct groups. After she did that, she asked the class to tell what they saw.

"All the trucks are red."

"And there are three spoons over there."

"One of the trucks has a wheel missing."

"And how many trucks are there?" Mrs. Steere asked. "Let's count them together—1, 2, 3. Are there more trucks or more spoons, Shelly?"

"They're the same."

Next the teacher brought out six beanbags and six pieces of chalk and asked the class to make more observations. With prompting, the class decided that the numbers in each group were the same. She repeated this procedure with several other equal sets of objects until a student finally noticed that the numbers in the matched sets were always the same. With that, Mrs. Steere introduced the term equal to them. She wrote the symbol on the board and used toothpicks for equal signs to show the students how the matched sets were always equal. Then she mixed up the objects, formed new sets, and asked the students to tell whether the sets were equal or not. Some were, and some weren't. Then she had the students form their own equal sets from the objects in front of them.

1. Identify the following steps in the lesson:

   a. Initial presentation of examples

   _____

   b. Presentation of additional examples

   _____

c. Students classify examples

_____

d. Students provide additional examples

_____

2. Mrs. Steere told them that the term for "the same number" was equal. Is this all right in a discovery lesson? Explain your reasoning.

_____

_____

Guided Discovery: Developing Thinking Skills

The development of student thinking has become a top priority in education (Perkins, 1987; Nickerson, 1988). A complete discussion of the "thinking-skills movement" is beyond the scope of this text, but we will use this section to present an overview of the movement, describe the processes involved, and illustrate how you might encourage your own students to think more critically and analytically.

The renewed interest in teaching thinking is a result of several factors. The obviously desirable goal of teaching students to think is a reaction to the long-standing emphasis on basic skills, and research indicating that recall of factual information is the dominant pattern in schools (Goodlad, 1984). Perhaps most important, however, are the reports of various national reform groups such as the Carnegie Forum Task Force on Teaching as a Profession and the Holmes Group, concluding that our future society will require a different type of citizen. Our students will need to function effectively in a high-tech, information-oriented society, with emphasis on flexibility, decision making, and the skills of adaptation and lifelong learning. The emphasis on thinking skills in the classroom is derived from these goals.

What are thinking skills, and how can they be taught? They can be classified into three broad categories: (1) essential cognitive processes, such as observing, comparing, inferring, generalizing, hypothesizing, and reasoning inductively and deductively; (2) higher order cognitive processes, such as problem solving, decision making, and critical and creative thinking; and (3) metacognitive processes, or literally, thinking about thinking (Eggen & Kauchak, 1997).

Within the context of your regular classroom activities, you can do much to encourage your students to think. Whenever you ask your students to look for relationships among examples or items of information, explain why a relationship exists, provide you with an additional example, explain why an existing example fits a pattern, or simply observe and describe, you're encouraging their thinking. These processes are developed with the kinds of questions you ask and the teaching strategies you use. As an illustration let's look at a teacher's lesson plan that focuses on thinking. The plan is illustrated in Figure 7.7. Now let's see how a teacher implements this plan in his teaching activity.

Unit: Spelling rules

Goals Objective: Fourth graders will understand the rule for making nouns ending in *y* plural, so when given a series of sentences they will correctly create plural forms of each.

Fourth graders will develop their thinking skills so when given a series of examples, they will identify the best description of the pattern illustrated in the examples.

Rationale: Students must be able to find patterns, form and assess conclusions, and think hypothetically to be prepared for an information-oriented society.

Content: When nouns ending in *y* are made plural, the *y* is replaced with *ies* if the *y* is preceded by a consonant, but only an *s* is added if the *y* is preceded by a vowel.

Finding patterns is identifying similarities in separate items of information. Assessing conclusions is determining the congruence between fact and conclusion. Thinking hypothetically is extrapolating from given information.

Procedures:

Display the following sentences for the students

There is a fly in my soup.
Put a cherry on your ice cream.
Look at the beautiful baby.

Ask the students to search for a pattern in the sentences. Display the following sentences.

Three flies are buzzing around my head.
I love fresh cherries for dessert.
A bunch of babies are in the nursery.

Have the students identify a pattern in the second set and compare the two sets. Display the third and fourth sets.

Gee! He's a good-looking boy.
Don't spill the stuff on your tray.
We had turkey for Thanksgiving.
All the boys in this class are good-looking.
Look, there are trays of food everywhere.
Hey, you turkeys! Don't any of you ever listen?

Have the students describe how the fourth set is different from the second set.
Have them explain why they think the differences exist.
Prompt them to identify the rule relating plurals and spelling.
Have them assess some hypothetical spellings.

Materials: List of sentences

Evaluation: Have students spell a series of words based on the rule. Give the students a unique set of information and have them identify the best conclusion based on the data.

Figure 7.7   Lesson Plan Emphasizing the Teaching of Thinking

Mark West begins his language arts lesson for the day by saying, "Today, we're going to practice being good thinkers. Do you think you can all do it?" he asks with a twinkle in his eye.

"YES!" the students shout in unison.

Mark quickly quiets them down and continues, "I'm going to show you some sentences, and if you're all good thinkers, you should be able to see some things about them
that are similar. Ready? Here goes . . . "

Mark then displayed the following sentences on the overhead.

> There is a fly in my soup.
> Put a cherry on your ice cream.
> Look at the beautiful baby.

"Now, what are some things that they have in common? Gloria?"

". . . They all begin with a capital letter and end with a period," Gloria responded
hesitantly.

"Good," Mark smiled supportively. "And what does that tell us, Kim?"

". . . They're complete sentences."

"Yes! Excellent, Kim. . . . What else do they have in common? Stacy?"

". . . They all have nouns in them," Stacy answered after studying the sentences
carefully.

"Very good," Mark nodded. "What are some of the nouns? Carl?"

". . . Fly, soup, cherry, ice cream."

"Any others, Rolan?"

". . . Baby."

"Those are excellent observations everyone. Now let's look at these," and Mark
then displayed the following sentences on the overhead.

> Three flies are buzzing around my head.
> I love fresh cherries for dessert.
> A bunch of babies are in the nursery.

"Now, what do these sentences have in common? Al?"

". . . They're all plural."

"Good. What do you see in the sentences that tells you that?"

". . . Well, it says 'three' in the first sentence, and it says 'bunch' in the third sentence."

"What else? Robin?"

". . . It says 'flies,' 'cherries,' and 'babies' in the sentences."

"Excellent observation, Robin. Now look carefully. What do the three nouns have
in common in our first set of sentences? Shawn?"

". . . They all end in *y.*"

"Excellent!" Mark exclaimed. "That's great thinking. Now, keep those thoughts in
mind, and I'm going to show you two more sets of sentences."

Mark then displayed the following on the overhead.

> Gee! He's a good looking boy.
> Don't spill the stuff on your tray.
> We had turkey for Thanksgiving.
> All the boys in this class are good looking.
> Look, there are trays of food everywhere.
> Hey you turkeys! Don't any of you ever listen?

"OK," Mark challenged. "Look very carefully now. What's alike and different about these compared to our first two sets?

. . . Mary?"

"There are plurals in the fourth set too?"

"Excellent! How are they different? . . . Steve?"

"Hmmm. . . ."

"How are the endings of the plural words different?"

". . . There is no *ies* at the end."

"Super, Steve! Very observant! Now, why do you suppose that's the case? Tammy?

". . . I'm not sure," Tammy responded hesitantly.

"OK, look, what kind of letters come before the y in 'fly,' 'cherry,' and 'baby'?"

"An *l*, an *r*, and a *b*."

"Good, and what kind of letters are they?"

". . . They're consonants."

"Yes! Excellent! And how about 'boy,' 'tray,' and 'turkey'? David?"

"Vowels," David responded quickly with a flash of insight.

"So what made the difference? . . . Kathleen?"

". . . It depends on whether there's a consonant or a vowel in front of the *y*."

"Yes! . . . You really are great thinkers," Mark praised them, raising his fists in Rocky-like triumph.

"Now, let's test ourselves a little. I'm going to make up a word, and you all write the plural for it. Remember this is just a made-up word."

He waited briefly and said, "The word is 'sliy.' "

After a moment he said, "OK, how do we spell it? Terry?"

". . . I think it is 'sliys.' "

"Why do you think so?"

"It has a vowel before the *y*."

"OK, good thinking. Now let's try 'flep.' "

Smiling to himself at the students' puzzled looks, he went on, "What's wrong here?"

"We can't use the rule," Nancy said uncertainly.

"Why not?"

"The word you made up doesn't end in *y*."

"Terrific, Nancy! That's super thinking. Our rule won't work here. It doesn't apply because our word doesn't end in *y*. I thought I had you, but you're getting really smart," he grinned at the class.

Mark gave the students three more examples to make plural. He then summarized the lesson by having the students verbally state the rule for making nouns ending in *y* plural, and he ended his lesson.

Let's look now at Mark West's teaching and see how it compares to other lessons we've examined in this chapter. First, let's examine his planning. We see that much of his planning is similar to the other plans we've seen in this chapter. The primary difference is in emphasis. We see that his plan focused on developing student thinking. This doesn't indicate a reduction in the significance of content; his content objective was as important as it would have been with a more "traditional" approach. Rather, it shows a dual emphasis—the teaching of content together with teaching thinking. This focus is first reflected in his objectives. In addition to his content objective, an objective that focused specifically on thinking was included as well.

Guided discovery strategies promote the student's ability to process information.

Thinking was further emphasized in his interactions with students. Mark not only wanted his students to reach his content objective, but he also placed equal weight on how they got there. He wanted them to practice comparing, inferring, documenting conclusions with evidence, hypothesizing, and generalizing while they were moving toward the content objective. He encouraged this practice when he conducted the lesson with questions such as the following:

". . . What's alike and different about these compared to our first two sets?"
". . . Why do you suppose that's the case?"
". . . What do you see in the sentences that tells you that?"
". . . Let's test ourselves a little. I'm going to make up a word, and you all write the plural for it."

By altering their approach slightly, teachers can significantly increase the emphasis on thinking regardless of the content areas or topics they're teaching. For example, Jane Morton did this in her lesson by giving her students information that allowed them to derive both the value of pi and the formula for the circumference of the circle on their own. At the same time she had them practice thinking skills by asking questions, such as:

"Look at the circles you have on the handout I've given you. What do you notice about them?"
"What patterns do you see there?"

Table 7.7   Questions Promoting Thinking Skills

Question	Skills
1. What do you notice?	Observing
2. How are these alike or different?	Finding patterns
3. Can you give me an example?	Generalizing
4. Why? (Why is this an example? Why does this relationship exist? What told you that? and a host of others)	Inferring/Documenting inferences
5. What would happen if . . . ?	Hypothesizing

". . . we see that the measurements aren't all exact. Why do you suppose that happened?"

"Now think about a formula we could use to find the circumference if we know the diameter."

These questions not only involved the students in the learning activity but also required them to practice observing, comparing, finding patterns, inferring (explaining), and generalizing (identifying a general formula)—all within the framework of inductive reasoning.

In comparing her lesson to Carl Hite's, we see that the content was identical and the goals were very similar. The difference was in their questioning and teaching strategies. With emphasis on certain questions, Jane prompted thinking in her students, and you can do the same thing within the context of virtually any teaching strategy. Questions that encourage the development of thinking skills are listed in Table 7.7.

We see that Jane Morton incorporated several of these questions in her lesson, and because she began her lesson with data and moved toward the general formula, her students were also involved in inductive reasoning. She could easily have asked the students for hypothetical thinking as well by asking a simple question, such as, "Now suppose that the radius were doubled. What would happen to the value of the diameter?" (or, "How would the diameter be affected?") "What would happen to the value of the circumference?" "How would pi be affected?" All these questions encourage hypothetical thinking on the part of the students. Jane could also have had the students engage in problem solving by giving them problems and requiring them to conclude that the solution called for finding the circumference of a circle, selecting the appropriate values, and making the calculations.

Notice, too, that we have discussed the emphasis on thinking within the context of guided discovery. However, there is nothing that prohibits the questions from being used in an expository lesson as well.

We hope this discussion both removes some of the mystery surrounding the notion of teaching thinking skills and illustrates how teachers can readily incorporate practice in thinking into the regular curriculum. Now, complete Exercise 7.5, which is designed to reinforce your understanding of this topic, before turning to the next section which presents discussion strategies.

EXERCISE 7.5

Using Table 7.7 look once more at Helen Cane's lesson and identify at least one question she asked that illustrates each of the question types listed in Table 7.7. Then compare your answers to the ones given in the feedback section at the end of the chapter.

1. _____

2. _____

3. _____

4. _____

5. _____

DISCUSSION STRATEGIES

We have now discussed both expository and guided discovery teaching. We found that they are planned essentially the same way but are implemented in different sequences. As a reference point for our present topic, the key common characteristics they share are that they are both strongly teacher-directed and that they are both designed to teach specific forms of content, such as a particular concept or generalization.

Discussion strategies are quite different. They are less effective than an expository or guided discovery procedure for teaching specific content because they are typically less teacher-directed and more time-consuming. However, other important goals exist in a classroom that go beyond or are different from acquiring specific content. For example, consider the following goals:

1. To become an active listener.
2. To develop paraphrasing skills.
3. To arrive at a consensus.
4. To handle controversy and differences of opinion.
5. To develop leadership skills.
6. To summarize group opinion.
7. To develop self-directed learning skills.
8. To develop analysis, synthesis, and evaluative skills.

Discussion strategies are designed to develop these skills, and you can see from the list that expository or discovery strategy are not as effective for reaching these goals. This marks the first major difference between these strategies and discussion techniques.

A second difference relates to the role of the teacher. In a discussion activity the teacher becomes less a director of learning and more a facilitator. In many ways this role is more difficult because the teacher has less control over the lesson's direction and pace. Nevertheless, the role of the teacher remains critical, for she must ensure the promotion of learning through student interaction and exchange of ideas. This can be accomplished by the teacher carefully initiating, regulating, informing, supporting, and evaluating the group activity. Let's now look at the planning and implementing phases of a discussion strategy.

Planning

While fewer actual materials are required to implement a discussion lesson than are required for either expository or discovery lessons, the thought and planning needed are greater, and ultimately determine the success or failure of discussion activities.

The bottom line in planning and implementing discussion lessons is organization. It is absolutely critical that the activity be carefully organized, or the activity will result in nonlearning at best or disintegrate into chaos at worst. The single biggest problem with discussions is the tendency of students to drift away from the central focus or topic of the lesson. Only careful organization can help prevent this problem.

Five crucial decisions must be made when planning and organizing a discussion activity. First, the teacher carefully considers goals. As noted previously, discussion goals include the acquisition of communication and social skills in addition to content goals.

Second, the teacher must decide if the activity would be best implemented in a large-group, teacher-led discussion or in small-group, student-led activities, which might include such forms as buzz groups, a mock trial, brainstorming, case studies, role-playing, or simulation. This decision relates to the goal. If the primary goal is to develop leadership skills, active listening, or other related interactive skills, small-group activities are more effective. On the other hand, the development of analysis, synthesis, or evaluation skills can probably be facilitated more through teacher-directed discussions.

Third, the teacher must consider the experience and development of the students. Young and/or inexperienced students need structure in the form of very explicit directions, a relatively simple task, and a short time period. As they acquire experience, they can take on more initiative themselves. Our discussion goals should be very developmental in this regard. A teacher hoping for success with the strategy needs a full grading period or more for students to develop the skills for effective discussions. A clear task that requires the students to produce something concrete in a short time period can help considerably with this problem.

Fourth, the discussion should result in a specific product such as a summary, list, series of conclusions, or something concrete that can be shared with the class.

Finally, the teacher should consider the time allotted for the activity. In general, the time allotted should be short. We have all had experiences where we were put into groups and we discussed the given task for a short time and then talked about everything from the weather to our clothes. This tendency to drift away from the task is one of the major problems with small groups.

Before proceeding on, please complete Exercise 7.6.

EXERCISE 7.6

Examine the following goals and determine if they are most appropriately taught through discussion (d) or through some other technique (o) such as the expository or discovery techniques. Then compare your answers to the ones given in the feedback section at the end of the chapter.

_____ 1. An ecology teacher wants his students to know the major causes of air pollution in a typical large city.

_____ 2. A middle school teacher would like input from his students in developing class rules for the year.

_____ 3. A language arts teacher wants his students to be able to summarize briefly the opinions of other students.

_____ 4. A literature teacher wants his students to understand the major characters in Steinbeck's *Tortilla Flat*.

_____ 5. A social studies teacher wants his students to determine the feasibility of nuclear power as an energy source.

Implementing

In implementing discussion strategies, teachers use lesson plans to provide structure and use questioning to guide students during the lesson. Examine the lesson plan in Figure 7.8 and then read the following teacher's implementation of the plan.

Mr. John Williams wanted his students to analyze and evaluate the president's constitutional right to impose a wage and price freeze without congressional approval.

He began the activity by saying, "Today we are going to analyze the president's right to make executive orders without the approval of Congress. I'm going to show you a video, and I want you to identify in the video the two positions taken and at least one item of information that supports each position . . . . Now tell me what you are going to do first, Tom?"

"We're going to identify the two positions on the issue."

"Exactly. Very good. Then, what will you do next, Mary?"

"We will identify one item of information that supports each position."

"Excellent, Mary. I think we're ready to look at the video."

After showing the video Mr. Williams asked, "All right, who can tell me what the two positions are?"

Tony volunteered, "Well, they are really simple. One position was that he had the right to impose the controls, and the other was that he didn't."

"OK," Mr. Williams said with a smile. "Now, give me an item that supports each position."

Jasmine raised her hand.

Unit: The executive branch of government

Goals Objective: American History students will understand the relationship between conclusions and evidence, so when given an issue they will take a position and defend it with evidence.
Students will understand leadership roles, so when placed in a position that requires leadership, they will help the group meets its goals.
Students will understand group consensus, so when given an issue, they will arrive at consensus.

Rationale: The ability to assess conclusions with evidence is important in developing analysis, synthesis, and evaluation skills. Leadership and the ability to arrive at group consensus are important skills in the work force.

Content: The president of the United States can only make executive decisions without the approval of Congress if a national emergency exists. What constitutes a national emergency is controversial and open to debate.

Procedures:
Introduce the issue of the president's right to make executive orders without the approval of Congress.
Show film illustrating the two positions.
Have the class identify the positions in the film and give one item of information that supports each position.
Break students into groups with the following charge:

Take a position on the issue and document it.
Summarize the information to be reported to the class.
Come to group consensus. If consensus is impossible, prepare a minority statement.

Monitor the groups to check their progress toward consensus.
Have the class present their findings.

Materials: Film illustrating the issue of presidential executive orders

Evaluation: Have students turn in papers that include a position, supporting evidence, and summary.

Figure 7.8   Lesson Plan Illustrating a Discussion Strategy

"Jasmine?"
"Inflation was running at a 12 percent annual rate, and some people on fixed incomes were being squeezed terribly. That supports imposing the controls."
"Hasam?"
"Technically, it's unconstitutional unless a national emergency exists. While the inflation is bad, it doesn't fit the standard definition of national emergency."
"Very good, everyone. Now listen carefully. This is what we are going to do. As you walked into class today, you selected a number from one to six. You also see the num-

bers one through six hanging on the walls of the room. When I tell you to move, I want all the people with ones to group themselves under the one, those with twos under the two, and so on. Now look at your numbers. In each group, all but one of you has the number in numeral form, and one has the number written out. The person with the number spelled out will be the group leader. This was done at random, and during the course of the year you'll each be a leader more than once. Leaders, it's your responsibility to appoint a recorder and lead the discussion. Recorders, you must summarize the information and report to the whole class. Each group's task is to take a position on the issues presented in the film, document the position in writing, and orally report your position to the whole class. Take either side of the issue. You must come to a group agreement. If one of you disagrees strongly, you may make a minority statement when reporting to the class."

Mr. Williams then reviewed the task with the class, as he had before showing the film. Finally, he said. "You have 15 minutes, starting now. Begin."

Mr. Williams then moved from group to group and announced the time at 5-minute intervals. At precisely the 15-minute point, he called the class together.

"We didn't have time to finish," Sharon complained.

"We couldn't come to a consensus," Pam said from another group.

"Hmm . . . " Mr. Williams said sympathetically. "Let's discuss both of those problems."

With that he explained why he only gave them 15 minutes and praised them for their diligence in the groups. He also explained that in time they would become more efficient. He then began a large-group discussion on ways of reaching a consensus. Finally, he had each group report their results and said they would analyze the results in greater detail the following day.

Exercise 7.7, which follows, analyzes Mr. Williams's lesson and reinforces your understanding of the content of this section.

EXERCISE 7.7 _____

Consider the lesson illustrated in the scenario you just read and answer the questions that follow. Then compare your answers to the ones given in the feedback section at the end of the chapter.

1. Mr. Williams had four goals that he wanted to develop in the lesson. Identify the four goals.

_____

_____

2. Mr. Williams used both large- and small-group techniques. Identify the portion of his lesson devoted to each.

_____

_____

3. Describe how Mr. Williams took the experience and development of his students into account.

_____

_____

4. What provisions did Mr. Williams make to ensure that the discussion was as effective as possible? There are at least four factors you should identify.

_____

_____

5. Consider our approach as authors. In presenting the description of implementing discussion activities, was our approach essentially expository, or was it more inclined toward discovery? Explain your answer, making reference to the text description.

_____

_____

INQUIRY TEACHING

An Overview

In earlier sections of this chapter we discussed guided discovery, expository, and discussion strategies and expanded our discussion of guided discovery by showing how it can be used to help students practice thinking skills. In this section we want to expand our discussion of teaching strategies by describing inquiry and how it relates to higher-order thinking through problem solving.

Inquiry is a process for answering questions and solving problems based on the logical examination of facts and observations. Inquiry strategies use these processes to teach content and to help students think analytically. Inquiry teaching begins by providing students with content-related problems that serve as the focus for the class's research activities. In working with a problem, students generate hypotheses or tentative solutions to the problem, gather data relevant to these hypotheses, and evaluate these data to arrive at a conclusion. In working in inquiry lessons, students learn not only content associated with the problem but also strategies for solving problems in the future. The planning steps for an inquiry lesson are listed under procedures in Figure 7.9 and illustrated in the classroom case study that follows.

Ms. Schmidt, a middle school teacher, was doing a unit on media and their effect on American life. During the course of the unit, her class had learned about the history of different media forms in America—the long life of the newspaper, the invention of the radio and its growth, and finally, the recent impact of television on our lives. As they investigated each of these topics, the role of advertising in each of these media was discussed. From students' comments about advertising, she realized that they didn't really understand how advertising functioned in the field of media. Therefore, she decided to have her students gather some information about this topic. She began the activity by saying, "We've mentioned advertising a number of times in our discussion of media. What are some of the things we've found out? Jack?"

"Well, advertising helps manufacturers tell people about their products."

"Also, it helps to pay for the cost of some media, like newspapers and magazines," Chadra remarked. "We don't have to pay as much for them because they have advertising in them."

"And TV and radio are almost totally paid for by advertising," added Jewel.

Unit: The effect of media on American life

Goals Objective: Middle school English students will understand the effect of the media on American life, so when given a question about television advertising, they will identify the relationship between programming and types of advertising.

Students will understand the inquiry process, so when given a hypothesis and data, they will identify which items support and which items detract from the hypothesis.

Rationale: Understanding the impact of advertising on consumer spending habits will help students make better purchasing decisions. Understanding the inquiry process will help students learn to make decisions based on evidence instead of emotion.

Content: Television advertising tends to be aimed at the group most likely to watch the type of programming being presented.

The inquiry process involves forming hypotheses to answer a question or solve a problem, gathering data, and using the data to assess the validity of the hypotheses.

Procedures:

Introduce questions about how often TV ads occur and what kinds of products are most often advertised.

Have the students form hypotheses that answer the questions.

Break the class into groups and have them gather data that will be used to assess the hypotheses.

Have the groups chart and display their data.

Have the students discuss the data and assess the hypotheses.

Generalize on the basis of the hypotheses and data.

Materials: TV commercials (students watch at home)

Evaluation: Give students a hypothetical sample of TV programming. Have them predict the type of advertising they are most likely to see. Give the students a hypothesis and data. Have them identify which items of data support the hypothesis and which items detract from the hypothesis.

Figure 7.9   Lesson Plan Illustrating an Inquiry Strategy

"Good, now I'd like for us to take a closer look at TV advertising and see if we can understand how it works. But first let's see how much we already know about TV commercials. Shanene?"

"Well, they're too long, and there are too many of them."

"Okay, anyone else? . . . No one, hmmm. Well, let's see if we can ask some questions that would help us find out more about TV advertising. Pretend that there is a man here from the network to answer questions. What kinds of questions might you ask him? Let's break up into our small groups and see if we can make a list of questions."

After a period of time, the groups came back together again to share their ideas. As they did this, they found that the following two questions commonly came up: How often do TV commercials occur, and What kinds of products are advertised most?

When Ms. Schmidt asked the class to form hypotheses about the answers to these questions, a heated debate arose. Some people thought that commercials came on every 5 minutes, whereas others thought they came on every 15 minutes. Also, the members of the class disagreed about the major products advertised on TV. Some said they were toys, others said beer and cars, and still others claimed they were food and detergents. To settle these arguments, Ms. Schmidt said, "A lot of you have different ideas about the answers to these questions. Let's write them on the board and call them hypotheses, and then let's try to gather some information to see which of these are correct."

Hypotheses

    1. Commercials occur every a) five minutes or b) fifteen minutes.
    2. The most commonly advertised products are
        a. toys
        b. beer
        c. cars
        d. food
        e. detergents

Then she added, "Well, at least we found that we don't all agree about the answers to some of these questions. Now how can we go about finding which of these hypotheses are correct? Any ideas?"

Some members of the class suggested that someone write to the stations for the answers. Others suggested that perhaps the answers could be found in magazines or books, while others suggested finding the answers by actually watching TV. After some discussion, they decided to break into teams to gather data by actually watching TV. In organizing for this, the class decided that each team would watch at different times and different stations. They agreed to use clocks to time the commercials and to write down what they found in notebooks to share with the class. After a week, they brought their information back to class, and Ms. Schmidt helped them to organize the information into a chart, a part of which is shown in Table 7.8.

Ms. Schmidt began the discussion by saying, "Look at the first three columns of the chart and tell me what you see. Tony?"

"Well, on the same channel there are different kinds of programs during the day."

"Anything else? Terry?"

"And there are different kinds of commercials during the day, too."

"Good, and why do you think there are different kinds of programs on at different times of the day? Josh?"

"Because different people like to watch different things."

"Anyone else? Cassie?"

"Also because people watch TV at different times. Like the only time my Dad gets to watch TV is at night and on weekends."

"And so what does the information we gathered tell us about our third hypothesis? What is the most commonly advertised product? Jim?"

"Well, it depends on when you watch. If it's during the day, the products are for kids and mothers, but at night they're for the whole family and for dads."

The class then continued to analyze the data they had collected, using the hypotheses they had formed to guide their discussion.

Let's pause now to see how this lesson was an example of inquiry.

An inquiry lesson consists of four parts. In the first, the teacher presents the class with a problem. Ms. Schmidt initiated this phase by asking the students how advertising functioned in the media.

Table 7.8   TV-Viewing Chart

Time of Day	Type of Program	Product Advertised	Length of Commercials	Intervals of Commercials
early morning	cartoons	cereal toys	20 sec. 30 sec. 45 sec.	10 min. 10 min.
midday	serials talk shows	detergents food household goods	20 sec. 30 sec. 45 sec.	10 min. 8 min.
evening	sit-coms specials movies	snacks beer cars	25 sec. 35 sec. 45 sec.	15 min. 12 min.
weekend afternoon	sports	beer cars	25 sec. 35 sec. 45 sec.	15 min. 12 min.

Table 7.9   Steps in Inquiry Lessons

Students: (with teacher guidance)

1. Identify problem
2. Form hypotheses
3. Gather data
4. Analyze data and form conclusion

Hypotheses are formed in the second phase of the activity. In a global sense, hypotheses are tentative notions about the way the world operates; in the classroom, they are tentative answers to the questions or solutions to the problems presented in the first phase of the inquiry activity.

In the third phase, data are gathered, which are used to assess the validity of the hypotheses. Ms. Schmidt's students gathered data by watching TV and noting the length and kind of commercials that occurred.

In the final phases of an inquiry activity, hypotheses are then analyzed using the data. In Ms. Schmidt's class, this phase began when the students' data were displayed and Ms. Schmidt asked them to look for patterns in the data. As the discussion continued, she guided the students' analysis of the hypotheses with questions such as, "And what does the information we gathered tell us about our third hypothesis?" These steps are summarized in Table 7.9.

The inquiry strategy can be a valuable tool in a beginning teacher's repertoire for several reasons. One is that it provides the teacher with a means of teaching students problem-solving skills. By seeing how problems are solved in the classroom, they are provided with a model to follow in solving problems in other areas of their lives. In addition, the stages in the inquiry model provide students with practice in information gathering and analysis, skills with wide application in other facets of life. Inquiry is an excellent means for helping students practice the higher order thinking skills we discussed earlier in the chapter. A third reason for using inquiry strategies is that they provide alternate means of teaching content to students who may already be saturated with more teacher-oriented, expository techniques. Because students are actively involved in each of the phases, inquiry activities can be a motivating alternative to other approaches.

EXERCISE 7.8

Read the following description of a college instructor using the inquiry approach and then answer the accompanying questions. Compare your answers with the ones given in the feedback section at the end of the chapter.

Mr. Hayes's methods class had been talking about factors that influence the effectiveness of textbooks. He began this new lesson by saying, "Now I'd like to have us take a look at factors that influence the readability of different texts. Let's take a second to think about factors that might influence how easy something is to read. Any ideas? Cal?"

"How about the number of pictures?"

"Okay, that's an idea. Anyone else?"

"Also the kinds of words. Longer words are usually harder to understand than shorter ones," added Leeann.

"And the length of sentences, too. The longer the sentence, the harder it is to understand," Mike contributed.

"Another thing is the number of graphs and charts," offered Cambrey. "These make a book hard to understand."

"Fine," answered Mr. Hayes. "Now does anyone have any suggestions on how we could find whether or not these ideas are correct?"

The class discussed the matter for a while and decided to look at textbooks at different levels in terms of the variables they had mentioned. They selected texts at the first-, fourth-, and eighth-grade levels and compared them to high school and college texts. In comparing them, they counted the average numbers of the following: syllables per word, words per sentence, illustrations per ten pages, and graphs or charts per ten pages. The results of this investigation were then compiled into the chart shown in Table 7.10.

The lesson then continued with Mr. Hayes asking, "What do the data tell us about our hypothesis linking grade level and number of syllables per word, Don?"

Table 7.10   Information on Texts

Level	Syllables	Words	Illustrations	Charts or Graphs
First Grade	1.2	6.2	6.0	0.0
Fourth Grade	1.3	8.4	5.1	0.0
Eighth Grade	1.4	12.8	4.4	2.1
High School	1.6	15.0	3.1	2.4
College	1.7	17.0	2.0	2.5

"It was correct because we can see that the number of syllables per word increases with each grade level."

"Okay, and how about the number of words per sentence? Kerry?"

The lesson continued with the class analyzing each of the columns in terms of the hypotheses they had formed.

Identify where the following phases occurred in the anecdote.

1. Problem identification _____

_____

_____

2. Formulation of hypotheses _____

_____

_____

3. Data gathering _____

_____

_____

4. Analysis of data _____

_____

_____

Planning

The first step in planning for inquiry activities is to identify a problem. Essentially this involves examining the content you are teaching and determining if any of these can be taught using a problem-solving approach. This isn't always possible, but when it is, it allows the teacher to teach both content and inquiry skills at the same time.

Often these problem situations arise spontaneously in the course of other lessons. When this happens, the teacher must recognize the opportunity in order to capitalize on them. For example, one of the authors observed an elementary science lesson in which the class was discussing some seeds they had planted weeks earlier. Some of the seeds had sprouted while others hadn't. The class was trying to figure out why. The teacher seized on this situation to initiate an inquiry lesson focusing on what factors cause seeds to germinate. The class then generated hypotheses about these factors (e.g., moisture, warmth, sunlight) and investigated them by germinating seeds under various growing conditions.

In this case, the inquiry lesson followed from a question or a problem that arose naturally in a previous lesson. This is an especially effective way to initiate inquiry lessons for two reasons. One is that students view the lesson as a functional response to a need rather than an artificial topic imposed by the teacher. In addition, students are able to see the utility of the inquiry process in solving problems that they encounter in their environment.

Often however, inquiry lessons do not arise naturally from problems encountered in class. Or, a teacher may have a particular topic that students need to learn. In situations like these, the teacher must recognize opportunities when inquiry activities are beneficial and structure the content appropriately. Inquiry strategies are most appropriate when there is some type of causal relationship involved in the content area. For example, in the science lesson, the inquiry lesson focused on factors that caused or influenced germination. In a similar manner, the lesson on readability focused on factors that influenced or affected readability. When areas of content are addressed in this way, the first phase of the inquiry lesson, identifying a problem, is already satisfied.

The second task in planning for an inquiry lesson is to arrange for data-gathering. Sometimes the materials needed are readily available, as was the case in the lesson on TV commercials. At other times, the teacher must plan ahead to make sure the necessary materials will be available when needed. For example, the instructor in the methods class had to make arrangements for the availability of textbooks at different levels, and the science teacher had to bring pots, seeds, and potting soil to class to allow her students to gather data about germinating seeds. Anticipating these needs ahead of time allows the process of inquiry to proceed with a minimum of wasted time and effort.

Some would argue that this efficiency imposes an artificial smoothness on the inquiry process. These critics contend that a major part of the value of inquiry lessons is to provide students with realistic experiences with problem solving. In other words, students should be given an opportunity to devise their own data-gathering procedures. Providing them with this freedom takes longer, but allows them to see how inquiry works in the real world. To make the problem-solving process too efficient artificially distorts the picture that students get of the inquiry process. Critics who take this position are more interested in the process of inquiry than in the content taught. More content-oriented teachers contend that time constraints limit the amount of time that can be spent in any particular lesson, and that teachers should go ahead and help students by arranging for the data-gathering procedures. This is another educational decision that you as a professional will have to make if you decide to use inquiry strategies.

EXERCISE 7.9

Examine the following topics and determine whether they could be taught using an inquiry approach (i) or whether a discovery or expository approach (d/e) would be more appropriate. Then compare your answers with the ones given in the feedback section at the end of the chapter.

_____ 1. An elementary teacher wants students to know factors that affect plant growth.
_____ 2. A language arts teacher wants students to understand the term *gerund*.
_____ 3. A health teacher wants students to know the relationship between exercising and pulse rate.
_____ 4. A home economics teacher wants students to know the effect volume buying has on the cost per unit.
_____ 5. A social studies teacher wants students to know the difference between capitalism and socialism.

Implementing

As previously described, the first phase of an inquiry lesson involves presenting a problem. The problem provides the focus for the remainder of the lesson as well as giving direction to the next phase of implementation—generating hypotheses. The problem can occur as the result of a situation encountered in a previous lesson or can be initiated by the teacher. When the latter is done, it is sometimes helpful to provide a focusing event that captures the students' attention. For example, the teacher who wanted to teach a lesson on the factors affecting the preservation of food might bring out two apples that had been cut open at the same time, one refrigerated and one not. The teacher would then ask the class to observe the condition of the two and try to explain why this occurred. The focusing event in this lesson provides a natural and tangible starting point for the inquiry lesson.

Similar events could be constructed for other types of inquiry lessons. For example, the teacher in the lesson on television advertising might have turned on a television before the lesson and asked the students to observe the commercials. In a similar manner, the methods instructor might have read two different passages on the same topic, one written at the fourth-grade and the other at the college level. His beginning question might be, "How and why are they the same? How are they different?" In all of the examples, the focusing event provides a concrete experience to which the students can relate. Focusing events can be motivating if they're eye-catching and can be helpful in getting students to see the relevance of the problem to the world around them. However the problem is introduced to the students, though, the formal statement of it should be written on the board or overhead for all to see and consider.

After students have had time to think about the problem, the teacher should encourage them to offer ideas about solutions. Often these hypotheses are produced spontaneously; at other times it is necessary for the teacher to prompt the students to offer them. For example, the teacher who wants his students to focus on factors affecting food spoilage and preservation might ask, "What kinds of things do we do in our kitchens to keep food from spoiling?" or "If you were going on a week-long hike, what kinds of foods would you take?" Answers to these questions help students to identify factors that might be included in hypotheses.

Once hypotheses have been formed, the next task for the class is to gather data to test these hypotheses. The data-gathering process can take place in several ways. It can occur as an in-class group activity or as an individual activity outside of class time. Probably the major factors to be considered here are time and equipment. If classroom time is scarce, or the equipment needed is unavailable in class, then the data-gathering process can be assigned as an out-of-class activity. Having students gather data in their homes can have several advantages. One is that it reinforces the idea that inquiry is not just something that's done in the classroom. Also, having students gather data at home provides an opportunity for parents to become involved in the activity.

The final inquiry phase is data analysis. The major goal of this phase of the activity is to examine the hypotheses, while analyzing the information gathered to determine if they agree. If they don't, hypotheses need to be revised and alternative conclusions offered. In essence, this part of the lesson involves a summing up of the activities of the lesson into conclusions that students can take with them. These conclusions then form the major content outcomes of the lesson. Because of this, these conclusions should be written on the board for all the class to see and write down in their notes.

As mentioned previously, organizing the data in some way facilitates the process of analysis. This can be done by placing the information in charts or by graphing it. The experience of wrestling with data and attempting to come up with an optimal organizational pattern is an educational experience in itself, in addition to its help in facilitating the data analysis. Often students will have had no previous experience with this process and will experience difficulty. The teacher who first tries to involve students in the analysis of data should not get discouraged; this is a skill that can be taught, and the best way of doing it is through the experience itself.

Summary

Chapter 7 has been devoted to a discussion of four different teaching strategies. Each strategy builds on and employs the questioning skills discussed in Chapter 6. All are designed to help the teacher reach specific goals. The first two, expository and guided discovery, are designed to reach the same goals but are sequenced differently and require different skills from both the teacher and students. Guided discovery is typically more motivational for students and is more effective for promoting student thinking skills than is expository. However, expository methods are usually more time-efficient.

Not all goals can be reached with guided discovery or expository methods, however. For goals involving organization skills, group work, interpersonal communication skills and the development of affective goals like open-mindedness and willingness to consider others' opinions, discussion strategies can be effective if they're carefully organized.

Inquiry methods are useful for developing problem-solving abilities in students within the context of the content they're learning. Inquiry problems often arise spontaneously during the course of typical learning activities, and alert and creative teachers can seize on the opportunities to develop inquiry problems as a natural outcome of other activities. When they don't arise spontaneously, they can be planned in advance and implemented using other activities as the context.

Questions for Discussion

1. How does the developmental level of students (i.e., first grade versus high school) influence the value or appropriateness of discovery versus expository strategies?
2. In which content areas are expository strategies more valuable or effective? In which content areas are discovery lessons more valuable or effective?
3. In which type of strategy—expository or discovery—are examples more important? Why?

4. How are discovery and inquiry strategies similar? Different?
5. What are the advantages and disadvantages of whole-class discussions? Small group discussions?
6. Can discussions be used effectively with lower elementary students? Why or why not?

Suggestions for Field Experience

1. Observe a teacher implementing an expository lesson.
   a. Outline the major points in the lesson.
   b. What was the teacher's primary content focus?
   c. How specifically did the teacher illustrate abstract ideas?
   d. How did the teacher involve students in the lesson?
   e. What suggestions do you have to improve the lesson?
2. Observe a teacher implementing a discovery lesson.
   a. Outline the major points in the lesson.
   b. What was the teacher's primary content focus?
   c. How specifically did the teacher illustrate abstract ideas?
   d. How did the teacher involve students in the lesson?
   e. What suggestions do you have to improve the lesson?
3. Design a lesson plan (see Chapter 4) for an expository or discovery lesson.
   a. Clearly identify your content focus.
   b. Clearly identify the examples you used to illustrate the abstraction.
   c. What questions did you use to involve students in the lesson?
4. Teach the lesson in Activity #3 and afterwards answer the following questions.
   a. Was your introduction clear and did it draw students into the lesson?
   b. Were your examples effective and adequate in number?
   c. Were students actively involved in the lesson?
   d. Did students achieve your lesson goal? How do you know?
   e. How would you change your lesson to make it more effective?
5. Examine a textbook or curriculum guide and identify several possible topics for a discussion lesson.
   a. What do these topics have in common?
   b. What kinds of background knowledge would students need to participate in the lesson?
   c. What kinds of questions would you use to: (i) begin the lesson, (ii) keep the discussion rolling, and (iii) wrap up the lesson.
   If possible, teach and critique the lesson.
6. Design a lesson plan for a discovery lesson. How in the lesson will you initiate the following phases:
   a. Problem presentation
   b. Hypothesis
   c. Data gathering
   d. Analysis of data?
   If possible, teach and critique the lesson.

Exercise Feedback

EXERCISE 7.1

1. (d) Discovery. The lesson began with the students gathering and analyzing data and forming the abstraction that the sum of the interior angles of a triangle is 180 degrees.
2. (d) Discovery. The sequence of the lesson was from examples to abstractions, and the class formed the abstraction themselves rather than having the teacher state it.
3. (e) Expository. The lesson began with the teacher defining the concept set and illustrating the concept with examples.
4. (d) Discovery. Students were provided with examples of inferences and then formed their own definition. Miss Kirk then reinforced the concept by having the class locate additional examples.

EXERCISE 7.2

1. The problem with the examples is that they don't show the interaction of the concepts in the generalization. The generalization links the concepts of strenuousness and calories. To illustrate this, the instructor would need to supplement the pictures with information about the calories burned in a given time period in each of the sports.
2. The examples used to illustrate this concept are inadequate because they only relate to one of the two kinds of verbs, action verbs. In addition, all of these verbs were in the past tense, thus giving students the impression that all verbs have to be in the past tense. These would need to be supplemented with additional examples like the following to give students a complete picture of the concept.

   The team was first on the floor.
   I am not going to be late again.

3. These two sequences of examples differ in terms of the order of difficulty or familiarity of examples. Because the initial examples used in sequence A are more familiar than the initial examples of sequence B, the goal would be attained more quickly using sequence A. Therefore, a teacher who wanted to teach this concept as quickly as possible or who wanted a more easily understood sequence for a given group of students would use sequence A.

EXERCISE 7.3

1. Mr. Kida was attempting to teach the concept *hyperbole*. He did this in an expository manner by first defining the concept and then illustrating it with examples.
2. He organized the content by linking the new concept to the superordinate concept of *figures of speech*. This told the class how hyperboles were similar to metaphors and similes.
3. In the lesson, Mr. Kida failed to let the students classify his examples. This wasn't a major mistake because he still had students explain his own classifications and also had students provide their own examples of the concept. However, by not having them classify his examples, he missed an additional opportunity to gather data about the students' knowledge of the concept.

EXERCISE 7.4

1. a. The teacher began the lesson by presenting the matched sets of blocks and books and asking the group to make observations.
   b. Additional examples were provided when she brought out the trucks and the spoons and then the other objects.
   c. The students classified the examples when they told the teacher whether the sets were equal or not.
   d. The students provided their own examples when they constructed equal sets of their own.
2. In discovery lessons, the responsibility for forming the abstraction is placed on the students. Mrs. Steere did this in her lesson when she had them come up with the idea that all the matched groups were the same in terms of number. This is really the concept of equal. Mrs. Steere was correct in providing the symbol and name for the concept since the students had already acquired the idea. No amount of prompting would have gotten them to arrive at the symbol or concept name if they hadn't already known it. It should be emphasized that what students discover in a discovery lesson is the meaning of the abstraction, not the symbol or word for it.

EXERCISE 7.5

The following questions illustrate the types specified in Table 7.7.

Observing	"Class, look at the words on the board and tell me what you see."
Finding patterns	"Now look at the other words and compare them to *beat*." "Can anyone describe the pattern we see in all these words?" (Notice in response to this question that Missy said, "If you have two vowels together, the first one is long." She *generalized* in making this response.)
Generalizing	"Now give me an example that fits our pattern."
Inferring/Documenting inferences	"Why do you say so?"
Hypothesizing	"Suppose that *boat* were spelled b-a-o-t. If we were following this rule, how would we pronounce the word?"

EXERCISE 7.6

1. This topic involves the transmission of information and would be best taught by a discovery or expository procedure. A next step for this topic could be to have students develop a plan to solve these problems.
2. Here is an example of discussion groups being used to elicit student input on classroom management rules, a topic discussed further in Chapter 9.
3. This is a goal that could be implemented in a large-group discussion activity. Large-group discussion would be preferable because it would allow the teacher to give immediate feedback to each student and other students could learn from the feedback as well. In a small-group activity the teacher would have difficulty determining to what extent the summary was accurate.

4. This goal involves sharing information and different perspectives about the characteristics and would be an excellent discussion topic.
5. This would be an excellent discussion topic.

EXERCISE 7.7

1. Mr. Williams's goals were for his students:
   a. to take and support a position with evidence
   b. to develop leadership skills
   c. to develop summarizing and speaking skills
   d. to develop strategies for arriving at a group consensus
   His first goal was stated explicitly, and the other three were more implicit.
2. Mr. Williams used a large-group activity initially when he showed the film and asked for one item of information that supported each position. He also used a large-group procedure in discussing procedures for moving to a consensus. He planned a further large-group discussion for the following day after the groups reported their respective positions. He used a small-group procedure in having the groups take and document a position. The small groups were also used in developing leadership, recording data, and summarizing information.
3. Because his students were inexperienced, Mr. Smith understood that his students wouldn't be efficient in this activity. He planned for their leadership development when he noted that each would have more than one chance to be a leader. Also, he discussed ways of increasing efficiency and strategies for reaching a consensus. Presumably, he would review all this prior to the next discussion lesson, and gradually the students' skills would increase with each discussion lesson.
4. Mr. Williams's organization and lesson development were excellent.

   First, he helped the students to have the necessary background by showing the film, which provided them with all the information needed to carry on the discussion.

   Second, he gave explicit directions prior to watching the film and reinforced the directions by asking students to repeat them before he turned on the projector. He also gave precise directions for getting into the groups and in identifying the task for each group.

   Third, Mr. Williams gave the class only 15 minutes to complete the activity. It purposely was short, perhaps too short. However, considering the students' developmental level, more time probably would have become inefficient. He knew that the students were inexperienced and planned to help them develop their skills through a series of discussion activities over the course of the year.

   Finally, Mr. Williams required a product. The students had to take their position and support it in writing. These results were then reported to the whole class.
5. We used a form of discovery approach in describing implementation of discussions. We presented an example in scenario form, and the conclusions are essentially described in this feedback. This is the reason we emphasized Exercise 7.7 and particularly its feedback.

EXERCISE 7.8

1. Problem identification occurred at the beginning of the lesson when the teacher asked the class to identify factors that affected the readability of a text.
2. Hypotheses were formulated when the class listed variables that would affect readability.

3. The class gathered data when they analyzed the different texts in terms of the variables listed in the hypotheses.
4. Mr. Hayes helped the class analyze the data by asking questions that required the students to compare the data in the chart to the hypotheses they had formed.

Several additional comments should be made about this lesson. First, note that the teacher identified the problem to be studied rather than having the class do it. This method of identifying the problem occurs when the teacher has a specific topic to be covered. Alternate ways of initiating the inquiry process are discussed in the planning section. Also, note that the teacher in this lesson organized the information that the class collected into a chart, as we have also seen earlier. Organizing data in this manner is not essential in an inquiry lesson but can be helpful when there are large amounts of data to consider. Organization makes the data easier to interpret and analyze in terms of the hypotheses formed earlier.

EXERCISE 7.9

1. (i) Inquiry. The teacher might begin the lesson by asking, "What kinds of things influence how fast a plant grows?" After hypotheses were formed, these could be investigated by growing plants and comparing their growth rates under different conditions.
2. (d/e) Discovery or Expository. Since a gerund is a concept, it would be more effectively taught using a discovery or an expository approach.
3. (i) Inquiry. This topic involves a cause-and-effect relationship. Such a lesson might begin with the teacher asking, "What things affect how fast your heart beats?" The class might then investigate this topic by surveying its members in terms of how much they exercise and then compare their respective pulse rates.
4. (i) Inquiry. The teacher could begin the lesson by asking, "What factors affect the price of a product?" The students could gather data relating to this question by checking the prices of different kinds and quantities of products.
5. (d/e) Discovery or Expository. Since these two terms are concepts, they would be better taught with a discovery or an expository lesson.

Chapter 8

Accommodating Learner Differences: Instructional Strategies

As Juanita Coleman prepared for her first year of teaching she looked over the cumulative folders of her fifth graders. "Whew," she thought, "I've sure got an interesting assortment of kids. They're all over the place on their achievement scores and previous teachers' comments tell me that they're not all A students. I can't wait to meet them and get the year started. I hope they'll like the curriculum I've got planned. With such a diverse group I think I'll use lots of group work. It will not only help build cohesiveness in the class but also let some of the higher achieving students help the others. We'll see how it goes on Monday."

Introduction _____

At one time in our imaginary past, all American children lived in a two-parent, two-child family and attended a traditional American school. In this fictional past, all children who came to our classrooms spoke English, were well-scrubbed and dressed, and were eager to learn.

Some teachers, in fact, have taught as if such a uniform society existed and all instruction was aimed at a homogeneous class. If this simplistic view of America were ever true, recent statistics document that it is no longer.

Students are not all clean and well-fed (Hodgkinson, 1991; Kellog, 1988). According to Hodgkinson and Kellog, one-fourth of all preschool children lived below the poverty level in 1991, the highest percentage in more than 20 years. Fifteen million children are being reared by single mothers whose family income averages $11,400 in 1988 dollars. Twenty percent of America's preschoolers have not been vaccinated against polio. Many of these children are homeless; experts estimate that on any given day between 50,000 and 200,000 children have no place to call home, and 40% of shelter users are families with children.

The family structure has also changed. The traditional two-parent, two-child family now constitutes only 6% of U.S. households. Almost 50% of our students will spend some years being raised by a single parent. Between one-third and one-fourth of our students go home after school to houses devoid of adult supervision. These so-called latch-key kids not only have no one to make them a snack when they come home after school, they often also lack someone to talk to and help them with their homework.

The ethnic composition of our classrooms has also changed. In the nation's 15 largest school systems, minority-enrollment levels range from 70% to 96%. By the year 2010 our school-age population will average almost 39% minority youths, with schools in the following areas exceeding that average: Washington, D.C. (93%), New Mexico (76%), Texas (57%), California (57%), and Florida (53%) (Hodgkinson, 1991).

This increase in the minority-student population brings with it a corresponding increase in the number of languages found in many classrooms. In the Los Angeles School District, for example, more than 81 languages are represented, with as many as 20 different ones found in some classrooms. By 1992, two of every three students in this district will come from a family that speaks a language other than English (Nazario, 1989). Nationwide, the number of students whose primary language is not English is expected to triple during the next 30 years (Pallas, Natriello, & McDill, 1989). This language diversity poses special problems for teachers who use language as a major vehicle to transmit ideas.

The overall picture that emerges is a rapidly changing, diverse student popula-tion that will provide opportunities for learning as well as present challenge for Juanita Coleman and America's teachers. Traditional teaching techniques like the lecture, which assume that students are homogeneous in terms of background, knowledge, motivation, and facility with the English language, will be less effective. Tomorrow's teacher will have to be skilled in a number of teaching strategies that recognize and build upon student diversity.

The purpose of this chapter is to introduce you to a number of teaching strate-gies that not only accommodate but also utilize students' diversity as strengths.

Objectives

After completing your study of Chapter 8, you should be able to:

- Understand the characteristics of an effective cross-disciplinary multicultural ap-proach
- Describe the essential characteristics of effective cooperative-learning activities
- Explain differences between the three major forms of cooperative learning
- Explain the essential components of mastery learning
- Describe the essential elements of inclusion

- Describe different ways that computers can be used to address diversity in the classroom
- Differentiate between various types of learning styles and explain how they influence learning

MULTICULTURAL EDUCATION

The United States has always been a nation of immigrants, but the recognition of the impact of this cultural diversity on schools and schooling is a fairly recent development. During the late 1800s and early 1900s, the concept of the "melting pot" predominated; the cultures that immigrants brought to America were expected to be assimilated into a homogeneous American society. This didn't occur, and educators recognized that this diversity both posed problems and offered the potential for enriching the school curriculum. This recognition has resulted in the concept of multicultural education.

> Ms. Pat Andrews' first-grade classroom reflects the diversity of the neighborhood in which she teaches. Her class of 28 students includes 11 Asian, 7 African American, 6 Hispanic, and 4 Caucasian children. They come from countries as diverse as Vietnam, Cambodia, Guatemala, Puerto Rico, and Mexico.
>
> On the bulletin board is a map of the world with strings connecting the names of students to their or their ancestors' country of origin. Above the blackboard, each child has a photograph with a story of her background and information about her cultural heritage.
>
> Ms. Andrews began the school year by openly discussing the diversity in her classroom. She described her own cultural background and had each student discuss his or her own family. Each member of the class took turns coming to the front of the room to a cardboard booth where they could see the most important person in the world—a mirror image of themselves. To conclude the discussion, Ms. Andrews stressed that despite this diversity, she expected everyone to be the same in one respect—to learn and to grow in her class.
>
> This multicultural approach permeates her curriculum as well. Some of the children attend the school's pull-out English as a Second Language (ESL) program, which is designed to help them gain proficiency in English so they can profit from instruction in the regular classroom. Others attend a two-way maintenance bilingual education program for an hour and a half every morning. In it they learn to read and write in both English and Spanish.
>
> Ms. Andrews tries to reinforce this multicultural approach in the rest of the curriculum as well. In math the whole class has learned to count to 20 in Spanish. In reading she had students dictate a story about their families. The stories were typed and then illustrated by each child. In social studies the class studies families from a different country every week, and Pat arranges to have parents and grandparents come in to share pictures, clothes, music, and even native dishes from their countries. The class learns to sing songs from different countries, and their art projects often focus on art forms unique to students' cultures.

Multicultural education is a multifaceted approach to teaching that has the following goals:

1. Recognition of the strength and value of cultural diversity.
2. Development of human rights and respect for cultural diversity.

3. Legitimation of alternate life choices for people.
4. Social justice and equal opportunity for all.
5. Equitable distribution of power among members of all ethnic groups (Sleeter & Grant, 1987).

These goals extend beyond any one classroom or subject matter and encompass the total school.

This approach to multicultural education developed out of earlier, less comprehensive strategies, one of which, teaching the culturally diverse, focused on helping minority students develop competence in the public culture of the dominant group. Major criticisms of this approach focus on its narrow emphasis on cultural diversity and inadequate exploration of other dimensions of diversity such as values and lifestyle. It also tends to leave the values and practices of the dominant group unexamined.

A second approach—focusing on human relations—also proved unworkable. This approach focused on ways of helping students of different backgrounds communicate, get along with each other, and feel good about themselves. A major problem with this approach is that it encapsulates multicultural education into a class or unit, failing to permeate or influence the whole school environment.

In contrast to these narrower approaches, cross-disciplinary multicultural education attempts to infuse the goals of multicultural education in all aspects of the curriculum (Banks, 1997). Pat Andrews used a cross-disciplinary multicultural approach when she focused on the positive aspects of her students' diversity.

Components of a cross-disciplinary multicultural instructional approach include:

1. The creation of a positive classroom environment in which all students are valued and respected.
2. The communication of positive expectations for learning for all students.
3. The recognition of cultural diversity in students and an active attempt to integrate this diversity into the curriculum.
4. The use of teaching strategies that build upon students' backgrounds and strengths.

Teachers in American classrooms can expect to work in culturally diverse classrooms. Probably the most important response to this diversity is the creation of a classroom environment in which all students are welcomed and in which there are positive expectations that all can learn. The research is clear on the subtle ways that teachers' expectations can directly and indirectly influence learning (Good & Brophy, 1997). Teachers who express their positive expectations for all students at the beginning of the school year and throughout the year give all students equal opportunities to learn and powerfully influence learning for culturally different students.

Effective multicultural teachers also actively recognize cultural diversity and respond to it in their classrooms. The curriculum reflects the fact that students come to class with different needs and interests and opportunities to explore. These are built into the curriculum. Home–school connections are forged through active channels of communication using periodic letters to parents and other caretakers, and these adults are encouraged to come into the classroom and contribute to the class (Epstein, 1990).

Effective multicultural teachers also recognize the importance of students' backgrounds and experiences. As opposed to a compensatory model that views different experiences as a deficit, effective teachers build upon students' interests and needs (Villegas, 1991). Teachers do that when they talk about and even celebrate holidays that are important to their students. Examples include African American Kwanza, Chinese New Year, Mexican Independence Day, the Tet holiday for Vietnamese students, and Ramadan for Muslim students. Discussion of these holidays is not only motivating for students, but it also helps to build valuable school–family connections.

Another way to foster multicultural goals and meet the diverse needs of students is through cooperative learning, which we discuss in the next section.

EXERCISE 8.1

Describe how Pat Andrews' class exemplified the following characteristics of an effective multicultural classroom. Then compare your answers to the ones given in the feedback section at the end of the chapter.

1. Cultural diversity of students valued _____

_____

2. Positive expectations _____

_____

3. Cultural diversity in the curriculum _____

_____

4. Use of students' background knowledge _____

_____

COOPERATIVE LEARNING

Cooperative learning is a generic term for a number of teaching strategies designed to foster group cooperation and interaction among students. These strategies are designed to eliminate the competition found in most classrooms, which tends to produce "winners and losers" and a classroom pecking order and which discourages students from helping one another (Slavin, 1995). Cooperative learning strategies are specifically designed to encourage students to work together and help each other toward common goals, and because of this, they have been found to be successful in fostering positive intergroup attitudes in multicultural classrooms. Let's see how cooperative learning might accomplish these goals in a junior-high classroom.

As Mrs. Harris examined the pretest she had administered at the beginning of her seventh-grade basic math class, she shook her head. Not only were her students ethnically diverse, they were also diverse in terms of their backgrounds in math. Some could do dec-

Cooperative learning promotes positive interactions among students.

imals and fractions while others were struggling with basic math operations like multiplication and division.

To take advantage of this diversity, she divided her students into groups of four, based not only on the pretest scores but also on their ethnic background. In addition to teaching math, she also felt strongly about the need to help her students know and get along with different ethnic groups.

The next day she began class by reviewing the procedures for multidigit multiplication. She knew for some that this would be an easy review, while others would struggle. After her initial presentation, she formed students into teams, gave each group worksheets, and explained how the performance of each team would be determined by the test scores of each member of the team. When some students groaned, she explained that the teams were specially designed for balance and that students would be evaluated on personal improvement and not direct competition with each other.

As the groups worked on their problem sheets, Mrs. Harris circulated around the room, encouraging cooperation, and giving students hints on how to help their teammates learn. At the end of the class period each student took a quiz, which Sasha graded and returned the next day. She incorporated the grades into team scores.

Cooperative learning can be used to accomplish many different but compatible goals. It can be used to teach traditional school goals—basic skills and higher level thinking skills. It also can be an effective strategy to teach cooperative group skills and to help different racial and ethnic groups to learn together. It has also been used to foster acceptance of special education students mainstreamed into the regular classroom (Slavin, 1995).

Whatever the goals of cooperative learning, three essential characteristics undergird all cooperative learning strategies (Slavin, 1995):

- Group goals.
- Individual accountability.
- Equal opportunity for success.

A group goal focuses students' energy on an agreed upon and shared learning task. Group goals motivate students to help each other and gives them a stake in one another's success. In support of this view, researchers found that successful groups had extensive interactions focusing on content, and group goals encouraged students to explain content to their teammates (Deering & Meloth, 1990; Webb, 1988). Group goals also encourage students to ask for and give help. Teachers can promote group goals by setting up reward systems that reward students for the whole groups' performance. The reward for team performance can be anything that is important to students, such as free time, certificates of achievement, or bonus points on their grades.

Individual accountability means that the success of the group is based on the individual learning of each team member. This occurs, for example, when the group reward is based on the average of the individual members' quiz scores. Without individual accountability, the most able students in the group may do all the work, with teammates being ignored or given a "free ride."

Equal opportunity for success means that both high- and low-ability students have an opportunity to contribute to the team and experience success. Ways of accomplishing this include grading on improvement and giving students different assignments. We will present more on this in the next section when we discuss the different forms that cooperative learning can take.

Types of Cooperative Learning

Cooperative learning takes many forms. One of the simplest, peer tutoring, uses students as supplementary instructors in basic-skills areas. The teacher's role is to present material as she normally would; pairs of students then use structured exercises and worksheets with answer sheets to reinforce the new material. Students take turns being the tutor and provide each other with immediate, one-to-one feedback (Miller, Barbetta, & Heron, 1994).

In Student Teams Achievement Division (STAD), which Mrs. Harris used, high- and low-ability students are paired on evenly matched teams of four or five; team scores are based upon the extent to which individuals improve their scores on skills tests (Slavin, 1995). An important feature in STAD is that students are rewarded for team performance, thus encouraging group cooperation.

The steps involved in implementing STAD are

1. Pretest students. This can be an actual pretest or work from previous units.
2. Rank students from top to bottom.
3. Divide students so each team of four has high-, low-, and medium-ability students and that groups are diverse in terms of gender and ethnicity.
4. Present content as you normally would.

5. Distribute prepared worksheets that focus on the content to be learned.
6. Monitor groups for learning progress.
7. Administer individual quizzes to each student.
8. Assign team scores based on individually gained scores.

STAD is one of the most popular cooperative learning strategies because of its wide applicability across most subject matter areas and grades. For a more detailed description of how to implement it in the classroom, see Slavin (1995).

Cooperative learning can also be used to promote higher level learning. Group investigations place students together on teams of three to six to investigate or solve some common problem. Examples here might include a science or social studies experiment, a home economics project, or the construction of a diorama or collage in art. Students are responsible for developing group goals, assigning individual responsibilities, and bringing the project to completion. Cooperation is fostered through common group goals, and grades are assigned to the total project.

In a variation on this idea, the Jigsaw Strategy places students in small groups to investigate a common topic. These are typically broad enough in scope (for example, the country of Mexico in geography, reptiles in science, or diseases in health) that individual members of the team can be assigned subjects within the topic. Individuals are then responsible for researching and learning about their area of specialization and teaching this topic to other members. All students are expected to learn all the information on the topic, and comprehensive quizzes can be used to supplement group reports to measure if this happens. These different forms of cooperative learning are summarized in Figure 8.1.

How do cooperative learning strategies accommodate diversity? They do this in several ways. First they place students on teams where interpersonal interaction and cooperation are rewarded. Second, they provide the teacher with opportunities to fo-

Strategies	Content Goals	Structure
Peer Tutoring	Facts, skills, goals	Drill-&-practice supplement to regular instruction
Student Teams Achievement Diversions	Facts, skills	Heterogeneous team reinforced for team performance
Group Investigation	Group problem solving/inquiry	Heterogeneous, with teams assigned to group projects
Jigsaw	Group investigation of broad topic	Individual team members assigned to facets of large topic

Figure 8.1   Cooperative Learning Strategies.

cus on diversity in composing teams. Finally, they allow students from diverse backgrounds to contribute in unique and individual ways.

This concludes our discussion of cooperative learning strategies. In the next section we discuss mastery learning, another teaching strategy designed to accommodate student diversity.

EXERCISE 8.2

1. Explain how Mrs. Harris applied each of the essential characteristics of cooperative learning in her class (described at the beginning of this section).
   a. Group goals _____

   _____

   b. Individual accountability _____

   _____

   c. Equal opportunity for success _____

   _____

2. Examine the following descriptions of classrooms employing cooperative learning and determine whether they are using STAD, group investigation, or jigsaw. Explain your answer using information from the description.
   a. Connie Evans' junior-high science class was studying ecosystems. To do this she assigned different ecosystems to each group, and each member of the group was responsible for investigating the weather, topography, vegetation, or animal life in one ecosystem. At the end of the unit, each group was responsible for constructing a report on each ecosystem.
   b. Part of Pat Jensen's language arts program was to focus on new vocabulary words. Every Monday she gave each group a list of words and their definitions. Each group was responsible for learning to spell the words, their definitions, and how to use them in sentences. On Fridays she gave a quiz that she returned on Monday with both raw scores and improvement scores.
   c. Sam Walton's basic science class was studying the different systems of the human body. He divided the class into groups and had each group select a system to study and present to the rest of the class. To help them do this, he gave each group key questions about each system to guide their study and their presentation. At the end of the unit, all students in the class were responsible for the key information in all units.

MASTERY LEARNING

One of the most important differences among students is in the time it takes them to master new content (Bloom, 1981). When a new topic is introduced, the brighter ones gallop through the new content leaving slower students behind. Pacing instruction appropriately is a difficult juggling act, made more difficult by the diversity of students in our classes.

Mastery learning is an instructional strategy that allows students to progress at their own pace through a unit of study. Formative quizzes are used to provide feedback about learning progress. When students pass the quizzes, they are allowed to continue; when they don't pass, they are moved into alternate learning activities. Summative exams are used to document final mastery of the content.

Because of its ability to accommodate different learning rates, mastery learning is being used in our nation's schools to accommodate diversity and ensure student success. School systems and individual schools throughout the nation are implementing mastery units of instruction and entire courses of study. An example of system-wide implementation is found in Johnson City, N.Y., and thousands of schools in Chicago, New York, Denver, New Orleans, Jacksonville, San Jose, and other cities are using variations of mastery learning.

A growing interest is also evidenced by the numbers of workshops, institutes, and presentations at local, state, and national conferences that involve mastery learning. One of the reasons for this widespread interest and implementation is the amount of research that continues to support its effectiveness. Block's books in 1971 and 1974, reporting his reviews of literature, were highly supportive. Okey's research, published in the *Journal of Teacher Education* (1977), involved more than 300 students in 26 classes. In every instance in which the teacher followed the mastery plan, the pupils outperformed the nonmastery pupils.

Hyman and Cohen (1979), in *Educational Leadership*, presented 10 conclusions after 15 years of studying the experiences in 3,000 schools with a learning-for-mastery curriculum. Two of their conclusions are that the learning-for-mastery curriculum is consistently more effective than traditional curriculums and that students in mastery-learning environments master more objectives during a given period of time than students in nonmastery environments.

Whiting and Render (1987) investigated the cognitive student learning outcomes of 16 semesters of a mastery-learning approach that involved 2,319 students. The data collected support the hypothesis that mastery learning produces successful learning experiences. Students who were not learning at the 25% achievement level before their exposure to mastery learning increased learning to more than an 80% achievement level.

Perhaps as important as the cognitive gains are the affective benefits that result from mastery learning. Researchers have found that students learning through a mastery approach have better attitudes toward learning, increased feelings of academic competency, and lowered absentee rates than others (Gusky & Pigott, 1988; Kulik & Kulik, 1990). To help you understand how mastery learning accomplishes these impressive results, let's compare it to traditional instruction.

The Traditional Model

In traditional instruction, all students are involved in the same activity at the same time. The teacher begins with a goal and presents information to the entire group. This is most often done in the form of lectures, textbook reading, teacher-led discussions, mediated presentations, drills, seatwork, or combinations of any of these.

After this initial instruction, the teacher administers an examination, referred to in mastery learning as a summative evaluation, in order to measure and evaluate stu-

Figure 8.2   The Traditional Learning Model

dent achievement. The teacher then moves on to the next objective regardless of the results of the examination on the first objective. As shown in Figure 8.2, this cycle of objective—instruction—examination—objective is repeated until the course content or curriculum has been covered.

Implementing Mastery Learning

Mastery learning is an instructional strategy that differs from traditional instruction, but it can be adapted and integrated into the regular classroom. It is an individualized approach that allows students to learn at their own pace. As with traditional teaching, the instructor using the mastery model begins with an objective. She then finds out what students already know through preassessment and adapts instruction. The purposes of preassessment are twofold: (1) to determine if students have the prerequisite skills to enable them to begin the unit of study and (2) to establish whether or not the students have already mastered the unit's objectives. The pretest is critical to mastery learning because it provides the teacher with information that allows her to place each student where they'll profit from instruction.

The mastery-learning teacher is now ready to start primary instruction, which begins the same way as traditional teaching. Lectures, readings, and other materials are offered, and all students are involved in the same activity. Because mastery learning begins with group-based instruction and not individualized programs, it is possible to incorporate it readily into the regular classroom.

In its basic form mastery learning contains the following components:

1. Objectives—specify learning goals.
2. Preassessment—determine student's background and prior knowledge.
3. Primary Instruction—usually group-based and teacher led.
4. Formative Evaluation—nongraded quizzes and exercises designed to provide feedback.
5. Alternative Instruction—additional instruction designed to help students who encounter problems on formatives.
6. Enrichments—learning activities for students who pass formatives early.
7. Summative Evaluation—test or quiz at the end of unit for a grade.

As we can see in Figure 8.3, these components can be easily integrated with regular or traditional instruction. Unlike traditional instruction in which formal testing takes place after group instruction, mastery learning relies heavily upon formative evaluations, sometimes referred to as progress checks or diagnostic tests. These evaluations are issued immediately after the primary instruction for each objective to determine if students are making progress. Because a unit of instruction includes a number of objectives, with subjects broken down into short, well-defined tasks that may be

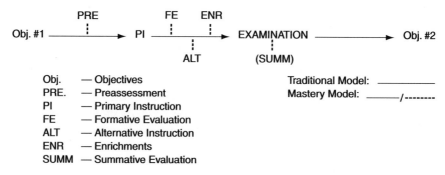

Figure 8.3   The Combined Traditional/Mastery Learning Model

sequential in nature, formative evaluations are used throughout the unit. In this way, problem areas are identified and remediated prior to formal or summative evaluations. These progress checks are not graded, so that the teacher may identify learning difficulties and provide feedback in a nonthreatening way. If the formative evaluation shows the student has mastered the objective at hand, that student might (1) move on to the next objective, (2) become involved in enrichment activities, or (3) formally test out on the objective completed.

If the formative evaluation reveals problem areas, the student is offered alternative activities, sometimes referred to as correctives. These activities allow for self-pacing or additional time and additional learning materials, two critical components of mastery learning. These two features, time and materials, together with preassessments, formatives, and enrichments, set mastery learning apart from traditional teaching and make it a powerful tool to deal with student diversity. Let's see how mastery learning works in a social studies class.

> Mrs. Shirley Heath, a middle school social studies teacher, was beginning a unit on map-reading skills. From working with her sixth-grade class, she knew that their experience with maps varied greatly. Some had worked with them with their parents on trips, and others had almost no contact with them at all.
>
> On the first day of the unit, she administered a pretest to find out where her students were. The next day she began by explaining how the unit would work. The whole class would start out at the same place, but then students could work at their own pace. She shared with the class her objectives for the unit and explained how students would be responsible for taking formative quizzes on their own. For those who needed more work, she had additional workbooks and tapes tied to each objective. For those who finished early, she had enrichment activities ready. The final test would be administered in two weeks for those who were ready.

Dealing with Different Learning Rates

To deal with diversity, mastery learning basically involves three tracks (presented in Figure 8.4): the main track; the alternative, or corrective, track; and the enrichment track.

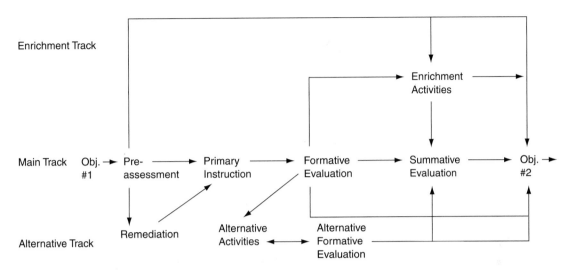

Figure 8.4 The Complete Mastery Learning Model

In the main track, instruction begins with establishing an objective and then pretesting students. For the student to be in the main track, the preassessment will have to establish both that the student has satisfied the prerequisite or entry-behavior skills and that the student is not familiar with the skills or objectives of the unit of instruction.

Immediately after the preassessment, the student encounters the primary instruction, which usually involves lectures, text readings, and various classroom activities or mediated presentations, or both. Once the primary instruction has been completed, the student takes a formative evaluation. At this point, the student would either proceed to the summative evaluation, if one is scheduled for the objective under study, or move on to the next objective. A summative evaluation might not be done then because it is not unusual to offer summatives for more than one objective instead of each one.

After taking the summative evaluation and moving on to the next objective, the student will have completed the main track for that given objective. If it is not possible to send the student to the next unit, the student moves from the main to the enrichment track, which is described later.

In the alternative or corrective track, the student begins with pretesting. If the preassessment data suggest the student does not have the needed prerequisite skills, the first part of the alternative track will be utilized. Here the teacher provides remediated instruction to make it possible for the student to begin the unit of study. If the student satisfies established entry-behavior levels and is not in need of additional information, she will move to primary instruction and on to the formative evaluation.

If the student is not successful in the primary track, she will go into the alternative track, which is designed to extend to students the two critical variables of mastery learning: additional time to master the skill and additional materials to facilitate their learning.

At this point the teacher must deal with two questions:

1. Why was the primary instruction insufficient in meeting the student's needs?
2. What materials or activities can be provided to solve the learning problem?

Considerations include

1. Were the objectives clear to the learner?
2. Did the pretest clearly establish the learner's mastery of the entry-behavior skills?
3. Did the primary instruction offer appropriate practice for the skill under study?
4. Did the primary instruction allow for a sufficient amount of practice?
5. Were feedback mechanisms employed?
6. Were possible motivational factors present or lacking?
7. Were there possible psychological or physiological factors that may have inhibited the student's learning or achievement? (Okey & Ciesla, 1975)

A powerful by-product of mastery learning is the emphasis it places on student success, a critical component of student motivation (Pintrich & Schunk, 1996). By examining instructional procedures with student mastery as the focus, the teacher can use the process of reflection to improve instruction.

When seeking alternative materials or activities, it is important to use other media and technologies as well as written instruction. If reading comprehension is a problem, methods other than books, such as computers, films, tapes, overheads, and models, can help students learn. (We'll find out why in a later section in this chapter on learning styles.) Enlist the aid of librarians, media specialists, curriculum directors and specialists, community sources, and colleagues when searching for resources. Many resources can be obtained at little or no cost.

Once the alternative instruction has been completed, the student undergoes additional formative evaluations and, assuming the learning problem has been solved, proceeds to either a summative evaluation or the next objective.

In the enrichment track, the student begins with pretesting. If preassessment shows the student already can exhibit mastery of objective 1, the student has "tested out" and can choose from the following alternatives found on the enrichment track:

1. Moving on to additional objectives in the unit.
2. Engaging in in-depth studies.
3. Engaging in peer tutoring.

If your classroom situation allows for flexibility regarding pacing, it will not be disruptive for the student to move on. However, if the management of the program is more uniform, which is particularly true if a basic curriculum is being emphasized, options 2 and 3 are best.

In addition to in-depth studies, which are generally undertaken on an independent study or small-group basis, students who have quickly mastered a given objective could be used in peer-tutoring situations. It is very reinforcing for one student to be able to "teach" another student, and there is some evidence that this tutoring also helps tutors extend and deepen their own learning as well (Slavin, 1991).

EXERCISE 8.3_____

Read the description of a teacher implementing mastery learning in the classroom and identify where each of the essential components occurred.

Brent Wilson looked over the recommended curriculum for his kindergarten class. In it he saw the goals "Know basic shapes" and "Know colors." As he thought about these, he decided that his students should be able to identify these verbally and match them with the correct word. The next Monday he began by passing out sheets that had different shapes on them. Students were to color the shapes the correct color and draw a line from the shape to the word. As he circulated around the room, he noted that some could perform the tasks with ease while others struggled.

On Tuesday he gathered the class around him at the front of the room and read a story about a man who had to find different shapes and colors in the forest. After the story he used the felt board to further illustrate the colors in the book. Then he described how there were two learning centers where students could listen to a tape about shapes and colors, and he explained how each student should complete a sheet when they were done.

As students completed these sheets, they handed them in to Brent, who would grade them that night. Students who did the sheet correctly played a game like Candyland in which they used shapes and colors to move from one place on the board to the next. Brent gathered students who were still having problems together at a table in the back of the room and had them cut out different colored shapes and paste them on the board. Two weeks later he had a parent volunteer come in and individually test each child so that he could report to parents which skills were mastered and which needed further work.

1. Objectives _____

   _____

2. Preassessment _____

   _____

3. Primary instruction _____

   _____

4. Formative evaluation _____

   _____

5. Alternative instruction _____

   _____

6. Enrichments _____

   _____

7. Summative evaluation _____

   _____

INCLUSION

Education changed markedly in 1975 with the passage of a law affecting people with disabilities. Now named the Individuals with Disabilities Education Act, the law requires that children with disabilities be provided with free and appropriate education. Let's see how this law changed the way we work with students with disabilities.

> Vicky Harrison was a first-year teacher in a large eastern U.S. city. Her first month had been spent on getting students adjusted to the first grade. Now she was ready to begin what she hoped would be an exciting start on reading and math.
>
> She had parents come in to work with her students on prereading and premath skills. As she analyzed the results, she found that she had some students who could already read while others struggled with even their name. Math was a similar story. Some could count and label groups of objects, while numbers were a mystery to others.
>
> As the school year proceeded, she noticed that three of her students were falling farther and farther behind. She tried extra help, even having them come in after school, but they still weren't learning. Vicky was feeling frustrated.
>
> She talked to her principal who suggested that they ask a special-education teacher and the school psychologist for their help. As the team discussed the three, they decided to involve the parents in the process. In meeting with the parents, it was decided that two of the three children should be tested in both Spanish and English to see if language contributed to the problem. When the results came back, the team sat down with the parents to plan a program of study for each child. For one, this program involved instruction in a pull-out program in both English and Spanish. For the other two, the special-education teacher teamed up with Vicky to help her adapt her instruction to meet the special needs of these students.

In the past, one way to accommodate student diversity was to create special classes. Special-education classes often existed as separate, self-contained classrooms next to regular classrooms. The majority of the students in these special-education classrooms were mildly disabled, needing only minor modifications in instruction to learn successfully (Hardman, Drew, & Egan, 1996).

Research on these separate classrooms revealed that students suffered in two ways. First, they didn't reach their full learning potential, and second, they were failing to learn to live in the "regular world." A third, negative by-product of separate classes was that other students weren't learning how to live with and accept exceptional students.

With enactment of the Individuals with Disabilities Education Act, often called P.L. 94-142, schools set up what is called a "least restrictive learning environment." This concept means that all children have the right to learn in an environment that fosters their academic and social growth to the maximum extent possible. Removal from the regular classroom environment is to occur "only when the nature and severity of the handicap is such that education in regular classes with the use of supplemental aids cannot be achieved satisfactorily" (Sec. 612, [5] [B]). This part of the law integrates or mainstreams students with disabilities into the regular classroom. The rationale for this provision is that students with disabilities' academic performance, self-concept, and peer acceptance all benefit from the contact with regular teachers and students (Hardman et al., 1996).

Initially this process of placing students with disabilities into "regular" class-rooms was called mainstreaming. Over time educators recognized that mainstreaming alone did not meet the total needs of students with disabilities. Out of this came the concept of inclusion. Inclusion is a comprehensive approach to educating students with exceptionalities that advocates a total, systematic, and coordinated web of services. The inclusion movement has three components:

1. Placing students with special needs in a regular school classroom.
2. Creating appropriate support and services to guarantee an adaptive fit.
3. Coordinating general and special-education services.

Inclusion into the regular classroom provides students with disabilities with valuable experiences in dealing with people and problems in the "real world," where they will ultimately live. Perhaps as important, it benefits regular students by providing them with opportunities to learn about exceptional students and develop relationships with them.

Inclusion directly affects the classroom teacher more than any other part of the law. It means, for example, that you will have students with mild disabilities in your classroom and will be asked to work with special educators in the design and imple-mentation of special programs for these students. The exact form that these programs take varies with the nature of the disabilities and the capabilities of the students. The important element here is that each child be considered individually in terms of her needs and capabilities.

In doing this, an essential element is the Individualized Education Program (IEP). An IEP is a comprehensive description of an individualized curriculum de-signed for each student. It must include: (1) a statement of goals, (2) a description of the educational services to be provided in relation to these goals, (3) a specification of when these services will begin and end, and (4) a delineation of the evaluation proce-dures to be used in placement and in the assessment of the program's effectiveness. The construction of each student's IEP is a team process involving a number of par-ticipants including parents, the classroom teacher, a special-education teacher, and the student. A major thrust of the IEP is to specify what special services will be provided to the handicapped children and by whom.

A final provision of P.L. 94-142 is the assurance of due-process procedures for children with disabilities and their parents. Procedural safeguards are required to pro-tect students and their families from decisions and procedures that could negatively af-fect their present education and their futures. These due-process safeguards require that parents be notified in advance of important educational decisions, that they have input into the decision, and that they have an opportunity to be heard if they have grievances. An important part of the due-process provision is the requirement that all services for children with disabilities be reviewed annually. This review evaluates the effectiveness of the present educational procedures and examines whether the student should be placed in a less restrictive environment.

How does this impact the classroom teacher? In all likelihood you will have stu-dents with exceptionalities in your classroom. What this means is that children with ex-ceptionalities who can benefit from regular classroom instruction will spend part or all of their day mainstreamed into your classroom. In addition, students already in your regular classroom who are not successfully functioning because of some learning problem may also be identified as needing special help. Here the classroom teacher's help is essential. These disabilities may range from speech and language disorders to hearing or visual impairments to mild learning and behavioral differences (Heward, 1996).

You will also be asked to alter your curriculum and teaching methods to help meet the needs of these students. Some of these are listed in Table 8.1, while others were introduced to you in the discussion of lesson planning in Chapter 4.

As you can see from Table 8.1, these adaptations reflect basic principles of good teaching for all students; their importance to students with mild disabilities is crucial.

A major help to the teacher in adapting her curriculum to the needs of these students will come from special educators either working in a consulting capacity or as a team-teaching partner in the classroom (Hardman et al., 1996). Before a student with disabilities is mainstreamed into the regular classroom, a multidisciplinary team, consisting of administrators, parents, special educators, counselors, school psychologists, and the teacher, meets to discuss the needs of the individual child. This team's function is first to assess the student's strengths and weaknesses and then to design an IEP that is compatible with these characteristics and able to be administered by the classroom teacher.

The role of the classroom teacher in these meetings begins with explaining conditions in his or her classroom and exploring how these conditions might help or hinder the student's success in the classroom. In addition, if the teacher has already dealt with the student in the classroom, the teacher can be a valuable source of information in the diagnosis of the student's problem. In addition, as the IEP is constructed, the teacher can help to ensure that the demands of the IEP are consistent with classroom practice and realistic in terms of the classroom's resources.

Finally, the teacher has an essential role as implementor of the IEP and evaluator of its effectiveness. As mentioned previously, these plans are reviewed annually to ensure that they are accomplishing the established goals.

Table 8.1 Instructional Modifications for Inclusive Classrooms

Modification	Description
Greater structure and support	Objectives need to be clearly laid out, and instruction adapted to ensure success.
Smaller steps with more redundancy	Break assignments into smaller steps and provide more opportunities for practice.
More frequent feedback	Monitor student progress through frequent assignments and quizzes.
Allow more time for learning	Accommodate different learning rates by allowing students more time to complete quizzes and assignments.
Emphasize success and mastery, not competition	Design assignments and quizzes to promote success. Grade on content mastery, not competition.

EXERCISE 8.4

Read the scenario about Vicky Harrison at the beginning of the section. In this scenario identify where or how the following concepts occurred.

1. Least restrictive learning environment _____

_____

2. Mainstreaming _____

_____

3. Individualized Education Program _____

_____

4. Due process _____

_____

COMPUTERS: TECHNOLOGICAL TOOLS FOR ACCOMMODATING DIVERSITY

Computers hold great promise, not only to improve teaching in general but also to accommodate instruction to meet the diverse needs of different students. The presence of computers in schools has grown considerably in recent years, and their ability to meet the needs of different students is being developed in such diverse areas as basic skills like math and reading and higher level skills like problem solving and inquiry. In this section, we examine the growth of computers in education and analyze how they can be used to meet the needs of all students.

Computer Uses in the Schools

Technology is changing the way we live and the way we learn and teach. Some examples of the dramatic growth of technology in schools include the following:

- Currently, there are about 5.8 million computers in American schools—about one for every nine students.
- Seventy-five percent of public schools have access to some kind of telecommunications.
- Nearly 50% of public schools are linked to the Internet.
- Almost every school in the country has at least one television and videocassette recorder.
- Forty-one percent of teachers have a television in their classroom (*Teachers & Technology*, 1995; Schrum & Fitzgerald, 1996).

The most dramatic area of growth has occurred with computers (Forcier, 1996). Initially computer literacy, or preparing students for life in the age of computers, was the focus of most computer use in the schools. Over time, instructional uses of computers have expanded to include

- Computer-assisted instruction, including drill and practice, tutorials, simulations, and multimedia instruction.
- Computer-managed instruction, including student record keeping, diagnostic and prescriptive testing, and test scoring and analysis.
- Design of instructional materials, including text and graphics.
- Information tools for students, including capabilities for information retrieval, processing, and multimedia learning.

Technology, in general, and computers, in particular, are being viewed as essential parts of instruction to help students develop critical thinking skills (Jonassen, 1996). Today's teachers need to be familiar with these technologies.

Teachers are optimistic about the potential of computers for teaching (Wirthlin Group, 1989). Eighty-two percent of a national survey felt they improved motivation, 86% believed that computers could be used to teach problem solving and other higher level thinking skills, and 64% felt that computer use could help reduce the drop-out rate by stimulating students who were most at risk of dropping out. Let's see how computers can accomplish these goals.

Instructional Use of Computers

Instructional use of computers varies from helping students learn basic facts to teaching them complex thinking strategies. Their value to students at both ends of the learning continuum—mildly handicapped and gifted and talented—comes from their ability to adapt instruction to meet the diverse needs of different students.

> The new Spanish-speaking student sat at the computer for a while and stared at it and then at the observer, who finally gave him a few simple directions in Spanish. He took off and with no more help began mastering the games on Muppetville. While working on "Zoo," it was evident that he didn't know all his numbers by sight. The observer showed him how to find the right number by counting on the screen and keyboard. He did this, got the right answer, and clapped his hands with glee. He really enjoyed his successes. He had the same problem during a different game—he could count and add but not always recognize the numbers. Without assistance, he transferred the same counting strategy he used at the "Zoo" and got the correct answers. Later, he had no trouble using this strategy again. Each time he was correct he clapped and smiled. He was one happy boy by the end of his 1/2 hour, uninterrupted computer use time.
>
> (Drexler, Harvey, & Kell, 1990, p. 9)

Computer-assisted instruction (CAI) is designed to develop automaticity, or spontaneous responses, in basic skill areas (Hasselbring, Goin, & Bransford, 1988). Math research reveals that a major problem facing slower students is an overdependence on finger-counting strategies in the computation of math problems. When students haven't mastered math facts to the point where they can readily retrieve them to solve math problems, they have to expend an inordinate amount of their attention on basic facts, leaving little time or energy for thinking about or solving the problem.

One computer program, called Fast Facts, attacks this problem in several ways (Hasselbring et al., 1988). It begins by pretesting to determine students' entry skills. Building on existing skills, it then introduces new math facts at a pace that ensures high success rates. When students fail to answer or answer incorrectly, the program provides the answer and then retests that fact. To develop automaticity and discourage finger counting, presentation rates are timed. As students become more proficient, their response times are shortened. When Fast Facts was tried with students with mild disabilities, the results were encouraging. Students who used the program outperformed control groups of students with disabilities, performed almost as well as students without any disabilities, and maintained their gains over a four-month summer break.

The key to the success of computer programs like this is that they are individually adaptive, adjusting to students' background knowledge, success rates, and response times. Adaptive programs are an improvement over what some critics call "electronic flashcard machines," which present the same information to all students at the same rate (Carlson & Silverman, 1986). If computers are merely used to replace flash cards, then time, energy, and money are being wasted.

The Apple Learning Series: Early Language software program uses the computer to teach beginning reading and writing skills (Drexler et al., 1990). This program pro-

Computers can be very useful in facilitating the diverse learning needs of students.

vides practice in letter, number, shape, and color recognition, matching upper- and lower-case letters, as well as word-processing skills that allow children to write their own stories. Students are encouraged to play with language in a nonthreatening manner, something that is especially important for limited English-speaking students who are less than confident about their language abilities. Mistakes are less threatening because they're not made in front of a whole class. As one teacher described it,

> The children seem to accept [feedback from the computer] . . . better than the class hearing them make a mistake, or me telling them they've made a mistake. . . . And when they make a mistake, they'll go over it, correct it, and go on (Drexler et al., 1990, p. 10).

This individualized feedback, tailored to each student, is one feature that makes computers so effective in meeting the needs of diverse students.

Computers can also be used to teach problem-solving and higher level thinking skills through the use of simulations. In one program, called Oregon Trail, students attempt to reach Oregon along the trail that pioneers used to travel from Independence, Missouri, to Fort Vancouver, Washington. Students have to budget food and supplies and practice their problem-solving skills through a series of simulated crises like Indian attacks and broken equipment. The goal of reaching Oregon is foremost to students but is incidental to the problem-solving skills and information gained by students as they progress through the program.

Computers have also been used to track students' educational progress. A persistent theme throughout the chapter has been that students learn at different rates and in different ways. A powerful way that computers can be used to improve instruction for students is as a data-gathering and tracking tool. Computers can be used to

- Plan and construct assessment instruments.
- Analyze assessment results.
- Maintain and update on a daily basis evidence of student learning progress (Merrill et al., 1992).

A related use of computers is in the construction and monitoring of IEP plans, discussed in the previous section on inclusion (Bluhm, 1987). Computers can be useful in the initial construction of the plan, in periodic monitoring and recordkeeping, and in writing the final report, which documents progress in meeting the objectives of the IEP.

EXERCISE 8.5

Explain how computers can be used to accomplish the following goals and give an example of each. Then compare your answer to the ones given in the feedback section at the end of the chapter.

1. Teaching basic skills _____

_____

2. Developing thinking skills _____

_____

3. Tracking student progress _____

_____

LEARNING STYLES

Introduction

Unquestionably, individual students come to us with different ways of attacking the tasks of learning and solving problems. Learning styles, also called cognitive styles, are the "preferred ways that different individuals have of processing and organizing information and for responding to environmental stimuli" (Shuell, 1981, p. 46).

> Jan Healy wanted to make science fun for her second graders. So her class spent an hour every Tuesday and Thursday afternoon investigating different topics in learning centers around the room. Some students planted seeds and measured their growth while others worked at the computer on simulations of experiments. Some of the time students worked alone, while other times they worked in groups.
>
> As Jan observed her students over time she noticed definite patterns. Some students always worked alone, while others were always in a group. Some liked to read, while others were happier doing things with their hands; the bigger the mess, the better—giving new meaning to hands-on science. Many were fascinated by the computer, but others avoided it. Jan wondered what these differences meant for her teaching in other areas.

Learning styles are the cognitive, affective, and psychomotor traits that indicate the ways learners perceive, interact with, and respond to the learning environment (Keefe, 1982; Schmeck, 1988). Students with different learning styles interpret and try to solve educational problems in different, relatively stable ways. In this section of the chapter we'll look at some different ways that learning styles have an impact on teaching learning.

The Work of Dunn and Dunn.   One of the most popular approaches to learning styles was developed by Ken and Rita Dunn (1978, 1987). These educators found that students differed in terms of their response to three key dimensions of learning: environment (for example, sound, light, and temperature), physical stimuli (for example, oral versus written), and structure and support (for example, working alone or in groups). Some of these key dimensions are in Table 8.2.

The existence of these different preferences of styles makes intuitive sense. We've all heard people say, "I'm a morning person" or "Don't try to talk to me before ten in the morning." In terms of learning modalities, we've also heard, "I'm a visual person. I need to be able to 'see' it," meaning someone learns most effectively through visual representation of concepts and other ideas. Other people tend to be more auditory, learning best through oral presentations. Some are tactile; they have to "feel" it. Each of these preferences can have powerful influences on learning.

To identify students' different learning styles, these researchers developed the Learning Style Inventory (Dunn, Dunn, & Price, 1985). This inventory asks students to respond to statements such as "I study best when it is quiet" and "I can ignore

Table 8.2   Learning Style Dimensions

Dimension	Learning Style Differences
Environment	
Sound	Is a quiet or noisy environment best for learning?
Light	Do students prefer bright or subdued light?
Temperature	Is a warm or cool room preferred?
Seating	Are individual desks or clusters of desks best for learning?
Physical Stimuli	
Duration	How does attention span influence the optimal length of activity?
Modality	Does the student prefer to read or hear new information?
Activity	Do students learn best when actively involved, or do they prefer more passive roles?
Time	Does the student work best in the morning or afternoon?
Structure/Support	
Motivation	Do students need external rewards, or are they internally motivated?
Monitoring	Do students need constant support and monitoring, or are they independent learners?
Individual/Group	Do students prefer to work alone or in a group?

sound when I study" on a Likert scale (that is, strongly agree, agree sometimes, disagree, strongly disagree). Teachers can develop their own inventories by focusing on the dimensions in Table 8.2 and can use the information to adapt instruction to individual students, groups of students, or whole classes.

Field Dependence/Independence. Field dependence and independence, another learning style dimension, involves students' ability to select relevant from irrelevant information in a complex and potentially confusing background (Witkin, Moore, Goodenough, & Cox, 1977). For example, when encountering word problems, a field-independent person is more likely than a field-dependent individual to extract and use relevant information in solving the problem while ignoring irrelevant information. A field-dependent person, by contrast, would have more difficulty in differentiating between relevant and irrelevant information in the problem.

The same difference occurs in student learning from teacher presentations. Field-independent learners are better at tracking the main idea of a lecture, tying important facts to it, and ignoring others. Field-dependent learners, by contrast, will often get lost in such a presentation, having trouble differentiating the forest for the trees. Correspondingly, the notes of field-dependent students are less organized and contain more irrelevant and extraneous information.

Field dependence/independence is influenced by development (Farr & Moon, 1988). Older and more mature learners are better able to keep track of the learning goal at hand; they are less likely to be distracted by irrelevant information. This suggests that this trait can be at least partially modified by the teacher, an idea we'll return to shortly.

Conceptual Tempo.   Conceptual tempo refers to the rate at which students respond to questions and problems (Kagan, Pearson, & Welch, 1970). Impulsive students rush to blurt out answers, and reflective students analyze and deliberate before answering. Error rates correspond to these differences. Reflective students think more before they answer; impulsive students take more chances and make more mistakes. Impulsive students perform better in speed games in which the target is low-level factual information; reflective students have an advantage when high-level problem solving is the task. In a similar way, impulsive students are more likely to plunge through a reading passage, ignoring inconsistencies or contradictions, while more reflective students go slower and are better at identifying these problems (Walczyk & Hall, 1989).

Left and Right Brains: Hemispheric Research.   Research on the left and right hemispheres of the brain also provides us with some insights into individual differences. The left hemisphere specializes in logical, sequential, analytical, and temporal processing of information; the right hemisphere focuses more on nonverbal, concrete, spatial, emotional, and aesthetic processing (Torrance, 1982). An overwhelming majority of school activities involve linear and verbal or printed instruction, which may be processed by the left hemisphere of the brain; nonverbal information may be a function of the right hemisphere. Printed materials might make learning difficult for students whose right hemisphere is more efficient than the left. A variety of mediated modes of instruction can be used to promote learning for these students.

Implications for Teaching

Unquestionably the students we teach differ in a number of ways. One of these is learning styles or the way they prefer to learn. In considering learning styles, a key question is, "How should teachers respond to this diversity?" or, after reading about all these differences, perhaps we should be asking, "How *can* teachers respond to these differences?"

Two polar positions on this question are equally unreasonable. One position ignores these differences and advocates teaching all students the same way—an ineffective response to diversity. The other position would take all instruction and tailor it to the distinctive needs of each student—an equally ineffective response because of its logistical impossibility.

We suggest several alternative responses. The first is more global and philosophical. Our knowledge of learning styles should serve as a constant reminder of the individuality and uniqueness of each of our students. As we become more sensitive to these individual differences, we can begin to treat each student as an individual human being and not just another face in a class of thirty.

The second implication suggests the need to vary our instruction. We have often heard that teachers who vary the way they teach are more effective than those who instruct the same way all the time. Alternatives such as cooperative learning, mastery learning, and computers provide flexibility in meeting individual learning styles. The importance of instructional variety is supported by research (Rosenshine, 1971). The existence of different learning styles helps us understand why.

A third implication is to help our students understand themselves as learners. By making them aware of how they learn best and their individual strengths and weaknesses, we are setting the stage for future and even life-long learning.

Let's see how this applies to some of the ideas we've been discussing. By making students aware of Dunn and Dunn's environmental, physical, and structure/support variables, we help them find ways to adapt that can help them understand and retain as learners. For example, if they have a big test to study for, should they stay up late at night or get up early the next morning? In a similar way, are they better off studying individually or in a group?

The same kind of self-awareness can be developed in impulsive students. Self-instruction training is one technique that can be used to help students understand the impact of conceptual tempo on their learning (Meichenbaum, 1986). Self-instruction training teaches students to monitor their thinking by talking themselves through a problem solution, such as "Now let's see . . . the problem asks for the distance around the circle. That's the circumference. Now, what's the formula for circumference?" By making students aware of their own thought processes, we reduce their tendency to be impulsive and also improve their general problem-solving skills.

EXERCISE 8.6

Examine the following statements about different types of learners and determine which type of learning style is being referred to: (a) Dunn and Dunn, (b) Field dependence/independence, (c) Conceptual tempo, (d) Left and right hemispheres. Note that in some instances more than one approach to learning style may apply. Then compare your answers to the ones given in the feedback section at the end of the chapter.

_____ 1. He won't check his answers. He just rushes through his assignments to get them done.
_____ 2. She's a real self-starter. I just have to give the assignment and she's off.
_____ 3. He has trouble with math but you ought to see his drawings.
_____ 4. She's good at taking a problem in science and analyzing it.
_____ 5. He's a really bright student but hates to work in groups.
_____ 6. When we're looking at biology slides under the microscope, she has a hard time identifying the structures.
_____ 7. He's a whiz on the computer. We were talking about a problem the other day, and he turned around and wrote a program to solve it.
_____ 8. She's a perfectionist. I have a really hard time getting her to let go of a paper. She wants to make sure it's perfect.

HOWARD GARDNER'S MULTIPLE INTELLIGENCES

Another way to describe differences in the students we teach is in terms of multiple intelligences (Gardner, 1983; Gardner, 1995). The idea behind multiple intelligences makes sense—different people are "smart" in different ways. We've all encountered students who were talented in math but not in speaking or writing or people who had great interpersonal skills but were not as talented in traditional academic subjects.

Howard Gardner has identified at least eight different ways that students differ in terms of intelligence (see Table 8.3). Teachers wanting to help students develop these different aspects of intelligence should

- Create multidimensional classrooms where students can succeed in different ways.
- Provide learning tasks that tap different dimensions of learning.
- Encourage students to express themselves in different modalities.
- Allow students options in demonstrating they have mastered a concept or skill.

As with learning styles, perhaps the most important message teachers should take from Gardner's work is that students are complex, multifaceted individuals who need to be treated with sensitivity and taught through a variety of teaching methods.

Table 8.3 Gardner's Theory of Multiple Intelligences (Adapted from Gardner & Hatch, 1989)

Dimension	Example
Linguistic intelligence	
Sensitivity to the meaning and order of words and the varied uses of language	Poet, journalist
Logical-mathematical intelligence	
The ability to handle long chains of reasoning and to recognize patterns and order in the world.	Scientist, mathematician
Musical intelligence	
Sensitivity to pitch, melody, and tone	Composer, violinist
Spatial intelligence	
The ability to perceive the visual world accurately, and to recreate, transform, or modify aspects of the world based on one's perceptions	Sculptor, navigator
Bodily-kinesthetic intelligence	
A fine-tuned ability to use the body and to handle objects	Dancer, athlete
Interpersonal intelligence	
The ability to notice and make distinctions among others	Therapist, salesman
Intrapersonal intelligence	
Access to one's own "feeling life"	Self-aware individual
Classification of nature intelligence	
Able to identify relationships in nature	Scientist

Summary

Student diversity, always an important dimension of teaching, is becoming increasingly important as the nature of the students in our classrooms changes. This diversity makes teaching not only more challenging but also more rewarding.

To meet these challenges teachers need a variety of instructional strategies designed to accommodate this diversity. Multicultural education attempts to build on student strengths to help students from all cultures achieve at their highest level. Cooperative learning, another teaching strategy, teams students of diverse backgrounds and abilities in learning activities. Mastery learning addresses student diversity by providing students with formative feedback, additional time, and alternate learning activities. Inclusion, a comprehensive approach to meeting the needs of exceptional children, integrates these students into the school and classroom with special assistance. Finally, computers provide an additional way to meet the instructional needs of different students.

In the final sections of the chapter, we looked at the way learning styles and multiple intelligences influence instruction. Learning styles remind us of the individuality of each student and help explain the effectiveness of a variety of instructional strategies. Multiple intelligences help us understand that there are many ways to be "smart" and encourage us to design classrooms where different kinds of intelligence can develop.

Questions for Discussion

1. Is multicultural education more important at some grade levels than in others? Why? Is multicultural education more important in some content areas than in others? Why?
2. For what types of students are cooperative learning strategies most effective? Least? Why?
3. How does the responsibility for learning shift in mastery learning? Is this shift a productive one?
4. Experts debate whether teachers should adjust instruction to match student learning styles or teach students to broaden their learning repertoires. Which approach is more desirable? Why?
5. Is technology more valuable at some grade levels than others? Which levels and why?
6. How does inclusion benefit
   a. students with exceptionalities
   b. regular students
   c. the teacher?
   What possible undesirable side effects might occur with these three populations? What can be done to minimize these side effects?

Suggestions for Field Experience

1. Interview a teacher about the diversity in his or her classroom. How do students differ in terms of
   a. culture
   b. home language

  c. socioeconomic status (SES)
  d. learning styles
  e. multiple intelligences?
  What does the teacher do to accommodate these differences?
2. Observe a classroom and focus on several minority students.
  a. Where do they sit?
  b. Who do they talk to and make friends with?
  c. Do they attend to the class and are they involved?
  d. Do they participate in classroom interaction?
3. Ask the teacher to identify several minority students. Interview these students and ask the following:
  a. How long have they been at this school?
  b. What do they like most about school?
  c. What do they like least about school?
  d. What can teachers do to help them learn better?
4. Observe a teacher using some type of cooperative learning.
  a. How did the teacher prepare students for the activity?
  b. How were students divided into groups?
  c. How did different groups differ in terms of gender and ethnic background?
  d. What activities were students involved in within the groups?
  e. How did the teacher hold students accountable?
  f. How could the lesson have been improved?
5. Interview a teacher regarding the use and availability of computers.
  a. Does each classroom have some or are they clustered in certain rooms?
  b. How many are there in the school?
  c. How modern and up-to-date are they?
  d. How modern and up-to-date are the software that go with them?
  e. How does the teacher use them instructionally?
  f. How does the teacher use them for recordkeeping?
6. Interview a teacher about inclusion.
  a. How many students with exceptionalities are included in the classroom?
  b. How has the teacher adapted instruction to meet the needs of these students?
  c. What assistance does the teacher have in working with these students?
  d. What suggestions does the teacher have to make the process more effective?

Exercise Feedback

EXERCISE 8.1

1. Cultural diversity of students valued. Pat's classroom communicated this both physically and instructionally. Her bulletin boards made a statement about the value of student diversity as did her curriculum, which focused on diversity as a theme.
2. Positive expectations. These were communicated on the first day of class when she said that she expected everyone to learn and grow.
3. Cultural diversity in the curriculum. Pat integrated cultural diversity in the curriculum in math, reading, social studies, art, and music.

4. Use of students' background knowledge. Pat accomplished this when she studied topics that students knew and cared about. Perhaps the best examples were in social studies when she focused on countries that were familiar to her students.

EXERCISE 8.2

1. a. Group goals. Sasha encouraged group goals by making team scores dependent on the performance of all members.
   b. Individual accountability. Students were held individually accountable when she administered a quiz to each student.
   c. Equal opportunity for success. All students could experience success in the unit because improvement points rather than raw scores were used.
2. a. This classroom was using the jigsaw strategy. Individual team members were responsible for individual topics which were then pieced together (like a jigsaw puzzle) into the final report.
   b. Pat Jensen was using STAD in her language arts class. The information to be learned was convergent and the members of each group helped each other learn the information for the quiz on Friday.
   c. This was an example of a group investigation. Each team was responsible for investigating a different topic, but note how the whole group was held accountable for essential information about each system.

EXERCISE 8.3

1. Objectives. Brent formulated objectives when he considered goals and translated these into specific objectives—to identify colors and shapes verbally and match them with the correct word.
2. Preassessment. Pretesting was done with a work sheet in which students colored and labeled shapes.
3. Primary instruction. This occurred when Brent read the class a story and illustrated shapes and colors on the felt board.
4. Formative evaluation. Brent initially evaluated student mastery of these concepts by having them do a worksheet and turn it in for grading.
5. Alternative instruction. Alternative instruction occurred when students cut out and pasted different colored shapes.
6. Enrichment. Students who already mastered the content were allowed to play a board game.
7. Summative evaluation. Brent ensured mastery of each skill by having a volunteer come in to test each student individually.

EXERCISE 8.4

1. Least restrictive environment. This provision of P.L. 94-142 ensures that children with disabilities will be educated in a classroom that is as normal as possible, while still meeting the individual needs of exceptional students.
2. Mainstreaming. This occurs when students are integrated into the regular classroom. This happened when the team decided to keep the two students needing special help in the regular classroom.
3. Individualized Education Program. This is a special program designed to meet the needs of students with disabilities. This program was a jointly constructed plan involving parents, teachers, and special educators.

4. Due process. This is designed to safeguard the rights and responsibilities of parents. This occurred when parents were involved throughout the process of diagnosis and placement.

EXERCISE 8.5

1. Basic skills. Computers can be used to develop basic skills through drill and practice or use of basic skills in adaptive programs. Programs designed to teach basic skills include Fast Facts and Apple Learning Series.
2. Thinking skills. Computers can be used with simulations to teach problem-solving and other higher level thinking skills. An example here is Oregon Trail.
3. Tracking student progress. Computers can be used to track student progress by keeping a running record of student performance. Examples are the work with mainstreamed students and in updating IEPs.

EXERCISE 8.6

1. c. This statement refers to an impulsive student, one dimension of conceptual tempo.
2. a. This refers to Dunn and Dunn's dimension of structure/support.
3. d. Creativity can often be explained by left brain/right brain differences.
4. b. Analytical skills are best described by the concepts of field dependence/independence. Analytical skills are also indirectly related to conceptual tempo since it takes time and reflection to be analytical.
5. a. This statement refers to Dunn and Dunn's structure/support.
6. b. Being able to find a figure embedded in a larger framework is one indication of field independence. In fact this is the most common test for this trait.
7. d. Writing a program on a computer is most closely related to logical, sequential, and analytical processing, which is typical of the left hemisphere.
8. c. This is an extreme example of a reflective person.

Chapter 9

Classroom Management: Prevention

Cheryl Poulos is a seventh-grade math teacher whose class is involved in a unit on converting fractions to decimals and percents. She has 32 students in a room designed for 24, so the students are sitting within arm's reach across the aisles.

As Ginger comes into the room, she sees a series of fractions with the directions, "Convert each to a decimal and then to a percent," projected high on the screen at the front of the room. She quickly slides into her seat just as the bell stops ringing. Most of the students have already begun working the problems.

Cheryl is finished taking roll by the time the bell stops ringing, and she hands back a set of papers as students busy themselves with the task. As she hands Jack his paper, she touches him on the arm and points to the overhead, reminding him to return from his window-gazing.

She waits a moment for the students to finish and then begins. She writes the fraction 7/12 on the chalkboard and as she says, "Let's think about this fraction. Let's estimate what percent 7/12 will be, . . . Donna?" she sees Scott, who sits behind Veronica, stick his foot forward and tap Veronica's leg. She also notices that Ellen is whispering something to Kristen at the back of the room.

In response to the tap, Veronica whispers loudly, "Stop it, Scott."

Cheryl moves down the aisle as Donna responds, "It would be . . . mmm . . . about sixty, maybe . . . I think." Cheryl stops at Scott's desk leans over and whispers softly but firmly, "We keep our hands and feet to ourselves in here," and then says, "Okay, good, Donna. . . . Explain why Donna's estimate is probably pretty good, . . . Jeremy?"

As Jeremy begins, ". . . Well, 7 is over half of 12 . . . yeah, . . . so, it would have to be more than fifty percent," Cheryl moves to the back of the room and stands by Ellen and Kristen.

Introduction

Understanding the topics you teach, and planning and implementing effective lessons are important abilities. However, an additional ability is so important that without it the carefully laid plans and strategies cannot work. This is the ability to effectively manage the learning environment.

A well-managed classroom supports learning. In it, students are orderly but not rigid, and they feel safe from both physical harm and the fear of ridicule. They speak their minds but understand limits. The classroom operates like a well-oiled machine, the focus is on learning, and the teacher seems to be making little effort to manage. In contrast, poorly managed classrooms are seas of chaos. The students are inattentive and perhaps disruptive, the teacher is frazzled and exhausted, and little learning is taking place.

Research indicates that once classroom management problems occur, it is often too late to maintain order, and effective managers organize and conduct their classrooms to prevent management problems from happening in the first place (Kounin, 1970). This chapter is devoted to a discussion of ways to prevent management problems. As you study the chapter, ask yourself how the information you're learning will help prevent management problems from occurring in the first place or will help prevent minor problems from expanding into larger ones.

Objectives

After completing your study of Chapter 9, you should be able to:

- Describe classroom patterns as competitive, cooperative, or individualistic
- Identify classroom incidents as related to teacher characteristics, classroom organization, or classroom environment

CLASSROOM MANAGEMENT: AN OVERVIEW

The Problem

From 1968 until 1986, Gallup polls identified school discipline as the most important problem teachers face; from 1986 to 1992, it ranked second only to drugs and inadequate funding; in 1995 it surfaced again as the number one problem (Elam & Rose, 1995). Management is particularly difficult for preservice and beginning teachers who typically feel ill-prepared to deal with issues related to classroom management and often find that their university preparation is incomplete (Kher-Durlabhji, Lacina-Gifford, Jackson, Guillory, & Yandell, 1997).

The reasons can be traced to changes in both schools and society at large. Unquestioned respect for authority figures has been replaced by attitudes of questioning, doubt, and hesitancy. Faith in the schools as instruments of socialization has been replaced by criticisms of education. Attitudes toward child rearing have changed, and these attitudes have found their way into the schools.

The student population has changed dramatically. Learners won't sit quietly through dull presentations, and motivation is an important consideration in both management and instruction. Students spend a great deal of time in front of television sets, and many urban classrooms have a majority of the students with native languages other than English (U.S. Department of Education, 1993; Fitzgerald, 1995). An alarming number of students come to school with home environments and experiential backgrounds that place them "at risk" of not succeeding (Slavin, Karweit, & Madden, 1989).

Classroom Management and Discipline

In this chapter we will emphasize the concept *management* over the commonly used term *discipline*. Management refers to the complex set of plans and actions that teachers use to ensure that as much learning as possible occurs. This includes the classroom routines and rules, teacher responses to student behavior, and instruction that promotes a learning-focused environment. In comparison, discipline refers to teacher responses to student behavior that detracts from classroom order or interferes with the opportunity to learn. These behaviors, or off task behaviors, include talking or leaving desks without permission, tapping pencils, passing notes, poking or hitting other students, making hostile or sarcastic remarks, or more seriously, fighting and assaults.

Outcomes of Effective Management

Increased Achievement.   The relationship between management and achievement is well documented (Blumenfeld, Pintrich, & Hamilton, 1987; Evertson, 1987). Purkey and Smith (1983) identified effective management as one of the four key characteristics of an effective school. Wang, Haertel, and Walberg (1993), in a comprehensive review of the literature on factors influencing learning conclude, "Effective classroom management has been shown to increase student engagement, decrease disruptive behaviors, and enhance use of instructional time, all of which results in improved student achievement" (p. 262). In short, effective management is an essential ingredient of effective teaching.

Improved Motivation.   Order and safety are necessary to promote student motivation. Brophy (1987) identified classroom management as an "essential precondition for motivating students" (p. 208). Classroom management is a foundation the teacher builds upon in creating motivating classrooms. In addition, by seeking student input on instructional and management issues, the teacher can promote student ownership and involvement, both of which positively influence student motivation (McLaughlin, 1994).

PREREQUISITES TO EFFECTIVE MANAGEMENT

Orderly classrooms don't magically happen. They must be carefully planned, and teachers who are caring, firm, and committed to the students and their learning are less likely to have management problems than their less professional peers. In this section we examine three prerequisites to effective management:

- Classroom climate.
- Teacher characteristics.
- The relationship between management and instruction.

Classroom Climate

Think back to your experiences in elementary and secondary school. Were you comfortable in some classes and uncomfortable in others? Did you look forward to some because they were interesting and stimulating while you dreaded others and watched the clock in them as the minutes dragged by? The answer for virtually all of us is "yes."

In some classes the emotional feeling is healthy, positive, and supports learning. The environment that supports these feelings represents the classroom climate. In classes with a positive climate students feel capable, included, and secure. A balance is maintained between teacher direction and student choice, students have freedom within well-defined limits, and learner responsibility is emphasized over rigid adherence to rules. The development of learner self-regulation is an overriding goal.

Positive climates don't automatically happen, however. They depend on the teacher and the kind of learning experiences students have.

Teacher Characteristics

We've all seen students go from one class, in which they're disruptive and out of hand, to another, in which they're orderly and on-task. The difference is the teacher.

Effective managers cover a spectrum of personalities. Some appear quiet and unassuming; others have voices like a drill sergeant. Although one type isn't necessarily better than another, effective managers usually have several important characteristics, such as

- Caring
- Firm
- Democratic
- Withitness
- Organized

Let's look at them.

Caring: The Foundation of Positive Classroom Climate.   It is virtually impossible to successfully manage a classroom or succeed in any part of teaching without genuinely caring about students and their learning. In one study, researchers asked fourth graders how they knew whether their teacher cared (Rogers, 1991). They described a caring teacher as one who

- Listens and tries to see things from a student's perspective.
- Creates a safe and secure learning environment.
- Helps with school work by making sense of learning tasks.

A caring teacher creates an environment in which students feel secure and free to learn. Students can't focus their energies on intellectual achievement if they feel physically or emotionally threatened.

Earning students' respect: Savage (1991) examines caring from a different perspective. Rather than focusing on caring per se, he states that in order to be truly effective

Providing opportunities for student ownership and involvement can positively impact upon classroom management.

managers, teachers must earn the respect of students rather than intimidate or coerce them into compliance with classroom rules. He offers several suggestions for earning this respect.

- Plan carefully so you thoroughly understand the topics you're teaching.
- Announce tests, be clear on what tests will cover, and avoid tricking students.
- Provide genuine encouragement and praise and avoid sarcasm.
- Learn students' names quickly and use them regularly.
- Provide appropriate rewards for good work.

Considering Learner Needs: William Glasser (1969, 1985) argues that all students come to school with a set of innate needs, one of which is belonging, and he links disruptive behavior to unmet belonging needs. Glasser suggests that a truly caring teacher will not accept excuses for misbehavior, regardless of student background and experience. A caring teacher communicates, "I care too much about your learning to allow you to harm yourself by being disruptive." This leads us to the concept of firmness.

Firmness: Helping Students Develop Responsibility.   Firmness means viewing students as capable of exercising responsibility and holding them accountable for their actions. A teacher who doesn't stand firm when a student breaks a rule communicates that the rule has no real purpose and that actions don't necessarily have consequences. These messages confuse students who are trying to make sense of the world. It is critical that a teacher follows through in making students responsible and accountable for their actions.

Democratic Teachers: Combining Caring and Firmness.   Rudolph Dreikurs (1968a), a psychiatrist well-known for his work in student discipline, argues that firmness combined with caring is one characteristic of a democratic teacher. Firmness indicates that teachers respect themselves, and caring shows respect for others. Dreikurs relates the two by connecting them in a democratic classroom. Let's look at an illustration.

> Gloria Durham greets her students with a smile at the classroom door. She surveys them as they take their seats and says, "Rico and Steve," in response to the students' loud whispering after the bell stops ringing. "One of the rules we all agreed on was 'Be ready to work as soon as the bell stops ringing.' "
>
> The students quickly stop, and Gloria continues, "We have much to do today, so let's get started. Each of you was responsible for one part of your team's presentation. Please give me a report of your progress. Go ahead, Team 1."

In this brief episode, Gloria displayed at least four characteristics of a democratic teacher:

- Her class was orderly, and limits were established.
- Students had input into the rules.
- She provided leadership in both maintaining order and guiding learning.
- She used her learning activity to promote a sense of ownership and belonging.

Withitness.   Kounin (1970) analyzed the classroom practices of effective and ineffective classroom managers and attempted to isolate variables that differentiated the two. One of the most important is *withitness*, which refers to the teacher knowing what's going on in all parts of the classroom all of the time, and to communicate this awareness to the students. Related to *withitness* is the variable called *overlapping*, which is the teacher's ability to do more than one thing at a time. Both involve dealing with individual problems while maintaining the attention of the class as a whole. Let's look back to our opening case study to see how Cheryl Poulos accomplished it.

Cheryl displayed demonstrated "withitness" in three ways. First, she intervened immediately. She caught Scott in the act and moved to prevent further disruption before the incident expanded. Second, she caught the "right one." She saw that Scott was the cause of the incident, so she ignored Veronica's comment. Third, she dealt with the potentially worst problem first. She first stopped Scott's disruption and then moved near Ellen and Kristen. Her proximity then stopped their whispering.

Cheryl quickly stopped the disruptions without interrupting the flow of her lesson, and in this way demonstrated overlapping. Most of the students in the class probably weren't even aware that an incident was occurring. These abilities are characteristic of effective managers.

Organization.   Let's look back at Cheryl's class in our opening case study. When students walked into the room, they found problems displayed on the screen as Cheryl started her beginning-of-class routines. The class began working on her warm-up activity without being told, and Cheryl moved quickly and smoothly from it to her lesson for the day. She demonstrated four important characteristics of effective organization. They are outlined in Table 9.1

Starting on time and having materials ready can eliminate the "dead time" at the beginning of classes, which is one of the times when management problems are most likely to occur (Doyle, 1986; Evertson, 1987). Careful organization maximizes opportunities for student involvement and learning and minimizes downtime that can lead to management problems.

Teachers who use several minutes at the beginning of class to take roll and complete other routines and who fumble with papers and demonstrations create the impression that they aren't sure of what they're doing and aren't fully in control of their classes. These teachers are inviting management problems.

Transitions are particularly important in orderly classrooms, and effective managers also help students make transitions from one activity to another quickly and smoothly. Often, teachers have a clear idea of where they are going, but they don't communicate this transition to the students. A great deal of confusion can be prevented by using the following techniques.

- Waiting until the whole room is quiet and attentive before making the transition.
- Clearly stating what transition is to be made.
- Writing important directions on the board if any aspects of the transition could be confusing.
- Carefully monitoring the transition as it occurs.

Distinctive times: Distinctive times are times during the school day or year when management problems are more likely to occur. Effective managers are especially alert and more carefully organized during these times. In addition to the beginning of class periods and transitions, some other distinctive times are

- Last period of the day (and particularly Friday).
- Few minutes just before lunch.
- Day before a big event or holiday.

Table 9.1   Characteristics of effective organization

Characteristic	Example
Having materials and demonstrations prepared in advance	Cheryl's problems were prepared and waiting when the students came into the room.
Starting on time	Cheryl was finished calling the roll before the bell stopped ringing.
Having well-established routines	Cheryl had a warm-up activity every day.
Making transitions smoothly and quickly	Cheryl moved quickly from her warm-up activity to her formal lesson.

- Beginning of a period following a rally, school assembly, or fire drill.
- Time before, during, and after report cards are distributed.

How these times are handled depends on the teacher's professional judgment, but some ideas include selecting strongly organized or highly motivating activities, giving seatwork or tests, and simply discussing these times with the students to make them aware of what you're doing and why.

Management and Instruction

Commonly overlooked in discussions of classroom management is the role of effective instruction. Research indicates that it is virtually impossible to maintain an orderly classroom in the absence of effective instruction and vice versa (Doyle, 1986).

In addition to the questioning skills that were discussed in Chapter 6, we want to examine some additional instructional factors that contribute directly to orderly classrooms. They are illustrated in Figure 9.1 and discussed in the sections that follow.

Lesson Focus.   Effective managers also use the chalkboard, overhead projector, charts, displays, and demonstrations to attract and maintain student attention. Called *lesson focus* (Kauchak & Eggen, 1998), it provides two functions. First, it promotes learning by helping maintain attention, and second, since students should be looking at the information display, inattentive students are easy to identify. In recalling some of the lessons from Chapter 7, we see that teachers used sentences displayed on the overhead, hierarchies written on the chalkboard, and even string and rulers as types of focus. Cheryl Poulos's fraction written on the chalkboard was a form of focus.

Lesson Momentum.   Lesson momentum refers to the force and flow of a lesson. Lessons that have momentum pull students into them and encourage their continued attention. Kounin (1970) found that students were attentive and involved when lessons followed a logical structure and moved along at a good pace, but problems occurred when the lesson's momentum was lost. Common reasons for loss of momentum include teachers wandering off the topic, repeating or reviewing material that was already understood, pausing for extended periods to gather thoughts or prepare materials, and interrupting lessons to deal with behavior problems or other concerns. Momentum underscores the need for teachers to clearly understand their goals and to select and implement strategies that will permit students to reach them. Nothing is harder to manage than a class of students who don't know why they are there or what is happening.

Interaction and Involvement.   With careful planning you ensure that your lessons have an internal logic and structure that can be communicated to the students. The

Figure 9.1   Instructional Factors that Contribute to Classroom Order

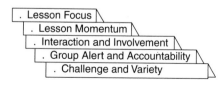

questioning skills and instructional strategies discussed in Chapters 6 and 7 can then be used to promote interaction and student involvement. At the same time that involvement increases learning, it also helps prevent management problems. It is virtually impossible to be effective at one without the other.

Group Alert and Accountability.   In calling on students, Kounin (1970) suggests creating suspense by posing a general question, looking around the room, and then calling on a student. He terms this "group alerting and accountability." He also suggests that students should be called on randomly rather than in a fixed order, with the teacher making a special effort to get around to everyone in the class frequently. These practices have been demonstrated as effective with students of all ages, including those at the university level (Kerman, 1979; McDougall & Granby, 1996). All of these suggestions not only get the students actively involved in the lesson but also communicate withitness.

Challenge and Variety.   The same ideas apply to the assignments students are given for seatwork. Student involvement in these activities depends on the challenge and variety that the work presents (Clifford, 1990). Students quickly become satiated with tasks that do not require thinking or challenge, especially if they are repetitive or lacking in value (Farrell, 1990). In addition, challenge has been identified as one of the sources of intrinsic motivation (Lepper & Hodell, 1989).

EXERCISE 9.1

Several teacher characteristics and strategies were identified in the chapter that help prevent management problems. Among them were *organization, withitness, focus, momentum, challenge and variety, interaction and involvement,* and *group alert and accountability.* For each of the following, identify the teacher strategy *best* illustrated in the example, and defend your answer. Then compare your answers to the ones given in the feedback section at the end of the chapter.

1. "OK," Mr. Izillo begins, "Why do you think the Battle of Gettysburg was the turning point of the war? . . . Teresa?"

_____

_____

2. "Take a look at the chart," Mrs. Moran directs, displaying a chart comparing a frog and toad, their characteristics, what they eat, and where they live. "How do the characteristics compare?"

_____

_____

3. "Man," Richard comments to Don, "She acts like she has eyes in the back of her head. You can't get away with anything in here."

_____

_____

4. "All right," Mrs. Evans announces. "Our math period is nearly over and it's time for language arts. Quickly put your math papers away and get your language arts books out." Mrs. Evans watches as the students put their papers away and get their books out. In two minutes they're ready to start language arts.

_____

_____

5. Mrs. Lynch's students are involved in a discussion of the geography of Europe. As the students examine a map showing the Pyrenees between France and Spain, Stewart asks, "What caused the Spanish Civil War?" Mrs. Lynch responds, "That's a very good question, Stewart. Hold that thought and I'll talk to you about it after class. Now, what effect might these mountains have had on the history of the two countries? Jack?"

_____

_____

PLANNING FOR EFFECTIVE MANAGEMENT

Nowhere in teaching is planning more important than in classroom management. Orderly classrooms don't magically occur; they are the result of careful and systematic planning—even for teachers who appear to be "naturals."

Preventing problems involves anticipating potential situations, such as during the distinctive times we discussed earlier in the chapter, and consciously planning for them. This idea is not new, as reflected in maxims such as, "Keep your students busy, so they won't have time to get into trouble," or "Don't smile until Christmas."

The first step in the planning process is creating a well-designed system of rules and procedures. Once the rules and procedures are in place, teachers should then plan for teaching and monitoring them.

Establishing and Implementing Classroom Rules

Classroom rules establish standards for student behavior. They are essential for effective management, and research consistently documents their value (Evertson, Emmer, Clements, Sanford, & Worsham, 1994; Emmer et al., 1994). Rules that are clearly stated and consistently monitored can do much to prevent management problems. Evertson (1987) offers several guidelines for preparing rules. They are outlined in the following sections.

Keep Class and School Rules Consistent.   This suggestion is self-evident. Teachers cannot develop rules for their classrooms that are inconsistent with the policies of the school or the district. Before preparing and presenting rules to the students, teachers should review district and school rules and then develop their own accordingly. For instance, if the school has a dress code, individual teachers are professionally obligated to enforce it. Teachers who feel strongly that the rule is inappropriate should work to get it changed, not subvert it.

State Rules Clearly.   Rules must be understandable, or they won't have any impact on students' behavior. Also, vague rules need to be constantly interpreted, which disrupts the flow of learning. For example, a rule that says, "Always come to class prepared," has an uncertain meaning, while "Bring needed materials to class every day" is much clearer. Even the second rule will need to be carefully discussed, reviewed, and reinforced to be effective.

Provide Rationales for Rules.   Explaining why a rule exists is important, particularly for classroom climate and the emotional impact it has on the students. When rationales are provided, students learn that the world is rational and sensible, and it helps satisfy their need for order. Rules presented without rationales leave the impression of an authoritarian world, and perhaps even an arbitrary and capricious one. This is true even for young children. While they may not fully comprehend the rationale at the time that it is presented, it is still important to state it. Doing so promotes a climate in which students learn that the world makes sense and provides the sort of experience that helps promote development.

State Rules Positively.   "Wait to be recognized by the teacher before answering" is preferable to "Don't blurt out answers." Rules stated positively create positive expectations and student responsibility. Further, negatively stated rules don't help students understand desirable behaviors; they only specify undesirable ones.

Keep the List of Rules Short.   This suggestion is pragmatic. Students commonly break rules because they simply *forget*. If rules are to be effective, the students need to be constantly aware of their existence, and this is possible only if the list is short. Teachers should be judicious about their rules and include only those that they intend to enforce fully. Superficial or peripheral rules left unenforced detract from the credibility of all the rules on the list.

Solicit Student Input in the Rule-Making Process.   Glasser (1985) suggests that students need to feel that they have some control over their existence, and one way of giving them control is to solicit their input as rules are developed. Further, Lepper and Hodell (1989) have identified control as one of the sources of intrinsic motivation. Developing rules in the format of a classroom meeting also helps develop social responsibility in the students, which has been linked to both improved student behavior and increased student achievement (Wentzel, 1991).

Establishing and Implementing Classroom Procedures

While rules provide standards for student behavior, procedures establish the routines the class will follow in their day-to-day activities. They address activities such as

- Beginning the school day.
- Dealing with absences and tardies.
- Entering and leaving the classroom.
- Making transitions from one activity to another.
- Turning in work.

- Sharpening pencils.
- Asking for help.

Procedures for dealing with these activities need to be so well-established that students follow them without having to be told. This frees teachers to devote their energies to instruction. If procedures are poorly established, teachers must spend time and energy reminding students, for example, how to turn in their work, to wait for help until they're finished with another student, or to avoid disrupting the discussion to go and sharpen a pencil.

Rules and Procedures: Developmental Considerations

As we all know, the behavior patterns of kindergartners and first graders are not the same as those for junior-high students. The needs and development of the two age groups are very different, and these differences should be considered as teachers plan their rules and procedures. In this section we consider the developmental characteristics of four different age groups and the implications these characteristics have for management. The stages are somewhat arbitrary, but they will give you a frame of reference as you make decisions about your rules and procedures (Brophy & Evertson, 1976; Brophy & Evertson, 1978).

Stage 1: Kindergarten Through Second Grade.   Young children are compliant and eager to please their teachers. However, they have short attention spans and often break rules because they forget that the rules exist. Rules and procedures need to be carefully and explicitly taught, practiced, monitored, and reinforced.

Stage 2: Grades Three Through Six.   Middle elementary students are becoming more independent, but they still like the attention and affection of teachers. They understand and accept rules and enjoy participating in the rule-making process. Rules need to be monitored and consistently and impartially enforced.

Stage 3: Grades Seven Through Nine.   Students at this stage are experiencing a mixture of social, physical, emotional, and sexual feelings, and as a result they can be capricious and perhaps even rebellious. They need a firm foundation of stability in the classroom. Rules need to be clearly stated, administered, and predictably enforced.

Stage 4: Grades Ten Through Twelve.   Older learners communicate effectively adult-to-adult. Their behavior has stabilized compared to the previous stage, and they respond well to clear rationales for rules. At this point, students respect teachers for their expertise and ability to communicate. Effective instruction is at least as important as effective management at this stage.

Teaching Rules and Procedures

Rules and procedures won't automatically work just because they exist and have been presented to the students. They should be treated as concepts and explicitly taught with examples just as you would do for teaching any concept (Dowhower, 1991).

Let's see how one teacher accomplished this.

> Jim Gallagher and his first-grade class have established the rule, "Leave your seat only when given permission," and Jim is now attempting to help his students fully understand the rule.
>
> He begins, "Suppose that you're working and you break the lead in your pencil. What are you going to do? Selinda?"
>
> ". . . I . . . I'll raise my hand and wait for you."
>
> "Yes, precisely," Jim smiled. "And why would Selinda do this? Grant?"
>
> ". . . The rule says stay in my seat."
>
> "OK, good. Why did we decide that rule was important? Joyce?"
>
> ". . . If people get up like out of their chair, . . .'er seat, it will, will make it so we can't learn as much," Joyce responded haltingly.
>
> "That's right, Joyce. Getting up can disrupt the class, so we won't learn as much. Very good. . . . Now suppose that you made a mistake on your work and you want to start over on a new piece of paper. What will you do with the old paper? Joe?"
>
> ". . . Keep it, . . . 'til lunch," Joe answered.
>
> "Good, Joe. What will you *not* do?" Jim continued raising his voice for emphasis.
>
> ". . . Crumple it up and go throw it away in the waste basket."
>
> "Excellent, Joe! Very good thinking."
>
> Jim then dealt with another example and moved on to the lesson for that period.

In this brief episode, we see how a teacher specifically taught a rule. He gave specific, concrete examples of compliance with the rule, and he also dealt with cases of noncompliance. If rules are explicitly taught in this way, the likelihood of students breaking them is significantly decreased.

Let's see how Kathy Francis, a first-grade teacher, taught her students a classroom procedure.

> I have a folder for each student and myself on a work table at the front of the room. I put the students' names in large letters on the front of them. They are told that when they finish a worksheet they are to take it to the front of the room and put it in the folder without asking my permission to do so.
>
> I then showed them what I want them to do by completing a short worksheet and taking it and putting it in my folder. We discussed what I did, and I then gave them a short assignment so they could practice putting their work away. I had them practice a couple times each day for the first week, and now I almost never have to remind them about putting their work away.

Just as Jim Gallagher did with his rule about remaining in their seats, Kathy Francis explicitly taught her procedure and helped cement it in the students' minds by modeling it herself and having her students practice it. As with teaching rules, this dramatically increases the likelihood that the students will follow the procedure.

The Beginning of the School Year.   To be most effective, teaching and reinforcing rules and procedures must begin immediately. During the first few days, the patterns—desirable or undesirable—will be established for the entire year (Doyle, 1986; Evertson et al., 1994). Some guidelines for beginning the year are as follows (Kauchak & Eggen, 1998):

- Make an effort to create a positive classroom climate by making explicit positive statements about your expectations, such as, "I have heard that you're all good kids, and I know you will be very well behaved in this class."
- Begin teaching rules and procedures the very first day. With young children, actively practice procedures. With older students, carefully illustrate and discuss rules and procedures.
- Monitor and enforce rules with complete consistency during this period. Intervene immediately when rules are broken or procedures are not followed. Follow through to ensure compliance. You want to make the environment completely predictable for the students during this time.
- Plan your instruction during the first few days for maximum control. Use large-group instead of small-group activities. Stay in the classroom at all times.

Monitoring Rules and Procedures

Merely presenting rules will prevent misbehavior from some students, and carefully teaching rules and procedures will eliminate even more problems before they get started. In spite of these efforts, however, incidents will periodically come up, and effective teachers continuously monitor their rules and procedures to prevent the incidents from expanding into problems (Emmer et al., 1994; Evertson et al., 1994). These teachers react to off task behavior immediately, stop it, and refer students to the rule, as Cheryl Poulos did by going to Scott and saying, "We keep our hands and feet to ourselves in here." The combination of the rules and procedures together with careful monitoring will eliminate most management problems before they get started.

Planning the Social Environment

The way a teacher organizes a classroom has significant implications for management. For example, a classroom filled with groups of students working on projects is apt to be noisier than one that has children doing individual seatwork. These are forms of social organization. Classroom social organization can be characterized in one of three ways: *competitive, cooperative,* or *individualistic.*

The competitive pattern of organization stresses individual excellence and achievement. It uses a system of assessment that compares each student with the others. There is always someone on top and someone on the bottom, with other students ranked between. Students are urged to do better than their neighbors, to keep reaching higher for a better position on the academic ladder. Classrooms that are organized competitively typically have students working alone or in small groups. Students work on separate tasks while striving for an acceptable standard within that classroom situation. The teacher is the initiator and director of the learning tasks. The pace, set by the teacher, is usually based on the average or slightly above average ability level in the class.

Most classrooms fit the competitive pattern with one exception. Rather than grading with a system that compares students with one another, most school districts have standards established for assigning grades, and teachers use these standards.

The cooperative pattern stresses students working together on problems. All members of the group are important, with all students capable of making unique contributions, no matter what their ability levels. Students are encouraged to contribute, to set group goals and tasks, to divide and assign work equitably, to listen to all viewpoints, and to weigh alternative solutions. The product of such an enterprise is viewed as a group accomplishment with the input of several individuals. Creativity, initiative, application of previous knowledge to the present situation, organization, and assessment are all tasks expected of students participating in this pattern. The teacher in this organizational pattern is a facilitator who asks for, listens to, and uses student ideas in planning instructional activities.

As we saw in Chapter 8, cooperative social organization has been the subject of considerable research, and the results are impressive. Not only does achievement increase in many cases, but relationships between students of different ethnic backgrounds, sexes, and academic abilities improves significantly (Slavin, 1995).

The individualistic pattern involves students working at their own levels and their own paces to achieve cognitive tasks. They must be able to follow directions, accept repetitive practice, and interpret self-assessments. The teacher is the director, diagnosing and placing students at their correct levels, assessing and encouraging

Interacting with students as individuals can promote a well-managed classroom.

progress, and serving as a source of information. Students usually work alone on a task that may be quite different from that of their neighbors. The objective of this type of organizational pattern is mastery of cognitive material, with steady progress upward.

Often in classrooms, a combination of several organization patterns may be observed. Teachers may use different patterns at different times of the day and for different instructional purposes. As noted earlier, the organizational pattern significantly influences the management considerations a teacher must make. A cooperative climate may lead to the appearance of some disorder but, at the same time, helps improve the students' socialization skills, creativity, and decision-making capabilities. An individualistic approach, in contrast, may prove most effective in terms of cognitive growth and would most likely result in fewer management problems. As with most considerations in teaching, the decision depends on your style and goals.

Planning the Physical Environment

An additional factor affecting management is the physical environment in the classroom. This often overlooked dimension of teaching not only affects how easily students are managed but also how well they achieve. An attractive, well-lit, comfortable, and colorful classroom is more conducive to a feeling of well-being than a dim, drab, and colorless one.

Other factors such as materials and the arrangement of seating can significantly affect management and learning. For example, learning materials that are attractive, accessible, and easily used influence students' overall feelings toward the classroom and their own capacity for learning. The visual impression received from features such as color, size of print, and spacing on the page can have an impact. Students respond positively to attractive learning materials, and you should consider this when choosing among the vast array of already prepared materials or when preparing your own. A positive reaction to learning materials certainly decreases the probability of management problems.

In designing the physical layout of the classroom, certain considerations should be kept in mind (Evertson, 1987):

Visibility

- Can students see the board and other visual displays?
- Does the teacher have a clear view of all instructional areas to allow monitoring?

Accessibility

- Do high-traffic areas (for example, pencil sharpener, door) allow for efficient movement in the classroom?
- Are these high-traffic areas designed so they minimize disruption in the classroom?

Distractibility

- Are potentially noisy areas separated from other areas?
- Do doors or windows invite students to drift off?

With these general considerations in mind, let's turn to some alternate ways to arrange desks.

The traditional setting with rows of desks and the teacher's desk at front, shown in Figure 9.2, focuses all attention upon the teacher and discourages communication among students. This might be ideal when a teacher is presenting a lesson to the entire class, but it can make group work difficult. Students at the rear of the room tend to be physically separated from the teacher and are most likely to be the ones causing problems.

Some classrooms use tables for seating, with the teacher's desk located somewhere on the periphery, as in Figure 9.3. This seating arrangement can be used by all organizational structures—competitive, cooperative, and individualistic.

An arrangement whereby students are provided their own work space with as little distraction as possible is often used in an individualized instructional situation, as shown in Figure 9.4. Access to materials and the teacher is maintained, and the side-by-side seating is not so distracting as across-table seating.

In considering seating arrangement, factors such as inclusion are important. Inclusion is one of a child's basic needs; a physical arrangement that promotes inclu-

Figure 9.2   A Traditional Seating Arrangement

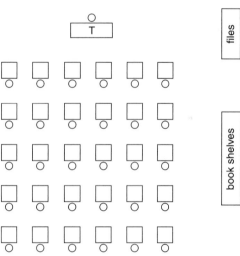

Figure 9.3   An Alternative Seating Arrangement

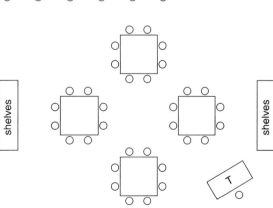

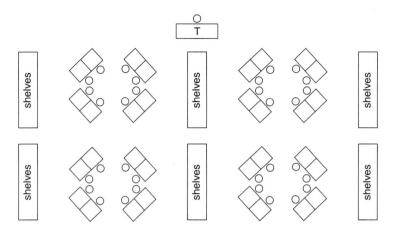

Figure 9.4   An Individualized Seating Arrangement

sion is conducive to a feeling of well-being while deterring management problems. Again, when considering the physical arrangement of your classroom, consider management and academic goals. What type of learning is required? Will students need to interact with one another? Will contact be primarily between the teacher and the individual students? Is communication among students desired? Are spaces for individual work as well as group activity important?

This completes our discussion of planning to prevent management problems. In Chapter 10 we consider interventions that teachers might use when management problems inevitably occur.

EXERCISE 9.2

The following example illustrates a teacher presenting his class rules at the beginning of the school year. Assess each of his rules and the way he presented them based on the criteria outlined in the chapter. In your assessment identify both the positive (if any) and negative (if any) features of both his rules and the way he presented them. Then compare your answers to the ones given in the feedback section at the end of the chapter.

Jim Harkness is working with his students in establishing the rules that will govern the students' behavior for the school year. He began the process by saying, "In order for us to learn as much as we can in this class, we need some rules that will provide guidelines for our behavior. So," he continued, "I have prepared a list for our class, and I want to discuss them with you this morning."
He then displayed the following list:

1. Always come to class ready and prepared to work.
2. Don't touch other students with your hands, feet, or any other part of your body.
3. Speak only when recognized by the teacher.
4. Don't leave your desk without permission.
5. Treat the teacher and your classmates with respect.

"Now," he continued, "Let's look at the first one. Why is a rule like this necessary?"

". . . If we aren't prepared to work, we won't learn as much as we could," Karen volunteered.

"OK, good. Can anyone give us another reason?"

Jim continued his discussion of the first rule, and then he led a similar discussion of each of the others in succession. Finally, he reviewed each and then moved to his instruction for the day.

EXERCISE 9.3

Read each statement below and decide if it is a feature of a competitive (cm), a cooperative (cp), or an individualistic (i) classroom. Then compare your answers to the ones given in the feedback section at the end of the chapter.

_____ 1. Students are valued for their unique contributions.

_____ 2. Achievement is expressed in terms of the highest grade assigned to the highest performing student and the lowest grade assigned to the lowest performing student.

_____ 3. Students must organize and evaluate their own instructional activities.

_____ 4. The teacher sets the pace for learning with certain set standards to be achieved.

_____ 5. The teacher serves a supporting, encouraging function.

_____ 6. The teacher helps each student find work at his or her own pace and speed.

Summary

In this chapter we have discussed classroom organization and management from the viewpoint that such planning is part of a totally integrated instructional plan.

We have defined management as helping students learn to understand and manage their own behavior. We have also described the relationship between management and learning. A developmental model of management was presented along with the patterns of organizational structure possible in classrooms. Considerations for choosing among these structures, characteristics of effective managers, and student interaction skills, including suggested activities for their development, were discussed. We also explained these specific techniques for preventing management problems: the establishment of rules, high-energy times, the effect of the physical classroom environment, and parent-teacher relationships.

Questions for Discussion

1. Helping learners develop responsibility and self-control is viewed as an important goal. Do classroom rules and procedures detract from that goal? Why or why not?

2. Why is it virtually impossible to maintain an orderly classroom if instruction is ineffective? Give an example to illustrate your description.

3. Why do orderly classrooms increase learner motivation? Explain based on your understanding of factors that increase motivation to learn.
4. Explain how a teacher can be simultaneously caring and firm.
5. Many experts feel that the willingness to give learners their time is the best indicator of caring that exists. Explain why this would be the case.

Suggestions for Field Experience

1. Interview a teacher. Some questions you might ask are
   a. How do you organize your classroom to prevent management problems?
   b. What are your rules and procedures? How did you arrive at them?
   c. How did you present your rules and procedures to your students? Did you solicit input from them in preparing the rules and procedures?
   d. How did you "teach" your rules and procedures? Was "teaching" them necessary, or did you merely present them?
   e. How did you communicate your rules and procedures to your students' parents?
2. Observe in a classroom. Identify and describe the procedures that you see. Ask the teacher how he or she taught the procedures.
3. Observe in a classroom and look for evidence of classroom rules. For example, are rules displayed? Did the teacher give the students a sheet with the rules written on it? Do the students have rules in a notebook?
4. Observe a teacher as she conducts lessons. How does she or he demonstrate withitness and overlapping? Specifically describe any examples that you see. Also describe any cases where the teacher appears to lack withitness or appears unable to demonstrate overlapping.

Exercise Feedback

EXERCISE 9.1

1. Group alert. Mr. Izillo asks a question, hesitates, and then identifies a student. While this process challenges students and promotes involvement, we don't have enough evidence from the short excerpt to conclude that challenge or involvement is a better response than group alert.
2. Focus. The chart gives the student something to focus on visually. Again, we don't have enough evidence to indicate that challenge or involvement would be better answers.
3. Withitness. The example suggests that the teacher knows what's going on in her classroom.
4. Organization—smooth transition. The students made the transition from math to language arts in two minutes. While it takes a well-organized teacher to accomplish this, we must infer organization, since we can observe a smooth transition.
5. The example illustrates momentum. Mrs. Lynch didn't allow herself to be sidetracked by Stewart's question.

EXERCISE 9.2

The positive features of Jim Harkness's rules are the following:

- His list was short. He only had five rules.
- He provided rationales for his rules as evidenced by the discussion he had with his students and questions such as, "Let's look at the first one. Why is this rule necessary?"

Jim could be criticized because he gave the students no opportunity to provide input into the development of the rules.
The following represents the assessment of the individual rules.

1. This rule isn't clearly stated. "Always come to class ready and prepared to work" is vague. A clearer description of this rule could be to divide it into two others stated as follows:

   - Bring all needed materials to class each day.
   - Sit quietly in your seat when the bell rings.

2. This rule is stated negatively. A better statement of the rule would be "Keep hands, feet, and other parts of your body to yourself."
3. This rule is well stated.
4. This rule is stated negatively. A better statement could be, "Leave your desk only when given permission by the teacher."
5. This rule is generally well stated. It could be argued that "Treat . . . with respect," is vague, but with careful discussion and illustration it would be acceptable. Also, the need to respect the teacher and classmates is so important that the rule is worthwhile even if it isn't precise.

EXERCISE 9.3

1. (cp) Cooperative
2. (cm) Competitive
3. (i) Individualistic
4. (cm) Competitive
5. (cp) Cooperative
6. (i) Individualistic

Chapter 10

Classroom Management: Intervention

SOURCES OF MANAGEMENT PROBLEMS

Cindy Daines's first graders were sometimes frustrating. Although she tried "alerting" the groups and having the whole class make transitions at the same time, each one took 4 minutes or more.

In an effort to improve the situation, she made some "tickets" from construction paper, bought an assortment of small prizes, and displayed the items in a fishbowl on her desk the next day. She then explained, "We're going to play a little game to see how quiet we can be when we change lessons. . . . Whenever we change, such as from language arts to math, I'm going to give you 2 minutes and then I'm going to ring this bell," she continued, ringing the bell as a demonstration. "Students who have their books out and are waiting quietly when I ring the bell will get one of these tickets. On Friday afternoon, you can turn these in for prizes you see in this fishbowl. The more tickets you have, the better the prize will be."

During the next few days, Cindy moved around the room, handing out tickets and making comments such as, "I really like the way Merry is ready to work," "Ted already has his books out and is quiet," and "Thank you for moving to math so quickly."

She knew it was working when she heard "Shh" and "Be quiet!" from the students, and she moved from the prizes to allowing the students to "buy" free time with their tickets to finally giving them Friday afternoon parties as group rewards when the class had accumulated enough tickets. She gradually was able to space out the group rewards as the students' self-regulation developed [Adapted from Eggen & Kauchak (1997). Reprinted by permission.]

Introduction

In Chapter 9 we discussed classroom management and the factors that affect its difficulty and complexity. We then suggested that effective managers prevent problems instead of eliminating them once they occur. We also said that management and effective instruction are interrelated and it is virtually impossible to have one without the other.

However, in spite of teachers' sincere efforts to prevent management problems by establishing a positive environment, being well organized in their instructional preparation, using high-interest materials, and getting their students involved in activities, management problems will periodically occur. It's inevitable; it happens to every teacher and it almost certainly will happen to you, particularly as an intern or a beginning teacher. How you deal with these problems is the subject of this chapter.

Objectives

After completing your study of Chapter 10, you should be able to:

- Describe sources of management problems as emotionally caused, teacher caused, or student caused
- Identify theoretical approaches to management as noninterventionist, interventionist, or interactionist
- Describe the characteristics of assertive discipline

SOURCES OF MANAGEMENT PROBLEMS

In order to be an effective manager, the teacher must first have a clear definition of management problems. For our purposes *management problems* are any situations that occur in the classroom that disrupt the learning environment or cause distress to either students or the teacher. These problems can be as simple as students sharpening their pencils during a class discussion or as serious as fighting. A list of common management problems encountered by teachers includes:

- Disruptive conversations.
- Passing notes.
- Refusing to comply with a request.
- Hostility between individuals or groups.
- One student overdepending on another.
- Fighting among students.

While this list isn't complete, it illustrates the scope of the problems teachers face. In this chapter we focus primarily on providing ways of coping with the routine problems that disrupt the teaching–learning process. While drugs, fighting, and attacks on teachers certainly do occur, the primary source of management problems are the not-serious but chronic things students do, such as students being off task, talking without permission, or frequently leaving their seats.

We will first discuss some general considerations in dealing with problems once they arise. Then we will describe three specific approaches to management problems and provide some particular things you should consider in handling them.

The specific approaches are presented as possible solutions to problems that you may face in the classroom. Knowing how to use them will provide you with some alternatives in solving management problems. We are offering alternatives, because we believe that there is no one best way to deal with all management problems. Rather, the strategy you choose should be based on your personality and management style.

The label *management problem* is sometimes a misnomer because what we typically describe as problems may in fact be symptoms of problems rather than the problems themselves. Behaviors teachers view as problems come primarily from one of three sources: (1) teachers themselves, (2) emotional problems, and (3) casual or capricious student actions. For example, a child's constant daydreaming or talking to her friends during a class discussion may indicate a boring activity, which is a teacher problem. The activity is the problem; the student's disruption is merely a symptom. On the other hand, a student who is frequently in fights may have an emotional problem. And, a child walking by his friend, thumping him on the shoulder, and being hit back may be nothing more than children's tendency to horseplay.

Understanding the source of misbehavior is important because it allows you to make better decisions about intervening. For example, you wouldn't treat an emotional problem in the same way as simple horseplay. Further, if you recognize yourself as a possible cause, you can make adjustments in your style, preparation, or the way you relate to students.

The best way to cope with emotional problems is by using the prevention techniques we discussed in Chapter 9. If clear expectations for acceptable behavior are established at the beginning of the year, and rules are enforced fairly and consistently, the management of almost all students is possible. In cases involving severe emotional problems, classroom teachers should seek the help of guidance counselors, who in turn will refer the student to an appropriate agency.

In dealing with teacher-caused management problems, the teacher characteristics and elements of effective instruction that we discussed in Chapter 9 are critical. Teacher-caused problems commonly result from a negative classroom climate, student perceptions that the teacher doesn't care, lack of organization, or ineffective instruction. Making special efforts to be well organized and conduct stimulating lessons will help a great deal with these problems.

Casual or capricious actions are the most common source of management problems in a typical school situation. Under normal conditions, you won't have a majority of your class composed of emotionally disturbed students. So, the most aggravating management problems for a well-prepared teacher are the "kids-will-be-kids" type. The main portion of our discussion focuses on these problems.

EXERCISE 10.1

Identify the following behaviors as coming from an emotionally caused (e), teacher-caused (t), or student-caused (s) source. Then compare your answers to the ones given in the feedback section at the end of the chapter.

_____   1. Getting out of seat without permission
_____   2. Saying negative things to peers

_____   3. Looking out the window during discussion
_____   4. Writing on desks
_____   5. Chewing gum when it is forbidden
_____   6. Blurting out responses without raising hand
_____   7. Throwing temper tantrum when told to wait to respond
_____   8. Being noisy around peers but quiet around teacher
_____   9. Continually using obscene language (although not in front of the teacher)
_____ 10. Refusing to respond to questions

SOLUTIONS TO MANAGEMENT PROBLEMS

General Considerations

The first factor in dealing with problems is perhaps as much prevention as it is treatment; the teacher and the students should be clear about what behaviors are acceptable in the classroom. This is the reason for establishing, teaching, and monitoring rules and procedures, which we discussed in Chapter 9. In addition, you should be clear about available options when management problems occur. Being clear allows you to act and communicate decisively when problems occur.

Intervention Guidelines

Intervening in the case of management problems is never easy. If it were, classroom management wouldn't remain among teachers' most intractable problems. Some guidelines can help, however. They are outlined as follows:

Brevity, Firmness, and Clarity.   Keep encounters as brief, firm, and clear as possible. Long interventions disrupt the flow of the lesson and detract from time devoted to instruction (Crocker & Brooker, 1986).

Clarity describes the precision of the teacher's communication with respect to the desired behavior. For example, "Jenny, we don't talk while others are talking," is clearer than "Don't, Jenny." It communicates to both Jenny and the rest of the class what the problem is and what is expected.

Firmness means the teacher is able to communicate that she means it. "Class there's too much noise. We need to settle down, NOW!" is more effective than, "Let's try to settle down and get quiet"; it better communicates that the teacher means what she says. The teacher's ability to communicate intent verbally and nonverbally is essential.

While clarity and firmness are effective, *roughness,* which is noisy expressions of anger, frustration, or hostility, are not. Kounin (1970) found that roughness was correlated with increased management problems. Rough and disruptive management interventions tend to have a *ripple effect* (Kounin, 1970), which means the disturbance spreads to the rest of the class when an individual is reprimanded. The ripple effect is more pronounced if the teachers use criticism or sarcasm in the reprimand (Rosenshine & Furst, 1971). Prolonged criticism of students wastes instructional time and disrupts students who are working.

Follow-Through.   Follow through on all interventions to be certain that the undesirable behavior has completely stopped. Two students who are whispering, for example, and are asked to stop, but only reduce their whispering, will soon be back at their former level, and a disruptive cycle often begins.

Maintain Consistency.   You hear this so often that it is nearly a cliche, but it is critical nevertheless. The need for consistency is obvious, but achieving complete consistency in the real world of teaching is virtually impossible. In fact, research indicates that interventions should be contextualized; they depend on the specific situation and student (Doyle, 1986).

Let's look at an example. Most classrooms have a rule "Speak only when recognized by the teacher." Suppose as you're monitoring seatwork, a student innocently asks a work-related question of another student and then quickly turns back to work. Do you intervene to let her know that you are "withit" and that talking is not allowed during seatwork? Failing to do so is technically inconsistent, but you don't intervene and you shouldn't. A student who repeatedly turns around and whispers, though, becomes a disruption. A "withit" teacher knows what is going on, discriminates between the two behaviors, and knows where to draw the line.

Avoid Arguments, Threats, and Ultimatums.   Avoid arguments with students. Once a directive is made, follow it through without argument. If students feel they've been treated unfairly, invite them to talk to you about it before or after school, or at some other time when you and the students can meet.

Threats and ultimatums can put you in a "no-win" situation. Because they are often impossible to carry out, they can eliminate the possibility of follow-through and consistency.

Teachers need to clearly communicate acceptable classroom behaviors.

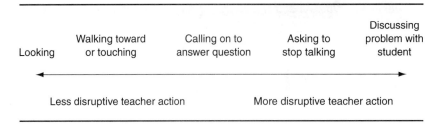

Figure 10.1   A Response Hierarchy for Talking in Class

Management Hierarchies

With these ideas in mind, we suggest that you develop a response hierarchy that is based on the severity of your response and the amount of disruption it will cause the class. Your actions should be based upon the student's misbehavior, and you should not attempt more severe measures before trying less disruptive ones.

A response hierarchy to deal with the problem of talking without permission appears in Figure 10.1. In using the hierarchy, you would begin by first looking at the students who were talking. If this didn't work, you could walk in the direction of the talking students and even touch them on the shoulder while continuing with the lesson. If that did not work, you could then call on one of the students to answer a lesson-related question. Note that all of these measures can be taken without disrupting the lesson. If none of these measures works, you could then move to other, more severe measures such as telling the students to stop talking, separating the students, or calling in parents for a conference.

A similar hierarchy can be developed in other management areas. For example, a response hierarchy to deal with the problems of cheating might look like Figure 10.2. In this hierarchy, you might face the problem of suspected cheating with a casual mention of the need for students to do their own work. If this wasn't effective, the next time you gave an assignment or quiz, you could briefly mention the problem of cheating in general terms and discuss the problems connected with it. This could be followed by a specific reference to the problem of cheating in the classroom and a class discussion of the problem. Finally, you could ask the involved students to meet with you privately to discuss the problem. In each of these examples, you choose a strategy that least disrupts learning. This approach also prevents minor problems from escalating into ma-

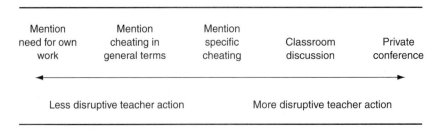

Figure 10.2   A Response Hierarchy for Cheating

jor ones and provides students with the opportunity to work out many situations in a nonthreatening atmosphere. Direct confrontation is used only when necessary.

In constructing hierarchies such as these, there are certain actions by teachers that are not recommended. These include corporal punishment, mass punishment, sarcastic remarks, forced apologies, and school tasks as punishers. Corporal punishment communicates that physical force is an appropriate way to resolve conflicts. Punishing the whole group for the actions of a few is both unjust and induces hostility in those who didn't misbehave. Sarcasm may temporarily solve the immediate situation, but it is devastating for classroom climate. Forced apologies are demeaning and require students to say things in front of the class that they don't really mean. Assigning school tasks for punitive purposes, such as doing math problems or writing sentences can result in school tasks being associated with negative emotions (Eggen & Kauchak, 1997), which over time can create negative attitudes toward academic tasks.

Finally, while these actions may temporarily suppress the symptoms, they won't solve the problem; in fact, they can create more problems than they solve.

DEALING WITH MANAGEMENT PROBLEMS: THEORETICAL APPROACHES

Depending on their assumptions about students and their role in guiding students' development, teachers take different approaches to dealing with management problems. Each suggests different actions by teachers in response to management incidents. The *noninterventionist,* the *interventionist,* and the *interactionist* are three of these approaches (Levin & Nolan, 1991). Let's look at an example focusing on a typical management problem: students who forget to bring materials to class.

> Joanne Bass is a seventh-grade geography teacher teaching a unit on the Middle East. Her students are expected to come to class every day with their texts, notebooks, and pencils or pens.
>
> Joanne began her Wednesday lesson by stating, "Look in your text at the pictures of the different groups found in the Middle East. Can someone describe the different types of people in the pictures on page 79?"
>
> The students began describing the pictures, and then Joanne asked, "Ron, what can you add?"
>
> Ron replied haltingly, "I didn't bring my book today."
>
> Joanne replied, "Ron, when you don't bring your materials, I have to stop the discussion, the class is disrupted, and I get frustrated." She paused for a few seconds and then went on, "Why didn't you bring your book to class?"
>
> "Well . . . ," Ron began, "I just forgot, I guess."
>
> "Do you often forget?"
>
> "No, I don't think so."
>
> This discussion continued briefly, and finally Joanne said, "I believe we ought to talk about this more after school, Ron. Can you stay a few minutes?"
>
> Later, when Ron and Joanne were discussing his failure to bring his book to class, she said, "I really did mean what I said earlier about being frustrated when students fail to bring their materials to class. Do you know why I feel that way?"
>
> "I think so."
>
> "Why is that?"

"Because we're . . . s'pposed to bring our books every day."

"And when you don't, what does that do to the class?"

"Causes trouble, because students who don't have books can't like be involved."

"That's right; that's why I get frustrated. Well, do you have any idea how we can avoid this problem?"

"I'm not sure."

"Well, why don't you think about that for a while. When you think you've got something, let me know. Meanwhile, I'll be grading papers here at my desk."

In a few minutes, Ron approached Joanne's desk and said, "I think I know what happens. Some nights I don't get my homework done. And then in the morning, I forget my books."

"You mean that sometimes at night you don't get a chance to do your homework, and so the next morning you're not prepared to come to school?"

"Yes, sometimes I try to do my homework in the morning, and there isn't time. So, then, I get rushed and forget."

The discussion continued with Ron's trying to figure out how he could avoid those disorganized mornings and Ms. Bass's helping in the process. In doing this, she attempted to be supportive by listening to his ideas and clarifying them but not trying to impose her own solutions. She felt this was important because the ultimate responsibility for the problem was with the student, and she wanted to give him practice in dealing with it.

Let's stop now and look at another teacher's approach to the same type of problem.

Jeff Gordon, fourth-grade teacher, was beginning his school year. He had gotten acquainted with his students in the first few days, had explained the grading system, and was ready to begin the instruction of his class.

He began by saying to the class, "In order for us to get the most out of school, we have to have a few basic rules. The rules are as follows:

1. Remain quiet while another student or I am talking.
2. Stay in your desk when we're in the middle of a discussion.
3. Raise your hand before speaking.
4. Write down all assignments.
5. Bring all necessary materials to class each day.

"I have this jar at the front of the room, and when the class is working together to follow these rules, I'll put a marble in the jar. When the class gets 30 marbles in the jar, we'll have a class free choice at the end of the day where everyone can choose his or her favorite activity like a game, puzzle, or quiet talking. When the jar is all full, we'll plan a class party.

"If I have problems with individuals who don't follow these rules, I'll put your name on the board. That's a warning. The second time I'll put a check by your name. You'll have to stay in for recess, then. If I put two checks by your name, I'll have to call your parents to come in and talk with me. The purpose of these checks is to remind you of the rules in the classroom and to help you to follow them. So, be on your best behavior and try to follow these rules as closely as you can."

Jeff implemented his plan, and the first time Chris forgot her notebook, her name went on the board. At the end of the day, Jeff reviewed the day's happenings and discussed particular problems with individual students and general problems with the class. When necessary, the rules were adjusted or were supplemented with additional details to help particular students.

Now let's contrast these two approaches to management with a third one.

Jacinta Williams is another seventh-grade geography teacher. She began her year through such activities as getting to know the students' names and explaining the grading system.

She then began her first actual instructional day by saying to her students, "In order for us to get the most out of our classes, get along with each other, and respect each other as human beings, we must have some rules that are fair to everyone and that will help us to behave appropriately in school. I want you now to break into the following groups of four, and each group is to prepare a list of rules that we will live by during this school year. Remember, they must be fair to everyone, and they should help us all learn as much as possible about our course work."

With that, the class broke into groups and began writing the rules. After a period of time, she asked each group to report to the whole class. In cases where one group suggested a rule that other groups did not, she asked the class if they thought it was a good rule and if it should be retained and incorporated into the final list. In several cases, particular rules were modified slightly until they became acceptable to everyone.

Finally, when the class was nearly finished, she noticed that no rule about bringing materials to class was mentioned. Jacinta then suggested to the students, that in order to avoid disruption caused by borrowing, a rule for bringing materials be included. The class agreed, and two of the students volunteered to write the rules in large letters on a piece of poster board.

The next day Jacinta referred the children to a page in their text and began a class discussion. During the discussion she noticed Kent was looking down at his desk and not responding.

She then said, "Everyone read page 96 in your text. Do that right now, and we'll continue the discussion in a few minutes."

She then went over to Kent and asked quietly, "What are you doing, Kent?"

"Nothing."

"Let's see now. You were doing nothing, but we were having a discussion. I see your book isn't in front of you. Did you forget to bring it today?"

"Yes, I did," he replied quietly.

"Do you know the rule about bringing your materials, Kent?"

"Yes."

"What is it?"

"We will always bring all our materials to class."

"Did you agree with the rule?"

"Yes."

"Okay, what do you plan to do tomorrow?"

"I will bring all my materials."

"Please write me a short letter telling me how you plan to do this. Then, at the end of the day, I'd like to discuss your plan with you."

Jacinta, after completing her discussion with Kent, went on with her class discussion. Kent wrote the letter and gave it to her at the end of the period. At the end of the day, they reviewed his plan and discussed its implementation in the future.

Let's analyze these examples now.

Noninterventionist

Joanne Bass would be called a *noninterventionist* because her approach was to work with students to develop their own solutions to management problems.

The noninterventionist approach, based on humanistic and psychoanalytic theories of development, suggests that the child develops from an inner unfolding of potential (Hamachek, 1987). The teacher's role is to facilitate this process by promoting strong, trusting relationships with children and helping them develop their problem-solving abilities.

The noninterventionist view has two distinctive features. The first is the assumption that children are innately good and trustworthy, and the second is that they should be in control of their own actions and futures. If given the appropriate opportunities, students will learn to develop on their own and will figure out ways to deal with their own management problems. Accordingly, the teacher does not evaluate the student's actions; instead, she works to establish a nonjudgmental atmosphere of trust so that students have the opportunity and freedom to deal with their own problems. The noninterventionist teacher facilitates rather than directs or orders.

Let's look specifically at how Joanne handled the incident. She first helped Ron identify the problem, being careful not to label him or his behavior as the problem or even the cause of the problem. Ron then suggested a solution and proposed a plan for implementing it.

She began the encounter with what Thomas Gordon (1975) calls an "I" message. In reacting to Ron not having his notebook she

- Described the behavior (the missing notebook).
- Identified the consequences of the behavior (disrupting the class).
- Stated her feelings (frustration).

She didn't "judge" Ron's behavior and carefully avoided any assessment of Ron's character or personality. Her goal was to listen and clarify the incident and then help Ron work through it on his own.

Throughout this process Joanne was an *active listener* (Sokolove, Garrett, Sadker & Sadker, 1990). She devoted her full attention to Ron and responded to both the intellectual and emotional contents of his communication.

The goal of the noninterventionist position is to enhance the personal growth and freedom of the individual. Management problems provide opportunities to function in a counselor–client relationship with students. In achieving this goal, the teacher remains as supportive and nondirective as possible.

Interventionist

The assumptions *interventionists* make are in direct contrast with those of the noninterventionists. Rather than believing that the learners are in control of their actions and their future, interventionists believe that the external environment is responsible for behavior. The teacher, instead of being a facilitator of student growth that comes from within the learner, creates an external environment to which learners respond.

Based on behaviorist views of learning—and sometimes called a behaviorist approach—it suggests that children develop as a result of externally imposed reinforcers and punishers. The teacher's role is to establish rules and procedures, clearly communicate them to students, and apply reinforcers and punishers appropriately. As students

respond to consistent applications of these rules, they learn to operate within the social structure of the classroom (McCaslin & Good, 1992).

This system places the teacher in a position of power and authority, responsible
for molding student behavior. While interventionists don't distrust students, the nonjudgmental atmosphere that is so critical for noninterventionists is not a consideration
for them.

Let's look now at how these factors came into play in Jeff Gordon's management
plan. First, he had established a set of rules that governed the students' behavior, and
he enforced the rules with reinforcers and punishers. He monitored the process with
a recording system using checks. When students followed the rules, they were given
marbles which could then be used to "buy" free-time activities. Failure to follow rules
resulted in the student's name being placed on the board, and subsequent checks
would bring after-school detentions or phone calls to parents. When Chris forgot her
notebook, her name went on the board, and if the pattern continued, punishers would
follow. On the other hand, compliance with the rules would be followed by rewards.

The interventionist position focuses on observable behaviors, not their causes. The
cognitive, or problem-solving, aspects of student behavior are for the most part ignored.

The goal of the interventionist approach is to maintain an orderly and productive classroom. The rules established and the rewards and punishments designed to
enforce these rules are not ends in themselves, but rather means toward the end, which
is an efficient learning environment.

Interactionist

Jacinta Williams was *interactionist*. She collaborated with the students in finding a solution to the problem. Interactionist approaches are based on social and developmental theories and hold that the child develops from the interaction of inner and outer
forces. While the teacher assumes full authority under the interventionist view and little authority as a noninterventionist, interactionist teachers share authority with their
students. They view students as capable of making decisions but needing guidance
from the teacher, and guiding students is their primary role in management.

As teachers guide learners, they attempt to help students understand their own
behavior and its consequences. Rules are established collaboratively and the development of student responsibility is a primary goal (Curwin & Mendler, 1988).

Jacinta Williams, for example, allowed and even encouraged participation from
the students in rule making but also provided her own input into the process. When
Kent came unprepared, she first asked him what he was doing and then asked him if
he knew the rule on bringing materials to class. She then got a written commitment
from him indicating that he would bring his materials in the future.

In contrast with Jeff, Jacinta didn't punish Kent, but in comparison with Joanne
she addressed the behavior directly. Jacinta was also prepared to take stronger steps if
necessary should the materials be forgotten again. This position is called interactionist because the teacher works on the problem of management in cooperation with the
student. However, in interacting with a student, the teacher does not give up her responsibility to direct or manage the student's behavior.

Summary of Theoretical Approaches

The goals of these three approaches are related to the different views about the sources of the management problems. The noninterventionist approach believes that management problems come from the incomplete development of the individual but does not blame the individual for these problems. Instead, the solution is viewed as a natural part of the growth process.

The interventionist views problems as emanating from incompletely or inefficiently developed learning systems. Rather than spending time trying to figure out the reasons for the misbehavior, behaviorists spend their time trying to develop more efficient systems.

The interactionist views management problems as being a normal consequence of 30 students with diverse backgrounds and interests being forced into the same classroom at the same time. The problems that arise are to be expected and should be dealt with as a normal part of the class's problem-solving activities.

The three approaches also differ markedly in their views toward teacher authority. The interventionist view emphasizes teacher authority and uses it to establish and maintain rules in the classroom. The interactionist views the teacher as being in charge of the classroom, but the authority is shared with students through collaborative rule making. Students are made responsible for working out solutions to problems, but the teacher doesn't disguise the fact that these rules must be acceptable to the teacher and the school at large.

The noninterventionist approach, by contrast, minimizes the authority of the teacher, instead emphasizing the relationship between teacher and students. The noninterventionist approach views the overuse of authority as an obstacle to this relationship (Kohn, 1996).

In presenting these views, we have attempted to take a balanced approach. Each is based on different theoretical assumptions, and the effectiveness of each depends on teachers and the context in which they work. This is the reason for advocating a models approach to management. Just as there is no single best way to teach, there is no single best way to manage a classroom. You should experiment with a variety of approaches until you find those that work the best for you. When armed with such a repertoire, you are then in a position to make professional decisions about your teaching.

Some researchers advocate the application of these different approaches in a developmental sequence (Wolfgang & Glickman, 1986). For example, you might begin with a tightly structured classroom (interventionist), and as the classroom becomes organized, shift more control and responsibility for rule setting to students (an interactionist approach). An alternate approach begins the year at an intermediate point in the teacher-student power continuum, allowing students to share in the process of rule setting. Subsequent movement from this interactionist position depends upon student behavior. If more structure is needed, the teacher can move the class toward the interventionist position by tightening class rules and procedures. If students are growing and assuming more responsibility for their own behavior, the teacher can concentrate on developing relationships with students and helping guide their personal growth (a noninterventionist position).

EXERCISE 10.2

Examine the following statements and determine whether they reflect a behaviorist (interventionist) (IV) position, an interactionist (I) position, or a noninterventionist (N) one.* Then compare your answers to the ones given in the feedback section at the end of the chapter.

_____ 1. Although children can think, a structured environment is necessary to help them learn.
_____ 2. Student creativity and self-expression are the most important goals of a classroom.
_____ 3. Students need help in formulating rules and in following through with them once established.
_____ 4. Management is a means to an end; my primary job as a teacher is to teach students knowledge and skills.
_____ 5. When a student doesn't complete an assignment, the teacher's role is to understand the reasons for this.
_____ 6. Students need to understand that teachers are persons, too, with rights and feelings.
_____ 7. The best way to motivate students to learn is through grades and assignments that can be completed successfully.
_____ 8. When students persistently talk out of turn, their inner needs aren't being met.
_____ 9. When students persistently talk out of turn, they don't understand the implications of this behavior for themselves or others.
_____ 10. When students persistently talk out of turn, the classroom reward system isn't working.

EXERCISE 10.3

Read the following anecdote and answer the questions that follow. Then compare your answers to the ones given in the feedback section at the end of the chapter.

Dan Rogers is a fourth-grade teacher in a typical school. He began his year by first getting to know his students and began to establish the procedures for his class.

On the first instructional day, he said, "In order to learn the most, we must have some rules that we all want to follow carefully." With that, he displayed a large poster board on which were clearly printed a list of rules for the class during the year. He then asked, "Do all the rules seem fair? Are there others we should add?"

The class then read the rules and after a short discussion agreed that the rules were okay as he presented them. Dan then went on with his class work.

A few days later during an explanation of a math problem, Susan was turned around talking to Shirley. Dan ignored the talking for a moment, but it continued. As the rest of the class was working on a problem, Dan went back to Susan and asked, "Susan, do you know why I've come to talk to you?"

Susan hesitated and then said, "Shirley and I were talking."

"Yes," Dan continued, "and I get upset when someone talks while I'm talking. Remember, we made a rule about talking while someone else is talking. Do you know what that rule is?"

Susan nodded.

"Now I want you to suggest some way that you can help yourself stay within the rules we agreed upon. Let me know after school."

Dan then continued with the lesson, and Susan stopped in at the end of the day and simply said she wouldn't talk anymore.

_____

*Adapted from Wolfgang and Glickman (1986).

The next day during the same class, as Dan was discussing another problem, Susan again turned around and began talking. Dan went to her after he had the rest of the class involved in an activity and said evenly, "Susan, this is the second infraction of the rules, so I'm going to have to put a check by your name. This means you won't be able to take part in our free-play activity this afternoon. Please try to obey the rules from now on."

With that, Dan again went back to his regular classroom activity.

1. Identify one place where Mr. Rogers illustrated characteristics of an interventionist.

_____

2. Identify one place where Mr. Rogers illustrated characteristics of an interactionist.

_____

3. Identify one place where Mr. Rogers illustrated characteristics of a noninterventionist.

_____

ASSERTIVE DISCIPLINE: YOU *CAN* CONTROL YOUR CLASSES

During the 1980s an approach to classroom management, called *assertive discipline,* became enormously popular. The approach is controversial; critics argue that it is punitive and stresses obedience and conformity over learning and self-control (Curwin & Mendler, 1988; McLaughlin, 1994). Others argue that it is inherently destructive (Kohn, 1996). Proponents disagree and contend that its emphasis on positive reinforcement is effective (Canter, 1988).

We neither support nor oppose its use. While it's popularity has waned in recent years, it continues to be well-known. It is a rare school district that hasn't had at least some experience with the program; estimates suggest that more than 750,000 teachers have been trained in the program (Hill, 1990). For this reason, we discuss it in this section.

Assertive discipline developed out of Lee and Marlene Canter's (1992) work in the area of assertion training. As they attempted to help their clients become more assertive, they encountered three characteristic patterns of reactions to conflict. *Passive* people were unable to express their wants or feelings or back up their words with actions. At the other end of the continuum, *hostile* people were able to express their wants and feelings but often did so by abusing others. An *assertive* response style, in contrast, clearly communicated wants and feelings but did so without harming other people. As they worked with teachers, they saw these response patterns in classrooms. Let's look at some examples.

Johnny has been told several times to keep his hands to himself in the classroom. The teacher turns around and sees Johnny poking at a student walking by his desk.

Passive Response: Johnny, I don't know what to do with you. Why can't you keep your hands to yourself?

Hostile Response: Johnny, there is something wrong with you; you just won't listen! I've told you a million times to keep your hands to yourself.

Assertive discipline can be effective in simplifying management tasks.

Assertive Response: Johnny, you've been warned before and now you've made the
choice to leave the room. Pick up your books and come with me.

Assertive discipline encourages teachers to use assertive rather than passive or
hostile responses. It is based on the premise that teachers have three rights:

1. The right to establish a classroom structure that is conducive to learning.
2. The right to determine and expect appropriate behavior from students.
3. The right to ask for help from parents, the principal, and other professionals to produce order in the classroom.

Using these rights as a foundation, assertive discipline advocates creating a
management system that is based on behaviorist views of learning, that is, similar to
the interventionist approach. Rules and procedures are clearly laid out at the beginning of the year and are enforced with reinforcers and punishers. Reinforcers can
include:

• praise
• awards

- notes or phone calls to parents (praising students)
- special privileges (for example, games, puzzles)
- material consequences (food, prizes)

Punishers can include:

- time out (preferably in another classroom)
- removal of a privilege (for example, P.E. or recess)
- after-school detention
- being sent to the principal's or dean's office
- notes or phone calls home (specifying misbehaviors)

Reinforcers and punishers are made clear to students from the beginning and are administered with names on the board, or some other checklist, much like the those used by interventionists.

In dealing with misbehavior, assertive discipline recommends a response hierarchy similar to the ones discussed earlier. At one end of a continuum are nondirective statements that call students' attention to a problem (see Figure 10.3); at the other end of the continuum are teacher demands that require immediate compliance.

Let's see what this continuum would look like in a classroom where students are having trouble staying in their seats:

Nondirective statement: Class, remember what we said about staying at your desks during seatwork.

Question: Would you get back in your seat right now?

Directive statement: Everyone needs to be in their seats right now.

Demand: Janey, get in your seat and get to work, or you'll choose to stay in for recess.

The way that the demand is made is important. It is neither threatening nor hostile, and it puts the burden of choice for behavior on the student.

A final aspect of assertive discipline should be mentioned—the "broken record." In dealing with problems, teachers can become sidetracked. To avoid this, teachers are encouraged to use a broken-record technique, in essence, repeating their request until the message is delivered. Here's what this technique sounds like in practice.

Ms. Jackson: Tom, you must stop fighting on the playground.

Tom: But, they're always calling me names.

Ms. Jackson: That's not the point. What gets you in trouble is *your* fighting. This has to stop.

Tom: But, they pick on me first.

Ms. Jackson: I understand. But still *your* problem is fighting. You must stop fighting.

|_Nondirective Statements___Questions___Directive Statements___Demands_|

Figure 10.3 Assertive Discipline Response Continuum.

If not overused (three repeats is the recommended maximum), this technique helps the teacher maintain focus in the middle of a management problem, without becoming distracted from the objective.

While most veteran teachers don't use a management system as rigid as assertive discipline can be, some researchers have recommended it, appropriate for beginning teachers (Wolfgang & Glickman, 1986). Its structure and clear delineation of alternatives simplifies the management task for teachers. The hope is that teachers use it as a foundation for growth, expanding their repertoire to more complex and truly educational alternatives, as the issue becomes not so much order but learner growth.

Summary

The purpose of this chapter has been to suggest ways of dealing with routine management problems. The discussion has been general because the number of specific situations that might arise is endless, and the manner in which they are confronted depends upon the environment established by the teacher as well as the students.

Nevertheless, three specific approaches were offered that should prove useful. The approaches included the noninterventionist, interactionist, and interventionist methods. For each, the role of the teacher was discussed in addition to underlying assumptions and suggestions for utilization.

It is critical to note that successful use of the approaches depends on matching the appropriate method to the teacher's philosophy of education. As discussed in the chapter, teachers hold certain philosophical attitudes toward the nature of the learner, and these attitudes should dictate a consistent methodology for addressing management problems. In concluding the chapter, we introduced you to the concept of assertive discipline which, when employed in your classroom, can foster an atmosphere of respect and further promote student achievement and growth.

Questions for Discussion

1. What proportion of the management problems that teachers face is "their own fault?" What could these teachers do to prevent those problems?
2. Are classrooms harder to manage, easier to manage, or similarly difficult to manage compared to five years ago? Ten years ago? If you believe they're harder to manage, why do you think so? If you believe they're easier to manage, why do you think so?
3. How important a problem is violence in schools? Why do you think so?
4. How significant a problem for learning is the threat to students of physical harm? Is this problem being described accurately in the public media and in professional journals? Explain.
5. To what extent are classroom management problems detracting from students' ability to benefit from instruction? Explain.
6. In some schools management problems seem to be very serious, whereas in others they don't seem to be a major problem. To what would you attribute the difference?

Suggestions for Field Experience

1. Interview a teacher. Ask her the following questions.
   a. How do you typically handle management incidents? Would you offer two specific examples?
   b. What do you feel are your most chronic problems?
   c. Is this class harder or easier to manage than your other classes (or last year's class)? Why are they harder or easier to manage?
   d. Have you ever had a serious incident, such as an attack on you or a fight between students? What did you do in response to the incident?
   e. What do you feel are the differences between effective and ineffective managers?
   f. Do you call parents about behavior problems with your students? If you do, how effective do you believe it is in intervening?
   g. Do you ever take points away from a student's average for misbehavior? If so, how effective is this practice?
   h. Do you ever give students extra points on their averages for desirable behavior? If so, how effective is this practice.
2. Observe in a classroom. Look for the following in your observation.
   a. Describe specifically how the teacher intervenes when a management incident occurs.
   b. Describe the differences in the way the teacher responds in the case of a minor compared to a more serious incident.
   c. How consistently does the teacher respond in the cases of management incidents?
   d. How much emphasis does the teacher place on the development of learner responsibility compared to maintaining control of the students' behaviors?

Exercise Feedback

EXERCISE 10.1

As with most of the area of classroom management there are few "cut-and-dried" answers; instead, a great deal of judgment must be employed. The answers we've provided are most appropriate in a typical situation, but extremes may suggest a much different source.

1. (s) Student-caused
2. (s) Student-caused. This is probably just "kids being kids"; however, if saying negative things to peers leads to a pattern of isolation of a child or fighting, this may indicate an emotional problem.
3. (t) Teacher-caused. Looking out the window during a discussion is almost certainly a teacher-caused problem. Perhaps the teacher isn't using any materials, the discussion lacks focus, or the topic is too abstract for the student. This problem is usually easily remedied with more careful preparation on the part of the teacher.
4. (s) Student-caused. Some amount of writing on desk tops is quite normal for students. A pattern of defacing property, however, indicates emotional disturbance.
5. (s) Student-caused

6. (s) Student-caused
7. (e) Emotionally caused. Temper tantrums, particularly if they occur frequently, indicate emotional struggling within the student.
8. (e) Emotionally caused. Children, of course, are more boisterous around their peers than their teacher, but a typical outgoing child will also tend to blurt out answers and continue to be quite outgoing in class. If the child dominates or bullies his peers while withdrawing from the teacher, he may have an emotional problem. Again, the teacher must judge this at the time it occurs.
9. (e) Emotionally caused. Obscenity indicates emotional problems, although nearly every child will swear on some occasion. The pattern is the indicator.
10. (e) Emotionally caused. Refusal to respond in class to the point of withdrawing signifies an emotional disturbance.

EXERCISE 10.2

1. (IV) This statement's emphasis on a structured environment indicates an interventionist position.
2. (N) The goals of creativity and self-expression would be most emphasized by a noninterventionist who believes in the natural unfolding of the individual.
3. (I) An interactionist believes in providing enough structure so that students can operate and grow in a classroom.
4. (IV) This view is most compatible with an interventionist's orientation because of its functional view of management.
5. (N) Understanding students is a primary goal for noninterventionists.
6. (I) Interactionists stress the consequences of behavior, especially regarding others' rights and feelings.
7. (IV) External motivation based on grades as rewards characterizes an interventionist's position.
8. (N) Explaining misbehavior on the basis of unmet personal needs is a humanist approach to management.
9. (I) The interactionist approach is based on students understanding the consequences of their behavior for themselves and others.
10. (IV) A management system based on rewards is consistent with a behaviorist view of behavior, on which the interventionist approach is based.

EXERCISE 10.3

1. When Mr. Rogers put a check by Susan's name he was, in effect, punishing her, which is an interventionist approach to management.
2. Mr. Rogers was using an interactionist approach when he discussed his rules with the students and encouraged them to consider whether or not they were fair. This process promotes understanding of rules and the need for them. An appeal to a need for understanding is characteristic of the interactionist approach.
3. When Mr. Rogers approached Susan, asked her if she knew why he came to talk to her, and explained his emotional response to her behavior, he was using a noninterventionist approach.

Learner-Centered Assessments

In the third unit, which is composed of a single chapter, we complete the planning-imple-menting-assessing cycle. In this chapter we encourage teachers to carefully think about the ways they will assess the extent to which students have met their goals and how they will communicate these results to the students and their parents.

While traditional paper-and-pencil measures are and will continue to be the dom-inant form of assessment in today's classrooms, they are being increasingly criticized, and alternative or authentic assessments are now being emphasized. As with the trend toward more learner-centered instruction, which was described in the introduction of Unit Two, authentic assessment reflects increasing learner emphasis in the processes of measuring and evaluating student growth.

Chapter 11 responds to these trends. Both traditional assessment and alternative as-sessments are discussed in detail. The chapter begins with basic concepts in assessment, con-tinues with a discussion of traditional measures, then examines authentic assessments, and closes by considering grading and reporting results to students and their parents.

Chapter *11*

Assessing Student Learning

Jim Gorman's class was passing their prealgebra homework in to him. They had exchanged papers, scored the homework, and had discussed the problems causing most difficulty.

"How many got all the problems right?" he asked the class.

"Good!" he smiled in response to their show of hands. "You get this stuff. Remember that we have a test on this chapter on Friday, but now we're going to move on to subtraction of integers."

Kelly Morris gives her chemistry class a one- or two-problem quiz every other day. She was scoring the students' answers to a problem in which the mass of an element in grams was converted to moles and number of atoms. "I need to do some more of these," she thought. "They can convert moles to grams, but they can't go the other way."

Barbara Fisher's fourth graders were working on the rules for forming plural nouns. After putting several words on the board, Barbara circulated among the students, making periodic comments.

"Check this one again, Nancy," she said when she saw that Nancy had written citys *on her paper. She continued this process for 10 minutes before she moved on to another activity.*

Later she commented at lunch, "My kids just can't seem to get the rules straight. They get so mixed up when they change the y *to* i *and add* es. *What do you do about it? If I spend much more time on it, we won't get all the objectives covered."*

Introduction

We are now at the third and final phase of the teaching cycle. Having considered both the planning and implementation of lessons, we now turn our attention to assessment, which includes the techniques for determining whether or not students reach the goals we specify during the planning phase.

Because this book is not a text in measurement and evaluation, we will not attempt to provide the coverage you would find in a book devoted solely to those concerns. We will, however, illustrate the assessment phase of teaching and show how the processes of planning, implementing, and assessing student learning are interrelated.

After completing your study of Chapter 11, you should be able to:

- Describe the relationship between measurement and evaluation
- Explain the differences between formal and informal measurement
- Discuss the differences between effective and ineffective measurement items
- Prepare items to measure concepts and generalizations
- Explain the assignment of grades based on assessment data

MEASUREMENT AND EVALUATION

In each of the examples in the opening scenarios, the teacher was trying to gather information about his or her students' achievement and progress. Jim decided to move on to the next topic based on the students' performance on the homework, and Kelly concluded that the students needed more practice. Sometimes in spite of conscientiously gathering information the teacher is left uncertain, which was Barbara's problem. She was caught in the dilemma of concluding that her students didn't understand the rules, but at the same time feeling the need to move on. There are no easy answers in these situations.

These examples lead us to the concepts of *measurement* and *evaluation*, two core ideas in the process of assessment. Measurement includes all the information teachers gather as part of the assessment process, and evaluation refers to the decisions teachers make based on those measurements. Traditional paper-and-pencil tests, homework, answers in class, and performance assessments, such as third-graders' handwriting samples are forms of measurement. Assigning grades is the most common example of evaluation, but deciding when to give a quiz, what items will appear on it, and even whom to call on in a discussion are also decisions and therefore are evaluations.

Returning to our brief scenarios, the students' scores on the homework in Jim's class, the answers to Kelly's two-problem quizzes, and the responses to the seatwork in Barbara's class were all measurements.

Jim's decision to move on to the subtraction of integers and Kelly planning to give her students some more practice were both evaluations. Barbara's dilemma left her without a decision. She was unable to make an evaluation based on her measurements.

Formal and Informal Measurement

Measurements differ according to whether teachers consciously plan to measure or whether they take the measurement as part of the flow of classroom activities. Tests and quizzes are the most obvious examples of the former, which are called *formal measurements.* However, noticing the reactions to a movie shown in class, gauging student responses in a question-and-answer session, watching students as they do seatwork, or noting significant changes in an individual's manner or dress also give teachers much information. These are called *informal measurements,* and they provide a great deal of information that is used for making decisions. For example, noticing changes in a student's manner or dress, a teacher suspecting possible drug use might decide to refer the student to a school counselor. This is a critical decision that cannot be made on the basis of formal measurement.

EXERCISE 11.1

Read the scenario that follows and decide whether each numbered statement describes an informal measurement (im), a formal measurement (fm), or an evaluation (e). Then compare your answers to the ones found in the feedback section at the end of the chapter.

Miss Anthony wanted her kindergarten students to be prepared for written symbol recognition so that they could pick out the symbol when its sound was made. Therefore, she needed to determine if her kindergarten class needed more work in sound discrimination before they went into recognition of the written symbols. (1)____ She decided to pronounce the words *bird, dog, ball, dad, man, none, nose,* and *milk* to the children individually and ask them to tell her which ones had the same first sound. (2)____ She then checked the students to see if they could match the sounds, and she found that 8 of her 20 students matched all four of the pairs of sounds correctly, while the other 12 incorrectly matched one or more of the pairs.

She separated the children into the group of 12 and the group of 8, which she started on written letter recognition activities. (3)____ Then in order to have smaller groups, Miss Anthony divided the group of 12 into those whose first names started with A through M and those whose names started with N through Z, which made six students per group. (4)____ She decided to practice first-letter sounds with both of these groups by presenting pictures of objects and pronouncing the words.

While Miss Anthony worked with the first group of six, she saw Joey poke Mary and pull her hair. (5)____ She also noticed Joey glancing at her as he performed his little disruptions. (6)____ She recalled that he had been making himself conspicuous in other activities as well. (7)____ She then decided that she wouldn't call more attention to Joey by reprimanding him. (8)____ She noticed that Mary seemed to be paying little attention to him.

After Miss Anthony completed her week-long activity with her two groups of six, she gave the children each a set of 15 pictures and told them to put all of the pictures that started with the sound of *b* in one pile, those that started with *d* in a second pile, those with *m* in a third, and those with *n* in a fourth. (9)____ Based on the results, Miss Anthony moved the top eight into symbol recognition but held the bottom four students back for more work.

Measurement Accuracy

As with all measurements, the ones teachers make differ in accuracy. For instance, a teacher can obtain more precise measurements of Juan's knowledge of multiplication tables than he can of Juan's creative ability. A child's knowledge of the alphabet can be measured more precisely than her reading comprehension.

Additionally, measurement accuracy is determined by the instruments used to make the measurements. For instance, standardized reading tests, when administered and interpreted correctly, can give a more accurate measurement of a child's reading level than informal methods.

Teachers should continually try to increase the accuracy of measurements. The purpose of this chapter is to help you learn to measure student understanding as accurately as possible.

PREPARING ACCURATE MEASUREMENT ITEMS

As we begin our discussion of preparing measurement items, we want to emphasize that the process is more complex than it appears on the surface. For example, a multiple-choice item actually measures at least three aspects of learning: 1) the learners' understanding of the content, 2) their ability to respond to multiple-choice items, and 3) reading ability. Each of these factors affects the accuracy of the measurement. Keep these factors in mind as you prepare items.

One way of dealing with the problem is to increase the frequency of your measurements and use a variety of formats. Increased frequency gives students practice with the particular format, such as multiple-choice, and variety allows them to capitalize on their strengths, for example, students who are good writers can capitalize on essay items.

Paper-and-pencil tests are widely used, not because they are more accurate than other forms but because they are more efficient. It's very time consuming to discuss a topic with each student in a large class, but giving a single paper-and-pencil test can be accomplished quickly. We neither support nor oppose paper-and-pencil tests; rather, we describe ways of making written items as accurate as possible. A good discussion of different item formats can be found in Gronlund and Linn (1995). Let's turn now to a more specific discussion of measurement.

Measuring the Learning of Facts

As noted in Chapter 2, facts are forms of information learned through drill, and measurement of their attainment exists only at the knowledge level on the Bloom et al. (1956) taxonomy. For example an appropriate item that could be used to measure whether or not learners know the American presidents during major events in history might be:

> The president during the Civil War was
> a. Alexander Hamilton
> b. Robert E. Lee
> c. Abraham Lincoln
> d. William Jennings Bryan

The example is a *recognition* item, meaning the learner merely had to "recognize" the correct choice. A question in the form of a *production* item for the same objective could be

Who was president during the Civil War?

In this case, the student had to "produce" the answer. Obviously, production items are more demanding that recognition items, and teachers should keep this factor in mind when considering their goals and assessment items.

Measuring Understanding of Concepts

First, while concepts can be measured at the knowledge level, they are most commonly measured at the comprehension level. This is accomplished quite easily by asking students to identify unique examples of the concept. (To refresh your understanding of comprehension, you might want to refer back to Chapter 4.) For example, suppose you want preschool students to understand the concept *between*. Their comprehension could be measured using the item in Figure 11.1.

Now let's turn to a discussion of measuring concepts at different levels. Note in the following discussion that some of the objectives go beyond the understanding of a concept per se and into the analysis of relationships. As we noted above, understanding concepts themselves is primarily a comprehension-level task.

Let's look at an example with the concept *noun*. Suppose your goal is for the students to "understand" nouns. What does this mean? Some possibilities are

1. Write the definition of nouns.
2. Identify the definition of nouns from a list of definitions.
3. In a list of words, circle all those that are nouns.
4. Write grammatically correct sentences using nouns.
5. Underline all the nouns in a list of sentences.
6. Describe the author's intent by interpreting the meaning of the nouns in the context of a written passage.
7. Select the best interpretation of the meaning of nouns in context when given several interpretations.

So, we see that deciding what "understanding" means isn't simple. We listed seven possibilities, and there are undoubtedly more. The decision depends on the teacher's careful judgment.

Figure 11.1 Recognition Test Item   Place an X on the picture where the dog is between the two boys.

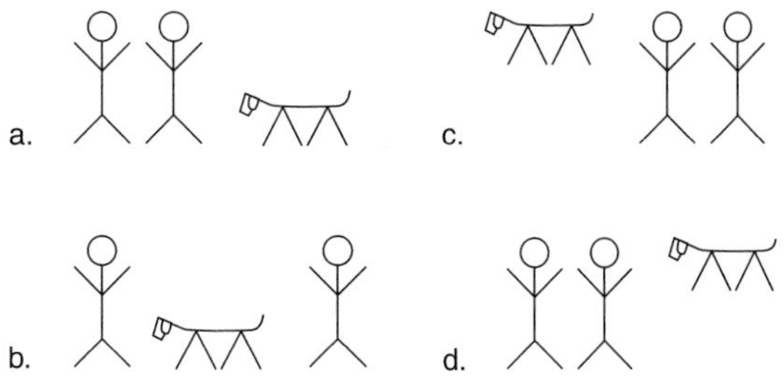

Let's look now at the seven possibilities on page 303 and discuss them in the context of the material we've presented so far. We can say several things about them.

First, each could become a formal measurement designed to provide data to help teachers assess their students' understanding of nouns. This is in contrast with informal measures such as observing the students at work or hearing a variety of responses from them.

Second, the possibilities represent different levels. Items one and two are knowledge level, three and five are comprehension level, four is application level, and six and seven are probably at the analysis level. As we noted in Chapter 5, exact determinations of level are sometimes difficult, so you shouldn't be overly concerned about whether items are at the application or analysis levels or at the analysis or evaluation levels. Our goal is for you to be aware of the higher levels of the taxonomy so you can encourage your students to improve their thinking skills.

Third, some of the possibilities require production, and others require only recognition. Items one, four, and six require production; the students were asked to produce, respectively, a definition, a sentence, and an analysis. Items two, three, five, and seven are recognition items; the students must recognize a definition, nouns in a list, nouns in a sentence, and a correct interpretation of a noun's use.

Let's look now at recognition and production in a bit more detail. First, production items are generally more difficult than recognition items at the same taxonomic level. Items one and two are both knowledge level, but recalling and stating the definition is more difficult than merely recognizing it. Another example of how recognition is simpler than production is found in our vocabulary. It is generally believed that our comprehension vocabulary is several times larger than our speaking vocabulary. This means that we recognize the meaning of many more words than we are able to use in conversation.

Second, recognition items are much easier for the teacher to score. A production item results in each student giving a slightly different response, leaving you in a position of having to decide whether the produced statement represents an adequate understanding of the concept. For example, compare item six to item seven. Item six puts much more demand on learners; they must interpret what is being asked, organize their thoughts, and put them down on paper. In item seven, they must merely select the choice they believe is best. Also, in item six, students will give a variety of responses since this is a divergent, not convergent, question, as in item seven. Therefore, the teacher needs to make more evaluation decisions with item six than with seven, where it would be much easier to be consistent in scoring.

One other factor to consider in deciding upon the item format is the amount of work involved. Production items are easier to prepare, but recognition items are easier to score. The decision of which to use depends on your goals. If you want to have students learn to express themselves in writing, you may choose to use a production item. You must keep in mind, of course, that you would be measuring writing ability in addition to the understanding of the concept.

These factors are not mentioned to suggest that accurate measurement is impossible. On the contrary, measuring can be an enjoyable task because it gives you in-

formation about your students and your own teaching. Instead, these factors are a reminder of considerations you must make in measuring—again, all in an effort to increase sound decision making.

EXERCISE 11.2

Look at the following two items designed to measure a kindergarten child's concept of a rectangle.
Assuming the directions are given orally, choose the better item and explain your choice. Then compare
your answers to the ones given in the feedback section at the end of the chapter.

1. Look at the three shapes on your paper and mark the one that is a rectangle.

2. Look at the four shapes on your paper and mark the one that is a rectangle.

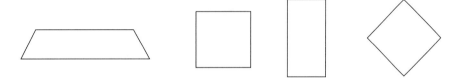

EXERCISE 11.3

Write a multiple-choice item to measure a kindergarten child's concept of mammal. Then compare your answer to the one given in the feedback section at the end of the chapter.

_____

_____

_____

Measuring Understanding of Generalizations

Generalizations, as with concepts, can be measured at the knowledge and the comprehension levels. In addition, however, they can readily be measured at the application level.

Let's look now at the different levels. Measuring a generalization at the knowledge level involves simply asking students to recall or identify one in a list. Measuring
generalizations at higher levels is quite another task. Let's look at the following goal:

Psychology students will understand the generalization that intermittent reinforcement
produces persistent behavior and slow extinction.

Effective teachers employ a wide-range of assessment techniques.

Consider the following item:

> Which of the following illustrates the generalization that intermittent reinforcement produces persistent behavior and slow extinction? Circle the letter of all choices that apply.
>
> a. Mrs. Williams was trying to encourage Johnny's seatwork. For a week she gave him a reward every 5 minutes whenever he was working quietly at his desk.
> b. Mr. Smith assigns homework nightly but checks it only periodically.
> c. Johnny, a spirited third grader, acts up often. Generally his teacher is firm but strict. Sometimes, though, Johnny's behavior is so funny, she has to laugh.
> d. When encountering a locked door, people generally wiggle it a few times and then leave or hunt for a key.
> e. Mr. Jones put 50 cents into the washing machine at the laundromat. It didn't come on, so he tried another machine.
> f. People who go to Las Vegas usually lose, but they win every once in a while.
> g. Mr. Anderson caught a fish in a particular spot in the St. Johns River. Now he fishes in that spot whenever he can and does fairly well.

In this recognition item, the students have to identify cases where the generalization is illustrated; in other words, they are identifying examples of the generalization. In this regard, the measurement is similar to having the students identify examples of a concept, which is also a comprehension-level task.

Note the format of the item. The student, in responding, makes a decision about each choice individually. The item then essentially operates in a true/false format. The directions could just as easily have read:

Mark as true the following cases that illustrate the generalization, intermittent reinforce-ment results in persistent behavior and slow extinction.

To make the item multiple choice, you would simply have to reduce the number of choices to four or five with only one of them correct.

The following is an example of using the multiple-choice format to measure ap-plication-level understanding of the generalization, reinforcement is most effective following desired behavior.

People in an institution were being paid 50 cents a day for doing maintenance work around the grounds. After the work was done, the trustee, who inspected the work, would come and pay the workers. After awhile, in that the work was always satisfactory and the workers always got paid, the administrators decided that they would just pay all the inmates in the morning at roll call and save the management the problem of paying people when the trustee came around.

Which of the following best describes the consequence of the change in routine?
a. There would be no change, and the operation would proceed more smoothly.
b. The inmates would like it better because they knew they would get paid, and conse-quently, they would work harder.
c. The inmates would work less hard because they got paid whether they did the work or not.
d. The inmates would work less hard because they would be insulted by the small amount they were being paid.

Notice in this example that students were asked to predict the consequences of the generalization, which is an application-level task.

EXERCISE 11.4

Read the following item and then answer the questions at the end. Compare your answers to the ones found in the feedback section at the end of the chapter.

Which of the following cases relate to the generalization, people who smoke tend to have a higher inci-dence of heart disease than those who don't?
a. Smith is a robust man in his late thirties. He runs two miles a day and lives a generally healthy life. He eats two eggs and has bacon for breakfast in order to get enough protein, and loves beef because "it keeps my energy level up." His only problem is that he has a heart murmur.
b. Mr. Jones has a generally healthy lifestyle. He has only two vices. He smokes a half a pack of ciga-rettes a day and has one strong drink before dinner. Otherwise he watches his diet by keeping fatty foods to a minimum and plays tennis four days a week. He is in his late thirties and is in excellent health.
c. Mr. Anderson lives a generally comfortable lifestyle. He smokes a few cigarettes each day but lays off the beer. He plays tennis, and everyone tells him how good he looks. However, he has two arteries par-tially clogged that his doctor says will eventually require surgery.
d. Mr. Holt is a generally healthy man in his early thirties. His only problem is he sometimes has heart fib-rillation. This is hard to imagine because he has a clean lifestyle. He is a vegetarian, and his weight is what it was in high school. He doesn't smoke and doesn't drink at all.

1. At what level is this item?

_____

2. Analyze the four choices in terms of the appropriateness of the distracters (incorrect choices).

a. _____

b. _____

c. _____

d. _____

Note in each of the previous examples that measuring understanding of a generalization required a short scenario either in the stem of the item or in the distracters. When measuring generalizations, this will often be the case since a generalization is broader and more inclusive than a concept. With practice, you will learn how to write scenarios that can be used in questions used to measure your students' understanding of generalizations.

Let's look now at an example that doesn't require a scenario. Refer back to pages 192–194, in which a teacher wanted her students to understand the following: when two vowels are together in a word, the first is long and the second is silent.

An item to measure this generalization could be as follows:

(Teacher reads) Look at the list of words in front of you. I'm going to pronounce each word, and you mark the ones in which this rule is generalized: when two vowels are together in a word, the first is long and the second is silent.

bought	sleigh	receive
either	protein	great
read	eight	load

Notice in this item that both the words and their pronunciations were required, because the rule linked the sound of the word to its spelling. Merely showing the students the words and asking them to state in which cases the rule applied wouldn't be appropriate. In order to respond correctly, a student would have to know how the word was pronounced; that being the case, the example couldn't be unique, which would mean the item was only at the knowledge level. This example is an excellent illustration of the teacher's need to think carefully about the measurement process.

EXERCISE 11.5 _____

Using a scenario, write a multiple-choice item to measure the following objective:

For students to understand the generalization, climate affects culture, so that when given a description of a culture, they will identify a statement that illustrates the generalization.

Then compare your answer to the one given in the feedback section at the end of the chapter.

_____

_____

Measuring Inquiry Skills

Now we will briefly consider the measurement of inquiry skills. This represents a departure from the themes of the text up to this point because measuring inquiry learning amounts to measuring an intellectual skill. The skill involved is the ability to relate data to a hypothesis or the ability to decide which of two or more hypotheses is most supported in light of the data. As an example, consider the situation shown in Figure 11.2 involving the relationship of data to hypotheses.

Both cities are on the coast and exist at the mouths of rivers. However, Jonesburg is a large and busy transportation center, whereas Williamsborough is small and insignificant. The following were proposed hypotheses that explained the reason for this difference:

1. While both Williamsborough and Jonesburg are on the coast and are at the mouths of rivers, Williamsborough's harbor is smaller than Jonesburg's, and the winds and tricky local currents made entrance dangerous in the early years when sailing ships were used.
2. The coastal range of mountains isolated Williamsborough but dwindled to foothills by the time they reached Jonesburg, which left it accessible to overland shipping.

The following data were gathered in reference to the hypotheses. Based on the data, decide which hypothesis is more logical and explain your choice briefly.

1. The current along the coast runs from north to south.
2. Jonesburg's harbor is larger than Williamsborough's.
3. About the same number of ships ran aground near Jonesburg as ran aground near Williamsborough in the sailing days.
4. Jonesburg and Williamsborough are over 100 miles apart.
5. The mountains around Williamsborough are more rugged than the mountains around Jonesburg.
6. The local winds around Jonesburg are more variable than they are around Williamsborough.

Keep in mind here that you're measuring the student's ability to relate data to hypotheses, which means the particular content of the item is not important. An inquiry lesson could present a topic in science while the item could involve social studies

Figure 11.2   A Partial Map of a Coastline

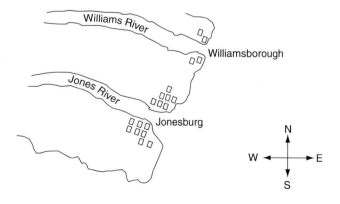

content. This is appropriate, because you're measuring an ability or an intellectual skill on the part of the students rather than information about an area of content. This is often a unique experience for a student and initially can be difficult. However, once this ability is developed, the students have acquired a powerful thinking skill.

EXERCISE 11.6

Read the following example of an inquiry situation and then respond to the data that follow. Compare your answers to the ones given in the feedback section at the end of the chapter.

A study reported an investigation of longevity in various groups of people around the world. The investigators found two particular groups with a wide disparity in the average life expectancy between them. Furthermore, Group A (the long-lived group) had a much lower overall standard of living than Group B (the shorter lived group). The average expectancies were Group A—85 years, and Group B—70 years. The investigators proposed the following explanation for this startling phenomenon:

While the standard of living for Group A is lower, they live in a manner conducive to good health. They are basically agrarian people, leading active and hard-working lives tending livestock and farms. Hence, they stay slim and avoid becoming overweight. They live in the mountains away from the psychological stresses of urban living. Their intake of potentially harmful items such as alcohol, tobacco, and high-cholesterol foods is kept at a minimum. On the other hand, Group B was sampled from an urban environment where psychological stress causing blood pressure problems is high, the air is dirty from factories, and the people lead sedentary lives. The following are data that were found relative to the two groups. In each case, decide if the data support the explanation (s) or do not (ns).

_____ 1. Group A people averaged about 5'10" and about 190 lb., while Group B people averaged about 6'0" and approximately 180 lb.

_____ 2. The average protein intake per capita per day was
  Group A: All sources—60 g.
                    Animal sources—1 g.
  Group B: All sources—100 g.
                    Animal sources—95 g.

_____ 3. Group A people average 6 oz. per person per day of an alcohol resembling a cross between gin and vodka.

_____ 4. Group A people spent an average of 12 working hours per day walking in the mountains as sheepherders.

_____ 5. The city from which the Group B sample was drawn was noted for its "soft" industry such as insurance companies and clearinghouses for photocopying companies rather than heavy industries such as steel making.

_____ 6. The companies noted in number five employed many supervisors and salespeople, with each company priding itself on its success in competing with rival companies.

_____ 7. The companies noted in numbers five and six also prided themselves on their comprehensive recreational programs including a variety of team and individual sports. They noted that each supervisor and salesperson averaged a minimum of five hours per week of vigorous physical activity.

_____ 8. Group A people enjoyed smoking a ground-up root resembling pipe tobacco in their leisure time. The investigators tried it and found it made them lightheaded when they inhaled, but the natives said it was easy to get used to.

_____ 9. In interviewing Group A people, a typical remark was, "It is good here where we can sit in the evening, watch the sun settle over our land, talk quietly, and watch our children grow."

_____ 10. In interviewing Group B people, typical remarks were, "I love my work. The only problem is that it's a bit of a hassle to be on the go all the time. It's really nice to get home and away from the grind. The traffic in this town is murder."

You've now seen what is perhaps a unique form of measurement for teachers and students—measurement of the inquiry process. Of course, the teacher could still measure the students' understanding of the content of a lesson in one of the conventional ways already discussed. Our purpose here is to give you a brief introduction to the idea of measuring inquiry skills. This introduction is sketchy because complete discussion of measuring for inquiry skills is beyond the scope of this text, but we hope this initial exposure will help you get started toward developing an important thinking skill in your own students.

ALTERNATIVE ASSESSMENT

Authentic Assessment

While paper-and-pencil tests continue to be used in education, they are being increasingly criticized. Some reasons include the following:

- Paper-and-pencil tests tend to focus on low levels of learning.
- Paper-and-pencil tests provide little insight into the way learners think.
- Paper-and-pencil tests don't measure learners' ability to apply their understanding to real world problems (Herman, Aschbacher, & Winters, 1992).

In response to these criticisms, *authentic assessments* are being emphasized. Often used interchangeably with *performance assessments* and *alternative assessments,* authentic assessments directly measure student performance through "real life" tasks (Herman et al., 1992; Worthen, 1993). Some examples include

- Explaining a real-world problem, such as why clothes tend to "stick" together when they come out of the dryer.
- Writing a letter to a penpal in another country.
- Designing and conducting an experiment to measure different effects on the growth of plants.
- Creating an original piece of sculpture.

In addition to products, such as the written explanation for the clothes sticking together, the letter, the description of the experiment or the sculpture, teachers want to examine learners' thinking when they use authentic assessments (Gronlund, 1993). For example, a portfolio of essays that illustrate improvement in writing, or systematic observation of students as they work, might be considered.

Let's look at two forms of authentic assessments: *performance assessments* and the use of *portfolios.*

Performance Assessment.

A middle school science teacher notices that her students have difficulty designing and conducting simple science experiments (such as determining which brand of aspirin dissolves faster).

A health teacher reads in a professional journal that the biggest problem people have in applying first aid is not the mechanics per se, but knowing what to do when. In an attempt to address this problem, the teacher has a periodic unannounced "catastrophe" day. Students entering the classroom encounter a catastrophe victim with an unspecified injury. Each time, they must first diagnose the problem and then apply first aid interventions (Eggen & Kauchak, 1997).

These teachers are using performance assessments to gather information about students' thinking. *Performance assessments* are authentic assessments that measure skill and understanding by directly measuring student performance in a natural setting.

Two common performance assessment methods are *checklists* and *rating scales*. *Checklists*—written descriptions of dimensions that must be present in an acceptable performance—extend systematic observation. When checklists are used, the students' behaviors are "checked off." For example, the science teacher wanting to assess learners' ability to design and conduct the experiment with plant growth might prepare a checklist such as the one that appears in Figure 11.3. (Notes could be added if desired, which would then combine elements of both checklists and systematic observations.)

Checklists are useful when the behaviors either exist or they don't, such as "Identifies variables that must be controlled." In cases such as, "Writes a description of results," the results aren't merely present or absent; some written descriptions will be better than others. This leads us to rating scales.

Rating scales are written descriptions of dimensions and scales of values on which each dimension is rated. They allow a more precise assessment of quality than is possible with checklists. A sample rating scale, based on the checklist in Figure 11.3 is illustrated in Figure 11.4.

While laborsome to construct, rubrics that are used as a basis for making decisions should be constructed for each of the dimensions. For example, definitions of values, such as the following might be used.

Rating = 5
The problem is stated clearly. Students appear to understand the topic and why the problem is important. It presents a framework for forming hypotheses.

Rating = 4
Problem is quite clear. It is adequate, but more important problems could have been identified. An adequate basis for stating hypotheses is provided.

_____ 1. Describes the problem
_____ 2. States hypotheses
_____ 3. Specifies variables that must be controlled
_____ 4. Clarifies independent and dependent variables
_____ 5. Makes at least three measurements of dependent variables
_____ 6. Organizes data in a chart or table
_____ 7. Writes a description of results

Figure 11.3   Checklist for Assessing the Design of an Experiment

---

Rate each item. A rating of 5 is excellent, and a rating of 1 is poor.

5 4 3 2 1   1. Describes the problem clearly.
5 4 3 2 1   2. States hypotheses clearly.
5 4 3 2 1   3. Controls variables effectively.
5 4 3 2 1   4. Gathers data appropriately.
5 4 3 2 1   5. Presents data clearly.
5 4 3 2 1   6. Draws logical conclusions.

Figure 11.4   Rating Scale for Assessing the Design of an Experiment

Rating = 3
The statement of the problem is uncertain. The basis for hypothesizing solutions isn't clear.

Rating = 2
The statement is made, but it isn't in the form of a problem. It isn't clear from the statement whether or not learners understand the significance of the problem.

Rating = 1
A problem isn't stated.

A rubric for each of the other dimensions would also be prepared in a form similar to what you see above. Using these descriptions, observers can achieve acceptable levels of reliability for both student performance and products.

Portfolio Assessment.   Portfolios are collections of work that are reviewed against preset criteria (Herman et al., 1992). They are a second type of authentic assessment. Using them allows students to be involved in the processes of collecting and assessing their own work. Portfolios are actually collections of products, such as samples of student writing; they are not the assessment. The assessments are the teachers' and students' evaluation of the products.

Portfolios have two characteristics. (1) They include products, such as samples of student writing, that have been gathered over a long period of time. (2) Students are involved in decisions about what materials will be included and how they will be evaluated.

Portfolios should reflect learning progress. For example, different essays indicate changes that occur during a grading period, semester, or entire course. These samples can then be used in parent–teacher conferences and as feedback for the students themselves.

GRADES AND GRADING

Grades and grading are somewhat controversial, and their merits have been argued for decades. Some argue that they're inherently destructive, pitting students against each other (Kohn, 1996). Grades are unlikely to disappear, however; parents and students both expect them. A variety of systems, such as "satisfactory," "satisfactory plus," and so on have been implemented, but they are little more than substitute terms for the traditional letter grades.

We won't debate the existence of grades in this text. They have always been a part of schooling, and they're likely to be a part in the future.

Norm- and Criterion-Referenced Evaluation

When decisions are made about student progress and grades are assigned based on how they compare to other students, the evaluation is *norm-referenced*. Most standardized tests are norm-referenced; the performance of learners in a class, school, or district on tests are compared to other students across the country.

Few classroom teachers write norm-referenced evaluations, however. They are more likely to use *criterion-referenced* evaluations, which are evaluations based on the extent to which learners have reached a preset standard.

A common form of criterion-referencing uses a percentage system, and this is what you're most likely to encounter when you begin teaching. A sample percentage system could be

93–100%	*A*
85– 92%	*B*
76– 84%	*C*
67– 75%	*D*

With this system a teacher determines each student's average percentage at the end of a grading period, and this percentage determines the grade. A thorough discussion of the issues involved in grading can be found in Gronlund and Linn (1995).

EXERCISE 11.7

Identify each of the ten functions listed below as characteristic of norm-referenced tests (n) or criterion-referenced tests (c). Then compare your answers with the ones given in the feedback section at the end of the chapter.

_____ 1. Determines whether or not a student is in the top 10% or bottom 10% of the group.
_____ 2. Must have predetermined standards.
_____ 3. Skills must be clearly demonstrated at a predetermined level.
_____ 4. Students are compared to standards.
_____ 5. Students are compared with other classmates or groups of students.
_____ 6. Students compete against each other.
_____ 7. Theoretically, all students could make an *A*.
_____ 8. The student's standing within the group is clearly identified.
_____ 9. Generally, one finds an equal distribution of letter grades.
_____ 10. More commonly used when teaching for mastery, competency, or the acquisition of skills.

Purposes of Assigning Grades

Feedback. First and foremost, grades provide feedback for students and parents. In doing so, a grade becomes an indicator of achievement in a given unit or course of study. If such feedback is to be useful, the students and their parents should be familiar with the grading system. The most common is the letter-grade system that uses *A, B, C, D,* and *F* grades. These letters have more or less represented *excellent, good, average, poor,* and *failing,* respectively.

In some areas, you might encounter a pass/fail (P/F) or an honors/satisfactory/unsatisfactory system (H/S/U). Whatever the system being used, its purpose is to communicate the educational progress of the pupil.

Other Uses for Grades. Grades are used not only to provide feedback to parents and students but also to meet a wide range of institutional needs. They are one of a number of factors used as a basis for grouping students. If a grade truly reflects achievement, it is legitimate to use such information when assigning students to math and reading groups at the elementary level and advanced or specialized courses at the high school level.

Grades are used by school systems to promote students from one grade level to the next and to graduate students from different levels within the system. Grades are often used to determine honor students and often serve as the basis for awards and scholarships. They may even determine whether or not a student is eligible to engage in extracurricular activities. Finally, grades are a major factor for college admission and eligibility to participate in athletics. For example, the National Collegiate Athletic Association, in implementing a rule called Proposition 48, has stated that any high school graduate with less than an overall *C* average is ineligible to participate in intercollegiate athletics at an NCAA member university. (A minimum score of 700 on the SAT or 17 on the ACT is also part of Proposition 48.)

Although the original purpose of grades was to provide information about student progress and achievement, there can be little doubt that as educational institutions have grown, grades have become a critical factor to the success in the adult world of today's students. This is true not only in the professions but also in any area that requires the student to exhibit mastery of a skill.

EXERCISE 11.8

In the spaces provided below, list five purposes for determining grades. Then compare your answers with the ones given in the feedback section at the end of the chapter.

1. _____

2. _____

3. _____

4. _____

5. _____

Inappropriate Uses of Grades

As stated previously, the primary purpose of grades is to serve as an indicator of achievement and to communicate this achievement to students and their parents. However, there are many other ways in which grades are used in classrooms.

Frequently, a higher, inappropriate grade is assigned to a student whose achievement has been low but whose effort has been high. In this way, the grade is designed as an incentive to keep trying regardless of the degree of achievement. When this takes place, the grade becomes more important than the achievement, which is often undesirable. The problem that arises from this situation is that a student might have solid grades yet very low scores on the standardized measurements, a situation that confuses and frustrates parents and aggravates administrators and school boards. If the function of a grade is to transmit information regarding student achievement, one must avoid communicating inaccurate information as this would do.

The teacher should also avoid using grades as a management axe. If a student achieves at the *B* level, it is illogical to report *C* achievement because of a lack of participation, poor attendance, or a management/discipline problem. Those situations should be handled in other ways, as discussed earlier in the text.

Affective areas must also be communicated in other ways. Grades should not be used to help students maintain a positive self-concept or help them move away from a negative one. Grades should not be given to reward the cooperative or to punish the uncooperative student.

The best way to support students is to review and upgrade the quality of instruction continually. This will allow increased numbers of students to achieve academically, which will then be reflected in higher grades.

EXERCISE 11.9

Place an X in front of the statements that reflect appropriate functions of grades. Then compare your answers with the ones given in the feedback section at the end of the chapter.

_____ 1. Grades should be awarded for effort.
_____ 2. Grades should be awarded to support a positive self-concept.
_____ 3. Grades should be awarded to help students conquer a negative self-concept.
_____ 4. Grades should accurately transmit academic achievement.
_____ 5. Grades could be lowered based upon participation and attendance.

Feedback Systems

Feedback to Students.   Students receive feedback from teachers in many ways. One of the most common is a grade on a formal measurement, such as a paper-and-pencil test. As stated earlier, the meaning of the grade must be clear and easily understood by the student so that it clearly communicates the level of achievement. Teachers also write comments on papers and provide verbal feedback. Again, the point is that all feedback regarding communication of achievement must be comprehensible.

In addition, the teacher's grading policies and system should be simple and clear to the student. As we have emphasized throughout this book, students have a right to understand their learning situations, the objectives they are expected to meet, and at what level they must perform in order to succeed. Feedback regarding performance and achievement should be continuous, and students should know their standing at all times. The "secret stuff" has gone on for too long; teachers must take the guesswork out of grades and grading schemes.

Feedback to Parents.   The most common form of communicating grades to parents is the report card. The high school report card offers grades that should be reflections of academic achievement, whereas the elementary report card serves the same function in addition to providing information on satisfactory or unsatisfactory performance in other nonacademic areas.

The parent should be familiar with as much performance information as the school can provide, most often presented in the form of grades. However, this information must be usable by clearly communicating levels of achievement. A letter grade of *B* in one class might not mean the same as a *B* in another class. As mentioned earlier, parents seeing satisfactory grades on report cards and low percentiles on standardized tests fail to understand how this could happen.

What teachers must keep in mind is that the reason for a report card or any other communication device is to increase parents' awareness of the educational progress of their children. The report card is only one way of achieving this goal.

Feedback should be constructive and supportive and need not always be in the form of a grade.

Another method of communicating progress is a written report. Such reports should be clear, easy to read, and void of any grade reporting as such. In everyday language, teachers must communicate the general academic situation, being concerned with not only what they are trying to say but also with the way they are trying to say it.

The most effective way of communicating with parents is through a conference. Face-to-face verbal communication allows the parent to ask questions and the teacher to provide understandable information. As stated earlier, parents need to know what grades mean, and in a conference, the teacher can very clearly discuss observable achievement as well as learning difficulties. The teacher should also realize that the parent conference is a two-way street and provides the opportunity to gain increased and valuable information about the student and his home environment. Such information may become instrumental in helping the teacher promote further achievement.

EXERCISE 11.10 _____

Which of the following three reporting systems is the most effective: report cards, written reports, or parent conferences. Give two reasons for your choice. Then compare your answers with the ones given in the feedback section at the end of the chapter. Most effective reporting system: _____

1. _____

2. _____

Communicating with Parents

Productive teachers communicate that both students and their parents are partners in learning. In a comprehensive review of variables affecting student learning, researchers concluded,

> Because of the importance of the home environment to school learning, teachers must also develop strategies to increase parent involvement in their children's academic life. This means teachers should go beyond traditional once-a-year parent/teacher conferences and work with parents to see that learning is valued in the home. Teachers should encourage parents to be involved with their children's academic pursuits on a day-to-day basis, helping them with homework, monitoring television viewing, reading to their young children, and simply expressing the expectation that their children will achieve academic success. (Wang et al., 1993, pp. 278–279)

Communication with parents or any other primary caregiver is no longer an appendage of the teaching process; it is an integral part of the teacher's job. Research indicates that students benefit from home-school cooperation in at least four ways:

• Higher long-term academic achievement.
• More positive attitudes and behaviors.
• Better attendance rates.
• Greater willingness to do homework (Cameron & Lee, 1997; Epstein, 1990).

These outcomes likely result from parents' increased participation in school activities, their more positive attitudes about schooling, and teachers' increased understand of learners' home environments (Weinstein & Mignano, 1993).

Strategies for Involving Parents.   Virtually all schools have formal methods for communication, such as interim progress reports, open houses, parent–teacher conferences, and report cards. There are at least two ways to do more, however. They are

- *Early Communication*—Send a letter home the first few days of school. Make the tone upbeat and describe class and school procedures.
- *Maintain Communication*—Send home packets of students' work. Have parents "sign off" acknowledging that they've seen the materials and have students return them.

Summary

In this chapter we've presented the third phase of the three-phase model of teaching. We discussed the differences between measurement and evaluation and then focused on measurement accuracy.

The idea of measurement accuracy was developed around sample items designed to measure the production or recognition of facts, concepts, and generalizations. A detailed discussion of multiple-choice items was woven into the description. We then closed this section with a brief introduction to the idea of measuring for inquiry skills.

A complete discussion of all the forms of measurement items, including various observational items, is beyond the scope of this text, and the reader wishing more information in this area should consult a text devoted primarily to measurement and evaluation.

The determining and communicating of grades, as discussed in this chapter, mark the last step of the three-phase model. When determining grades, teachers must first decide whether they are going to compare students to students or students to preset standards. Once this decision is made, the next step is to select an appropriate grading system that allows the teacher to assign letter grades objectively. It is important to note that a certain amount of subjectivity is always present, no matter how objective the grading system.

Once letter grades have been assigned, the next step is to clearly and understandably communicate them to both students and parents. The critical point here is that the letter grade must accurately represent student performance. Once this step is accomplished, the utilization of the three-phase model is complete.

As a final point, it should be understood that using this model involves a never-ending process. Although the process of assigning and communicating grades completes the assessing phase, the teacher must now examine student achievement in order to plan, implement, and evaluate subsequent instruction. Therefore, the utilization of the three-phase model is a circular situation in which the teacher is engaged in an endless instructional series. Only through such a process can teachers hope to improve instruction on a continual basis and thereby promote student achievement and a success-oriented environment.

Questions for Discussion

1. Does assessment enhance, detract from, or have no effect on the amount that students learn? Provide evidence to support your position.
2. Does assessment enhance, detract from, or have no effect on learner motivation? Provide evidence to support your position.
3. To what extent should assessment be used for motivational purposes? Explain why you feel this way.
4. To what extent should you use assessment for grading and reporting compared to using assessment to enhance learning? Explain.
5. Traditional paper-and-pencil tests are commonly criticized as measuring low-level learning in students. Do you agree with this criticism? Explain.
6. Since traditional paper-and-pencil tests are so strongly criticized, do you believe that they will eventually no longer be used? Explain why or why not.
7. Imagine 5 years and then 10 years from now. Do you believe that authentic assessments will be more or less prominent than they are today? Why do you think so?
8. Why do you believe that traditional *A, B, C,* etc., grading has endured for so long? Will these traditional grades eventually disappear? Why or why not?

Suggestions for Field Experience

1. Interview a teacher. Questions you might ask are
   a. How important do you feel assessment is for promoting learning?
   b. How do you assess? Would you describe your assessment system? How do you include homework, projects, and tests and quizzes in your assessment system?
   c. Do you use authentic (or alternative or performance) assessments in your system? If so, how do you count them in your grading?
   d. How do you communicate assessment results to parents (beyond sending home report cards and interim progress reports)?
   e. Do you do any specific test-preparation for your students before you give tests (such as the day before)?
   f. Do you go over tests with your students after you give them? Why or why not?
   g. How often do you test?
2. Observe a teacher the day before she gives a test. Does she do anything to prepare the students for the test?
3. Observe a teacher the day she hands a test back to the students. Does she discuss the test with them? If so, describe specifically what she does as part of the discussion.
4. Gather a sample of teachers' tests. As you study them, you might consider the following questions:
   a. At what level in the cognitive taxonomy are most of the items written? Are they primarily knowledge level, or do they measure higher level thinking?

b. What format is used for most of the items? Are they primarily objective, such as multiple-choice, matching, or true-false, or do they use another format, such as fill-in-the-blank or essay?

c. Are most of the items clear (i.e., is it unlikely that they would be misinterpreted)?

5. If the teacher uses portfolios of students' work, examine the contents of a portfolio. Describe the contents and be prepared to discuss them with your peers.

Exercise Feedback

EXERCISE 11.1

1. (e) Evaluation. A decision was made based on some previous measurement.
2. (fm) Formal measurement. Miss Anthony consciously planned to gather some information about her students and did so by checking to see if they could match similar first sounds.
3. (e) Evaluation
4. (e) Evaluation
5. (im) Informal measurement. The teacher, in an unplanned way, gathered some information.
6. (im) Informal measurement
7. (e) Evaluation
8. (im) Informal measurement
9. (e) Evaluation

EXERCISE 11.2

Item two is better than item one. In item one the correct choice is obvious since it is the only four-sided figure. In item two, the children must discriminate among four different four-sided figures. Also, they must know the difference between a rectangle and a square and between a rectangle and a trapezoid. A teacher could be quite certain the children had a concept of rectangle if they marked item two correctly, while he might be mistaken with a correct response to item one.

EXERCISE 11.3

The following would be an appropriate item to measure a small child's comprehension of the concept *mammal*. Of course, your item is probably somewhat different, but it should have good distracters.

Circle the animal that is a mammal. (Assume this would be read to the students and that the four choices would be in pictorial form.)
a. Frog
b. Cow
c. Alligator
d. Eagle

The correct answer, of course, is *cow.* The distracters are good ones, though, because a frog is an amphibian, an alligator is a reptile, and an eagle is a bird. Each represents a concept coordinate to the concept *mammal* and measures the child's ability to discriminate among coordinate concepts. (For a review of coordinate concepts refer to Chapter 2.)

EXERCISE 11.4

In order to respond correctly, students must relate smoking and heart disease.

1. The item is written at the comprehension level.
2. a. Heart disease but no smoking
   b. Smoking but no heart disease
   c. Correct—heart disease and smoking
   d. Heart disease but no smoking

If the distracters were written without any reference to either smoke or heart disease, the students could respond correctly without understanding the generalization. This would make the item invalid and could give the teacher some misinformation about student understanding.

EXERCISE 11.5

The following is an item that could be used. In this case, as with many others in this chapter, there are a number of appropriate possibilities.

The Tahitians have a peaceful, fun-loving culture. Life in Tahiti hasn't changed much in the last 100 years. Many Tahitians still fish for a living. Because it is warm, many wear a sarong the year round, just as their ancestors have for centuries.

The sentence that illustrates the generalization, climate affects culture, is
a. Tahitians have a peaceful, fun-loving culture.
b. Life in Tahiti hasn't changed much in the last hundred years.
c. Many Tahitians still fish for a living.
d. Because it is warm, many wear a sarong the year round, just as their ancestors have for centuries.

EXERCISE 11.6

1. (ns) Does not support. The explanation says Group A people are slim, but according to the data, their weight-to-height ratio is higher.
2. (s) Supports
3. (ns) Does not support. The explanation says Group A people drink little, but the data say they drink an average of four drinks per person per day.
4. (s) Supports
5. (ns) Does not support. The explanation says Group B people breathe dirty air, but the data say the city in which they live is noted for "soft" industry, which is nonpolluting.
6. (s) Supports
7. (ns) Does not support. The explanation says Group B people are sedentary, but the data say they exercise.

8. (ns) Does not support. The explanation says Group A people avoid harmful items like tobacco, but the data say they smoke.
9. (s) Supports
10. (s) Supports

EXERCISE 11.7

1. (n) Norm-referenced. With criterion-referenced tests, bottom and top percentages are not identified.
2. (c) Criterion-referenced
3. (c) Criterion-referenced
4. (c) Criterion-referenced
5. (n) Norm-referenced
6. (n) Norm-referenced. The highest scores receive a letter grade of *A* and the lowest a letter grade of *F*.
7. (c) Criterion-referenced. If the highest score, based upon 100%, was 99% and the lowest was 95%, all might be awarded the letter grade of *A*.
8. (n) Norm-referenced.
9. (n) Norm-referenced. The usual grade distribution is mostly the letter grade of *C* with some *B*s and *D*s and a few *A*s and *F*s.
10. (c) Criterion-referenced. These approaches require the establishment of predetermined standards.

EXERCISE 11.8

Any of the following would be acceptable responses:

1. Inform students of educational progress.
2. Inform parents of educational progress.
3. Guide further course work.
4. Provide a basis for grouping.
5. Provide a basis for promoting.
6. Provide a basis for graduating.
7. Provide a basis for college admission.
8. Provide a criterion for honors.
9. Provide a criterion for extracurricular participation.
10. Provide a motivational factor.
11. Identify student strengths and weaknesses.
12. Provide a basis for employment.

EXERCISE 11.9

1. No X
2. No X
3. No X
4. X
5. No X. If the grade accurately reflects student achievement, there can be no legitimate reason for lowering the grade. However, teachers often build participation and attendance into their grading scheme.

EXERCISE 11.10

The most effective reporting system is the parent conference. Any two of the following are acceptable reasons:

1. Allows parent questions and teacher answers
2. Allows parents to learn exactly what a grade means
3. Allows the teacher to explain both progress and problems
4. Allows the teacher to learn more about the student and his home environment.

References

Alexander, P., & Murphy, P. (1994, April). *The research base for APA's learner-centered psychological principles*. Paper presented at the Annual Meeting of the American Educational Research Association, New Orleans, LA.

Armstrong, D. (1989). *Developing and documenting the curriculum*. Boston: Allyn and Bacon.

Ashcraft, M. (1989). *Human meaning and cognition*. Glenview, IL: Scott, Foresman.

Association for Supervision and Curriculum Development. (1962). *Perceiving, behaving, becoming: A new focus for education*. Washington, DC: Author.

Banks, J. (Ed.) (1995). *Handbook of research on multicultural education* (pp. 525–547). New York: Macmillan.

Banks, J. (1997). Multicultural education: Characteristics and goals. In J. Banks & C. Banks (Eds.), *Multicultural education: Issues and perspectives* (pp. 3–31). Boston: Allyn & Bacon.

Bardwell, D. (1987). The development and motivational function of expectations. *American Educational Research Journal, 21*(2), 461–472.

Bean, R., Fulmer, D., Zigmond, N, & Grumet, J. (1995, April). *How experienced teachers think about their teaching: Their focus, beliefs, and types of reflection*. Paper presented at the meeting of the American Education Research Association, San Francisco, CA.

Berk, L. (1994). *Child development* (3rd ed.). Needham Heights, MA: Allyn & Bacon.

Berliner, D. (1985, April). *Effective teaching*. Pensacola, FL: Florida Education Research and Development Council.

Berliner, D. (1987). Simple views of effective teaching and a simple theory of classroom instruction. In D. Berliner & B. Rosenshine (Eds.), *Talks to teachers* (pp. 93–110). New York: Random House.

Berliner, D. (1988). *The development of expertise in pedagogy*. Washington, DC: American Association of Colleges of Teacher Education.

Berliner, D. (1994). Expertise: The wonder of exemplary performances. In J. Mangieri & C. Collins (Eds.), *Creating powerful thinking in teachers and students* (pp. 161–186). Ft. Worth, TX: Harcourt Brace.

Beyer, B. K. (1987). *Practical strategies for the teaching of thinking*. Boston: Allyn and Bacon.

Beyer, B. (1988). Developing a scope and sequence for thinking skills instruction. *Educational Leadership, 45* (7), 26–30.

Block, J. H. (Ed.). (1971). *Mastery learning: Theory and practice.* New York: Holt, Rinehart & Winston.

Block, J. H. (Ed.). (1974). *Schools, society and mastery learning.* New York: Holt, Rinehart & Winston.

Bloom, B. (1981). *All our children learning.* New York: McGraw-Hill.

Bloom, B., Englehart, M., Furst, E., Hill, W., & Krathwohl, D. (1956). *Taxonomy of educational objectives: The classification of educational goals: Handbook 1. The cognitive domain.* White Plains, NY: Longman.

Bloom, B., Hastings, J., & Madaus, G. (Eds.). (1971). *Handbook on formative and summative evaluation of student learning.* New York: McGraw-Hill.

Bluhm, H. (1987). *Administrative uses of computers in the schools.* Englewood Cliffs, NJ: Prentice-Hall.

Blumenfeld, P., Pintrich, P., & Hamilton, V. L. (1987). Teacher talk and students' reasoning about morals, conventions, and achievement. *Child Development, 58,* 1389–1401.

Borich, G. (1996). *Effective teaching methods* (3rd ed.). Englewood Cliffs, NJ: Prentice-Hall.

Brophy, J. (1987). On motivating students. In D. Berliner & B. Rosenshine (Eds.), *Talks to teachers* (pp. 201–245). New York: Random House.

Brophy, J., & Evertson, C. (1976). *Learning from teaching: A developmental perspective.* Needham Heights, MA: Allyn & Bacon.

Brophy, J., & Evertson, C. (1978). Context variables in teaching. *Educational Psychologist, 12,* 310–316.

Bruning, R., Schraw, G., & Ronning, R. (1995). *Cognitive psychology and instruction* (2nd ed.). Upper Saddle River, NJ: Prentice-Hall.

Buser, K., & Reimer, D. (1988). Developing cognitive strategies through problem solving. *Teaching Exceptional Children,* 1988.

Cameron, C., & Lee, K. (1997). Bridging the gap between home and school with voice-mail technology. *Journal of Educational Research, 90*(2), 182–190.

Canter, L. (1988). Let the educator beware: A response to Curwin and Mendler. *Educational Leadership, 46*(2), 71–73.

Canter, L., & Canter, M. (1976). *Assertive discipline: A take-charge approach for today's educator.* Seal Beach, CA: Canter & Associates.

Canter, L., & Canter, M. (1992). *Assertive discipline.* Santa Monica, CA: Lee Canter & Associates.

Carlson, S., & Silverman, R. (1986). Microcomputers and computer-assisted instruction in special classrooms: Do we need the teacher? *Learning Disability Quarterly, 9*(2), 105–110.

Carr, K. (1988). How can we teach critical thinking? *Childhood Education, 65*(2), 69–73.

Chenfield, M. (1990). My loose is tooth—kidding around with kids. *Young Children, 56,* 60.

Clark, C., & Peterson, P. (1986). Teachers' thought processes. In M. Wittrock (Ed.), *Handbook on research on teaching* (3rd ed., pp. 255–296). New York: MacMillan.

Clark, C., & Yinger, R. (1979). *Three studies of teacher planning.* East Lansing, MI: Michigan State University, Institute for Research on Teaching.

Clarke, A. (1994). Student-teacher reflection: Developing and defining a practice that is uniquely one's own. *International Journal of Science Education, 16*(5), 498.

Clifford, M. (1990). Students need challenge, not easy success. *Educational Leadership, 48*(1), 22–26.

Cohen, S. (1987). Instructional alignment: Searching for a magic bullet. *Educational Researcher, 16*(8), 16–20.

Combs, A. (1962). Motivation and growth in self. In *Perceiving, behaving, becoming.* Association for Supervision and Curriculum Development Yearbook (pp. 83–98). Washington, DC: National Education Association.

Crocker, R., & Brooker, G. (1986). Classroom control and student outcomes in grades 2 and 5. *American Educational Research Journal, 23,* 1–11.

Cromer, J. (1984). *The mood of American youth.* Washington, DC: National Association of Secondary School Principals.

Curwin, R., & Mendler, A. (1988). Packaged discipline programs: Let the buyer beware. *Educational Leadership, 46*(2), 68–71.

Deering, P., & Meloth, M. (1990). *An analysis of the content and form of students' verbal interactions in cooperative groups.* Paper presented at the annual meeting of the American Educational Research Association, Boston.

Denham, C., & Lieberman, A. (1980). *Time to learn.* Washington, DC: National Institute of Education.

Dillon, J. (1981). To question and not to question during discussions: Non-questioning techniques. *Journal of Teacher Education, 32*(6), 15–20.

DiVesta, F. (1987). The cognitive movement and education. In J. Glover & R. Ronning (Eds.), *Historical foundations of educational psychology* (pp. 203–230). New York: Plenum.

Dowhower, S. (1991, April). *The beginning of the beginning: A comparison of classroom management practices of novice and experienced kindergarten teachers the first month of school.* Paper presented at the annual meeting of the American Educational Research Association, Chicago.

Doyle, W. (1986). Classroom organization and management. In M. Wittrock (Ed.), *Handbook of research on teaching* (3rd ed., pp. 392–425). New York: Macmillan.

Dreikurs, R. (1968a). *The courage to be imperfect* [Speech]. Tempe, AZ: Arizona State University.

Dreikurs, R. (1968b). *Psychology in the classroom* (2nd ed.). New York: Harper & Row.

Drexler, N., Harvey, G., & Kell, D. (1990). *Student and teacher success: The impact of computers in primary grades.* Boston: American Educational Research Association.

Duffy, G., Roehler, L., Meloth, M., & Vavrus, L. (1985). *Conceptualizing instructional explanation.* American Educational Research Association.

Dunn, R., Beaudry, S., & Klavas, A. (1989). Survey of research on learning style. *Educational Leadership, 46*(6), 50–58.

Dunn, R., & Dunn, K. (1978). *Teaching students through their individual learning styles.* Reston, VA: Reston.

Dunn, R., & Dunn, K. (1987). Dispelling outmoded beliefs about student learning. *Educational Leadership, 44*(6), 55–62.

Dunn, R., Dunn, K., & Price, G. (1985). *Learning style inventory.* Lawrence, KS: Price Systems.

Eagly, A., & Chaiken, S. (1993). *The psychology of attitudes.* Ft. Worth, TX: Harcourt Brace.

Eby, J. (1996). *Reflective planning, teaching, and evaluation.* Upper Saddle River, NJ: Prentice-Hall.

Eggen, P., & Kauchak, D. (1996). *Strategies for teachers: Teaching content and thinking skills* (3rd ed.). Needham Heights, MA: Allyn & Bacon.

Eggen, P., & Kauchak, D. (1997). *Educational psychology: Windows on classrooms* (3rd ed.). Upper Saddle River, NJ: Prentice-Hall.

Elam, S., & Rose, L. (1995). The 27th annual Phi Delta Kappa/Gallup poll. *Phi Delta Kappan, 77*(1), 41–49.

Ely, J. (1994). *Reflective planning, teaching & evaluation for the elementary school.* New York: Merrill.

Emmer, E., Evertson, C., Sanford, J., Clements, B., & Worsham, M. (1994). *Classroom management for secondary teachers* (3rd ed.). Upper Saddle River, NJ: Prentice-Hall.

Epstein, J. (1990). School and family connections: Theory, research, and implications for integrating sociologies of education and family. In D. Unger & M. Sussman (Eds.), *Families in community settings: Interdisciplinary perspectives* (pp. 99–126). New York: Haworth Press.

Eschermann, K. (1988). Structuring classrooms for success. *Vocational Education Journal, 63,* 36–38.

Evertson, C. (1987). Managing classrooms: A framework for teachers. In D. Berliner & B. Rosenshine (Eds.), *Talks to teachers* (pp. 54-74). New York: Random House.

Evertson, C., Emmer, E., Clements, B., Sanford, J., & Worsham, M. (1994). *Classroom management for elementary teachers* (3rd ed.). Upper Saddle River, NJ: Prentice-Hall.

Fairbain, D. (1987). The art of questioning your student. *Clearinghouse, 61*(1), 9.

Fantini, M., & Weinstein, G. (1968). *The disadvantaged: Challenge to education.* New York: Harper & Row.

Farr, C., & Moon, C. (1988). *New perspectives on intelligence: Examining field dependence/independence in light of Steinber's Triarchic Theory of Intelligence.* Paper presented at the annual meeting of the American Educational Research Association, New Orleans.

Farrell, E. (1990). *Hangin' in and dropping out.* New York: Teachers College Press.

Fitzgerald, J. (1995). English-as-a-second-language learners' cognitive reading processes: A review of research in the United States. *Review of Educational Research, 65*(2), 145–190.

Forcier, R. (1996). *The computer as a productivity tool in education.* Columbus, OH: Merrill.

Fraenkel, J. (1980). *Helping students think and value: Strategies for the social studies* (2nd ed.). Englewood Cliffs, NJ: Prentice-Hall.

Frankena, Wm. (1965). *Three historical philosophies of education.* Glenview, IL: Scott, Foresman.

Gage, N., & Berliner, D. (1992). *Educational Psychology* (5th ed.). Boston, Houghton Mifflin.

Gardner, H. (1983). *Frames of mind: The theory of multiple intelligences.* New York: Basic Books.

Gardner, H. (1995). Reflections on multiple intelligences: Myths and messages. *Phi Delta Kappan, 77,* 200–209.

Gardner, H., & Hatch, T. (1989). Multiple intelligences go to school. *Educational Researcher, 18*(8), 4–10.

Gestwicki, C. (1995). *Developmentally appropriate practice: Curriculum and development in early childhood education.* Delmar, NY: Delmar Publishers.

Gilman, D. (1988). The educational efforts of a state supported reduced class size program. *Contemporary Education, 59,* 112–116.

Glasser, W. (1969). *Schools without failure.* New York: Harper & Row.

Glasser, W. (1985). *Control theory in the classroom.* New York: Perennial Library.

Good, T. (1983). Research on classroom teaching. In L. Shulman & G. Sykes (Eds.). *Handbook on teaching and policy* (pp. 42–80). New York: Longman.

Good, T., & Brophy, J. (1997). *Looking in classrooms* (7th ed.). New York: HarperCollins.

Goodlad, J. (1984). *A place called school.* New York: McGraw-Hill.

Gordon, T. (1975). *T.E.T.: Teacher effectiveness training.* New York: Wyden.

Gorham, J., & Christophel, D. (1990). The relationship of teacher's use of humor in the classroom to immediacy of student learning. *Communication Education, 39*(1), 46–62.

Greenwood, G., & Fillmer, H. (1997). *Professional core cases for teacher decision-making.* Upper Saddle River, NJ: Prentice-Hall.

Gronlund, N. (1993). *How to make achievement tests and assessments.* Needham Heights, MA: Allyn & Bacon.

Gronlund, N. (1991). *How to write and use instructional objectives* (4th ed.). New York: Macmillan.

Gronlund, N., & Linn, R. (1995). *Measurement and evaluation in teaching* (7th ed.). Upper Saddle River, NJ: Prentice-Hall.

Gusky, T., & Pigott, T. (April, 1988). Research on group-based mastery learning programs: A meta-analysis. *Journal of Educational Research, 8*(4), 197–216.

Hagaman, S. (1990). The community of inquiry: An approach to collaborative learning. *Studies in Art Education, 31*(3), 147–149.

Hamachek, D. (1987). Humanistic psychology: Theory, postulates, and implications for educational processes. In J. Glover & R. Ronning (Eds.), *Historical foundations of educational psychology* (pp. 159-182). New York: Plenum Press.

Hardman, M., Drew, C., & Egan, W. (1996). *Human exceptionality* (5th ed.). Boston, MA: Allyn & Bacon.

Harrow, A. (1972). *A taxonomy of the psychomotor domain: A guide for developing behavioral objectives.* New York: David McKay.

Hasselbring, T., Goin, L., & Bransford, J. (1988). Developing math automaticity in learning handicapped children: The role of computerized drill and practice. *Focus on Exceptional Children, 20*(6), 1–70.

Herman, J., Aschbacher, P., & Winters, L. (1992). *A practical guide to alternative assessment.* Alexandria, VA: Association for Supervision and Curriculum Development.

Heward, W. (1996). *Exceptional children* (5th ed.). Upper Saddle River, NJ: Merrill/Prentice-Hall.

Hill, D. (1990). Order in the classroom. *Teacher, 1,* 70–77.

Hirsch, E. (1987). *Cultural literacy.* Boston: Houghton Mifflin.

Hodgkinson, H. (1991). Reform versus reality. *Phi Delta Kappan, 73*(1), 8–16.

Hunter, M. (1982). *Mastery teaching.* El Segundo, CA: TIP Publications.

Hyman, J. S., & Cohen, S. A. (1979). Learning for mastery: Ten conclusions after 15 years and 3,000 schools. *Educational Leadership, 37*(2), 104–109.

James, W. (1914). *Talks to Teachers.* New York: Holt.

Jarolimek, J., & Foster, C. (1997). *Teaching and learning in the elementary school* (6th ed.). Upper Saddle River, NJ: Prentice-Hall.

Jewett, A., & Mullan, M. (1977). Movement process categories in physical education in teaching-learning. *Curriculum design: Purposes and procedures in physical education teaching-learning.* Washington, DC: American Alliance for Health, Physical Education and Recreation.

Jonassen, D. (1996). *Computers in the classroom.* Columbus, OH: Merrill.

Jones, E. (1995, April). *Defining essential critical thinking skills for college students.* Paper presented at the annual meeting of the American Educational Research Association, San Francisco.

Kagan, J., Pearson, L., & Welch, L. (1966). Conceptual impulsivity and inductive reasoning. *Child Development, 37,* 123–130.

Kauchak, D., & Eggen, P. (1998). *Learning and teaching: Research based methods* (3rd ed.). Needham Heights, MA: Allyn and Bacon.

Keefe, J. (1982). Assessing student learning styles: An overview. In National Association of Secondary School Principals (Ed.), *Student learning styles and brain behavior* (pp. 18–21). Reston, VA: Author.

Kellog, J. (1988). Forces of change. *Phi Delta Kappan, 70,* 199–204.

Kendsvatter, R., Wilen, W., & Ishler, M. (1988). *Dynamics of effective teaching.* New York: Longman.

Kerman, S. (1979). Teacher expectations and student achievement. *Phi Delta Kappan, 60,* 716–718.

Kher-Durlabhji, N., Lacina-Gifford, L., Jackson, L., Guillory, R., & Yandell, S. (1997, March). *Preservice teachers' knowledge of effective classroom management strategies.* Paper presented at the annual meeting of the American Educational Research Association, Chicago.

Kohn, A. (1996). *Beyond discipline: From compliance to community.* Alexandria, VA: Association for Supervision and Curriculum Development.

Kounin, J. (1970). *Discipline and group management in classrooms.* New York: Holt, Rinehart & Winston.

Kulik, C. C., & Kulik, A. (1990). Effectiveness of mastery learning programs: A meta-analysis. *Review of Educational Research, 60,* 265–299.

Laboskey, V. (1994). *Development of reflective practice: A study of preservice teachers.* New York: Teachers College Press.

Larson, K. (1989). Task related and interpersonal problem solving training for increasing school success in high risk young adolescents. *Remedial and Special Education, 10,* 32–41.

Lawson, A. (1995). *Science teaching.* Belmont, CA: Wadsworth.

Lepper, M., & Hodell, M. (1989). Intrinsic motivation in the classroom. In C. Ames & R. Ames (Eds.), *Research on motivation in education* (Vol. 3, pp. 73–105). San Diego: Academic Press.

Levin, J., & Nolan, J. (1991). *Principles of classroom management: A hierarchical approach.* Englewood Cliffs, NJ: Prentice-Hall.

Mager, R. (1997). *Preparing instructional objectives: A critical tool in the development of effective instruction* (3rd ed.). Atlanta, GA: The Center for Performance, Inc.

Mager, R. (1962). *Preparing instructional objectives.* Belmont, CA: Fearon.

Marzano, R. (1992). *A different kind of classroom.* Alexandria, VA: ASCD.

McCaslin, M., & Good, T. (1992). Compliant cognition: The misalliance of management and instructional goals in current school reform. *Educational Researcher, 21*(3), 4–17.

McCutcheon, G. (1980). How elementary teachers plan their courses. *Elementary School Journal, 81,* 4–23.

McCutcheon, G. (1982). How do elementary school teachers plan? The nature of planning and influences on it. In W. Doyle and T. Good (Eds.), *Focus on Teaching* (pp. 260–279). Chicago: University of Chicago Press.

McDougall, D., & Granby, C. (1996). How expectation of questioning method affects undergraduates' preparation for class. *Journal of Experimental Education, 65,* 43–54.

McLaughlin, H. J. (1994). From negation to negotiation: Moving away from the management metaphor. *Action in Teacher Education, 16*(1), 75–84.

Meichenbaum, D. (1986). Cognitive behavior modification. In F. Kanfer & A. Goldstein (Eds.), *Helping people change: A textbook of methods* (3rd ed.) (pp. 346–380). New York: Pergamon.

Merrill, P., Hammons, K., Tolman, M., Christensen, L., Vincent, B., & Reynolds, P. (1992). *Computers in education.* Needham Heights, MA: Allyn and Bacon.

Miller, D., Alway, M., & McKinley, D. (1987). Effects of learning styles and strategies on academic success. *Journal of College Student Personnel, 28,* 399–404.

Miller, D., Barbetta, P., & Heron, T. (1994). START tutoring: Designing, training, implementing, adapting, and evaluating tutoring programs for school and home settings. In R. Gardner, D. Sianato, J. Cooper, W. Heward, T. Heron, J. Eshleman, & T. Grossi (Eds.), *Behavior analysis in education: Focus on measurably superior instruction* (pp. 265–282). Pacific Grove, CA: Brooks/Cole.

Mintz, A. (1979). *Teacher planning: A simulation study.* Unpublished doctoral dissertation, Syracuse University.

Moore, K. (1992). *Classroom teaching skills* (2nd ed.). New York: McGraw-Hill.

Nazario, S. (1989). Failing in 81 languages. *Wall Street Journal, 213* (63).

Neale, D., Pace, A., & Case, A. (1983, April). *The influence of training experience, and organizational environment on teachers' use of the systematic planning model.* Paper presented at the annual meeting of the American Educational Research Association.

Nickerson, R. (1988). On improving thinking through instruction. In E. Rothkopf (Ed.), *Review of Research in Education* (pp. 3–57). Washington, D.C.: AERA.

Noddings, N. (1984). *A feminine approach to ethics and moral education.* Berkely, CA: The University of California Press.

O'Keefe, P., & Johnston, M. (1986). *Teachers' abilities to understand the perspectives of students: A case study of two teachers.* Washington, DC: American Educational Research Association.

Okey, J., & Ciesla, J. (1975). *Mastery teaching.* Bloomington, IN: National Center for the Development of Training Materials in Teacher Education.

Okey, J. R. (1977). Consequences for Training Teachers to Use Mastery Learning Strategy. *Journal of Teacher Education, 28*(5), 57–62.

Ormrod, J. (1995). *Human learning* (2nd ed.). Columbus, OH: Merrill.

Ornstein, A. (1987). Questioning: The essence of good teaching. *National Association of Secondary School Principals Bulletin, 71,* 71–79.

Pajares, M. (1992). Teacher's beliefs and education research: Cleaning up a messy construct. *Review of Education Research, 62,* 307–332.

Palincsar, A. (1987). Can student discussions boost comprehension? *Instructor, 96,* 56–60.

Pallas, A., Natriello, G., & McDill, E. (1989). The changing nature of the disadvantaged population: Current dimensions and future trends. *Educational Researcher, 18,* 16–22.

Papalia, D., & Wendkos-Olds, S. (1996). *Human development* (6th ed.). New York: McGraw-Hill.

Perkins, D. (1987). Thinking frames: Integrating perspectives on teaching cognitive skills. In J. Baron and R. Sternberg (Eds.). *Teaching thinking skills: Theory and practice* (pp. 41–61). NY: Freeman Press.

Peterson, P., Marx, R., & Clark, C. (1978). Teacher planning, teacher behavior, and student achievement. *American Educational Research Journal, 15,* 417–432.

Pintrich, P., & Schunk, D. (1996). *Motivation in education: Theory, research, and applications.* Upper Saddle River, NJ: Prentice-Hall.

Pittman, R. (1987). Perceived instructional effectiveness and associated teaching dimensions. *Journal of Experimental Education, 67,* 34–39.

Porter, A., & Brophy, J. (1988, May). Synthesis of research on good teaching: Insights from the work of the Institute for Research on Teaching. *Educational Leadership,* 74–93.

Presidential Task Force on Psychology in Education. (1993). *Learner-centered psychological principles: Guidelines for school redesign and reform.* Washington, DC: American Psychological Association.

Purkey, S., & Smith, M. (1983). Effective schools: A review. *Elementary School Journal, 83,* 427–452.

Raths, L., Harmin, M., & Simon, S. (1966). *Values in teaching.* Columbus, OH: Merrill/Macmillan.

Redfield, D., & Rousseau, E. (1981). A meta-analysis of experimental research on teacher questioning behavior. *Review of Educational Research, 51,* 237–245.

Rich, J. (1988). Competition in education. *Educational Theory, 38*(2), 183–189.

Rodriguez, G. (1988). Teaching teachers to teach thinking. *Curriculum Review, 1,* 13–14.

Rogers, D. (1991, April). *Conceptions of caring in a fourth-grade classroom.* Paper presented at the annual meeting of the American Educational Research Association, Chicago.

Rosenshine, B. (1971). *Teaching behaviors and student achievement.* London: National Foundation for Educational Research.

Rosenshine, B., & Furst, N. (1971). Research in teacher performance criteria. In B. O. Smith (Ed.), *Research in Education* (pp. 37–66). Englewood Cliffs, NJ: Prentice-Hall.

Rosenshine, B., & Stevens, R. (1986). Teaching functions. In M. Wittrock (Ed.), *Third Handbook of Research on Teaching* (3rd ed.) (pp. 376–391). New York: Macmillan.

Rowe, M. (1974). Wait-time and rewards as instructional variables, their influence on language, logic, and fate control: Part one—Wait-time. *Journal of Research in Science Teaching, 11,* 81–94.

Rowe, M. (1986, January/February). Wait-time: Slowing down may be a way of speeding up. *Journal of Teacher Education,* 43–50.

Savage, T. (1991). *Discipline for self control.* Englewood Cliffs, NJ: Prentice-Hall.

Schmeck, R. (Ed.). (1988). *Learning strategies and learning styles.* New York: Plenum.

Schrag, F. (1989). Are there levels of thinking? *Teacher College Record, 90* (4), 529–533.

Schrum, L., & Fitzgerald, M. (1996). *Educators & information technologies: What will it take for adoption & implementation?* Paper presented at the annual meeting of the American Educational Research Association, New York.

Schunk, D. (1991). *Learning theories.* Columbus, Ohio: Merrill.

Science Curriculum Guide (1982, p. 31) Jacksonville, Florida: Duval County School System.

Shavelson, R. (1973). What is *the* basic teaching skill? *Journal of Teacher Education, 24*(2), 144–151.

Shavelson, R. (1983). Review of research on teachers' pedagogical judgments, plans and decisions. *Elementary School Journal, 83*(4), 392–413.

Shuell, T. (1981). Dimensions of individual differences. In F. Farley & N. Gordon (Eds.), *Psychology and education: The state of the union* (pp. 32–59). Berkeley, CA: McCutcheon.

Shulman, L. (1986). Those who understand: Knowledge growth in teaching. *Educational Research, 15*(2), 4–14.

Shulman, L. (1990). Paradigms and research programs in the study of teaching. In M. Wittrock (Ed.). In *Handbook of Research on Teaching* (3rd ed.). New York: MacMillan.

Slavin, R. (1991). *Educational psychology* (3rd ed.). Englewood Cliffs, NJ: Prentice-Hall.

Slavin, R. (1995). *Cooperative learning* (2nd ed.). Needham Heights, MA: Allyn & Bacon.

Slavin, R. (1997). *Educational psychology* (5th ed.). Boston: Allyn & Bacon.

Slavin, R., Karweit, N., & Madden, N. (Eds.). (1989). *Effective programs for students at risk.* Needham Heights, MA: Allyn & Bacon.

Sleeter, C., & Grant, C. (1987). An analysis of multicultural education in the United States. *Harvard Educational Review, 57*(4), 421–444.

Soar, R. (1973). *Follow-through classroom process measurement and pupil growth, 1970–1971: Final report.* Gainesville, FL: University of Florida.

Sokolove, S., Garrett, S., Sadker, M., & Sadker, D. (1990). Interpersonal communication skills. In J. Cooper (Ed.), *Classroom teaching skills* (4th ed.) (pp. 186–219). Lexington, MA: Heath.

Sternberg, R. (1994). Allowing for thinking styles. *Educational Leadership, 52,* 36–40.

Sternberg, R., & Lubart, R. (1995). *Defying the crowd.* New York: Free Press.

Stipek, D. (1993). *Motivation to learn* (2nd ed.). Needham Heights, MA: Allyn & Bacon.

Strahan, D. (1989). How experienced and novice teachers frame their views of instruction: An analysis of semantic ordered trees. *Teaching and Teacher Education, 5*(1), 53–67.

Strother, D. (1989). Developing thinking skills through questioning. *Phi Delta Kappan,* 324–327.

Student Performance Standards of Excellence for Florida Schools (1984, p. 85). Tallahassee, Florida: Department of Education.

Teachers & Technology (1995). Washington, DC: U.S. Government Printing Office.

Tennyson, R., & Cocchiarella, M. (1986). An empirically based instructional design theory for teaching concepts. *Review of Educational Research, 56,* 40–71.

Tom, A. (1984). *Teaching as a moral craft.* White Plains, NY: Longman.

Torrance, E. (1982). Hemisphericity and creative functioning. *Journal of Research and Development in Education, 15*(3), 29–37.

Tyler, R. (1949). *Basic principles of curriculum and instruction.* Chicago: University of Chicago Press.

U.S. Department of Education. (1993). *Fifteenth annual report to Congress on the implementation of the Individuals With Disabilities Act.* Washington, DC: U.S. Government Printing Office.

Villegas, A. (1991). *Culturally responsive pedagogy for the 1990s and beyond.* Princeton, NJ: Educational Testing Service.

Walczyk, J., & Hall, V. (1989). Is the failure to monitor comprehension an instance of cognitive impulsivity? *Journal of Education Psychology, 81*(3), 194–198.

Wang, M., Haertel, G., & Walberg, H. (1993). Toward a knowledge base for school learning. *Review of Educational Research, 63*(3), 249–294.

Wang, M., Haertel, G., & Walberg, H. (1995, April). *Educational resilience: An emerging construct.* Paper presented at the annual meeting of the American Educational Research Association, San Francisco.

Webb, N. (1988). *Small group problem-solving: Peer interaction learning.* Paper presented at the annual meeting of the American Educational Research Association, New Orleans.

Weinert, F., & Helmke, A. (1995). Learning from wise mother nature or big brother instructor: The wrong choice as seen from an educational perspective. *Educational Psychologist, 30*(3), 135–142.

Weinstein, C., & Mignano, A. (1993). *Elementary classroom management.* New York: McGraw-Hill.

Wentzel, K. (1991). Social competence at school: Relation between social responsibility and academic achievement. *Review of Educational Research, 61*(1), 1–24.

Whiting, B., & Render, G. F. (1987). Cognitive and affective outcomes of mastery learning. *Clearing House, 60*(6), 276–290.

Wirthlin Group. (1989). *The computer report card: How teachers grade computers in the classroom.* McLean, VA: Wirthlin Group.

Witkin, H., Moore, C., Goodenough, D., & Cox, P. (1977). Field dependent and field independent cognitive styles and their educational implications. *Review of Educational Research, 47,* 1–64.

Wlodkowski, R. (1984). *Motivation and teaching: A practical guide* (2nd ed.). Washington, DC: National Education Association.

Wlodkowski, R., & Jaynes, J. (1990). *Eager to learn.* San Francisco: Jossey-Bass.

Wolery, M., Bailey, D., & Sugai, G. (1988). *Effective teaching principles and procedures of applied behavior analysis.* Boston: Allyn and Bacon.

Wolfgang, C., & Glickman, C. (1986). *Solving discipline problems* (2nd ed.). Boston: Allyn and Bacon.

Wolfinger, D., & Stockard, J. (1997). *Elementary methods: An integrated curriculum.* White Plains, NY: Longman.

Worthen, B. (1993). Critical issues that will determine the future of alternative assessment. *Phi Delta Kappan, 74,* 444–454.

Yinger, J. (1977). *Middle start: An experiment in the educational enrichment of young adolescents.* Cambridge, NY: Cambridge University Press.

Zahorik, J. (1996). *Constructivist teaching.* Bloomington, IN: Phi Delta Kappa Ed Foundation.

Zeichner, K. (1991, April). *Conceptions of reflective teaching in contemporary U.S. teacher education program reforms.* Paper presented at the annual meeting of the American Educational Research Association, Chicago.

Index